The Polish Presence in Canada and America

The Polish Presence in Canada and America

Edited and with an
introduction by
Frank Renkiewicz

The Multicultural History Society of Ontario
Toronto
1982

ISBN: 0-919045-13-8

Published 1982.
Printed in Canada.

The Multicultural History Society of Ontario
43 Queen's Park Crescent East
Toronto, Ontario M5S 2C3

Canadian Cataloguing in Publication Data

Main entry under title:
The Polish Presence in Canada and America

ISBN 0-919045-13-8

1. Polish Americans - History - Addresses, essays, lectures.
2. Polish Canadians - History - Addresses, essays, lectures.*
I. Renkiewicz, Frank, 1935- II. Multicultural History Society of Ontario.

E184.P7P64 973′.049185 C83-094004-9

Contents

Religion and Culture

Family

The Post-Immigrant Generation

Ethnicity in Post-Industrial Society, 1940-80

Work

Preface

In October of 1980 the Multicultural History Society of Ontario and the University of Toronto Ethnic and Immigration Studies Program sponsored a conference entitled "Poles in North America." The gathering drew scholars, especially historians of Polonia, from throughout the world. Along with historians and sociologists from Canada and the United States who tried to reconstruct and understand the North American experience, the shared history of Poland's "fourth province," there were scholars from Australia and from Polish universities.

The conference was one in a series of such gatherings sponsored by the Multicultural History Society to encourage ethnic studies in North America. Previous conferences on the Italians, Dutch and Finns had shown the value of bringing scholars and community together to discuss their ethnicity in a North American perspective, to reflect upon the state of the art of immigration studies and to hear directly about the many frontiers of valuable research upon which students of each immigrant and ethnic group labour.

A healthy tradition of amateur historical scholarship about Polonia, begun in the United States first by the Polish clergy and in Canada by the postwar national intelligentsia in exile, has given birth to a community of university scholars, usually of Polish descent, who have combined the best of the older "little history" of communities and parishes with the methods and objectivity of modern scholarship. Most of these scholars have moved away from filio-piety but not beyond empathy for their parents' and grandparents' ethnoculture. When Professor Robert F. Harney, the director of the Multicultural History Society, sought a person to coordinate a conference on the Polish experience in North America, the choice was easily made. Professor

Frank Renkiewicz had, through his literate and far-sighted editing of the journal *Polish American Studies* (formerly the *Polish American Historical Review*), provided a focus for the best new work on Poles in America for a number of years.

Under the direction of Professor Renkiewicz and with the help of the Canadian Polish Research Institute, the conference took shape. The articles published in this volume of proceedings represent the fruit of the conference. In their variety of topics and methodologies, the papers represent the difference in preoccupations and insights among scholars of Polonia in the United States, Canada and Poland respectively. For example, the Canadian papers, mostly sociological in method, reflect the concerns of a Polish community largely created since World War Two, one in which a sense of ethnic history involves the extinction of the independent Polish republic, the war against Nazism and the Soviets, and the effort to survive as a coherent people in a Canada which describes itself as multicultural but wears away the Polishness of the younger generation. On the other hand, the historians from the United States showed a sense of their longer North American history. No one spoke about the men "fetched out of Prussia and Poland" to Virginia in the sixteenth century, mentioned by Richard Hakluyt in *The Voyages of the English Nation in America.* It was clear though, from the subjects they chose and the sophistication of their methods, that American Poles knew that they were long in the land and that their ethnocommunity life and historiography were mature. The scholars from Poland contributed the unique perspective of the sending country—the view of the North American ethnic group as lost to the homeland, or as attempting to cling to the old country rather than evolving in the new world. Their view found strange points of congruence with the idea held by some others at the conference that Polonia in the world, despite differences among the nations of immigration to which Poles have gone and the gulf between the modern Polish state and those settled abroad, remained an integral and useful concept.

Amidst the academic sessions and the good discussions that filled the three days of meetings, there occurred one extraordinary event, an evening symposium on the idea of "Polishness" itself which drew a large audience. By serendipity or shrewdness the organizers had invited the poet Czeslaw Milosz to participate in the symposium well before the announcement that he had been awarded the Nobel prize. Milosz was joined on the dais by other Polish poets in North America and by several younger scholars. The participants represented such a breadth of Polish sentiment, background and attitudes that those assembled gained new insight into their human variety as Poles, but also into the modes of thought, historical memories and values which constituted for each his or her "Polishness." The tape recording and subsequent transcriptions of that session do not come close to recapturing the strength and beauty of the discussion, or the manner in which audience participation swelled and gave resonance to the words of those on the dais. Like Polishness the symposium about it exists best as ideas and images remembered or felt. A disjunctive or doctored transcription cannot do the session justice. It is with regret then, but with a certainty of the rightness of our editorial choice, that we do not include the transcription of that extraordinary session with the academic papers presented here.

On behalf of all those who participated and attended, I would like to thank the Multicultural History Society of Ontario and the University of Toronto Ethnic and Immigration Studies Program for organizing and sponsoring the conference.

Benedykt Heydenkorn
Canadian Polish Research Institute

Introduction

Frank Renkiewicz

Canadian and American Poles have been the subject of thousands of published studies. A review of the literature in 1975 listed well over a thousand titles in English alone, and the number threatens to grow rapidly. The most recent bibliography of Polish- and English-language publications reaches to nearly five hundred items. Early on, Poles in North America were the objects—some would say the victims—of the first classic example of empirically based sociology in the United States, William I. Thomas's and Florian Znaniecki's *The Polish Peasant in Europe and America.* Despite the title and like many early studies in the United States, it dealt implicitly with Canadian Poles as well.

The earliest attempts to interpret the great Polish immigration overseas in the late nineteenth century, inspired by speculation about the future of the Polish nation, were extensions of the internal debate on the Polish Question. The survivors of the failed insurrections, some of whom influenced the formation of the first popular Polish American institutions, often thought they saw a Fourth Province abroad, a base for protecting the national culture and liberating the partitioned homeland. Their dream faded as an immediate possibility by the 1880s in the face of the unrelentingly hostile interests of the Russian and German empires. Variants of the Fourth Province interpretation survive to this day, but North American Poles have never decisively affected the fate of the homeland. That dream was succeeded briefly in the 1880s and 1890s by visions of a New Poland, usually in Latin America. That view faded still more rapidly with reports of disastrous living conditions in Brazil, but they too, maintained a curious half-life through the 1930s.

By the turn of the century, as reports of exiles, travellers, journalists, missionaries and artists began to accumulate, the general Polish view of the immigration was that of an untamed and disorganized growth, for the most part lost to the homeland, but which might serve it in more modest ways. Immigration relieved the agrarian crisis, notably in southern and eastern Poland, by lessening the pressures of population growth and through remittances of money to those who remained. Eventually, with the encouragement of emigrant protective associations in major Polish cities, that concern generated important narrative and descriptive studies which anticipated research population policy in independent, interwar Poland.

The earliest research-based overview of Polish immigration to North America took shape from 1899 to 1908 within the ethnic community itself. It was the Reverend Waclaw Kruszka's *Historya Polska w Ameryce* (Polish History in America), which in the fashion of the day associated Polish settlement in Manitoba and Ontario with that in the prairie and industrial northeastern states to their south. Flawed by his passionate struggle for a greater Polish role in the governance of the Catholic church–it exaggerates the number of immigrants and accepts the accounts of local Polish sources uncritically–Kruszka's work represents, nevertheless, a first attempt to define at length a Polish identity within a culturally plural American society. It incorporates the histories of hundreds of settlements within that framework. No gathering of Poles is too small or too remote to escape his attention. What may have seemed an inchoate scattering to others achieves coherence and strength within a Polish tradition of localism. In this tradition nests (*gniazdy*) of decentralized settlements are grouped around some major centre (a church), person (priest), or geographical feature. These groups are integrated less by centralized institutions than by shared loyalty to a tradition.

The context in which Kruszka's views emerged was Polish as well as American. Throughout the late nineteenth century, Poles were adopting a modern, ethnically exclusive and socially inclusive view of nationality in place of the elitist, cosmopolitan definition which prevailed in the old Polish state. The earlier understanding had it that the nobility (and later the intelligentsia from which it derived) were the bearers of the national culture as well as owners of the national soil and keepers of political power. The masses, with their variety of folk cultures, were perceived even by social reformers as auxiliary to the nation, as indeed they were literally the auxiliaries who worked the noble estates. The German burghers of Danzig or the polonized gentry of Lithuania might, therefore, be Polish; the peasants of Mazovia and Little Poland were not. That view of the nation was increasingly irrelevant after the failure of the insurrection of 1863. Industrialization, urbanization and immigration altered the social and material basis for the traditional national self-image. Meanwhile, other cultures within the Polish lands–Ukrainian, Lithuanian, Jewish, Byelorussian, German, Czech–sought separate national identities.

Kruszka seems to have accepted the newer, more exclusive idea of nationality—a German can no longer be a Pole—but his pluralistic definition of America is reminiscent of the multinational Poland which was a realistic alternative for many until the 1940s. His analysis of pluralism rests on the interaction of a supporting environment, the United States or Canada, and an active, shaping social and psychological identity, in this case Polish. Like most popular theorists of cultural pluralism, he could not go for long without resorting to metaphorical explanation. America is described as the soil which nurtures a forest where a variety of trees grow according to their inherited characteristics. Like a forest the differences among the trees are not nearly as apparent from afar as they are close—a caution still valid for all comparative studies of ethnic groups. Trying to define the Polish American type or the new ethnic identity, Kruszka falls upon a more fruitful metaphor in the family. He describes America as a mother—a true parent whether she is adoptive or genetic—who gives of her abundance and provides material security. At a distance she gives a superficially similar and new appearance to her children. The metaphor frankly acknowledges the material appeal of the new land, whose values and morals were frequently criticized by Poles of all social classes. Extending the metaphor in a fashion which seems quaint eighty years later, Kruszka locates the source of true national identity—the "characteristic disposition" or "internal nature" as he calls it—in a Poland described as a father. That continuous, active, shaping role is symbolized by the child's adoption of the father's surname.

What is the core or distinguishing quality of one's Polish paternity? What differentiates the Polish tree in the American or Canadian forest? It cannot be soil or geography, no matter how fondly remembered, otherwise many Germans would be Poles and many Poles would be Americans. Neither can it be behaviour or language, the "embankment" which protects the fortress of national identity, given their variations and the ability of Polishness to survive language change. And, despite Kruszka's clerical calling, the division of his history according to ecclesiastical provinces and the special piety of Poles, he rejects Catholicism as the identifying mark. He may be too aware of the divisions within his native Catholicism, not to mention the controversy surrounding him in the American church, to choose that standard of Polishness. Instead he argues that the core of Polish identity anywhere lies in consciousness of a common past which transcends language, religion and the existence or not of a Polish state. The remembered past allows Poles of all regions, dialects and custom as well as Poles several generations removed from the homeland to think of themselves as parts of a single nation. It was important, as Kruszka realized, for showing how ethnicity could change, persist and accommodate variety whilst preserving a common, non-coercive loyalty. Pluralism in America required pluralism within Polonia. History, like the old commonwealth, seemed to command the allegiance of many kinds of people. Poles in North America, of course, share a new element of history—their immigration—which sets them apart. That experience had generated creative adaptions of Polish institutions and values.

Kruszka's pluralism had implications for his ethnic community. Believing that Poles had "grown up" by 1900, well before the heaviest immigration, he wondered whether they had "measured up and matured socially." He assumed, for example, that they had an active part to play in the operations of the Catholic church. Instead their clerical leadership preoccupied itself with the appointment of Polish bishops effectively serving only Polish interests and with a system of segregated parishes governed by powerful pastors in cooperation with a neighbourhood middle class. The restoration of the Polish state in 1918 further cleared the ground for inward-looking development. The parish educational system turned its back on immigration history in favour of Poland's less relevant kinds and ancient glories.

Even the historians of the Polish American school focused increasingly on the mythic past. Miecislas Haiman, the outstanding member of that school after Kruszka, contributed an enormous amount of painstaking research, devised a scheme for periodizing Polish American history, initiated archival preservation of materials and founded the Polish American Historical Association. However, he dealt mainly with the era before 1865—an age of Polish firsts, heroes, contributions and achievements in the new world which continue to distort the perceptions of outsiders. His articles in the Polish *Dictionary of Biography,* an institutional history of the Polish Roman Catholic Union, and a biography of Thaddeus Kosciuszko held a promise of focusing on the core of immigrant history.

Haiman's associates in the Polish American Historical Association seldom escaped the trap of filiopietism or dealt with the large issues raised by Kruszka. Their normally clerical background encouraged them in a Catholic nationalist interpretation of both Polish and Polish American history. Much the same may be said of the many M.A. theses from the 1930s to the 1950s which lie buried in Canadian and American university libraries. Almost alone among Haiman's young associates, Reverend Joseph Swastek sought during the Second World War to adapt Kruszka's insights on the Polish American identity. When Swastek began to write, what Kruszka had predicted from isolated cases had come to pass more generally. The use and quality of Polish were declining. Customs were disappearing, and signs had emerged that many Polish Americans would not be shored up in their ethnicity through life in geographic neighbourhoods. Much of the best work he edited for *Polish American Studies,* the journal of the Polish American Historical Association, for example, Helen Busyn's on Chicago politician Peter Kiolbassa or Helen Zand's ethnographic surveys—demonstrated implicitly the adoption of new standards of behaviour, belief and value.

In the 1950s, the dominant interpretations of the Polish American school continued to be the work of social workers and sociologists, who had been the first at the turn of the century to come in contact with Polish immigrants. Most of their work—for example, the Pittsburgh Survey and Peter Roberts's studies of coal miners—was done within prevailing nations of the biological inferiority of immigrants. Social disorganization and abnormal behaviour, which appear typical, were attributed to physically immutable racial traits. The best of the genre, Emily Green Balch's *Our Slavic Fellow Citizens,* avoids the presumption of ethnic guilt without escaping the prevailing tone of condescension. If the earliest Polish views of the immigration had made it an extension of the Polish Question, the first American studies created a new Polish American Question.

Within a few years, sociologists mostly associated with the University of Chicago largely overturned earlier and overwhelmed later American interpretations of the Polish immigrant. They shared only a few general ideas and common concerns: an empirical approach to social reality; an interest in social policy, notably in the rapidly growing urban environment of Chicago, and an emphasis on social process rather than structure. Still, their impact was enormous. William I. Thomas, the intellectual light of the first generation of Chicago sociologists, took the nearby Polish population of the city to illustrate the explanatory power of the new discipline. Explorations of the Chicago terrain and several trips to Europe led to an association with the young Polish social philosopher, Florian Znaniecki. The fruit of their labour, *The Polish Peasant in Europe and America,* was published in five volumes from 1918 to 1922.

Justly renowned, *The Polish Peasant* offered both a method and a theoretical structure for the study of modern urban society. It turned away from fashionable theories of biological determination and Freudianism as explanations of social psychology and social change. Though concerned with the dynamics of modernization, it did not yield to the simplistic and value-laden siren song of *gemeinschaft/gesellschaft.* Its less ambitious analysis of change in nineteenth-century Western society through a continuous process of social disorganization and reorganization still serves in some form to explain abnormal social psychological behaviour. That process, that reshaping of social reality, was conceived as the product not of some force as the theorists of the nineteenth century might devise, but of subjective factors of perception and consciousness. Though failing to define individual motivation adequately, Thomas and Znaniecki accompanied their work with a rich collection of peasant letters, life histories and other translated documents. It has influenced American sociology and ethnography ever since. Together with its adversary Marxist school, it generated a rich literature of peasant and worker memoirs, autobiographies and correspondence. The approach enjoyed a remarkable late flowering in Canada in volumes edited by Benedykt Heydenkorn and others. Oddly, *The Polish Peasant* itself was not translated (retranslated in the case of the documents) into Polish until the 1970s.

The academics at Chicago in the 1920s and the 1930s, continued to influence the study of Polish Americans through their work on the processes and patterns of urban life. Robert Park, Thomas's successor as intellectual innovator between the wars, refined the theory of social change in the city through a four-stage cycle of group competition, conflict, accommodation and assimilation. Together with the department's surveys of the neighbourhoods of Chicago, this led to a theory of urban ethnic succession: as groups stabilized socially and improved their economic position, they moved out steadily from the centre of the city and were replaced by less well-organized newcomers. It was an influential formula which provided a rationale, a framework, and perhaps an intellectual straitjacket for thinking about the American city and its ethnic groups from the 1950s to the 1970s.

In the immediate aftermath of publication, criticism of *The Polish Peasant* focused on epistomological issues: failure to integrate ethnographic data with the theoretical overview, shaky support for the motivational aspects of the social behaviour—weaknesses which the authors freely admitted and which sustained further research. In the longer view, the deficiencies of *The Polish Peasant* appeared to have more to do with an excessive emphasis on social disorganization in the immigrant Polish community and unwarranted or simplistic assumptions about the nature of assimilation in the future. It was the natural error of outsiders, perhaps of sociologists. Even Znaniecki, despite his credentials as a Pole, was socially alien to the mass of his subjects and might well fail to take their values, institutions and adaptive powers at face value.

The major criticisms stem from limitations in the outlook of the Chicago sociologists. Operating from essentially progressive political assumptions, they underrated the socially conservative, moderating and compromising character of modern urban politics; the ability of power brokers to accommodate newcomers and mediate among elements of the social structure. And, while recognizing the nationalist goals of immigrant Polish institutions, they missed the power and historic depth of the tradition which legitimized the work and authority of the Polish intelligentsia in the new world. That tradition, however defined, had a residual strength not comparable to the Carpatho-Ruthenian, Byelorussian, Macedonian or any number of local cultures which struggled toward nationhood in the nineteenth century. Similarly, though Thomas and Znaniecki recognized the American parish-neighbourhood as the successor to the European village as a mediator between immigrant workers and American society, they underestimated the traditional authority of religious belief, clerical power and devotional practice. These not only survived but flourished in the immigrant generation. The consequence of their ahistorical attitude was to underestimate the survival power of communal ethnic institutions, their ability to compromise with external forces and to retard assimilation, their refusal to wither away.

Academia corrects itself, at least partially and on its own terms. Thirty years after *The Polish Peasant,* Helen Znaniecka Lopata completed a dissertation at the University of Chicago which explained the survival of ethnic Polish institutions long after Thomas and her father had predicted their demise. They had, she found, developed new missions in the 1920s: as agencies of individual welfare through expanded insurance, mortgage and social service programs; as cultural, non-political links between Polonia and Poland; as non-threatening representatives of American culture. Still, gaps in research and the bias of her discipline left the impression that immigrant Polonia provided almost no worthwhile material, social or psychological support to its members. Much of the research of the next quarter-century was dedicated to closing those gaps and placing even the most recent manifestations of ethnicity in historical perspective for the first time.

Following a break during the war and immediate postwar years, Polish social historians renewed their investigations of the agrarian problems of the nineteenth century. The efforts of People's Poland in the 1950s to mobilize a rural work force into an industrial system lent their research contemporary significance and a certain realism in spite of attempts at a Marxist-Leninist framework. Polish sociologists meanwhile concentrated on the social mechanisms and consequences of industrialism. An early work of Hieronim, for example, concluded that sudden involvement in a modern industrial system by no means detached workers from their traditional culture and economy.

The social reaction to emigration and industrialization was not strictly the maintenance of old ways. Social historians of early Polonia in the United States since the 1960s and increasingly in Canada have given their best efforts to explaining how ethnic identification, though rooted in older regional and status loyalties, developed in conjunction with industrial and urban life. In doing so they have evoked the memories of the "ancient" ethnic past, as Father Kruszka might have put it, which created the first Polish type in North America.

The Polish Presence in Canada and America seeks to grapple with this question of ethnic identity and assimilation in the new world. Some of the writers in these volumes place the emergence of ethnic identity in a Polish context. Joanna Matejko notes that some Galician Poles in rural Alberta had an older sense of being Polish, one in which they did not distinguish themselves too clearly from Ukrainians, while others had a modern, exclusive sense of their nationality. Anthony Kuzniewski and Laurence Orzell both describe the spirit of perceived oppression among many nineteenth-century Poles coming to the United States, the reckless and unsuccessful attacks on authority and its social assumptions by Kruszka and Francis Hodur, their "realistic" submissions to authority in middle age. It makes as much or more sense to interpret their behaviour constructively in Polish terms than it does as a breakdown of social order in the face of external pressures. Well before the First World War Polish Americans had begun to settle for toleration of tolerance; for most, within the Roman Catholic Church; for the minority National Church of Bishop Hodur, within Polonia itself. The result was a generation of practical separatism within the Roman Church and of permanent juridical separation in the case of the Polish National Catholic Church. Daniel Buczek has described the outcome, the segregated parish of the 1920s in which the early signs of that formula of structural assimilation and cultural pluralism, predicted by Kruszka, made their appearance.

Writers in the last decade or two have re-emphasized other ways in which Polish immigrants carried their cultural baggage into a new world. In Back of the Yards, Chicago, in Johnstown, and in three separate areas of Buffalo, Dominic Pacyga, Ewa Morawska and Eugene Obidinski describe for us how traditions of local autonomy and neighbourhood self-sufficiency took on new meanings and vitality in the new urban environments of the United States. Even the fraternal insurance associations, whose early Polish American functions Donald Pienkos describes, never quite outgrew their regional origins. Helen Lopata has emphasized the power of traditional status arrangements to order Polonia and give continuity as late as the 1970s. These were elements of institutional completeness and low mobility which were often deplored as disunity or disorganization. In fact they were sources of strength in winning the support of immigrants. Pastors, for example, who ignored Polish realities did so at their own peril.

Several contributors to this symposium, notably John Bodnar and Joseph Parot, describe how Polish and other Slavic families found new purpose and strength in meeting the harsh challenges of the early industrial system. According to Bodnar, their adaptation varied significantly according to area of origin in Poland, American environment, age at emigration and place in the generational ladder. His conclusions serve as an antidote to the Chicago model which has dominated both sociologists and historians. Parot emphasizes the differences according to sex by showing how women mobilized a variety of resources—the traditional piety of the Marian cult, an anti-materialist ethic, early marriage, the companionship of church societies—to sustain themselves in Chicago. It was not simply an urban phenomenon. The household economies of Alberta described by Janina Matejko and of Brazil by Marcin Kula may have provided the margin of survival for their members.

In their own terms most Polish immigrants succeeded well enough. Though many returned disappointed with the New World, the consensus, as Irena Spustek puts it, was that their decision to leave Poland assured them a relatively better life. Brazil, whose economy according to Kula offered less opportunity than the developed capitalism of North America, also seemed on balance to offer more than the old country.

Of course, Polish "success" was on the margins of Canadian and American prosperity. The crisis of the Great Depression made that clear and compelled Poles, now often of the second generation, to refine the definition of themselves as permanent members of the working class. Arguing, like Buczek, for a new ethnicity in the interwar period, Thaddeus Radzialowski analyses the origins of the struggle with employers in Detroit in the 1930s for job security and union recognition. Economic conflict also locked second-generation workers into a fateful confrontation with blacks over jobs and housing. Employers used racial and ethnic division to undermine labour solidarity, and government used public housing for blacks needed in defense production. Both threatened the hard-won gains of the previous thirty years.

Just as early and mature industrialism evoked somewhat different ethnic identities in the immigrant and second generations, post-industrial society eventually called forth yet a third. The studies in the second half of this symposium deal with issues raised in the new milieu, here dated from the 1940s. They are concerned heavily with traditional questions of assimilation; nevertheless, their authors appear to be more conscious of the imprint of historical experience upon the values, beliefs, perceptions of reality and status which they seek to analyse and measure.

All studies agree that since the 1940s the Polish population in North America has shifted location and become more complex. In Canada, as Rudolph Kogler describes it, more Poles were now to be found in southern Ontario than in the prairie provinces (Alberta/Manitoba) where they had largely settled at first. They are also more urban, more likely to be employed in services and professions, less likely to be found in rural occupations. In the United States they have moved from old neighbourhoods near the industry which employed them without, however, entirely abandoning many of those areas. New blue-collar and middle-class suburbs have appeared farther out to house them in what appears to be a fulfilment of the theory of urban ethnic succession. Meanwhile, American Poles have witnessed the relative decline of the old industries, sought higher education in record numbers, and increasingly joined the newer service and technological economies. Their structural assimilation conforms to general trends in both countries; but, as Grzegorz Babinski concludes, it is not as simple as all that. The overall rates of change are only relatively the same as other groups and national norms. They also conceal significant variations according to sex and generation.

The gradual movement of descendants of the old immigration into white-collar occupations is one way to describe the new employment and geographic patterns. Another has been new immigration, especially in Canada, where it has clearly altered the mix of the far smaller Polish population. Both have had their impact upon the institutional life of the ethnic community and its self-image. In Canada it has meant the regeneration of old institutions and the emergence of new ones such as the Canadian Polish Congress. Organized Polonia in Sudbury, as Henry Radecki shows, was threatened with extinction when the newcomers of the 1940s and 1950s appeared. In the United States, where the early immigration was far larger and more concentrated, the old fraternals, which Donald Pienkos describes, continue to demonstrate strength even if they seem unable to adapt to the newer demographic structure. Here, too, the newer immigration has made itself felt. Stanislaus Blejwas and Henry Radecki particularly point out the gulf which opened up between the descendants of the old immigration and the members of the new. Collaboration is restricted to cultural events, usually with a national Polish flavour, and to membership in a common church. Alexander Matejko deals particularly with the utter failure of the Polish intelligentsia tradition, the enlightened social leadership of the educated, to take hold among Polish Canadians or Americans in the last forty years. Representatives of that tradition abound in both countries. Only the audience has disappeared.

The recent proliferation of ethnic identities frequently encourages writers on the subject to suggest programs for action. Usually they have to deal with cultural maintenance and meliorating the tensions between generations which often lead the youth to abandon their older identification. Nowhere in this symposium does one's birth and current residence seem more a factor. Canadian Poles and immigrants whose formative years were spent in Poland appear preoccupied with maintenance questions. American-born Poles who have lived with and studied the question longer are relatively indifferent. Polish scholars are interested and sympathetic, but uncertain that it much matters. Andrew Woznicki, for example, argues a philosophic rationale for a Catholic Church able to accommodate identities in other ways than the geographic parish which is suited to a less mobile society. While Helen

Lopata outlines the sources of conflict and cohesion in the Polish American family in ways that describe the trends of the last fifty years, Danuta Mostwin argues for pluralism as a social worker concerned for individual and family health. Jan Fedorowicz suggests ways in which Polish language, institutions and culture may be renewed. On their own evidence and that of others, however, language and institutions are declining both absolutely and relative to the growing Polish-origin population. Even new immigration, as Matejko suggests, is not likely to reverse the trend. Perhaps their decline is related, as Jerzy Zubrzycki puts it, to the perception that involvement in a structured ethnic community, the pluralism of 1910 or 1940, is a mobility trap. The old ethnicity may offer psychological satisfaction and even economic reward at first; eventually it appears to perpetuate second-class politics and status. Elsewhere in a study of a contemporary working-class suburb in Detroit, Paul Wrobel notes that Polish Americans no longer encourage children to pursue the same job and status objectives as their parents. There is some greater hope for cultural maintenance, or at least for a slower rate of decline, adapted to the mobile nature of post-industrial society.

Perhaps, as Father Kruszka argued eighty years ago and as Eugene Obidinski reminds us now, Polish ethnicity in the long run has less to do with place and institutions—old neighbourhoods wherever they be—and more to do with the world of symbols and memories through which we express our innermost selves. At the nadir of the Polish state over two centuries ago, Jean-Jacques Rousseau advised the Poles: "If you cannot prevent your enemies from swallowing you whole, at least you must do what you can to prevent them from digesting you." Canada and the United States can hardly be called enemies. Indeed they are models of hospitality compared to the rapacious powers which have surrounded Poland in modern times. Their toleration may explain their ability to digest many Poles even as they allowed so many others in so many ways to be Polish.

Immigrants in Industrial Society

Entry

The Socio-economic Base of Polish Emigration to North America, 1854-1939

Krzysztof Groniowski

Emigration: An Overview

Mass emigration from Poland to the United States—in contrast to the movement of individuals and waves of political exiles—is commonly dated from 1854 with the arrival in Texas of the first of several bands of settlers from the Opole Regency in Upper Silesia. Kaszubs from Bytów county in western Pomerania assumed that pioneering role in Canada when, in 1858, they settled in the neighbourhood of Barry's Bay and Wilno in central Ontario.[1]

Overwhelmingly, overseas Polish emigration—nearly 85 per cent of the total before 1914 or about 2.2 million people—found its way to the United States. The number rose rapidly from 144,000 in the 1860s and 1870s, to 613,000 in the 1880s and 1890s, to 1,327,000 in 1900-14. On the eve of the First World War, the flood showed no sign of abating. Nineteen-thirteen witnessed the arrival of record numbers of Polish immigrants in America.[2]

The central demographic part of Polish emigration was its regional character. The Kaszubs and Silesians of the 1850s were soon joined and eclipsed by other rural folk from Prussian Poland, especially Great Poland (Poznań) and West Prussia. By the time emigration from Prussia declined in the 1890s, over 600,000 Poles from its eastern provinces had arrived in the United States, largely to settle in the new farms and cities of the Middle West. They were joined between 1880 and 1914 by 900,000 from the Russian partition (the so-called Congress Kingdom) and 700,000 from Austrian Poland (Galicia). The newer arrivals were far more likely to settle in such industrial centres as the Great Lakes ports (notably Chicago), the mining regions of Pennsylvania, the Atlantic coast ports and the textile mill towns of New England. The

United States census of 1910, based for the first time on the mother tongue of respondents, revealed the predominance of Russian Poles (44.3 per cent) over Austrian (34.9 per cent) and Prussian (20.1 per cent) in the immigrant Polish American population. Reflecting the shifting currents of migration just before and after the First World War, the census of 1920 showed a preponderance of Poles from the Austrian sector.[3]

It was also Austria and Russia that from 1896 onward provided the bulk of Polish immigration to Canada, some of it by way of the United States. The Canadian census of 1901 recorded 6,285 Poles, chiefly in Ontario (2,918) and Manitoba (1,674). By 1911, the number of Poles had climbed to 33,652, with Manitoba outstripping Ontario 12,321 to 10,631—a sure sign of the strongly rural character of early Polish settlement in Canada. When international migration resumed freely at war's end in 1918, Poles continued to migrate more heavily—in a ratio of about eight to one—to the United States. It was only the introduction of restrictive American immigration laws combined with a liberal Canadian policy that reversed the trend in the late 1920s, though many of those bound for Canada probably hoped to make their way indirectly into the United States.[4]

The Canadian census quickly registered the changing patterns of migration. In 1921, it showed 53,403 Poles, 71.2 per cent of them in the prairie provinces. By 1931, the number had nearly tripled to 145,503, and their location had begun to change as both the children of early immigrants and the recent arrivals reoriented themselves socially. Though Manitoba, Saskatchewan and Alberta together were home still to a majority of Polish Canadians, industrial and urban Ontario was the most attractive single province.[5]

American policy probably also diverted would-be Polish immigrants to Latin America. For example, 96,976 of the 157,579 Polish immigrants to Argentina in this period arrived there from 1926 to 1931. Together with the fitful migration to Brazil in the late nineteenth century, it hinted at the creation of a formidable Latin American Polonia. But the world economic crisis of the early 1930s ended that possibility.

The Economic Roots of Emigration

The regional character of the great overseas migration was evident also in its root cause—the transformation of the agricultural economy of east-central Europe in the third quarter of the nineteenth century. Superficially, serfdom and the monerial economy ended everywhere in the Polish lands by the late 1860s. Nevertheless, each partition responded to different political imperatives and separate economic developments in the ruling monarchies. Prussia was the first of the three to undertake the emancipation of the labour force and to introduce a modern capitalistic system in the rural economy. It was a long process, however, begun under the impact of the Napoleonic wars in 1807, accelerated in 1825-40, and only completed in the 1850s, after the revolutionary upheavals of 1848.

Though liberated from obligations to landlords and empowered to move about freely, Prussian Polish peasants lost one-fifth of the land they had farmed as well as rights in commons lands. They were burdened, moreover, with high taxes and heavy indemnity payments for their economic freedom. Only about one-third of the rural population actually acquired real property under such conditions. Most poorer peasants simply lost the land they had farmed traditionally under long-term agreements. The consequences were inevitable: the emergence of a large and poor if mobile rural work force; and the expansion of commercially profitable great estates whose landlords were the mainstay of the Prussian monarchy. Great Poland provided a particularly vivid example of the agricultural revolution. Peasants there in 1861 held only 39 per cent of the soil while the landless numbered 600,000 or 60.1 per cent of the agricultural population. Working for wages on the large farms and estates was the first solution for most but such work was seasonal. At that, employers came to prefer the flexibility and lower cost of temporary migrant labour from the Kingdom and Galicia. Except for Upper Silesia, which had begun to industrialize by mid-century and escaped most of the consequences of rural change, Prussian Poland had few towns or cities to absorb surplus population. Great Poland, where the number of towns was greatest, was still only 29.8 per cent urbanized in 1890.

In those circumstances even modest increases in population might create a social crisis within a generation. However, the freedom of movement which accompanied emancipation provided an answer. Overseas migration from Prussia's Polish provinces equalled 36.8 per cent of the population increase in the 1860s, 41.3 per cent in the 1870s and 78.3 per cent in the 1880s. In Great Poland alone in the 1880s it reached a rate of 82.8 per cent. That decade also witnessed the beginning of changes which brought overseas migration to a halt. Imperial tariffs on agricultural produce and the easing of debt burdens associated with emancipation brought about an improvement in the standing of richer peasants. Self-help organizations and rural credit facilities gradually appeared to make up for the traditional contractual arrangements which had once governed village life. The growth of large estates declined and holdings by Polish peasants increased early in the twentieth century as part of national resistance to Germanization. Above all, the rapid industrialization of western Germany, especially the Ruhr Valley, opened opportunities for work much closer to home than North America. Only the

Kaszubian region south of Gdansk and in western Pomerania remained a poor, rural backwater.[6]

Congress Poland, the heart of modern Poland, was the most populous of the partitions. In order to win the loyalty of small farmers and to punish the gentry who had led insurrections in 1830 and 1863, the Tsarist government liberated the peasants on terms more favourable than those in Russia proper. The newly liberated peasant-landowners held 44 per cent of soil after their enfranchisement in 1864 and acquired an additional 311,000 hectares in the next thirty years. In 1890, the government-sponsored Peasants' Bank began to provide credit for land acquisition though its work was frustrated by steadily increasing prices. There were other factors as well which encouraged migration. Even in the immediate post-emancipation period, 21.8 per cent of the farms in the Kingdom were too small to support normal families and their owners had to seek additional sources of income. In 1901, the population of villages and small farm towns with no land at all reached 1,432,000. Not unlike many peasant societies on the verge of modernization, there was a decline in mortality and a rapid growth in population. The number of inhabitants of the Kingdom doubled from six million in the emancipation period to just under twelve million on the eve of the First World War. The peasant population grew proportionately from four to eight million.

The pressure of population upon land varied widely by region. It was strongest in the non-industrialized provinces nearest the frontiers, least in the vicinity of such highly developed cities as Warsaw and the great textile centre of Łódź. Płock, for example, adjoining West Prussia, had an unusually high number of farms (34 per cent) which provided less than a subsistence livelihood.

Seasonal migration across the border to Germany and for the longer term to the United States took hold as early as the 1870s. At the end of the 1880s, emigration from Płock to the United States reached an annual rate of 1,300 and included a number of Jews, a significant demographic fact in Congress Poland; by 1892, when the overseas movement had spread widely through Russian Poland, it stood at 2,200. At that time, landless peasants accounted for 60.9 per cent of the emigrants, farm owners 18.4 per cent, industrial workers and craftsmen 3.8 per cent. Increasingly in the twentieth century, emigration and re-migration were institutionalized in village life. In some villages of the Kurpie region in the great forest of the north in the Kingdom, 15 to 20 per cent of the inhabitants had gone to America before 1914. Income from the American emigration in the form of remittances and the savings of re-migrants was significantly greater than in Prussian Poland. The evidence also suggests that here the emigrants were younger and that though many men among them were married they went abroad singly.[7]

Galicia was yet another case. There, the Austrian government, hoping to undermine the influence of the nationalist gentry, abruptly liberated the peasantry on favourable terms in 1848. Peasants received all arable soil, though disputes long continued over rights to pasturage and forests on the great estates. Emancipation failed, however, to solve many of the fundamental problems of the peasants. As the government in Vienna reverted in the late 1860s to dependence on the socially conservative oligarchy to rule Galicia, it was less well motivated to come to the aid of small landowners. Meanwhile the population grew rapidly, doubling between 1850 and 1914, but on a far narrower base of material resources than in Russian Poland.

Indeed, emancipation and property rights may have exaggerated the troubles of peasants by opening the way to the division of land holdings, a practice formally sanctioned by law in 1868. Tradition may have dictated passing a property intact to one son, usually the eldest—it was a major factor in the eventual emigration of many younger children—yet the number of small and inefficient farms grew steadily through division. In 1859, 61 per cent of peasant holdings were less than five hectares and only 15.1 per cent were larger than ten hectares. Samples of villages in 1882-83 showed that the number of farms smaller than five hectares (usually the property of farmer cottagers) may have reached 70 to 80 per cent of the total, while those greater than ten hectares fell to between 5 and 6 per cent. Another measure of the size of holdings—the area of land in farm units larger than ten hectares—fell from 50.7 per cent of the total in the same period.

Rural Galicia simply could not support or feed its people by the turn of the century. Grain alcohol was its most profitable commercial product. Local crafts such as weaving were undermined by foreign competition. Outside of the oil fields in the heavily Ukrainian east and some mining and manufacturing adjacent to Upper Silesia, there was no major investment in industry in the province. Usurous interest rates, a high level of foreclosure, and alcoholism were the most obvious symptoms of widespread distress in the countryside. Farms earning one to two thousand crowns yearly—and they were the majority—were unable to maintain a normal sized family. Emigration—European and seasonal at first, North American and increasingly permanent eventually—was almost the only realistic alternative. Limited only by the obligation of young men to military service, emigration to North America grew steadily in the 1880s. It assumed the character of a mass movement in 1896-1914 when 433,000 Poles and 146,000 Ukrainians left.

Nowhere in Poland did the cycle of emigration and re-migration become as important in the local economy as it did in Galicia. Just prior to the First World War, one-quarter of the people of the province depended in some way on income from emigration. Earnings from that source reached an annual rate of 160 million crowns ($32 million). Mostly the money went for the building of houses, the purchase of cattle and land, and the repayment of debts. Ironically, it had the effect of driving up the price of land and the cost of owning a farm beyond the reach of most emigrants.[8]

Independent Poland

The outcome of the First World War, by undoing the partitions, was a political triumph for Polish nationalism. Economically, however, the war was a disaster. As the principal battlefield of eastern Europe, the restored nation found itself physically in a shambles. Though the worst of the havoc was remedied quickly enough as industrial employment rose in early 1919 from 14 per cent of prewar levels to 90 per cent in 1921, independent Poland enjoyed only brief periods of prosperity: from 1921 to the summer of 1923, from the spring of 1926 to the autumn of 1929 and in the very late 1930s.[9]

The new Poland also faced major structural economic problems. It was compelled to weld together the three quite different and unequal economies of the partition area. The demographic and social trends of the late nineteenth century continued unabated. Interwar Poland had one of Europe's highest rates of population growth, expanding from about 27 million to 35 million people. It was also a heavily rural economy. In 1921, 75.4 per cent of the population lived in the villages and countryside, and 63.8 per cent were occupied in agriculture. The size of farms was still pathetically small. Over one-third (33.9 per cent) were less than two hectares in size; nearly as many (30.7 per cent) were two to five hectares. Ten years later, 61.9 per cent of Poles worked in agriculture, one of the highest proportions in Europe. Agricultural workers, 72 per cent of them employed on great estates, numbered 2,700,000 or 10.8 per cent of the working population. Peasants represented 52.5 per cent of the total. In 1939, over 70 per cent of Poland's people lived in rural areas.[10]

The old solutions to the problems of the countryside seemed to serve the new nation less well than its predecessors. During the interwar period, one and one-half million people migrated to cities and towns, but they represented only one-fifth of the population increase. There was even a return to the villages in the early 1930s, though the agricultural economy suffered relatively more than the industrial during the depression. Emigration abroad also relieved pressure on the labour market and the land in the 1920s but overall it failed to benefit the country in the form of remittances and investments as it had prior to the war. It was also a less effective tool as receiving countries became more selective and offered fewer opportunities for Poland's rural overpopulation. Canada, for example, absorbed far more peasants compared to the United States in the late 1920s, but it could not bring the total remotely close to the pre-1914 American levels.[11]

Land reform, not surprisingly, ranked high on the agenda of early Polish governments as the long-range solution to rural social problems. It came in two spurts: in 1922-23, following the law of July 15, 1920; and, less effectively, in 1926-28, after the law of December 28, 1925. Altogether, 2,700,000 hectares or about 20 per cent of the great estates were divided among the peasants. Implementation of the land reform varied significantly along prewar boundaries. The rate of division was highest in old Russian Poland. In Galicia it was lower than it had been under Austrian rule, and it was lowest of all in the more progressive, western, formerly Prussian provinces. The depression of the 1930s slowed the pace of the reform substantially as it did the older remedies for rural distress.[12] Finally, political events, as they had so often in modern Polish history, set the stage in 1939-45 for a new overseas migration, rapid urbanization and yet another effort to grapple with the problems (or problem) of the Polish peasant.

Notes

1. T. Lindsay Baker, *The First Polish Americans. Silesian Settlements in Texas* (College Station, Texas, 1979); Izabela Jost, "Osadnictwo Kaszubskie w środkowym Ontario" ["Kaszubian Settlement in Central Ontario"], in Hieronim Kubiak and Andrzej Pilch, eds., *Stan i potrzeby badań nad zbiorowościami polonijnymi* [The State of and Needs for Research in Polonian Studies] (Wrocław, 1976), pp. 451, 460.
2. Mieczysław Szalewski, *Kwestia emigracji w Polsce* [The Emigration Question in Poland] (Warsaw, 1927), p. 17.
3. Thirteenth Census of the United States 1910. Bulletin. Population, pp. 890, 978-81.
4. Centralnyj Derzawnyj Istoricznyj Archiw Ukrainskoji RSR w m. Lwowi, Galićke Namistnyctwo 2476 [Central Historical Depository of the Archives of the Ukrainian Soviet Socialist Republic in the city of Lwow, Galician Division 2476], p. 107; see examples of individual experiences in *Pamiętniki emigrantow Kanada* [Memoirs of Emigrants to Canada] (Warsaw, 1971), pp. 283, 385; Janina Matejko, ed., *Polish Settlers in Alberta* (Toronto, 1979), pp. 12-14; Jan Derengowski, "Ruch migracyjny pomiędzy Polską a Stanami Zjednoczonymi Ameryki Północnej" ["The Migration Movement between Poland and the United States of North America"], *Statystyka Pracy* [Labor Statistics] 6 (1927), p. 45.

5. Roman Mazurkiewicz, *Polskie wychodźtwo i osadnictwo w Kanadzie* [Polish Emigration and Settlement in Canada] (Warsaw, 1929), pp. 29-44; Benedykt Heydenkorn, ed., *Pamiętniki imigrantów polskich w Kanadzie* [Memoirs of Immigrant Poles in Canada] (Toronto, 1978) III, pp. 183-253.
6. On developments in the Prussian partition see: Stanisław Borowski, *Kształtowanie się rolniezego rynku pracy w Wielkopolsce w okresie wielkich reform agrarnych 1807-1860* [The Formation of the Agricultural Labor Market in Great Poland in the Period of the Great Agrarian Reform, 1807-1860] (Poznań, 1963), p. 387; Stanisław Borowski, "Rozwój demograficzny i problem maltuzjański na ziemiach polskich pod panowaniem niemieckim w latach 1807-1914" ["Demographic Growth and the Malthusian Problem in the Polish Lands Controlled by Germany in 1807-1914"], *Przeszłość demograficzna Polski* [Polish Demographic History] III (1970), p. 141; Lech Trzeciakowski, *Walka o polskość miast Poznańskiego na przełomie XIX i XX wieku* [The Struggle for Polishness in the City of Poznań at the turn of the 19th and 20th Centuries] (Poznań, 1964), pp. 17-18. Also see Mack Walker, *Germany and the Emigration, 1816-1885* (Cambridge, Mass.: Harvard University Press, 1964).
7. On conditions in the Russian partition see: Juliusz Łukasiewicz, "O structurze agrarnej Królestwa Polskiego po uwłaszczeniu" ["The Agrarian Structure of the Kingdom of Poland after the Uprising"], *Przegląd Historyczny* [Historical Review] 62, no. 2 (1971), p. 299; Krzysztof Groniowski, "Przemiany gospodarczo-społczne na Kurpiach na przełomie XIX i XX wieku" ["Socio-economic change in Kurpie at the Turn of the 19th and 20th Centuries"], *Przegląd Historyczny* 54, no. 1 (1963), p. 57.
8. On conditions in Galicia see: Wincenty Styś, *Rozdrabnianie gruntów chłopskich w byłym zaborze austriackim od roku 1787 do 1931* [The Break-up of Peasant Lands in the Former Austrian Sector from 1787 to 1931] (Lwów, 1934), p. 300; Andrzej Pilch, "Migrations of the Galician Populace at the Turn of the Nineteenth and Twentieth Centuries," in Celina Bobińska and Andrzej Pilch, eds., *Employment-Seeking Emigrations of the Poles Worldwide XIX and XX C.* (Kraków, 1975), p. 81; R.F. Leslie, ed., *The History of Poland since 1863* (Cambridge, 1980), p. 16; Franciszek Bujak, *Rozwój gospodarczy Galicji 1772-1914* [Galician Social Development 1772-1914]; Krzysztof Groniowski, "Motwy emigracji w świetle dzieła Williama I. Thomasa i Floriana Znanieckiego, *Chłop polski w Europie i Ameryce*" ["Motives for Emigration in Light of the Work of William I. Thomas and Florian Znaniecki, *The Polish Peasant in Europe and America*"], *Przegląd Zachodni* [Western Review] 5-6 (1977), pp. 13-31; Jerzy Zubrzycki, *Polish Immigrants in Britain* (The Hague, 1956), p. 11. On emigration from specific areas and communities see: Franciszek Bujak, *Limanowa* (Kraków, 1902), p. 159; Franciszek Bujak, *Żmiąca, wieś powiatu Limanowskiego* [Żmiąca, A Village in the County of Limanowa] (Kraków, 1903), p. 99; Franciszek Bujak, *Maszkienice, wieś powiatu brzeskiego. Rozwój od r. 1900 do r. 1914* [Maskienice, A Village in the County of Brzesko. Development from 1900 to 1914] (Kraków, 1914), pp. 9, 76, 91; Krysztyna Duda-Dziewiarz, *Wieś małapolska a emigracja amerykańska* [The Countryside

of Little Poland and the American Emigration] (Warsaw, 1938), pp. 23, 27, 68; Kazimiera Zawistowicz-Adamska, *Społeczność wiejska* [Rural Society] (Łódź, 1948), p. 145.

9. Zbigniew Landau, "Zasadnicze tendencje rynku pracy i płac w Polsce w latach inflacji (1918-1923)" ["Fundamental Tendencies in the Labor Market and Wages in Poland in the Years of Inflation (1918-1923)"], *Z Pola Walki* [From the Battlefields], I (1966), p. 15.

10. Ludwig Landau, *Skład zawodowy ludności Polski jako podstawa badania struktury gospodarczej* [Occupational Make-up of the People of Poland as the Basis for Research on Social Structure] (Warsaw, 1931), p. 16; Janusz Żarnowski, *Społeczenstwo Drugiej Rzeczypospolitej 1918-1939* [The Society of the Second Republic, 1918-1939] (Warsaw, 1973), pp. 190, 342.

11. Zbigniew Landau, "Kryzys rolny w Polsce (1929-1935)" ["The Agrarian Crisis in Poland, 1929-1935"] *Zeszyty Naukowe SGPiS* [Scientific Publications of the SGPiS] 37 (1962), p. 69; Maria Ciechocińska, *Próby walki z bezrobocim w Polsce międzywojennej* [The Ordeal of the Struggle with Unemployment in Interwar Poland] (Warsaw, 1965), p. 32; *Pamiętniki chłopów nr 1-51* [Peasant Autobiographies, nos. 1-51] (Warsaw, 1935), pp. xxxvii, 387; Józef Orczyk, *Produkcja rolna Polski w latach wielkiego kryzysu gospodarczego (1929-1935)* [Farm Production of Poland in the Years of the Great Economic Crisis (1929-1935)] (Poznań, 1971), p. 205.

12. Mieczysław Mieszczankowski, *Struktura agrarna Polski międzywojennej* [The Agrarian Structure of Interwar Poland] (Warsaw, 1960), p. 69.

Immigrant Perceptions of Life in North America

Irena Spustek

The great progress in ethnic studies in North America in recent years is encouraging, but it still seems that some major problems have not received sufficient attention. We lack studies showing the ethnic Polish group in relation to the broad trends of American history and in comparison to other ethnic groups, especially those which arrived in the same period and under similar conditions. Such elements of culture as hierarchy of values, level and scale of aspiration, way of life—not only customs and ceremonials—require research and analysis. Relations with other ethnic groups who had lived in or had been neighbours of Poland also demand attention. This essay focuses on the expectations and hopes of Polish peasants of the great emigration to the United States, the realities of their lives in America, and how they themselves evaluated their failures and achievements.

Mass emigration from the Polish territories to the United States, unlike that to Canada and Brazil, took place in a time of relative decline in agricultural opportunities. Meanwhile, rapid urbanization and industrial development in the United States created a market for cheap labour. Immigrants, despite their rural provenance, did not generally settle on the land but joined the American economy as unskilled workers. The difficulty of integrating the newcomers with American workers subjected the immigrants to manipulation on the labour market, condemning them to the lowest wages, job insecurity and poor relations with the trade union movement.

The expression "culture shock" is too weak to emphasize the experience of immigrants arriving in America, directly from remote Polish villages with backward socio-economic structures and primitive living conditions. The peasant, who had seldom left his hamlet, and for whom the port of embarkation was usually the first big town he had seen, was deposited after a difficult voyage in the radically different environment and social structure of the American city. The transplantation of rural peoples to industrial cities within the same society was difficult enough, but migration to America aggravated the problem. In the new world, they were not only ignorant of the language, laws, institutions and culture, but they were unfamiliar with the new factory discipline and the rapid pace of a dynamic, highly developed industrial society.[1] Immigrants from Poland were further handicapped, until 1919, by the absence of support from their own national state and, except for Austrians, by consular protection as well.

Politics—in the Polish case, partition among the three neighbouring European empires—also directly influenced emigration. National or religious persecution and flight from military service were frequently factors in the decision to leave Poland. The fairly large emigration brought on by the failure of the revolution of 1905-07 was especially important since it included a substantial number of intelligentsia and skilled workers. They played an important role as stimulators of cultural and political life in Polonia, bringing new values and vigour to its organizational life.

Political emigrés, of course, thought of their stay in the United States as temporary. The expectations, hopes and plans of the "average" immigrant were somewhat different. Many went abroad temporarily, they thought, to earn enough money to purchase farmland, a workshop or a small business upon their return. It seemed, to some at least, that politics, the lack of an independent state, were responsible for their economic status at home and that the restoration of Poland would make their return feasible.

The character and institutions of the immigration were also shaped by the political and social structure of the partition, sometimes the very village, from which it derived. The immigrants from Prussian Poland, for example, were distinguished by higher levels of prosperity, literacy, craft and business skills, and knowledge of modern agriculture. They were also better prepared to create self-help institutions and, because they often knew German, to deal with foremen and church officials in the United States. The differences among the Prussian, Russian and Austrian sectors were especially apparent in the political orientations of immigrants toward the Central Powers or Allies during the First World War.

How much had the newcomers known about the country of their choice? Very often their knowledge about America was derived from a letter from relatives and friends in the United States. Sometimes it took concrete form through the well-dressed "Amerykan" who returned to his family village with tales of eating meat three times a day and fancy cakes as often as he liked. The externals of their vision were the most realizable. On arrival in the United States, the immigrant was immediately commanded by his American contact to dispose of his old country (*starokrajskie*) clothes, even though these were often of good quality and purchased just prior to departure. With his last few cents, even with borrowed money, the newcomer was clothed in American garments, the country maid jammed into a corset and tight shoes with high heels. A son, recently arrived from a long stay in Brazil, sought to kiss his father's hand in public as was the custom in Poland, but the somewhat Americanized father was embarrassed and ashamed at the public confession of his origins. As a rule the immigrant tried to make himself one of the American crowd, albeit superficially.[2]

The need to mimic American ways is understandable, but the effort was largely a failure. The most serious barrier was language. The lack of knowledge of English condemned immigrants to take whatever jobs—even the worst kind—were available, exposing them to exploitation by agents and bosses, easily misunderstanding the orders of foremen. The newcomer only realized his problem fully after arrival. "The children cry the very same manner as in Poland, even the children of Negroes, but the people speak a quite different language," complained one peasant-immigrant with astonishment. Another, a highly qualified brazier (or smith-silver, as he called himself) failed to find work for a long while because no one in his circle knew the English term for his craft. He even wrote to the editor of a Polish newspaper in Chicago but never received an answer. Finally he learned the word from a Jewish salesman from Poland. Nor were many immigrants able to attend classes in English at the start for they were often ill-prepared by previous schooling and preoccupied with most basic problems of survival and adaptation.[3]

Many of the cleverer or better educated immigrants complained about the indifference and apathy of their compatriots.[4] However, though immigrants mostly expected hard work in America, their previous experience did not provide even an approximate idea of the realities—the scale of difficulties, the divergence from the old ways, the character of work—in the new world. They were especially unprepared for the uncertainties of their place in the labour market. Economic fluctuations and the perennial danger of unemployment—"green-horns" were always the first to be laid off—shaped their lives and personalities. Easy victims of ridicule and discrimination, new immigrants were easy scapegoats for the disappointments and frustrations of others. Vulnerable and demanding relatively little to live, they were seen as competitors for jobs and, with some justice at first, as strikebreakers.

Periods of relative prosperity alternated with unemployment, search for work and indebtedness. Money brought from home seldom exceeded the minimum required by the immigration authorities. The costs of the voyage, the necessities of life before regular work was found, and the expense of bringing families to America exhausted any savings and often drove immigrants into debt. Indebtedness combined with instability of earnings to jeopardize the best-laid plans, delay the reunion of families or the return to Poland, and often encouraged personal demoralization. Above all, it hindered or delayed achievement of their American Dream—the purchase of at least a modest piece of real estate—which they had brought with them from the old country and had nurtured during the struggle to establish themselves. A guarantee of safety, stability and family security, the ownership of land represented success in terms which the immigrants could understand and realistically attain. Time and again, notably in the Great Depression of the 1930s, their hard-won achievement was threatened. "Bent on survival," as one writer put it, "they narrowed their lives to the thinnest line of existence."[5] It is no wonder that the children and grandchildren of Polish immigrants, in contrast to longer-established, middle-class Americans, value "stability" more than "satisfaction from work."[6]

The immigrant seldom decided to go to America without the promise of support from someone there, but his hopes were not always realized. Sometimes the promise of a job which motivated his move faded in the changed economic environment of arrival. In any case, help was usually limited to a few days of hospitality, and assistance in finding shelter and work. The single newcomer became a *bortnik* (boarder), often subletting a bed which was shared by someone working another shift. "Here, in America," as one man put it, "every working man must think for himself about himself and is not to count on anyone else."[7] The adage that "everyone with money has friends" was a truth quickly learned by newcomers. In the recollections of immigrants, it is clear that established Polonia institutions helped their members mainly. Except for warm memories of St. Joseph's Immigrant Home in New York, new arrivals seldom encountered any organized community help. There are some examples of socialist circles aiding political immigrants, but more frequent were complaints that societies did not even want to meet and talk with the unemployed.[8] Nevertheless, new immigrants depended on the ghetto settlements because of the regional character of emigration (or one might say that the regional character of emigration encouraged neighbourhood dependence in America).[9] Even when work was not available in that first environment, language barriers, relative ease in making new contacts, and the desire to satisfy less easily defined spiritual needs, encouraged immigrants to settle in other Polish communities.

A newcomer was sometimes shocked to discover changes which the sojourn in America had wrought in an old friend. It was difficult to accept a situation in which "after work everyone calculates how many hours he worked and how much he was paid."[10] For many men, the only distraction was the saloon, the Polish *knajpa.* An unemployed worker might be stood a beer by his companions, but it was not consistent with old country manners "to drink at another's expense and not to stand for it himself."[11] Lacking proper clothes and money, the new immigrant might be embarrassed to attend church where he found the materialism of American life most shocking. Even after many years in the United States, he might find it difficult to accept the spirit in which the offertory envelope was inscribed "give as much as you value your faith."[12] The bitterness of the new life led to some harsh evaluations: "Here a human being is only called a human being, but he is not a human. Here a man is a machine in perpetual motion, a man who forgets about himself and lives only for the dollar . . . "; "Here the people who do not estimate your knowledge, but your money, if you have some, they would call you omniscient."[13] Others were disgusted with the manners of Polish Americans. Disappointed because he had expected a quite different style of life, one peasant from a remote village in the Wilno region sharply criticized the primitive nature of dancing parties, the absence of good manners and improper behaviour toward women by the standards that prevailed in his home.[14]

Yet the myth of America persisted. European experience seemed to prove that there was a greater degree of legal and social equality, more peaceful intergroup relations, fairer civil administration and a more tolerant attitude to religious diversity. The immigrant, working beyond his strength, conscious of social injustice and the permanence of his social status, concluded in spite of all, that the possibilities for material advancement were greater in America than elsewhere. Despite some reservations, he admired the industriousness, ingenuity and capacity for organization which appeared to lay at the foundation of the higher standard of living. During the First World War, some Polish societies prepared their members to return to independent Poland through lectures and courses on American methods and skills. Even in the economic crisis of the 1930s, the unemployed immigrant rated his standard of living above what he had known in Poland. The very hardships of the first years in the United States and (to an outsider) a relatively low level of aspiration, accentuated and perhaps exaggerated the progress they had made since the beginning. The illiterate peasant from northeastern Poland who, after decades of work, could cover his wife with a fur coat, and his floor with a "linoleum carpet," rent a three-room apartment with electricity and running water, where he enjoyed a player piano (*fortepijan na rolkach*) and a radio, was genuinely proud of his achievement. His American standard of living was higher, he thought, than the imagined comfort of the "count" in the old country.[15] In the United States, "it seems to me," wrote one immigrant, "the situation is the best, better than anywhere in other countries."[16]

Notes

1. Witold Kula, Nina Assorodobraj-Kula, and Marcin Kula, eds., *Listy emigrantów z Brazylii i Stanów Zjednoczonych 1890-1891* (Warsaw, 1973), p. 88.
2. *Pamiętniki emigrantów. Stany Zjednoczone* II (2 vols.; Warsaw, 1977), pp. 54-55, 390, 609.
3. Ibid., II, p. 462; I, p. 288.
4. Ibid., I, p. 337.
5. Thomas C. Wheeler, ed., *The Immigrant Experience. The Anguish of Becoming American* (Baltimore, 1972), p. 8.
6. Renata Siemińska, *Siła tradycji i siła interesów. O źródłach białego ruchu etnicznego w Stanach Zjednoczonych* (Warsaw, 1978), p. 155.
7. *Pamiętniki,* I, p. 288.
8. Ibid., I, p. 356.
9. Tadeusz Makarewicz, "Emigracja a macierzysta grupa parafialna," *Przegląd socjologiczny* 4, nos. 3-4 (1936), pp. 521-46.
10. *Pamiętniki,* II, p. 458.
11. Ibid.
12. Ibid., II, p. 469; I, p. 414.
13. Ibid., I, p. 344.
14. Ibid., I, pp. 335-36.
15. Ibid., II, p. 469.
16. Ibid., I, p. 492.

New-Old Communities

Villages of Steel Mills and Packinghouses: the Polish Worker on Chicago's South Side, 1880-1921

Dominic A. Pacyga

By 1900 Chicago had joined the ranks of great industrial cities. Visitors often came not to see the impressive downtown, magnificent park system, or beautiful lakefront, but to witness the city's industrial might. Chicago was already the meatpacking centre of the nation and was presenting a serious challenge to Pittsburgh's leadership in steel-making. Tours through the huge plants were musts on any tourist's itinerary. The South Side of the city contained the great industrial nexus centring on the Union Stock Yards and on the huge steel mills which lined the lakefront south of 79th Street. The development of industry meant the creation of thousands of jobs which in turn meant the arrival of workers and the formation of working-class neighbourhoods adjacent to the slaughterhouses and mills. Every wave of immigration that touched Chicago and the country was reflected in the populations of South Chicago and the Back of the Yards.

Chicago passed Cincinnati in the slaughtering of hogs in 1861 and became the leading meatpacker of the nation. When the Union Stock Yards were opened four years later the livestock business became consolidated in the southwest of the city, in an area bounded by 39th Street on the north and 47th Street to the south with Halsted Street and Racine Avenue making up the eastern and western boundaries. Most of the packing plants were located about two miles to the northeast in Bridgeport along the south branch of the Chicago River. Once the yards were opened, new plants began to be erected in the area just west of the sale pens. Eventually all of the large packers settled here in the district known as Packingtown.[1]

The Union Stock Yards and the industry grew rapidly. In 1866, the yards' first full year of operation, 1,564,293 head of stock passed through the sale pens. This number grew to 14,622,315 in

1900, reaching an all-time record for a livestock market in 1924 with 18,643,539 head. In 1900 the original 320 acres had grown to 475 acres with a pen capacity for 75,000 cattle, 50,000 sheep, 300,000 hogs, and 5,000 horses. By this time about 32,000 people worked in the industry; this number grew to approximately 60,000 during the First World War.[2]

While meatpacking was becoming the predominant industry on the near South Side, to the southeast of the slaughterhouses the steel mill district was also expanding rapidly. In 1880 the North Chicago Rolling Mill Company opened its South Works on 74.5 acres of lakefront below 79th Street. By 1898, and after a merger which created the Illinois Steel Company, the South Works covered 260 acres. The complex eventually expanded to over 600 acres. Other mills followed the South Works to South Chicago.[3] These gave the entire region the ambience of a steel town; they dominated the skyline and polluted the atmosphere of the neighbourhood. Eventually the steel industry spilled over the Illinois-Indiana boundary. There a new town, Gary, was developed by the huge United States Steel Corporation which was created by a merger that included Illinois Steel in 1900.[4]

The plants attracted wave after wave of immigrants. The first to settle in the Back of the Yards were the Irish who entered the packinghouses in large numbers in the 1870s and 1880s. Many of them followed the industry when it moved from Bridgeport to the area west of the new stockyards. In 1881 the Irish founded the parish of St. Rose of Lima on 48th and Ashland Avenue. At about the same time German Catholics were establishing the parish of St. Augustine, and German Lutherans were soon to erect the church of St. Martini. The neighbourhood had a German and Irish atmosphere, and for a time the two groups dominated the packing industry. They were soon joined by other groups, however, including the Poles.

By the turn of the century the neighbourhood had become predominantly Polish and Slavic. The first Polish parish of St. Joseph was established in 1889, to be followed later by the parishes of St. John of God and the Sacred Heart. While the first Poles were generally from Prussian Poland, by the period of the First World War most of the Polish immigrants were Highlanders from the Tatra Mountains, and many of them settled in the parish of the Sacred Heart. This parish later served as the meeting place for the First Congress of the Polish Highlanders Alliance in 1930.[5] By this time the Back of the Yards contained twelve Roman Catholic parishes in the area of only about two and one-half square miles.

South Chicago was also a receiving area for the huge migrations of the nineteenth and twentieth centuries. The Irish and Germans were among the early settlers in the neighbourhood, followed by the Poles after the establishment of the South Works in 1880. Two years later there were some thirty Polish families in the district. At that time there was no Polish parish in South Chicago and the immigrants were under the care of the priests at St. Stanislaus Kostka on the North Side of Chicago. Indeed, there were only three Polish parishes in the whole of Chicago, and all were located far from the emerging steel district. As a response to this, the growing community of Polish Catholics organized the St. Vincent Benevolent Society in 1881, it was this group that took the initial steps toward creating the first Polish parish in South Chicago, the Immaculate Conception, in 1882.[6]

The community grew and spread throughout South Chicago. In 1891 it was evident that another parish was needed and the church of St. Michael the Archangel was created on 82nd Street and South Shore Drive. Two other Polish parishes were founded —St. Mary Magdalen in 1910 and St. Bronislava in 1928. The Polish population became more dominent in South Chicago than in Back of the Yards. Both neighbourhoods were shared, however, with other ethnic groups.[7]

In the nineteenth century and well into the twentieth the Polish peasant lived in a world based on the church, the community and the family. These three institutions marked, within the rhythm of the seasons, the frontiers of rural society and formed the communities' world view. Throughout much of the nineteenth century peasants lived in self-contained villages, but slowly outside influences affected them, especially after the abolition of serfdom. Nevertheless, traditional society did not give way easily, old customs persisted and many of them were transplanted to America. Of course the new milieu influenced traditional lifestyles, which became modified in time to meet the new reality. A similar process occurred at the same period in Poland as that country underwent industrialization and became gradually absorbed into the developing Western capitalist order.

When Poles found themselves thrust into an alien urban environment they responded in much the same way as other immigrants—they created neighbourhoods. The identification with a local community was extremely important and the kind of communities formed had much to do with the manner in which Poles migrated to the United States and Chicago. An intricate system based on primary relationships was created. As successive waves of immigrants came to North America, they gravitated to communities that had been settled by their relatives and neighbours in the old country.[8] This is the reason why, for example, the Highlanders settled in the Back of the Yards while Kujawiaks tended to go to South Chicago.[9]

The neighbourhood-building experience of Polish workers in Chicago sheds light on the development of working-class districts in the industrial cities of the North. While the word "neighbourhood" has been used as a generic term it has not been precisely defined. To understand the historical process through which Polish and other ethnic groups have passed during the periods of large working-class migrations, it is important to differentiate between a "neighbourhood" and a "community."

The neighbourhood first of all is a geographical unit. It is this geography which to a large extent determines behaviour. In the large industrial cities like Chicago this environment was man-made, the product of the economic development of the area. In the Back of the Yards and South Chicago the ecology was dominated by the industries located in them. The packing industry gave the Stock Yard District a special ambience. The streets were lined with working-class balloon, or wooden-frame dwellings. These were primarily cottages and two-family dwellings. The neighbourhood was cut off from the rest of the city by the stockyards to the east, the open sewer, Bubbly Creek to the north, and by garbage dumps to the west. City services were poor. Alleys were rarely cleaned and many homes were not connected with the municipal water and sewer works.[10] In 1904 when Upton Sinclair visited the area he referred to it as "the Jungle."[11] The geography dictated the future development of the Back of the Yards, a future very different from other nearby communities such as Hyde Park on the lakefront to the east of the Stock Yard District. And it was this geography that molded the response of the Polish community to its position in American society.

The Polish response was a communal one, and one where the church played a central role. A parish was more than a religious institution, it was a meeting place and a cultural centre. It gave the new community a physical and spiritual focal point in the neighbourhood. The parish provided an outlet for the concerns of the peasant immigrants. In response to the fear expressed by Złotopolski in Sienkiewicz's *Za Chłebem* that the immigrant young would be lost to Poland,[12] a school was established in an attempt to maintain Polish culture and traditions among the youth. The parish also contained various fraternal and religious groups which helped to continue a sense of *Polskösċ* among adults. Plays, operas, poetry readings and libraries were common in Polonia. Later sports became an outlet for children and young adults.[13] In response to the assimilationist tendencies of industrialization Polish peasants used the church as a solid rock upon which to build their new neighbourhood-villages.

Other institutions also played important roles in the communal movement. Saloons and stores were among the most important of these. The tavern was an important institution in the Polish village and in the Polish-American community. Here labour unions and political parties were organized. The saloon was also a news-gathering place where immigrants could come to exchange local gossip and where new settlers could find the address of relatives and friends from the bartender. It was a central social institution for the communal neighbourhood.[14]

Stores were also used as meeting places. Both the Back of the Yards and South Chicago contained large east European Jewish populations which settled along the main commercial streets. Polish Jews played much the same role in the new neighbourhoods as they had in the Polish countryside. The relationship between Polish Jews and Christians was often strained, but remained important. With the emergence of a middle class entrepreneurial group in Polonia there was some attempt to take business away from the Jewish stores, but as in Europe it was not as successful as hoped. The Polish peasant understood the Jewish merchant, and often preferred to do business with him in the traditional manner.[15]

In order to understand the concept of neighbourhood it is necessary to see the importance of the individual block within the neighbourhood itself. The block was the area where primary relationships took place. The architecture of the apartments and houses was conducive to an active street life. Families sat on the stoops in the evenings; children and adults used the alleys as playgrounds and short cuts. The block was like a small village and indeed often contained the population from the same village in the old country. Gangs became the military arm of the block and patterned themselves after adult organizations.[16]

The most important institution was the family. As in most rural communities, the familial group had played an important role in Poland; it was the basis of the peasant agricultural economic unit.[17] In Chicago it was the reason for the creation of all other neighbourhood institutions. The church and the block reinforced the power of the family. The family was, of course, instrumental in the migration process itself. It is not suprising that its stability was so important for Polonia.

The Polish workers, then, struggled to build a community within the framework of the neighbourhood. The neighbourhood itself was a collection of several communities. Poles lived next to older German and Irish settlements. In fact there is some evidence that Poles were attracted to neighbourhoods where German Catholics were already maintaining institutions. In turn Poles were joined by Lithuanians, Slovaks, Ukrainians and other east European groups. Their immediate neighbours in Europe became their new neighbours on Chicago's South Side.[18]

The working conditions in the mills and packinghouses were deplorable. In the stockyards the work day was irregular. Down in South Chicago the twelve-hour day, seven-day week prevailed.[19] Wages were low and fluctuated with the economy.[20] Industrial accidents happened with a frightening frequency in the mills, and diseases associated with work in the slaughterhouses threatened all workers, adult and child.[21] Poles filled the unskilled positions in both industries at the turn of the century.[22]

The communal nature of Polish society in North America led naturally to the organization of labour unions once the community had passed through an initial settling-in period. By 1904 the Poles were active in the Amalgamated Meat Cutters and Butcher Workmen locals in Chicago. One reason for their active participation was the fact that the union allowed unskilled workers to join.[23] Mechanization and improvements in production made the unskilled crucial for any organizational drive in the large mass-production industries.

Polish workers took part in both the 1904 and 1921 meat strikes. In 1921 they were among the most loyal union members in a long winter strike which badly hurt the community.[24] In 1919 Polish steelworkers supported a union movement revived by reforms which allowed the recruitment of unskilled men and by a wartime emergency which saw the government aiding the workers in order to avoid the shut down of a vital industry.[25] When the postwar reaction set in, the steel unions were among the first to be attacked. The 1919 strike, called to secure formal recognition of the union as a bargaining agent and to improve the working conditions, was a tremendous failure. But once again Polish and east European workers stood steadfast behind the union. David Brody has described the strikes in detail, but what emerges from a study of them is a common pattern in the types of violence associated with them. Riots that occurred were communal ones; the entire neighbourhood was involved. The Polish community in particular was very active in the fighting.

Street battles between the Chicago police and working-class crowds were features of the 1904, 1919 and 1921 strikes. The 1921 meatpacking walkout is an especially good example of the communal strike. Crowds of women and children supported the strikes. Polish women clutching their babies faced mounted police.[26] Many of the women were workers themselves, but more importantly they were community members. The entire community felt threatened after a period of relative economic stability brought upon by unionization and wartime prosperity. Churches had been beautified during this period, parish debts eliminated, and Polish workers had purchased homes, thereby making a definite commitment to the neighbourhood.[27] The threatened pay cut and the possible destruction of the union could undermine everything that had been struggled for. The Polish urban worker acted much the same way that the villagers in Reymont's novel *Peasants* had when they battled the local gentry for control of forest land.[28] In each case the Poles had felt themselves threatened; their community was under attack. In each case the entire community responded regardless of age or sex. The rural and urban manifestation of communalism meant unity when the life of the village was in peril.

The Polish worker living on the South Side of Chicago created a new society based on his past communal experiences. It was not a reproduction of the Polish village because it operated in a new urban milieu, but it contained social institutions Poles were familiar with. Since the one-time peasants were now members of the working class, they were forced to make adjustments. This meant joining unions with other ethnic and racial groups. It also meant communal support of the labour organizations by every stratum of the neighbourhood from the churches, schools, saloons, stores, on to the families. While the labour riot was not a jacquerie, it was a distant cousin, and a community affair.

Notes

1. Phyllis Bate, "The Development of the Iron and Steel Industry of the Chicago Area" (Ph.D. dissertation, University of Chicago, 1949), p. 9; William Parkhurst, *History of the Yards 1865-1953* (Union Stock Yard & Transit Company, 1953), p. 11.
2. Union Stock Yard & Transit Company, *81st Annual Livestock Report, 1946* (Chicago: U.S.Y. & T. Co., 1946); pp. 8-9; Commission on Chicago Historical Landmarks, *Report on the Union Stock Yard Gate* (Chicago, 1971), p. 4.
3. Bate, "Development of Iron and Steel Industry," pp. 10-11; Victor Windett, "The South Works of the Illinois Steel Company," *Journal of the Western Society of Engineers* 3 (Chicago, 1898), p. 789.
4. The Iroquois Iron Company plant was built in the 1880s on the south side of the Calumet River; in the 1890s it moved to a new site opposite the South Works. Three large mills located in the area around 106th Street: the Wisconsin Steel Division of the International Harvester Co., the Federal Furnace Company, and the Interstate Iron and Steel Company. The Youngstown Sheet and Tube Company also located in South Chicago. See Bate, "Development of Iron and Steel Industry," p. 13, and John B. Appleton, "The Iron and Steel Industry of the Calumet District—A Study in Economic Geography" (Ph.D. dissertation, University of Chicago, 1925), pp. iii-iv.
5. "The Back of the Yard Area," p. 21, in the University of Chicago Settlement House Papers, Chicago Historical Society, Box 1, Folder 1 (hereafter cited as Settlement House Papers). Bertram B. Fowler, *Men, Meat and Miracles* (New York: Julian Messner, Inc., 1952), p. 79; Vivian Palmer, comp., "Documents: History of Bridgeport," Document no. 1; Department of Development and Planning, City of Chicago, *Historic City: The Settlement of Chicago* (Chicago, 1976), pp. 49-50; "The Foreign Born: Immigrants in the Packing Industry," n.d. in Mary McDowell Papers, Chicago Historical Society, Box 2, Folder 12 (hereafter cited as McDowell Papers); Louis J. Schwartzkopf, *The Lutheran Trail* (St. Louis: Concordia Publishing House, 1950), pp. 330-31; *Pamiętnik 2-Go Sejmu Związku Podhalan w Pol-*

nocnej Ameryce [Memorial Book of the Second Convention of the Podhale Alliance in North America] (Chicago, 1933), p. 15.

6. *Diamond Jubilee 1882-1957 Immaculate Conception B.V.M. Parish* (Chicago, 1957), pp. 21, 26.
7. Ibid., pp. 27, 33, 40.
8. Frank J. Sheridan, "Italian, Slavic, and Hungarian Unskilled Immigrant Laborers in the United States," *Bulletin of the Bureau of Labor* 72 (September 1907), pp. 479-80; Marja Gliwicowna, "Drogi Emigracji" ["Paths of Emigration"], *Przegląd Socjologiczny* [Sociological Review] 4 (Warsaw-Poznan, 1936), pp. 509-11.
9. Although it is nearly impossible to trace the origin of these Polish mountaineers, the census data, the location of the principal mountaineer organizations and meetings of their conventions on Chicago's South Side indicate their location in the Stock Yard District. Sacred Heart parish in the Back of the Yards was a favourite meeting place for the Podhalan clubs. See *Sacred Heart of Jesus Church Golden Jubilee Book, 1910-1960* (Chicago, 1960). A similar overview was expressed by Rev. Stanley Orlikiewicz, the main speaker at the Graduate Reunion and Dinner Dance (all classes, 1912-66), Sacred Heart Grammar School, September 4, 1976. For South Chicago see Józef Chałasiński, "Parafja i szkoła parafialna wśród emigracji polskiej w Ameryce. Studium dzielnicy polskiej w Połudnowym Chicago" ["The Parish and the Parish School among Polish Emigrants in America. A Study of Polish Children in South Chicago"], *Przegląd Socjologiczny* 3 (Warsaw, 1935), p. 637.
10. Sophinisba Breckinridge and Edith Abbott, "Housing Conditions in Chicago: III, Back of the Yards," *American Journal of Sociology* 16 (January 1911), pp. 434-35; Mary E. McDowell, "Standard of Living" (typed manuscript), p. 4 in McDowell Papers, Box 2, Folder 13; Eleanor Kroll, "The History of the University of Chicago Settlement House" (typed manuscript), p. 10 in McDowell Papers, Box 1, Folder 3A.
11. Upton Sinclair, *The Jungle* (New York: The Viking Press, 1947; reprint of 1905 edition), passim.
12. Henryk Sienkiewicz, *After Bread,* trans. Vatslaf A. Hlasko and Thomas Bullick (New York: R.F. Fenno & Co., 1897), p. 101.
13. See the various parish histories.
14. Chałasiński, "Parafja Polski w Ameryce," p. 638; Helen Stankiewicz Zand, "Polish American Leisureways," *Polish American Studies* 18 (January-June 1961), p. 35; E.C. Moore, "The Social Value of the Saloon," *The American Journal of Sociology* 3 (July 1897), pp. 4-5.
15. Edward R. Kantowicz, *Polish-American Politics in Chicago* (Chicago: University of Chicago Press, 1975), pp. 118-19.
16. Frederick M. Thrasher, *The Gang* (Chicago: University of Chicago Press, 1927), p. 174.
17. William I. Thomas and Florian Znaniecki, *The Polish Peasant in Europe and America* 1 (Chicago: University of Chicago Press, 1919), pp. 87-90.

18. Victor Greene, *For God and Country* (Madison: The State Historical Society of Wisconsin, 1975), pp. 58-59, 150.
19. U.S. Congress, Senate, *Final Report and Testimony Submitted to Congress by the Commission on Industrial Relations* S. Doc. 415, 64th Cong., 2nd sess., 1916. Vol. 4, p. 3464; David Brody, *Steelworkers in America: The Nonunion Era* (New York: Harper & Row, 1969), pp. 35-37.
20. *Industrial Relations Report and Testimony,* p. 3464.
21. William Hard, "Making Steel and Killing Men," *Everybody's Magazine* 17 (November 1907), p. 579; Floyd Erwin Bernard, "A Study of Industrial Diseases in the Stockyards," (M.A. thesis, University of Chicago, 1910), passim.
22. Carroll D. Wright, "Influence of Trade Unions on Immigrants," *Bulletin of the Bureau of Labor* 56 (January 1905), p. 2.
23. David Brody, *The Butcher Workmen* (Cambridge: Harvard University Press, 1964), pp. 38-41.
24. Dominic A. Pacyga, "Crisis and Community: The Back of the Yards, 1921," *Chicago History* 6 (Fall 1977), p. 176.
25. David Brody, *Labor in Crisis: The Steel Strike of 1919* (New York: J.B. Lippincott Company, 1965), pp. 54, 70-71.
26. *Dziennik Związkowy* [Alliance Daily] (Chicago), December 8, 1921.
27. Pacyga, "Crisis and Community," p. 176.
28. Ladislas Reymont, *The Peasants* 2, trans. Michael A. Dziewicki (New York: Alfred A. Knopf, 1925), pp. 268-84.

"T'was Hope Here": The Polish Immigrants in Johnstown, Pennsylvania, 1890-1930

Ewa Morawska

Several facets made Johnstown, Pennsylvania a typical small city in late nineteenth-century America. The Cambria Iron Works, opened in 1853 to exploit the vast local deposits of iron ore, coal and limestone, expanded its operations so rapidly that by the 1880s Johnstown was counted among the first six of the nation's steel centres. The industrial growth of the city was accompanied by a corresponding increase of its population: from 8,380 in 1880 to 21,805 in 1890, 35,936 in 1900 and 55,482 one decade later. Like other industrial centres, Johnstown also attracted a number of immigrants from Europe: first from Britain, Germany and Ireland, later from southern and eastern parts of the Continent. In 1890 the town recorded 4,482 persons of foreign birth and 5,978 natives of foreign parentage. Of the former, only about 1,000 were "new" immigrants. By 1900 the number of foreign-born persons increased to 7,318 and that of the native-born of foreign parentage to 9,629. Of the former, 3,509 came from western Europe and the remaining 3,350 were east Europeans. Of the second generation, 4,826 were sons and daughters of British, German and Irish immigrants; 882 came from other west European families and 3,600 were children of the new immigrants. A decade later, Johnstown's foreign population reached 15,316, of whom 8,117 had come from southern and eastern Europe. The second generation numbered 13,467, of whom 3,714 were children of the new immigrants.[1]

The industrial expansion and rapid population growth made Johnstown similar to other American cities. It also possessed some particular traits, which gave the city its own local character. These determined to a large extent the opportunities and means of adjustment accessible to the immigrant workers.

One of Johnstown's outstanding characteristics was the town's dependence by the 1880s on the Cambria Iron Company. The influence of the company, which had been further strengthened by the destruction of the local unions, stretched far beyond the economic realm. Not only did Cambria have on its payroll 75 per cent of the city's labour force involved in manufacturing pursuits; it also developed its own railroad system which brought coal and ore to the mills; it owned a woollen factory in the city as well as a flour mill and the largest general store. Company managers held several public offices in Johnstown and took a leading part in the social and cultural life of the community. They built and patronized the city hospital and the public library, constructed hundreds of houses for their workers, presided over most of the Johnstown banking and loan institutions. In short, by the end of the century Johnstown had become a perfect company town and stayed so for almost fifty years.[2]

Closely related was another characteristic: an unusually large percentage of the population at the turn of the century had resided in town for twenty years or longer. The residential stability of Johnstowners was undoubtedly related to Cambria's efficient paternalism and to its deliberate hiring policy which until the late 1880s gave a priority to the native American workers from the nearby area.[3] With no substantial shift from 1890 until the 1930s, the native Americans of native parentage constituted a solid 50 per cent of the city's population. From the foundation of Johnstown until the 1940s, the community life, its public opinion, political orientations, social and cultural sentiments were overwhelmingly influenced by this stable, native American element.

These, then, were the general conditions encountered by the east European immigrants settling in Johnstown at the turn of the century. Their chances of advancement, their prospects of success, if measured by native American standards, were largely predetermined. Their low socio-economic standing and the company's hiring policies which had reflected the business cycle as well as the changing demands of technology, set definite limits to the immigrants' movements. The technological changes in American industry in the last two decades of the nineteenth century demanded an increasing supply of unskilled labour. The Cambria steel plants "could not, according to the statements of its representatives, have been operated at all without the aid of immigrants," stated the United States Immigration Commission which had visited Johnstown in 1908.[4] The immigrants' chances in Johnstown were further limited by strong nativistic sentiments pervasive in the community. The Cambria Company did not conceal its attitudes toward the immigrant labour: "Natives are considered superior to all races for executive positions, from the 'labor bosses' up," stated the same report. "In all skilled occupations the preferences are stated to be for native labor first, and

English, Welsh, Scotch, Swedes, Germans and Irish in the order named."[5] The same sentiments dominated at city hall, in the downtown business elite and in the American neighbourhoods. The local newspapers consistently referred to recent immigrants as "Huns" or simply "foreigners." The *Johnstown Tribune*'s reports from the immigrant section invariably confused the various ethnic groups: "Magyars interfered with a ball picnic conducted by Huns," or "Rev. Father Dembinski, Pastor of St. Casimir's Russian Catholic church identified forty-seven of his parishioners killed in the recent mine explosion."[6] The term "Hun," applied indiscriminatedly to all east Europeans, did not necessarily imply contempt; more often it expressed the ignorance and the indifference of the host community toward the newcomers.

Following a natural impulse in an alien environment and because they were shut out from participation in the community at large, the immigrants created their own world, as in-bound and separate as the American one. It was the world governed by the values and rules transplanted from Europe, frequently reinforced by the conditions they found in America. Limited from the outside, the inside world of the immigrants offered a range of prospects and opportunities. While the external conditions restricted the social and economic space in which the immigrants were permitted to move, to them their own territory seemed promising and quite extensive. The world they had created was thick in texture, rich in joys and dramas, with "great careers" and equal notorious bankruptcies, which found but a remote and dim reflection in the Johnstown newspapers and, subsequently, in local opinion.

For many immigrants settling in Johnstown at the end of the century, America had in a way been an extension of their old country village. They had travelled in groups and naturally had chosen the place where their countrymen were already settled. Families, neighbours and sometimes large portions of many villages and even counties were thus transplanted. The first Slavic groups had settled in Johnstown as a result of contracts between the Cambria Steel Company and the New York labour agents. The great majority of Slovaks came from the counties of Spiska, Sariska and Liptovka; the Rusins from Gemer, Blazov and Ungvar; Croatians from Karlovac, Jaska and Carniola. The Poles settled in Johnstown in three subsequent waves: the earliest group came from the Poznan region; the second, much larger group, from the Galician counties of Krosno, the Tarnów and Rzeszów. The "Russians," predominantly from County Mława in northeastern Poland, arrived last. Explaining his father's decision to settle in Johnstown rather than in Pittsburgh where the opportunities might have been somewhat greater, an old Polish miner points to a simple necessity: "What did he know about the world, poor little peasant, what was Pittsburgh or Johnstown or other. . . . He just went where his people were." Stanislas P. came with his parents as a little boy: "They were heading for Chicago but on the boat somebody talked them into coming here and so we went. They said they had friends in Johnstown so this would help."[7]

The city's foreign colony—four wards stretched on both sides of the Cambria plants—had housed immigrants since the 1870s. The Welsh, Germans and Irish who had lived there first, by the end of the century were being rapidly replaced by the east Europeans. In 1900, 85 per cent of all Slavs lived in Cambria City (Wards 15 and 16) and in Minersville (Wards 13 and 14). Many of them lived in the "little shabbies"—company houses rented to them for $10 to $12 a month. In 1908 the Immigration Commission reported on living conditions in the "Croatian" section of the city: "Whole families cook, eat, sleep and live in one room, some of them in very damp basements.... Many of the rooms were dark, badly ventilated, and kept in a very dirty condition, and nearly all the houses were in bad repair."[8] Crowded together and indistinguishable to an outside observer, the Slavs soon formed separate ghettoes within the foreign colony. From one block to the next, the Serbs gave way to the Slovaks and then to the Poles. In 1908, 60 per cent of Polish immigrant families in Johnstown kept boarders and lodgers; quite often fifteen or more in a single household.[9] "In these two little rooms we had lived with the boarders, young men—where should they turn if not to their own—they all slept on the floor," recalls Anthony C., tears coming to his eyes at the remembrance of his first years in Johnstown.

Soon after their arrival the Slovaks, Rusins, Poles and Hungarians, like all immigrant settlers, began organizing their communities. The first Polish society in Johnstown was founded in 1892 and soon after ten more were established. In 1902 the Polish immigrants celebrated the consecration of their own church, St. Casimir's. Three years later the parochial school was opened.

The function of the immigrant societies were threefold. Firstly, they had provided benefits for sick and injured workers and cared for the families of those who had been killed in mill accidents. Secondly, they fulfilled the immigrants' need to cling to their own. As they had settled in Johnstown in groups from different parts of the old country, the Polish immigrants soon formed three separate societies: one composed of the "Prusaki" who did not wish to mix with the "greenhorns," one of the "Krosnaki" who came together in a large group and one of the "Ruski" who had arrived last and did not feel comfortable with the "oldtimers."[10] Thirdly, by organizing under the Polish banner, the whole group was defined as separate from others and given the purpose as well as the authority of the collective representation.

St. Casimir's Church in Cambria City, with one thousand parishioners by 1905, served as a rallying centre for the Polish immigrants who often travelled several miles every Sunday to attend services, to meet their compatriots or to seek advice from the priest, the spiritual leader of the community and its political representative. The Polish church—one of the biggest and most spectacular buildings in the "foreign colony"—was an object of immense pride for the whole congregation. The visible symbol of Polishness, it witnessed the achievements and the good standing of Poles among other immigrant groups. At a time when immigrant labourers were earning on the average between $10 to $15 a week, the Polish community had duly contributed up to $1,000 a month for their church in the form of dues, pew collections and various holiday donations.[11] "Our Polish church," with its loud bells and high towers overlooking the neighbourhood re-created for the immigrants the familiar old-country surroundings and at the same time established their place in the new environment.

A few days after they had arrived in Johnstown, the immigrants would usually go to work. In the mines they worked twelve or more hours a day, six days a week; in the mills as well as working ten to twelve hours a day for six days a week, once a fortnight they had to do a 48-hour shift. The same networks of kin and village friendships which brought them over to Johnstown were now used to get a job. Without exception, all the Polish immigrants questioned pointed to family members or neighbours as their "job agents." After they had settled they would in turn place others in one of the Polish "gangs" at the mills. The local priest served as the important link in this informal yet most efficient employment network. "Our Polish Priest had some connections in Cambria Company . . . if only one of his people had lost the job or a new man came seeking employment, it was enough for Father to write a little note to the management and job was there for the asking, from the priest."[12] The priest's role as a go-between which he was to perform for the next two decades was profitable to the Polish community as well as to the Cambria Company: ". . . the Polish priest, with the consent of his congregation, made an arrangement whereby the Company was to deduct a dollar from the wages of every Polish Catholic on the regular fortnightly pay days. The result of this policy was one of the finest immigrant church buildings in the city, and the willingness of the company to aid was compensated by certain services on the part of the priest in securing labor when called upon."[13]

According to the Immigration Commission in 1908, 75 per cent of adult Polish males in Johnstown were employed in the iron and steel manufacturing plants, while 22 per cent worked in the mines. Of those employed in the steel mills, 87 per cent were unskilled labourers; the figure for the miners was 94 per cent. A sample of 254 adult Polish males drawn from the 1900 manuscript census of Johnstown revealed a slightly higher percentage of unskilled labourers, the difference due to the fact that the sample contained more unattached boarders than the government study. (Only eighty members of the sample were married men living with their wives.) By 1910 the great majority (90 per cent) of the Polish immigrants who had been living in Johnstown a decade earlier, were still employed as the unskilled labourers, while only 4 per cent had moved to semi-skilled positions. The remaining 6 per cent earned their living from small local business. For about 3,000 skilled and semi-skilled positions available in the iron and steel manufacturing industry in Johnstown, there were (not counting the 7,000 adult male Americans) some 4,000 candidates from the English, Welsh, Scottish, German and Irish groups who had priority before the Slavs. Even if we subtract from this number 4,000 people needed to fill the city's white-collar jobs, the remaining figure is still much greater than the number of more prestigious and better jobs in the industry.[14]

Even though they did not dream of moving into the higher positions at the Cambria Company, the immigrants knew perfectly well which of the jobs available to them were "better" than others and which would offer better prospects. First, there were financial considerations. The wages paid to the unskilled labourer in Cambria's various departments ranged from $8.50 to $12 a week to $20 and over. In the open hearth division, in structural and railroad departments as well as in the brickyards, the majority of Slavic workers earned $10 to $12 a week. The rolling and bessemer mills, car shops and foundries were better: two-thirds of the Polish labourers there earned from $15 to $18 per week. The best jobs, however, were in the blast furnaces and mines. While work there was either dangerous and hot or dirty and wet, 75 per cent of the Poles who worked there averaged over $20 a week.[15] "At that time five dollars more a week made the whole world of difference, so people stuck to these hard dirty jobs," says Wladyslaw W. who at the age of 14 was already working with his father in the mines. Financial considerations were not always the most important, however. "My uncle, I remember," recalls Anthony C., "preferred working in the mines because, so he thought, it was more independent. He was his own boss. In the mills one had to do what others told you, do this do that, he did not like it." In general, however, the miners had the lowest prestige among the immigrants: "People would say, oh, he is just a coal miner," explains Anthony C., "it was a lowly, dirty job, so many preferred the factory." There, too, some jobs were better than others. "Well, even though you got good pay, the blast furnaces were bad, red hot all day, the hardest work. . . . Finishing department, mechanical shop, these were better jobs, cleaner, lighter."

As limited as they were in their occupational opportunities, the immigrants did have some choice: they could stay in the mines and with a pick and shovel work for 13-14 hours a day to bring home more money. Or they could go to the mills and through friends or relatives try to get a cleaner and lighter job or else a job in a department where wage increases were more certain.

In 1915 only 8 per cent of the Polish immigrants who had lived in Johnstown in 1900 were found in the semi-skilled and skilled occupations. By 1920 this percentage had risen slightly to 9.1 per cent. At the Cambria Steel Company an immigrant's chance of moving into a higher position was minimal. For the total number of 4,200 semi-skilled and skilled jobs available to non-Americans in 1920 in the iron and steel industry in Johnstown, there were nearly 3,500 candidates of British, German and Irish descent. For 4,500 downtown white-collar jobs available for men in the same year, there were three times as many candidates of American, British, German and Irish backgrounds.[16]

Restricted in their movements, the immigrants nevertheless perceived the opportunities opening for them. The old world they had left behind was not like that contained in a popular American cliché: the isolated, shut-in hamlets where people spent their whole lives unaware of or unaffected by outside changes. In fact, before leaving for America, a number of east European peasants in the last quarter of the nineteenth century had repeatedly used the seasonal migration as means of material improvement. The money was used to buy more land, to grow more grain, to raise more cattle or build a bigger house. "America" had meant the promise of a much larger fortune, the opportunity to fulfill the peasant ambitions already awakened and growing. "The inquiries have revealed," reported the Immigration Commission from Johnstown in 1908, "that in the communities in the foreign countries where the immigrants lived before coming, the United States has been known as a country of opportunities for earning money, and for economic and political independence, and consequently there has grown up a feeling that it is a country for the dissatisfied and ambitious."[17]

The reality the immigrants encountered in America did not exactly correspond to the villagers' vague dreams of the "glass houses" and the "golden streets." Yet despite the exhausting work, the ugly, unclean surroundings and the shabby housing, the immigrants held to their hopes. Certainly, it was a realistic optimism, trimmed to fit the conditions around them, but optimism nevertheless, whereby the American opportunities, measured by the economic standards of the old country, appeared promising. "Maybe we did expect more and maybe we did not," muses an 81-year-old immigrant woman after she had recollected her initial disappointment with Johnstown and its foreign section, "but for sure there was more bread here and a better future for us."

With the irregular employment—in the steel industry probably more so than elsewhere—and with the big families to be taken care of, the immigrants valued steady work beyond anything else. To have a healthy family and a steady job were the two things immigrants enumerated first as the values most cherished in life. And yet steady employment was not the ultimate goal. For despite the fact that they certainly did not like it, amazingly enough the immigrants were able to *survive,* with the help of friends, relatives and the company store during the times of the industrial depressions, through months of idleness after they had been laid off. "The storekeepers in the neighborhood and the Penn Traffic [the company store], they had always kept selling to us on credit," recalls Mary G., "for weeks and even months sometimes when work at the mills was slack." Explaining how his family had coped with the recurrent unemployment, Ignaz P. explains: "We had chicken and geese and two pigs and my mother used to give away eggs and milk and pancakes to the neighbors when times were hard. Or else they would feed us children when we came around and so it went." Rather than the expression of the survival orientation, as some ethnic historians suggest, a steady job had been perceived as the means of achieving a better life, either back in Europe, where some of them had returned with their savings, or in America, in the immigrant community.[18] Here it had meant a house of one's own, clean and nicely furnished, a well-kept garden, elegant suits, a golden watch (or two), good entertainment, some savings, good respect among the neighbours, a beautiful church.

The immigrants were aware of the maximum promise the outside world held for them: a steady job and, hopefully, gradually increasing wages. Their own inside world, however, offered even greater promise. Within it, and by means of the income flowing from the steady jobs in the mills, they could further adorn their churches and build their clubs, they could have noisy picnics, give great weddings, attend concerts and theatre performances in their Polish hall, support their choirs, bands and orchestras. They could also, with the help of their friends and with a little luck, open a local business and gain greater respect in the community, possibly even reach a position of authority over the whole group. If they were not doing well enough in the business they could return to the mills which "always had jobs for everybody" and build their savings. Viewed from the inside of the immigrant society and through the eyes of its inhabitants, America had offered chances of "getting ahead" that remained within their reach. But among the immigrants—just like in the outside American society—there would always be the "achievers" and the "stagnants." There would be people who tried harder, who were determined to better their lives faster, to "make it big," and there would be others who were quite satisfied with what they had. "It is just something inside people," reflects Anthony C. "Some of them, I remember, they had this drive, this push, while others had had it much less. ... And there were also people who did not have it at all. Some always wanted more from life, so they tried harder and harder and others just lived on what they got, day after day, the whole life, the same thing. I don't know what it is that makes similar people so different. ... "

For those who were willing to risk, the immigrant world offered a range of possibilities. The growing number of the immigrants settling in Johnstown every year created opportunities for small local business. In 1900 there had been no more than eighteen east Europeans among nearly eighty storeowners in the foreign colony: seven Jewish and eleven Slavic "oldtimers" who had lived in Johnstown since the 1880s. By 1905 in the four wards comprising the immigrant section, the number of east European businesses increased fourfold. There were now sixty-eight groceries, variety stores, cigar stands, butcher shops, clothing and jewelry stores, etc. Of the latter, the Poles owned seven: two bakeries, two butcheries, one bookstore with a notary, one pharmacy and one photographic agency. The Immigration Commission reported: "Employees of immigrant business establishments are, with very few exceptions, of the same race as the proprietors," "... the stock carried by immigrant merchants is more or less adapted to the peculiar needs of the immigrant consumers. An examination of a general store, for example, would reveal a comparatively large stock of brightly coloured cloth, handkerchiefs, miners' supplies, etc.; rough shoes and clothing for workingmen; religious pictures, small personal articles, such as tobacco, pipes, etc.... potatoes, sauerkraut, garlic, onions, cheap coffee, and other kinds of food used in a large measure by the foreigners; as well as cheap household and kitchen articles."[19]

The impressive proliferation of immigrant enterprises became possible because, in the opinion of the immigrants, "to open a small business in the neighbourhood did not require any substantial investment." The father of Andrey J. had only $140 when he opened his butcher shop in 1910 in the Fifteenth Ward. He was able to supplement his savings by borrowing from his brother-in-law. "Our family was very well known in the neighbourhood and my father was trusted here. He went to the local wholesalers and asked them and they gave him whatever he needed on credit. They knew him well and did not doubt he would repay them, which he did." After they had borrowed the money to open a store, the immigrant merchants would in turn sell to their customers "on the book" and would extend their credit "as long as was necessary for them to be able to pay." Regular customers of grocery and meat stores, such as the families or boarding houses, "were given store books and the gross amounts had been entered upon the merchant's day books for periodical settlements." Many immigrants cultivated their own gardens (or even the fields outside of Johnstown proper), kept chickens, geese, pigs and cows; and quite frequently they would bring their produce—tomatoes, lettuce, milk, eggs—to a local merchant who would exchange them for meat, flour or sugar.

The same informal, *Gemeinschaft*-type relations among the immigrants had governed their other pursuits. The Immigration

Commission's findings on immigrant investment in real estate revealed conflicting trends among east European immigrants, Poles included. The records of real estate transfer in the Cambria County courthouse are clearer.[20] The total figure for the east European homeownership in Johnstown was only 7 per cent in 1905 and almost 14 per cent in 1910. For the Polish group the respective figures were 9 per cent and 10.5 per cent.[21] Yet, those allegedly backward peasants, foreigners unacquainted with the modern world of finance, had engaged in complex real estate operations with amazing skill and shrewdness, selling one house, buying it back with an adjacent one, reselling it somewhat later with profit, purchasing one lot, doubling its value, leasing it for a while and eventually selling in exchange for one half of a boarding house. Often several people together—relatives or simply neighbours—had been recorded as buyers and sellers of the same property.

A comparison of the number of real estate transfers among immigrants recorded in the courthouse between 1890 and 1910 with that of loans and mortgages taken in the same period, indicates beyond doubt that in the majority of cases the money needed for purchase had been obtained from private hands or else through immigrant bankers. Relatives, friends, local businessmen, even the priest would provide a prospective buyer with the required sum. "The priest gave my uncle $600 and this is how he bought his house," recalls Ignatz P. "My parents had some money put away but not enough so my mother's sister gave them the rest. She just then got the death benefit for her husband who had been killed in the mills and she did not need it right away." Seventy-five-year-old Maria W. still lives in the house her parents bought in 1912. The immigrant banks (there had been no less than six of them in the foreign colony in 1907) also advanced loans on real estate. In that year alone immigrants made a total of $120,000 in deposits in their banks, of which a good part was used for down payments and mortgages.[22]

Restricted as it was and confined to its own limits, the immigrant world nevertheless provided the opportunities for small as well as "large-scale" careers. With the help of the others, the determined and the ambitious could try their luck in local business, in real estate or in banking. Between 1895 and 1910 several immigrants had risen to the positions of respected businessmen and community leaders. According to the Immigration Commission, several immigrant businessmen gained:

> considerable influence among their countrymen by gradually increasing their interests. The most conspicuous example is a Serbian of the foreign section, who, possessing little education, and starting as a common labourer in the principle steel company some years ago, . . . became in a short time the local agent of a prominent foreign banker and steamship agent. In a few years he severed his

> connection with this firm and established a banking house and steamship agency of his own in the foreign section. . . . He embarked also on several other ventures until he operated, in addition to his bank and steamship agency, a Croatian general store, a butcher shop, a Croatian weekly paper, a hotel and barroom, besides considerable real estate holdings.[23]

This was a spectacular and a prominent career. There had been also smaller ones, which found a faint echo in the Johnstown newspapers: "Valentine M., the well-known Polish real estate owner and meat dealer, stated today to a representative of the *Tribune* that he carried $6,000 insurance on his 14-family tenement house which was destroyed by fire this morning."[24] And smaller yet were those of the local storeowners unknown to the people outside their community, "our merchants," who became officers in the immigrant societies and enjoyed the authority of their position. There were even the millworkers who, to fulfill their cherished goals, thriftily lived on one-fourth of their monthly earnings, saving the rest so that they could send for their families or take the money to Europe or purchase a house in Johnstown.[25] There were, finally, the careers of those who had secured positions in "better" departments at Cambria mills and were respectfully envied by their compatriots.[26]

The world created by the immigrants at the turn of the century expanded and deepened in the next two decades. Although Johnstown had long since become a permanent home of the east European workers, the "foreigners" remained almost as isolated from the native American community as they had been before. "The line between the natives and foreigners is very sharply drawn in Johnstown. The native population as a rule know scarcely anything about the foreigners, except what appears in the newspapers about misdemeanours committed in the foreign section.[27] Left to themselves, the immigrants—familiar now with their environment and feeling a part of it with their neighbourhoods, churches and schools, with their jobs in the mills—continued to pursue goals they valued and considered accessible.

Around 1915, following the lead of the Slovaks who had been in the city much longer, the Polish immigrants began moving in increasing numbers from Cambria City and Minersville—the original foreign colony—into the more desirable sections of the city. The east Europeans chose the unclaimed areas in Morrellville and Coopersdale and parts of Brownstown and Lower Yoder. In the chain pattern much like the one they had followed in crossing the ocean, families, neighbours, large groups of people bound by the ties of friendship or interest began moving into the new locations. The new place suited them well: much more spacious, it allowed for the big gardens so necessary to the immigrant household economy. "Almost everyone had gardens and we also kept chicken and geese," recalls Catherine C. "We children would get up in the morning and go with a basket from house to house selling tomatoes, lettuce, eggs, parsley, onions. There was competition, too, if you were late; other children came first with their baskets and got more money." Florence W., who in 1917 had a household of five to feed, tells how every year she and her neighbours would get together and "can things for winter, put sauerkraut in the barrels, marinate beets and make pickles."

Every year more and more immigrants were buying homes in Morrellville which became the new "foreign section." From 10.5 per cent in 1910, Polish homeownership increased to 15 per cent in 1915, 18.6 per cent in 1920 and, the immigrants were now more likely to take out loans from the American banks downtown: from Johnstown Savings Bank, Peoples B&L Association, Friendly City and Loan Association, U.S. Trust Company of Johnstown. The loans ranged from $1,000 to $3,000 and it often took the mortgagees several years to repay their debts. A closer inspection of the Mortgage Books at the Courthouse Recorder's Office reveals the repetitive pattern in the immigrants' efforts to become homeowners. In a typical sequence, John P. in 1906 took a $250 loan from Mr. Amos C., whose house he had bought for $500. In 1907 he sold the house to William K. and bought himself another one for $3,700 from Mrs. Lavignia P., who made him a loan of $2,700. Unable to pay it back, in 1909 he took another loan of $2,400 from Conemaugh B&L Association with which he satisfied his mortgagor. Five years later, still unable to free his house of the mortgage, he took two other loans for a joint sum of $1,700 which he had used repaying the previous loan he took. His final payment on the loan he had taken in 1914 was entered in 1927.[27] Through all these years John P. had been only nominally the owner of his house; but, like many others, he had held to it until eventually it was his own.[28]

In the years following the First World War, the social and organizational network of the Polish community in Johnstown, already quite extensive, became even stronger. St. Casimir's Church remained the pillar and unifying force in the Polish community. Its pastor, who had held his position for more than twenty years from 1902 until 1923, as before directed his people in a strong, authoritarian manner. In 1913 the immigrants built their first "Dom Polski" (Polish Home), and it soon became the centre of the social, cultural and patriotic life of the local Polonia. It was known as Ojczyzna (Fatherland) and people said: "Tonight at Ojczyzna..." or "We are going to Ojczyzna now..." Soon three more Polish Homes were erected and new branches of the Polish societies were founded in those parts of the city where Poles had settled.[29]

Every month the Dramatic Club of the Polish Youth Circle (Kółko Młodzieży Polskiej) gave a theatre performance which attracted large crowds from all over the city. The Polish band played at picnics held every Sunday on the nearby hills. Every Saturday the youth choir sang for the congregation in the church basement and on Fridays it often gave concerts in the Polish Home. Several billiard and poolrooms, bars and cafes—there were nearly forty of them in the foreign section—also provided entertainment and served as centres for social gatherings. There was even in Johnstown a short-lived Polish weekly, *Postep* (later *Wola Ludu*) which between 1924 and 1927 carried news about community events. Not a month passed without weddings and christenings which invariably provided occasions for gatherings. These joyous and noisy events were sometimes reported by the local newspapers.

Local businesses, previously confined to Cambria City and Minersville, expanded rapidly into the new areas of immigrant settlement. By 1915 there were well over one hundred east European small enterprises in greater Johnstown, including poolrooms and restaurants, both Jewish and Slavic. Ten years later, their number increased to more than two hundred. The immigrant-owned enterprise offered a full range of services so that each group could patronize its own businessmen or could choose at will among the others. In 1921 Poles had their own butchery, bakery, photographer and bookstore. There were two Polish funeral homes, four groceries, three automobile rental agencies, two public notary offices, a jeweller, tailor, barber, hotelkeeper, shoemaker and at least three bars with billiards and pool. By 1926 the number of Polish-owned businesses in greater Johnstown increased from twenty to thirty-three. The immigrant community looked up to its merchants and held them in respect. Even though they constituted no more than 6 per cent of the gainfully employed, the businessmen and entrepreneurs were disproportionately represented among the group leaders: more than 60 per cent of the local PNA officers in the years 1910 to 1930 were local merchants.[30]

To acquire a self-employed status, to open a store, a bar or a poolroom had been a dream of many immigrants. "Those who had gotten their own business, even a small, tiny-weeny one," says Wladyslaw W., himself a son of a storekeeper, "were better off than the rest. It was a good thing and they were respected." The career of a small merchant in the neighbourhood, so appealing to many, was not an unrealistic goal, accessible within the confinements of the immigrant world. Around 1925 no more than $1,000 was needed to open a store and if one had some savings or the friends from whom to borrow, it could be done without much effort. The competition, however, was keen, and the risks involved in carrying a business which to a large extent depended upon shifting industrial conditions at the mines and mill, were much too great for many entrepreneurs. The annual Mercantile Appraiser's Lists for the city of Johnstown reveals a high turnover in immigrant businesses. With no significant differences throughout the whole period from 1915 to 1930, from one year to the next more than 50 per cent of store and restaurant owners would disappear from the list and their place would be taken by others trying their luck.[31] For instance, of one hundred immigrant businesses listed in 1923, only about fifty would have had persisted until 1924; but those fifty who had given up were promptly replaced by an equal or even greater number of new ones. Many of those who decided to fold their business in one section of the city, would later try in another place and then again in another. Others, more successful, would subsequently open one, two or even three more stores in different immigrant neighbourhoods, often in partnership with members of their own family.

The process by which the immigrants adjusted to and simultaneously created their environment in Johnstown was the outcome of the interplay between local socio-economic conditions and internal cultural devices they had used to achieve their goals. In order to understand their world, it is necessary to view it and interpret it from the inside, through their own eyes and their own value systems. The range of the immigrants' movements and the scope of their opportunities in the external, American society was severely limited by the general and local industrial conditions as well as by the attitudes of the host community. Yet the opportunities they found in America were, by the Polish peasant immigrants, perceived and evaluated against the comparative framework of, first, the old-country conditions and second, their own immigrant community. Hardworking and recurrently insecure, their existence in this country had still appeared more promising than the one they had left behind. Unintegrated into the Johnstown socio-cultural network and largely left to themselves, even in the mills, the first generation defined their goals and measured their achievements in terms of the values prevailing inside their peasant-immigrant community. They came to America to make a better life for themselves. The price they paid for it was certainly very steep. But with peasant perseverance they sought this better life, step by step, through many set-backs, for many years, pursued and realized among their own, within their immigrant world.

Notes

This paper sums up part of the initial phase of the investigation of Slavic immigrants in Johnstown, Pennsylvania from 1890 to 1940. Research for the first stage of the project has been made possible by a grant from the American Council of Learned Societies.

The quantitative portions of the study are derived from a sample composed of 5,400 east Europeans recorded in the manuscript census for Johnstown in 1900. The residential and occupational movement of those immigrants and their children was traced at five-year intervals in city directories from 1905 to 1940. The Polish part of the sample included 466 individuals: 254 immigrant males; 85 immigrant females; 127 second-generation children from between 1890 and 1900.

1. Tenth Census of the United States: 1880, *Population,* pp. 309, 454; Eleventh Census of the United States: 1890, *Population,* pp. 292, 426-27; Twelfth Census of the United States: 1900, *Population,* Part I, pp. cxxi, 334, 676; Thirteenth Census of the United States: 1910, *Supplement to Pennsylvania,* pp. 579, 610, 646, and *Statistics for Pennsylvania,* p. 628.
2. John Bennett, "Iron Workers in Woods Run and Johnstown: the Union Era, 1865-1895" (Ph.D. dissertation, University of Pittsburgh, 1977), especially Part II.
3. Ibid.
4. U.S. Immigration Commission, *Reports* 8, p. 439. On changes in the steel industry see: John Fitch, *The Steel Workers* III of the Pittsburgh Survey (New York, 1910); David Brody, *Steelworkers in America. The Non-Union Era* (New York, 1960), chapters 1-3; Katherine Stone, "The Origin of Job Structures in the Steel Industry," *Radical America* 7, no. 6 (1973), pp. 19-64.
5. U.S. Immigration Commission, *Reports* 8, pp. 400-01.
6. *Johnstown Tribune,* 5 July 1900, p. 1; *Johnstown Democrat,* 12 July 1902, p. 1.
7. This quotation and those below are derived from interviews with long-time Johnstown residents conducted by the author from 1979 to 1980. Copies of the interviews are in the possession of the author. On the beginnings and sources of Slavic settlement in the city see: N.D. Shappee, "A History of Johnstown and the Great Flood of 1889" (Ph.D. dissertation, University of Pittsburgh, 1940), p. 87; the marriage and funeral records of St. Casimir's (Polish) Church, St. Mary's Greek Catholic Church, St. Stephen's (Slovak) Church, St. Rochus (Croatian) Church, all in Johnstown, from 1895 to 1914; Anthony Cyburt, "Historia Polonii w Johnstown, Pa." ["The History of Polonia in Johnstown, Pa."], 1966, p. 7, typescript in possession of the author.
8. U.S. Immigration Commission, *Reports* 8, p. 404. On housing conditions among immigrants, see: US Senate, *Report on Conditions of Employment in the Iron and Steel Industry in the United States* 2 (S.Doc. 110, 62nd Cong., 1st sess.); Commonwealth of Pennsylvania, Secretary of Internal Affairs, *Annual Report, Part III. Industrial Statistics,* pp. 12-15; Commonwealth of Pennsylvania, Bureau of Industrial Statistics, *Annual Report 1909,* pp. 140-65.
9. U.S. Immigration Commission, *Reports* 8, p. 409.
10. Cyburt, pp. 7-8.
11. St. Casimir's Financial Book, 1902-08, available at St. Casimir's parish rectory.
12. Cyburt, p. 38.

13. U.S. Immigration, *Reports* 8, p. 454.
14. Computed from Thirteenth Census of the United States: 1910, *Special Reports: Occupations* IV, pp. 238-42.
15. U.S. Immigration Commission, *Reports* 8, pp. 377-81. On wage differentials for unskilled labour in departments of steel mills see: Isaac Hourwich, *Immigrants and Labor* (New York, 1922), pp. 288, 398, 448; Fitch, p. 301; Frank Sheridan, "Italian, Slavic and Hungarian Unskilled Immigrant Laborers in the United States," *Bulletin of the Bureau of Labor* (September 1907), p. 428.
16. Computed from Fourteenth Census of the United States: 1920, *Occupations* IV, pp. 276-82.
17. U.S. Immigration Commission, *Reports* 8, p. 333.
18. The most persuasive exponent of the survival thesis is John Bodnar, especially in these works: "Immigration, Kinship, and the Rise of Working-Class Realism in Industrial America," *Journal of Social History* 14, no. 1 (Fall 1980); "Beyond Mobility: Immigrant Access to Industrial America," paper read at the meeting of the Organization of American Historians in San Francisco, 1980; "Materialism and Mobility: Slavic-American Immigrants and Education, 1890-1940," *Journal of Social History* (Winter 1976); "Immigration and Modernization: the Case of Slavic Peasants in Industrial America," *Journal of Social History* 4 (Fall 1976); with Michael Weber and Roger Simon, *Migration and Urbanization: Blacks, Italians and Poles in Pittsburgh, 1900-1950* (Urbana, Ill., 1981).

    The size of re-emigration remains largely unknown. In 1900-10, for example, over 30 per cent of all east Europeans who went to America later returned to their villages. See Hourwich, pp. 90, 558; Sheridan, p. 481. Though there were failures among re-emigrants, the research has emphasized that those who returned were usually successful and had a positive effect upon their village economies and the further flow of people to America. See: U.S. Immigration Commission, *Reports* 4, pp. 58, 386; Hourwich, pp. 270-71; Krystyna Duda-Dziewirz, *Wieś Małapolska a Emigracja Amerykańska* [The Countryside of Little Poland and the American Emigration], (Warsaw, 1938); Tadeusz Makerewicz, "Emigracja Amerykańska a macierzysta grupa parafialna," *Przegląd Socjologiczny* 4, nos. 3-4 (1936), pp. 521-46.
19. U.S. Immigration Commission, *Reports* 8, pp. 458-591. On growth of local business, see "Mercantile Appraiser's Lists for the City of Johnstown," in *Johnstown Tribune,* 24 May 1900, p. 7; 13 May 1905, p. 6; 20 May 1912, pp. 12-14. Also see: Program and Banquet Book of the Kółko Młodzieży Polskiej [The Polish Youth Circle], 1911.
20. U.S. Immigration Commission, *Reports* 8, pp. 477, 479.
21. The percentages are based on computations for 1905 and 1910 from the sample of Polish families living in Johnstown since 1900. Also see: Cambria County Recorder, Grantee and Grantor Indexes, 1804-1923. There are many instances of immigrants buying property valued at more than $2,000.
22. U.S. Immigration Commission, *Reports* 8, p. 463.
23. Ibid., pp. 460-61.

24. *Johnstown Tribune,* 2 June 1910, p. 10.

25. On the high rate of savings among immigrants see: Sheridan, pp. 474-75. On large remittances to Europe see: Hourwich, p. 269.

26. On individual "status envy" among Polish Americans in contrast to the more collective (family) style of Italians see: Helena Znaniecka-Lopata, *Polish Americans: Status Competition in an Ethnic Group* (Englewood Cliffs, N.J., 1976); Irwin Sanders and Ewa Morawska, *Polish-American Community Life: A Survey of Research* (Boston, 1975), pp. 185-206.

27. Emma Duke, *Infant Mortality. Results of a Field Study in Johnstown, Pa. based on births in one calendar year* (Washington, D.C., 1915), p. 27.

28. Cambria County Recorder, Mortgagor and Mortgagee Books, 1880-1930. See: Mortgagor Books, 53/126, 53/56, 57/409, 79/390, 73/527; Grantee Books, 201/95, 203/68. Of a sample of sixty immigrants, only about 10 per cent lost their houses before 1930.

29. Cyburt, p. 33.

30. Mercantile Appraiser's Lists for the City of Johnstown, in *Johnstown Tribune,* 14 June 1915, pp. 14-15; 27 May 1920, pp. 16-17; 4 June 1925, pp. 22-23. East European business totals include Jewish storekeepers and merchants, which significantly affect the ethnic pattern. Also see: *P.N.A. Advertising Book* (Johnstown, 1926) which indicates that the immigrant social and economic network extended well beyond Johnstown; PNA Lodge 832, *Memorial Album—Dom Polski "Powstań Ojczyzno"* (Johnstown, n.d.).

31. Mercantile Appraiser's Lists for the City of Johnstown, in *Johnstown Tribune,* 8 June 1914, p. 14; 14 June 1915, pp. 14-15; 27 May 1920, pp. 16-17; 25 May 1921, pp. 14-15; 9 June 1923, pp. 16-17; 4 June 1925, pp. 22-23, 12 June 1926, pp. 21-22; 21 June 1928, pp. 22-23; 3 July 1930, pp. 21-22; 16 June 1932, pp. 23-24.

Polish Farmers in Alberta, 1896-1939

Joanna Matejko

Arriving first in the 1890s, Polish immigrants to rural Alberta are relatively new members of Canadian society. As country folk, part of the lower classes economically and with little formal education, they resembled other central and east European immigrants, Ukrainians especially. Overwhelmingly, they came from Galicia, the Austrian partition of Poland, where they were beset in the second half of the nineteenth century by overpopulation, low productivity, high taxation and the division of land holdings into units well below subsistence levels for the enlarged families. The dream of owning or enlarging a parcel of land ceased to be a realistic possibility for the majority of peasants, and with little in the way of industrial opportunity in nearby towns, peasants were forced to look for work outside their region, abroad and, finally, on other continents.[1]

Settlement Patterns

Almost all Poles who settled on the land in Alberta had been involved in agriculture in Poland, but they were not a cross-section of the rural population in the mother country. The majority were petty and non-inheriting farmers who had sold all they possessed to buy tickets for themselves and their families. Some had borrowed money from friends and relatives to send a son or a father to Canada where he was supposed to earn money to pay off debts incurred in bad years, to enlarge the size of family holdings in Poland or to assist the immigration of others in the family. Others, who were members of propertied families, reached Alberta with enough cash to buy railway land and the necessary agricultural implements soon after arrival. Most by far who took up homesteads or purchased railway land before World War One emigrated with their whole families and intended to stay in Canada. Single men who left in order to return home with their earnings looked for jobs in the cities, in mines, on road construction or as seasonal farm labourers. The prospects of their making money in a short time on a homestead were slight. Whatever their background, most of the Polish immigrants came directly from Poland. A few, however, were recruited by agents of the Canadian Pacific Railway from the United States.[2]

Though the majority of Polish settlers were scattered individually and in small groups throughout central Alberta, some twenty-one clusters of Polish settlement emerged from the late 1890s to the late 1920s. All but two were established prior to World War One. The earliest settlements—Wostok, Rabbit Hill (or Rabbit Hills), Skaro and Round Hill—were founded just before the turn of the century.[3] The Wostok pioneers came in 1896 from the Czortków district of Galicia, an area of mixed Polish and Ukrainian population. Settling among Ukrainians northeast of Edmonton, they were culturally close to their neighbours. Some even spoke Ukrainian at home. Though they built a Roman Catholic chapel in 1905 (the mission was called St. Michael), when they added a belfry in 1912, it was in the Ukrainian style. Encouraged by Father Paul Kulawy (who served the mission from Round Hill), they put up a new church in 1915. Penniless and with little formal education when they arrived, the Wostok Poles did not learn English for a long time. Archbishop O'Leary, who visited the church in 1922, carried on most of his discussions with the parishioners through an interpreter.

The settlement in Rabbit Hill, now in the Nisku area south of Edmonton, stemmed from the arrival of the Stanislaus Sarnecki family in 1897. Soon after establishing a farm, they wrote encouraging letters to their native village of Laszki in the Jarosław district of Galicia, stimulating the immigration of sixteen farm families in the spring of 1898. Most of the pioneer families of Rabbit Hill possessed some financial resources, and some were able to buy better pieces of land from the Canadian Pacific Railway. The Halwa family, for example, bought a partially cleared homestead with a house and farm buildings for $500. Three families shared the house until they found suitable homesteads in the Glidehurst area where Frank Halwa opened the first post office. Rabbit Hill was long known to Poles as "Torbowina," from the Polish *torba,* meaning bag. The name derived from the fact that the pioneers used to walk the twelve to eighteen miles to Strathcona carrying their products in for sale and bringing back their groceries.

The Poles of Rabbit Hill were surrounded by Germans and Ukrainians, and after several years in Canada, they tended increasingly to speak Ukrainian. However, the arrival of the energetic young Jan Wojnarowski to spend the winter with relatives in 1913 helped to reverse that trend. Wojnarowski organized a choir, founded a drama group which staged several plays and taught his friends and cousins to read and write Polish while they taught him English. Young people began to meet regularly to read Polish, English and Ukrainian newspapers. The result was that the second generation preserved the mother tongue quite well and the third generation still understands Polish. Social life at Rabbit Hill also centred on the church. A log chapel in 1905, and a rectory for visiting missionaries added in 1907, were the first buildings. A more solidly built church was erected in 1915-17 and when that burned down in 1930 it was replaced in two years.

The core of the Skaro community in the Star (formerly Edna) area was the Wawrzyniec Mreczak family from Trybuchowce in the Buczacz district of Galicia and Jerzy Turczanski who emigrated by way of Brazil. Both settled in Skaro in 1897; by 1899 there were twelve new Polish families in the colony, among them the Jan Wachowicz family which had lived in North Dakota briefly after leaving Trybuchowce. They replaced their first chapel, built in 1904, with a more substantial structure in 1917, which served their needs until 1963 when the children and grandchildren of the pioneers constructed the present church. Father Anthony Sylla, a well-known Oblate missionary in western Canada, added a replica of the grotto of Lourdes in 1919, creating what is still a popular pilgrimage centre in the province.

Tom and John Banach were the founders of the Round Hill colony in the Lake Demay area in 1899. Their father, Stanislaus, had emigrated at first from Poznań to Tacoma, Washington, and in 1895, to Alberta where he is believed to have been the first Polish settler in the Edmonton region. The Banach brothers were joined in 1901-03 by families from Galicia. When Francis Olszewski, the first resident Polish missionary in Alberta, helped them to organize a parish in 1903, he listed thirty-nine adult men in the congregation. The majority of them had arrived without money. They found temporary shelter at the homesteads of earlier settlers and worked at first for better-established farmers in exchange for a few chickens, a piglet, a bushel of potatoes or the wreck of an old wagon. Typically, they soon organized a parish (St. Stanislaus) and in 1904-05 built a church and rectory. Father Paul Kulawy took up permanent residence in 1907 and for several years visited Polish settlements in central Alberta from Round Hill. He also established a school where he taught the Polish language and catechism, though here too there is evidence (from the names of witnesses to homestead ownership in the Township General Register) of significant Ukrainian contacts.

Four other colonies of Galician origin continued the patterns of the pioneer settlements in 1902-05.[4] In Waugh, northeast of Legal, Grzegorz Zadunayski and his father-in-law Roman Medynski together with two Marczak brothers settled on the Athabasca Landing trail. They were followed soon by other families, and in 1908 the community erected the church of St. Hedwig. Polish settlers arrived in Kopernik (near Holden, southeast of Edmonton; the name was given to the former post office of Kopperville in 1910 through the efforts of Father Kulawy) in the spring of 1903. They came from ethnically Polish villages in the Mosciska district, east of Przemysl—six families from Trzciniec and four from Lacka Wola—with enough resources to buy horses, wagons and agricultural implements soon after their arrival. In 1905 they established a cemetery and organized a committee to build a chapel which was completed in 1907. As the number of settlers increased, they dedicated a new church in 1910, converting the old one into a rectory and later into a community hall. A few years later they opened the Polska School where, from 1919 to 1921, Victoria Wachowicz taught Polish, Ukrainian and catechism. About 1905 several Poles filed for homesteads in the Opal district. Mostly they were sons of the Skaro pioneers who were old enough to farm on their own. In Opal itself, a small Polish business community emerged: the Wachowicz family which operated a general store and the post office, four merchants, a restaurant operator and one miller. They were soon joined by new immigrants, and in the 1920s there were some twenty-five Polish families in the area. Several Polish families also settled in the Mundare area among Ukrainians where, about 1906, they built first one church (unofficially called Dabrowa) and then, in 1915, a second.

Between 1908 and 1912, a distinctly Polish settlement was established in Tide Lake, east of Brooks in southern Alberta. A majority of the settlers had been recruited by the Canadian Pacific Railway from Buffalo, New York and from Pennsylvania, where they had mined coal. Settling at first on forty-acre plots in Strathmore, east of Calgary in a settlement called Krakow, they found the farms too small to develop and moved to Tide Lake where the government had opened new land for homesteads. By 1911 there were ten Polish families with thirty-one children and six single persons who had taken homesteads there. Relatives and friends, some directly from Poland, joined the first colonists in the years that followed. The community built both a school, called Polonia, and a small chapel served from Canmore between 1911 and 1917 by Father Anthony Sylla.[5]

Other Poles, also from the United States, established themselves in Acadia Valley around 1909, growing into a community of some twenty families in the 1920s, and in more dispersed fashion near Fourways, Pakowski and Empress. Unlike earlier Polish immigrants, some of these came from Silesia and the Russian partition. The community which was established in Flat Lake in northern Alberta also drew its members from diverse sources—

Alberta and other provinces, the United States and directly from Poland—and continued to grow into the 1920s. Small Polish colonies were also founded prior to World War One by miners at Burmis in the Crow's Nest district, by other miners from Zaolzie and Cieszyn in Richmond Park in the Athabasca region, and by peasants near Warwick, Peguis, Derwent, Chipman (southeast of Lamont) and Naples (in the Barrhead district). With one exception, their church life followed the conventional pattern. The Acadia Valley group built a Catholic church and supported a Polish priest for many years. At Flat Lake a church was erected in 1918-22 and served by a resident priest, with a few intervals, from 1935. The Chipman colonists built and shared a church with German Catholics in 1916; those at Naples, using lumber donated by sawmill owner Jozef Majkut, did the same with local Italians in the early 1930s. The Richmond Park Poles, the only Polish Protestant community in Alberta, joined the Anglican church in Athabasca.[6]

Poles in the Peace River country were dispersed throughout the region, except for a concentration in the Clairmont area, until after World War One. Then, in 1926, the arrival of Joseph Kozlowski in Webster initiated a settlement known for a time as Kozlowo. By 1930 the Webster-Sexsmith area held some forty Polish families who had come from Poland directly or from other places in Alberta such as Derwent and Vermilion. In addition to a church in the early 1930s, they put up a Polish hall and (during the Second World War) founded an active lay association and a small library. The other late Polish farm settlement was begun in the late 1920s by twenty-three homesteading families in the Ardmore neighbourhood, east of Bonnyville in northern Alberta. The majority of them came directly from the Ropczyce area in the Rzeszow district, but some had moved east from Bonnyville where they had farmed for a few years. They built a school and, in 1938, a church.[7]

Most post-World War One peasant immigrants preferred the city to the country, possibly because they were less likely to emigrate as families or find homesteads when they reached Canada. Still, the ratio of rural to urban Poles continued to increase until 1931. In 1911, 1,684 (73.3 per cent) of the 2,297 people of Polish origin in Alberta lived in the country. The percentage grew to 75.5 in 1921, and to 78.5 in 1931, when the number of Poles in the province numbered 21,157. Ethnic Poles were far less urbanized than the population as a whole; in 1931 only 68.9 per cent of Alberta's people were found in rural areas (see Table 1). The high percentage of Poles in the countryside was due not only to the Canadian immigration policy but also to the economic situation and the character of Polish immigrants. When the Great Depression took hold it was easier to survive on a farm where a garden, a cow, some poultry and game supplied food for the family. Some Polish families even moved from Edmonton to farms for fear of deportation. In 1941 the percentage of Poles in the country declined as members of the second or third generations drifted away from the land or into other occupations. The immigrants who arrived in the wake of the Second World War accelerated the trend by settling almost entirely in towns and cities.

Table 1: Polish Ethnic Group in Alberta by Rural and Urban Population, 1901-71

	Rural			Urban		
Year	No.	% of total ethnic group	% of Alberta average	No.	% of total ethnic group	% of Alberta average
1901	391	81.1	83.8	79	28.9	16.2
1911	1,684	73.3	70.6	613	26.7	29.4
1921	5,414	75.5	69.9	1,758	24.5	30.1
1931	16,597	78.5	68.9	4,560	21.5	31.1
1941	19,903	74.1	68.5	6,942	23.9	31.5
1951	18,135	62.1	54.2	11,526	38.9	45.8
1961	16,118	39.8	36.1	24,421	60.2	63.9
1971	12,460	28.1	26.4	31,865	71.9	73.6

SOURCE: *Census of Canada, Government of the Province of Alberta*; *Alberta Bureau of Statistics, Alberta Industry and Resources, 1970*, p. 133.

Rural Household Economies

Poles, like other east European peasants, passionately loved land. The intensity of their attachment to land—the source of economic well-being, psychological satisfaction and social esteem—conditioned their behaviour in the new world. The acquisition, development and expansion of homesteads constituted the greatest achievements of their lives in Canada. Polish farmers tended to purchase their farms as soon as possible, many of them applying for their patents after three years of homesteading. The number of Polish-born farm operators in Alberta rose gradually from 611 in 1921 to 994 in 1926, rapidly to 7,757 in 1931 and more slowly to 8,419 in 1936.[8]

Though some were better off financially than others, the beginnings of farm life on the Alberta prairies were not easy for any Polish settlers. Most of course had barely enough resources to start farming. The clearing of land for cultivation, acre by acre, took years. Unfamiliarity with the climate bred such disasters as the destruction of the first wheat plantings by early frost in Rabbit Hill. The settlers at Round Hill were plagued at the start by an inadequate and poor quality water supply from local sloughs. The response of Polish immigrants took several forms: persistence and the willingness to learn from failure and the example of earlier settlers. Also, in the difficult early years they relied heavily on other sources of income. Many worked for established farmers. Others sold lumber from cleared land for fence posts and cordwood or engaged in truck gardening if they were near enough to Edmonton. Wild game and food were often available. Sawmills, road and railway construction offered some opportunities. Some of the men in the Athabasca area and many of those in the Crow's Nest region worked in coal mines during the long winter; and a few of the pioneers in Waugh prospected with occasional success for gold in the Saskatchewan River.

In the longer run, almost all Polish farmers put their faith in mixed farming which gave them the security and self-sufficiency they prized. They had been used to that kind of farming in the mother country. In Alberta they cultivated some wheat, oats and barley, potatoes and other vegetables while raising cattle, pigs, sheep and much poultry. The system guaranteed the supply of basic consumer goods, most obviously in times of economic crisis like the Great Depression. Of course Poles did not bring with them the experience of specialized knowledge required for ranching or commercial farming. Nor did they have or want to borrow the venture capital to begin such operations. Only after many years of old-fashioned mixed farming did some Poles, among them the better educated immigrants of the 1920s, start to specialize. Still, in 1936, 40 per cent of Polish farms in Alberta were self-sufficient and another 30 per cent derived their main income from general products. Only 15 per cent of Polish farm operators specialized in growing wheat, and just 9 per cent in livestock.[9]

Finally, Polish farmers drew upon the cooperative traditions of their culture to succeed in Alberta. Mutual assistance in the spirit of the village frequently sustained newcomers and eased difficult moments afterwards. Above all, each member of the family contributed a share to the improvement of the farm. Wives had far more to do than rear children, working in the fields with and often instead of the men. The lack of capital to establish a farm was frequently so acute that men had to look for work outside. They earned money, learned better techniques of farming and improved their command of English, but women had to carry the burden, often with babies on their backs, of farm work and management. Quite often also a man ran the neighbouring farm of his absent brother or cousin.

Women and children helped in clearing new land to increase

Table 2: Farm Operators of Polish Origin in Alberta, Classified by Size of Farms and compared to Ukrainian and British Farm Operators, 1936

Size of farm	1-50 acres	51-100 acres	101-200 acres	201-299 acres	300-479 acres	480-639 acres	640 acres and over	All farms
No. of Polish operators	77	45	1,882	94	653	170	171	3.092
% of Polish operators	2.49	1.45	60.87	3.04	21.12	5.50	5.53	100%
% of Ukrainian operators	2.69	2.40	58.01	5.52	23.67	4.82	2.89	100%
% of British origin operators	3.26	1.22	33.10	3.23	28.68	11.58	18.93	100%
% of all Alberta operators	3.05	1.96	40.30	3.46	26.41	9.68	15.14	100%

SOURCE: *Census of the Prairie Provinces, 1936* I (Ottawa 1938), p. 1239.

the acreage under cultivation. In the summer they gathered berries for sale and mushrooms to dry. Vegetable gardens, poultry and dairy products were traditionally the responsibilities of women in Polish peasant families. Dairy goods were processed for consumption at home and for sale or barter. Grain was also processed by handmill and bread baked at home. During the winter, wool was spun and dyed, and clothes were made for everyone. In near-cashless families, women sometimes made their clothes from sugar sacks. The distribution of lesser family chores among the children was by sex. Girls assisted their mothers in household tasks of preparing meals, house-cleaning, washing, gardening and caring for younger children. Boys helped out in the fields and stables. At the age of 14 or 15, and sometimes earlier, children began to work full-time on parental farms or on other farms as domestics and labourers. Ordinarily, working children turned over all or a substantial portion of their earnings to their parents.

The efforts of Polish farm families were rewarded with some success prior to World War One. Their achievements were reflected in the replacement of dugouts and sod cabins with more solidly built houses, in the increased level of contributions to the church, in the purchase (often cooperatively) of a few steam threshing machines and automobiles and in the construction of mills. A small middle class of businessmen appeared by 1920, and a few of the children of the pioneers took up their own homesteads, skilled occupations or the professions in the years that followed. The census data on place of birth are not always helpful in tracing their progress since they confuse Poles, Ukrainians, Austrians, Russians and Germans. In the 1920s many Polish farmers, possibly still without a clear national consciousness, probably gave Austria as the country of their birth. In the 1930s many Ukrainians and some Germans born on Polish territories were included in the category "Polish-born farm operators." The later data using the category "Polish ethnic origin" are more reliable. There were 3,092 farm operators of Polish ethnic origin in Alberta in 1936. Most of them (81 per cent) owned their farms; nearly 9 per cent were tenants; and 10 per cent were partly owners and partly tenants. Only an insignificant number (4) were managers.[10] The size of Polish farms in Alberta was smaller than the provincial average. The majority of Polish farmers in 1936 operated quarter-section farms; 61 per cent were in the range of 101-200 acres. Only 33 per cent of the British-origin farm operators and 40 per cent of all Alberta operators were in the same category. About 6 per cent of Polish farm operators compared to 19 per cent of the British had large farms of 640 acres or more. Poles resembled Ukrainians in the size of their holdings as they did in so many other respects (see Table 2).

Religious Life and Institutions

Though Polish immigrants failed to reproduce the social structure of their homeland, they succeeded in bringing their Roman Catholic religion and its cultural style with them. The church where they prayed in their own language and confessed their troubles to a Polish missionary was the only familiar landmark in a strange environment. It was, moreover, the locus of that ritual which plays such an important role in Polish Catholicism. Church holidays were celebrated with great solemnity; and old customs were attached to each holiday. Traditional Polish saints, hymns, prayers and treasured pictures of the Madonna rounded out their religious practice.

A church was not only the site for the expression of religious aspirations; it was also a symbol of achievement in the new country. For centuries, landlords in Poland had sponsored the founding of churches. Peasant immigrants continued to see that act as highly honourable, and a majority of the Alberta colonies donated the scarce cash and services necessary to build chapels or churches within a few years of their establishment. The many Polish farmers who were scattered throughout the province were compelled to join Greek Catholic or other Roman Catholic parishes.

The first and most ambitious Polish mission in Alberta was established at the turn of the century by Father Francis Olszewski at Krakow, northeast of Edmonton. Father Olszewski's dream was to create a Polish religious and cultural centre with an educational institute and convent. In order to support the institution he took a homestead and secured five quarters of fertile land. The Polish farmers of Skaro and vicinity contributed labour and farm machinery while Father Olszewski himself managed the farm and worked in the fields with his parishioners. In 1902 a large building was erected with a small chapel, schoolroom, kitchen, lodging for the children and nuns, and a room for the priest. Krakow also became the site of a post office. Father Olszewski encouraged several farmers' daughters to join the convent and sent some of them to St. Mary's High School in Edmonton to prepare them for teaching careers. Others worked on the mission farm. A boarding school was opened in 1906, but there were only a few students enrolled since the immediate area was occupied by Ukrainians. Polish families were some miles distant, and the idea of sending children away from home was not attractive to parents. In any case the government soon opened a school closer to the Polish settlement. In the summer of 1910, the mission buildings were destroyed by fire. Though Father Olszewski began reconstruction, he and the nuns eventually left for Fried in North Dakota.[11]

Polish consulates were not established until after the First World War of course, and missionaries naturally assumed broad leadership roles among Polish immigrants. Polish priests in Edmonton, for example, were instrumental in organizing a delegation to the premier of Alberta in February 1919, to seek recognition of the Poles as a separate national group and not, as before, as subjects of the three partitioning powers. The best-known missionaries were two Oblates, Father Paul Kulawy (1877-1941), who worked in the province from 1904 to 1921, and Father Anthony Sylla (1881-1978), who first served Slavic Catholics in the south from 1909 to 1917 and then Poles in central Alberta until 1927 when he left for Winnipeg. Like other missionaries, they encouraged farmers to subscribe to immigrant Polish Catholic newspapers and to build elementary schools. Father Kulawy established a school in Round Hill and helped set up the Polska School in Kopernik. Father Sylla played a part in founding the Polonia school in Tide Lake. Father Kulawy moreover actively defended both Polish and Ukrainian farmers against discrimination.

The missionaries identified themselves with the lives of the people they served, and for many years worked under difficult pioneer conditions. The measure of the esteem in which they were held was apparent in the willingness of parishioners to contribute two to four dollars yearly for church support, though occasionally they were too poor to do so. Immigrant parents, aided by missionaries, also sent several of their sons to St. John's College in Edmonton to prepare for the priesthood. When a German priest with indifferent Polish was assigned to Wostok, parishioners forced his removal by the bishop; and when a German at Chipman was perceived as hostile to Polish nationality, Polish parishioners simply refused to attend his services.

Polish-Ukrainian Relations

Polish pioneers had little contact with Anglo-Saxons or with other ethnic communities in Alberta except the Ukrainians. Poles and Ukrainians had long co-existed in the old country. Many immigrants came from the regions in eastern Galicia with mixed Polish and Ukrainian populations, where they had known each other, spoken or understood both languages, and were sometimes related. The national consciousness of some Polish and Ukrainian peasants was not well developed. Many identified themselves with the region they had come from rather than with Poland or Ukraine. Some felt that they were loyal subjects of the Austrian Emperor Franz Joseph and even named their sons after him.

The most important distinction between the Polish and Ukrainian settlers was religion. Both groups were aware of the difference between Greek Catholic and Roman Catholic liturgies, and tried to preserve the difference. The missionaries in Alberta who had come from the Prussian partition and did not speak Ukrainian, despite their sympathy for the Greek Catholic rite, tried to prevent Poles from joining Greek Catholic congregations, the more so since there was a strong tendency among some Polish farmers to integrate into the Ukrainian community. Only a few rural communities established a basis for a Polish institutional life concentrated around the Polish church, and in those, marriages between Poles and Ukrainians were not unusual. Intermarriage was more common among Polish immigrants dispersed in small groups among predominantly Ukrainian farmers. Poles, it must be remembered, were a minority among "Galicians" in Alberta.

Some families were divided by conflicting national and religious loyalties, and many Polish families spoke Ukrainian at home. John Liss, a Polish pioneer who travelled across Alberta as an itinerary salesman of Slavic books, described his impressions of Polish-Ukrainian relations in his reminiscences:

> During the years 1915-1916, I visited almost all of the Polish and Ukrainian settlements east of Edmonton, with my father. Poles living there told us that they always were, and always would be Poles, even though they were talking Ruthenian at home. They bought Polish books and taught their children to pray in Polish. When I asked them why they did not speak Polish at home, they explained that back in Poland they spoke Polish, but here, being surrounded by Ruthenians, in order to keep good neighbourly relations, they had started to speak Ruthenian. It also made it easier for the young people to mix.[12]

According to Rose Dul, whose parents settled in the Opal area in 1907:

> Ruthenians were the predominant group in the vicinity. All Poles spoke Ukrainian and almost all Ruthenians spoke Polish. Many Polish settlers spoke Ukrainian at home; however, they considered themselves Polish. There was no hostility between the two nationalities. The Ruthenian settlers helped the Poles to build a church in Opal in 1919, and they attended Roman Catholic services held by the Polish missionaries visiting Opal from Edmonton. The services were in Polish and Latin; but outside the church, after Mass, everybody spoke Ukrainian again.[13]

In spite of their differences Polish and Ukrainian farmers cooperated in many fields, even in fulfilling their religious needs. They helped each other with building churches, shared some churches and attended church services when a Greek Catholic or Roman Catholic priest arrived in the colony. For instance, when the Ukrainian settlers of Rabbit Hill decided to build a church at the turn of the century, Polish pioneer Stanislaus Sarnecki donated two acres of his land to the project, and the Polish farmers helped to construct the church. They also shared this church with the Ukrainian community until they erected a church of their own. The Ukrainians allowed the Polish settlers to use their cemetery. In Round Hill Poles and Ukrainians attended church services of both rites by turns. The Ukrainian farmers of the Skaro area helped their Polish neighbours erect a church and a grotto. The farmers of Waugh decided to build a chapel for both ethnic communities in 1903. After some money was collected, the Ukrainians took back their money and separated, but when the first service was performed in the Polish church on Christmas Day of 1908, they attended the Mass. Later on they invited a Polish priest, Father Anthony Sylla, to celebrate a Christmas Mass in the Ukrainian church.[14]

There were instances of communal conflicts also. Poles and Ukrainians in Hay Lakes argued over the construction of their common church. The Ukrainians wanted an onion-shaped steeple and an altar one could circle about. The Poles insisted on a gothic-style steeple and the traditional Polish altar against the wall. The disagreement resulted in separation of the two groups.[15] Polish-Ukrainian relations deteriorated considerably after the First World War for several reasons. During the war the Ukrainians and Poles from Galicia were prevented from obtaining patents for their homesteads and denied Canadian citizenship. The situation changed for Poles after Poland regained independence. Ukrainians, however, continued to be excluded from naturalization by the act of 1920. The clause could be circumvented by an admission of Polish nationality, but for many Ukrainians that constituted treason toward their homeland. During the collapse of Austrian rule in Galicia, and in 1919, fighting between Poland and Ukrainian nationalists broke out over eastern Galicia, a subject of constant controversy. During the entire interwar period Ukrainians remained unreconciled to Polish rule, and the Polish authorities mistrusted the Ukrainian minority. The new immigrants, both Poles and Ukrainians, who came to Canada in the 1920s transplanted their European controversies and antipathies. Newly arrived Ukrainians tried to cut all ties with the Polish consulate as soon as they arrived on Canadian soil. The discord started in the cities and spread to the rural communities. During the depression ideological differences further divided the two communities. Probably because of the influence of the Polish clergy, the radical leftist ideology was much less popular among Poles than among Ukrainians in Alberta.

The Second Generation

The second generation of the Polish pioneers mostly settled on farms, though quite a few children in each settlement became teachers, priests or nuns in what was considered a respectable way of social advancement. To be a teacher was perhaps the easiest way for farmers' children to advance. There were not enough teachers in Alberta and only one year of study was necessary after completion of high school. Some young men moved to the urban centres and ended as blue-collar workers, or operators of small groceries and various small businesses. Very few became professionals in the second generation, but it was not unusual among the children of farmers who immigrated in the twenties.

Conclusions

Polish farmers came to Alberta in two waves: between 1896 and 1914, and in the 1920s. The overwhelming majority came from southern Poland, known prior to the First World War as Galicia. The majority of the postwar settlers also came from the same region; many were friends, relatives or acquaintances of the early immigrants.

Though most Polish farmers were scattered throughout central and northern Alberta in small groups of two, three or four families of friends or relatives, they established twenty-two distinctly Polish communities, strong enough to build a chapel, a church, a community hall, or to organize occasional visits of Polish missionaries. The Polish colonies were located mostly in central Alberta, south, east and north of Edmonton. Only three settlements, including the small community of Burmis established by Polish miners, were located in southern Alberta, and one was in the Peace River country. All but two were created by the settlers who had come prior to the First World War. Polish farmers tended to practise mixed farming on units which were smaller (though large in their own eyes) than the provincial average. Relying heavily on the cooperation of neighbours and the family, they created self-sufficient farms which served them usually until retirement or death.

The cultural importance and centralizing power of the Roman Catholic church and clergy cannot be overemphasized. The church was the only Polish institution established by immigrant farmers, and the missionary clergy were a network of social leaders which linked the colonies and preserved or created a sense of Polish identity which survives to this day.

A Note on the Sources

In spite of the fact that the literature on Polish ethnic groups in Canada is quite extensive, Alberta has been neglected even in the most recent publications.[16] Unlike the Ukrainians, available statistical data on Polish settlers in Alberta have not been fully researched.[17] Another source, the Township General Register, can provide information not only on the economic situation of homesteaders, their progress in breaking the land, but also on the problem of naturalization and even inter-ethnic relations (through the nationality of witnesses on applications). However, the main difficulty in using the Township General Register is time. It would require a large team of researchers. In this paper information from the register has been used only to provide a few examples. Church records do not provide much information. Instead, many published and unpublished memoirs, reminiscences, family life stories and biographies (in Polish and in English) provide a mine of source material.

Notes

1. On emigration from Galicia see: Celina Bobińska and Andrzej Pilch, eds., *Employment-Seeking Emigrations of the Poles World-Wide XIX and XX C.*, trans. Danuta E. Żukowska (Krakow, 1975).
2. Major general works on Polish immigration to Canada which bear on Alberta include Roman Mazurkiewicz, *Polskie wychodźtwo i osadnictwo w Kanadzie* [Polish Emigration and Settlement in Canada] (Warsaw, 1929); Victor Turek, *Poles in Manitoba* (Toronto, 1967); Melchior Wankowicz, *Three Generations,* trans. Krystyna Cekalska (Toronto, 1973); Benedykt Heydenkorn, ed., *Pamiętniki imigrantów polskich w Kanadzie* [Memoirs of Polish Immigrants in Canada], 3 vols. (Toronto, 1975-79); Joanna Matejko et al., eds., *Polish Settlers in Alberta: Reminiscences and Biographies* (Toronto, 1979). Also see: Joanna K. Krotki, comp., *Local Histories of Alberta: An Annotated Bibliography* (Edmonton, 1980).
3. On the first four communities see: Anthony Sylla, "Memoir," 3 vols., unpublished MSS., unpaginated, vols. 2 and 3, in Archives of the Oblate Fathers, Canadian Province of Our Lady, Toronto; the Township General Register, deposited in the Provincial Museum and Archives of Alberta in Edmonton: T.48 R.18 M.4 and R.19 M14; *Wachowicz Centennial Project* (Edmonton, 1967); *50th Anniversary—Skaro Shrine—Star, Alberta* (Edmonton, 1969); Joanna Matejko and Tova Yedlin, eds., *Alberta's Pioneers from Eastern Europe: Reminiscences* II (Edmonton, 1977), pp. 13-19; "Cairn Honors Polish Pioneers of Nisku-Rabbit Hills," *Western Catholic Reporter,* 16 November 1975; Joanna and Alexander Matejko, "Polish Pioneers in the Canadian Prairies," *Ethnicity* 5 (1978), pp. 351-69; J. Matejko et al., eds., *Polish Settlers in Alberta,* pp. 89-94, 273-75.
4. Sylla, "Memoir," vol. 2; J. Matejko et al., eds., *Polish Settlers in Alberta,* pp. 27-28, 275-80, 293-98; author's interviews with Rev. T. Rataj, September 1976, with Mrs. Rose Dul, December 1978, with Mrs. H. Tomusiak, September 1978.
5. Howard Palmer, *Land of the Second Chance* (Lethbridge, 1972), p. 65; J. Matejko et al., eds., *Polish Settlers in Alberta,* pp. 106-09, 293-98; author's interview with Mr. Donald Olekszyk, 15 October 1973.
6. Sylla, "Memoir," vol. 2; J. Matejko et al., *Polish Settlers in Alberta,* pp. 56, 96-97, 108-09, 127-29, 141-44, 298-99, 311-13; *Biuletyn Kongresu Polonii Kanadyjskiej—Okreg Alberta* [Bulletin of the Polish

Canadian Congress—Alberta Branch], no. 6, 11 November 1964 (reminiscences of John Liss); Father Boniface, OFM, *Pioneering in the West* (Vancouver, 1957), pp. 49-76; author's interviews with Rev. J. Kochan, October 1973, with Mr. Andy Solikoski, September 1980.

7. J. Matejko et al., eds., *Polish Settlers in Alberta,* pp. 318-19; *Daily Herald Tribune,* 2 November 1976, p. 16; *Rural Route,* 30 November 1977, p. 12; *Biuletyn KPK—Okreg Alberta,* no. 10 (1961), p. 7; author's interviews with Mr. Antoni Wozniak, 19 July 1977, with Mr. Leonard Ostaszewski, July 1975, with Rev. Joachim Michalowski, 21 September 1977, with Mr. and Mrs. Donald Olekszyk, October 1973, with Mr. and Mrs. Antoni Szydlik, October 1973.
8. *Census of the Prairie Provinces, 1936* I (Ottawa, 1938), p. 1138. The discussion which follows is culled from material cited above.
9. Ibid., p. 1240.
10. Ibid.
11. Sylla, "Memoir," vol. 2; J. Matejko et al., eds., *Polish Settlers in Alberta,* pp. 270-73. On Polish missionaries and churches in Alberta see: Emile J. Legal, *Short Sketches of the History of the Roman Catholic Churches in Central Alberta* (Winnipeg, 1914), pp. 117-19; Edward M. Hubicz, *Polish Churches in Manitoba* (London, 1960); Joanna Matejko, "Rola misjonarza wśród polskich pionierów w Albercie," *Migrant Echo* 3, no. 1 (1974), pp. 41-51.
12. J. Matejko et al., eds., *Polish Settlers in Alberta,* pp. 349-50.
13. Author's interview with Mrs. Rose Dul, November 1978.
14. Sylla, "Memoir," vol. 2.
15. Ibid., vol. 3.
16. Henry Radecki and Benedykt Heydenkorn, *A Member of a Distinguished Family: The Polish Group in Canada* (Toronto, 1976); Henry Radecki, *Organizational Dynamics: The Polish Group in Canada* (Waterloo, Ont., 1976).
17. William Darcovich and Paul Yuzyk, eds., *Statistical Compendium on the Ukrainian in Canada 1891-1976* (Ottawa, 1977), typescript, which also includes some statistics on Poles; W. Roman Petryshyn, *Changing Realities: Social Trends among Ukrainian Canadians* (Edmonton, 1980).

Polish Emigration to Latin America

Marcin Kula

Scholars involved in immigration studies have been concerned to analyse the underlying circumstances in the homeland which influenced groups to choose certain destinations when they decided to emigrate. In this respect, a comparison of the vicissitudes experienced by various emigrant groups seemed to yield useful results. Therefore, an examination of the lot of Polish emigrants in Latin America in comparison with Poles in the United States and Canada should be instructive because of similarities between emigrants at the point of departure and because of significant differences between the groups for many years after their arrival in their adopted countries.[1]

Polish emigration to Latin America—particularly the mass exodus at the end of the nineteenth century and the beginning of the twentieth—has many different facets. It includes the little-known contribution made by a small number of Polish volunteers to the Latin American independence movements at the beginning of the nineteenth century. It includes the emigration of political refugees after the Polish uprising of November 1830, among them Ignacy Domeyko. It includes the work of Polish engineers in Peru and Bolivia in the second half of the nineteenth century and Polish naturalists and geologists in the nineteenth and twentieth centuries.

Large-scale emigration was probably initiated by the departure of a group of peasants from Siołkowice village in Opole Silesia, who sailed from Hamburg for Brazil on June 10, 1869. The first group to Argentina left in 1897 from Małopolska (Little Poland) where a few Poles had arrived earlier through Brazil. Both these countries were popular areas of settlement for Polish emigrants. In Brazil they were concentrated mainly in the southern states: Parana, Rio Grande do Sul and Santa Catarina; in Argentina they settled in Misiones. Poles also went to Uruguay, Paraguay, Mexico and Cuba in lesser numbers, and scattered groups were in many other Latin American countries. Not all the Latin American Polonias were intended to be permanent. Centres in Mexico, Cuba and Paraguay, at least in the first period of their existence, could be considered "centres of transfer." Emigrants who arrived in these countries initially planned to go either to the United States or to Argentina, but their plans were frustrated by adverse circumstances.

Data related to the number of Poles who emigrated to Latin America are incomplete and difficult to interpret. Usually it is not known whether emigrants listed by Argentina, for example, as coming from Poland, included ethnic minorities such as Jews, Ukrainians, Germans or Lithuanians, and immigration records in the receiving country are sparse and unreliable. Until further research has been done into primary sources in the emigrant communities themselves, it will not be possible to establish with any certainty the size of the Polonias and their ethnic composition in Latin America.

Despite these limitations, several estimations, based on Polish archival sources and publications, can be made. By 1914 Brazil had received about 100,000 people from Polish territories; in the interwar period the figure was about 40,000. In Argentina on the eve of World War One, it is known that about 5,000 Poles and 5,000 Ukrainians lived in Misiones; in the interwar period, the number rose to 160,000. In other Latin American countries, the numbers prior to 1914 are insignificant. In the interwar period, however, immigration increased, 12,000 people coming to Paraguay, 8,600 to Uruguay, 7,500 to Cuba, 4,500 to Mexico, 700 to Columbia, 500 to Peru, 300 each to Costa Rica and Chile and over 100 each to Venezuela and Bolivia. (Panama, Honduras, Ecuador, Curacao and Trinidad received less than 100 each.) This means that since the beginning of mass emigration till 1939, about 330,000 people left from Polish territories for Latin America.

For the period of World War Two and after, the information is fragmentary. It is known that at the beginning of the war a certain number of Poles, mainly of Jewish origin, managed to reach Latin America from Portugal, and a small group arrived at Santa Rosa camp in Mexico via the Near East. It is also known that after the war, soldiers of the Polish Armed Forces in Europe and survivors from the labour and death camps of Germany, arrived in Latin America, a few settling in Argentina and several thousands in Brazil. Most of them arrived between 1947-49, and it was to be the last wave of Polish emigration to Latin America.

This considerable influx of emigrants during the twentieth century created what has become known as "Latin American Polonia." It is worth remembering, however, that this phenomenon existed only in a statistical sense. In the sociological sense, the separate Polonia communities that have arisen in Latin America are tied more closely to Polonia in the United States or to Poland than to one another. Even those that were quite close geographically found communication difficult, especially in the interwar period. For example, the settlements in southern Brazil and the community at Misiones in Argentina were about ninety miles away, but the journey through the wilderness between them could take from five to eight days.[2] Even within one country, Polonia was often divided into separate groups. Communications between groups in Sao Paulo or Rio de Janeiro and Parana was minimal, as was the connection between Buenos Aires and Misiones. Neither was there any sense of continuity in the various communities. For example, Polish engineers had been working in Peru in the nineteenth century. But when the Polish government tried to organize the mass emigration of peasants to Peru after World War One, the Polish groups already there did little to help prospective settlers, nor did these later emigrants benefit even from the status obtained by the earlier migrants.

Economic Status

Most of the Polish emigrants were peasants who had suffered many years of privation in their homeland. They arrived in the direst poverty and were destined to remain poor in their new homes. Even in Brazil, often referred to as an example of the Polish settlers' success, the agricultural community they created remained relatively poor and very traditional. While the Polish peasants were concentrating on owning more and more land, Italian emigrants built Sao Paulo industry and developed an agricultural economy that was much more intensive, commercialized and profitable than the one established by Poles in the same southern region. "One of our manias is to declaim about the contribution of Polish peasants to Parana, to Brazil," a settler wrote in *Gazeta Polska* (The Polish Gazette) in 1935:

> Undeniably they proved to be persistent, being grafted in the tropical wood, where they snatched an expanse of plough-land away from the wild nature and stayed, by the strength of their insurmountable resistance and superhuman laboriousness. Let us have a look, however, at this famous farm. Can we see there progress imposed by knowledge: Are we equal to our nationals of German, Italian or French origin? Every year tracts of forest, the source of national wealth, are destroyed by fire. Thin ears of corn toss melancolically in the fields and a group of our children transformed into beasts of draught, lunge out with hoes at the dried soil.

Although the statistical evidence is not available to verify this rather impressionistic statement, there is sufficient corroboration from other sources to show that it contained at least a kernel of truth.

Brazil was not the only Latin American country where the circumstances of Polish peasant settlers were very hard and, contrary to legend, Polish peasants were not held in high repute as farmers in all countries. Government officials in Chile, even if they did not dispute the industriousness of the Poles, stressed the low level of Polish agricultural development. Attempts during the interwar period to organize peasant settlement in Peru came to nothing, although this failure may not have been the fault of the peasants. It seems that only in Argentina at Misiones did a Polish settlement achieve any measure of prosperity.

Polish emigrants living in Latin American cities did not fare much better. In general they entered the lowest positions of the social hierarchy. They were employed in poorly paid jobs requiring few skills. Only Poles employed in the oil industry in Ecuador during the twenties managed to acquire some status as skilled workers. Others had the tendency to become outcasts. At the end of the nineteenth century Antoni Hempel described the life of the Poles in Sao Paulo as "dull, gloomy due to uncertainty of future, and somehow exceptionally restricted, among representatives of other nationalities, stronger by their knowledge of the language and relations."[3] Till the end of 1914, Polish enterprises of any consequence in Sao Paulo could be counted on one's fingers: a restaurant, several stores, a shoemaker's shop, one fairly sizeable electrical shop. In the interwar period the situation was improved a little by the arrival of several Polish engineers who became employed in their profession.

Certain Polish urban communities, for example the one in Havana, lived in utter poverty in the interwar period. In 1924 the General Consulate of the Polish Republic in New York, which had Cuba within its jurisdiction, stated:

> Poles are left to their fate, helpless, with no aid from outside, with no knowledge of the language, with no care whatsoever, therefore they are fated to utter poverty and treated worse than the Blacks. For weeks and weeks, they lie on beds of misery in stinking and stuffy sheds, or in parks and in the fields, they rummage street and park tidies in order to find fusty scraps and appease their hunger.[4]

At that time, Melchior Wańkowicz, after he had visited Cuba as a young journalist and stated that in the past this was a slave country, wrote bitterly: "Now, these are the times of long ago. A Black is the citizen of Cuba. The subject of contemporary slavery is un polaco—the Polish peasant."[5]

Other minority groups from Poland, such as the Ukrainians, in general shared the fate of Poles. Jewish emigrants were often in a better situation; many of them got employed in commerce, starting as pedlars and sometimes becoming managers of larger enterprises. They were also sometimes supported by Jewish organizations, which were stronger than the Polonia ones, and more ready to give practical help.

After 1939 the situation of the Polonias of Latin America had changed to a certain degree. New emigrants, coming mainly to cities, came from a different socio-economic background. They had greater potential chances for upward mobility. On the other hand, during and after the war, the countries of Latin America experienced a period of prosperity which provided an economic advantage to both urban emigrant centres and former agricultural ones, as their products were in larger demand. As a journalist wrote in 1943, after a visit to the Parana interior:

> In houses and vendas [stores, saloons] at Ivai river-basin, talks among neighbors focus on fattened hogs and their prices. In [the colony of] Getulio Vargas—on potatoes and cotton and in Londrina, the interest is concentrated on coffee and the prices of land, increasing from day to day. There are also talks about the war. About Poland, too, but the main interest is focused on one's own and the neighbor's farming. One has to admit that forest colonies experience the period of prosperity due to the war. Settlers are well off, very likely, as never before.[6]

Socio-economic Values in Polonia

There were several reasons for the initial, difficult position of Polish emigrants in Latin America. The lack of resources and of education in the homeland, the low level of aspirations, the internalized system of values of a Polish peasant which raised land ownership into an end in itself, the lack of tradition to unite to resist exploitation, and few outside organizations to offer help—all these were undoubtedly factors that determined the position of the group.

In Brazil the Polish emigrants went south because the work in coffee plantations in Sao Paulo state in the north reminded them of the feudal system of their homeland, the memories of which were still green. In Parana, Rio Grande do Sul and Santa Catarina, they received free grants of land, even though, had they stayed in Sao Paulo, with its greater economic opportunities, they would have had better chances for advancement. But it was proverbial hunger for land, the effort to enlarge the farm, which so often proved uneconomical and against their own interests. One observer, referring to Misiones, noticed ironically in 1901: "All hungry of land, find enough of it here. And they take such an amount of it, as well as of forests, that even in 200 years they will not be able to cultivate."[7] The author of a short story on Polish settlement in Brazil, a witness of the events, put in the mouth of a Brazilian protagonist of his story the statement that Poles "would like to buy the whole land."[8] Inevitably this attitude was counterproductive, since it was not the land itself that counted, but the cultivated part of it. To the Polish peasant, however, such economic argument was of little importance; he was only motivated by the desire to attain an ambition which was beyond his reach in Poland—the position of a landowner, master, squire, the status of which was marked, first of all, by the ownership of large estates. Having obtained a large farm in Brazil, a peasant was able to proudly inform his family at home: "My dear brothers, I would not change my farm into yours now. Now, I am the Squire, it is not as it was in Poland."[9]

Peasant emigrants brought with them from Poland their system of values but not the financial means to implement it. They had neither money to start any business, nor any marketable skills, especially in the cities. As Warren Dean pointed out, the story of Matarazzo, the man who, starting with nothing, became the pioneer of Brazilian industry, even if true in this particular case, as a general rule is only a myth. Most of the industrialists of foreign origin had previously in their mother countries lived in towns, belonged to middle-class families and received at least some technical education and experience in trade.[10]

What is equally important, Polish peasants also lacked a desire for social upward mobility. In the late 1920s the Polish Consul in Sao Paulo wrote:

> When an emigrant of another nationality, after several years spent in Sao Paulo, becomes the owner of a workshop or a factory, the emigrant Pole contents himself with the position of a foreman in this enterprise. Almost never he tries to attain anything more than what is necessary to exist.[11]

This attitude, too, we can assume, is a throwback to conditions the emigrants had experienced in Poland. "Our laborious Polish peasant, used in the Country to poverty, greedy for land, satisfied by anything, not needing a lamp yet to read a newspaper in the evening, lives here and is happy that he is better here than in Europe," was the view of Roman Dmowski, a Polish politician visiting Brazil in 1900.[12]

Other observers have noted that the Polish peasant in Brazil contributed to his own exploitation. Although he did not wish to work in the plantations, he was in great demand, mainly because of the "low level of culture and the lack of ability to demand his rights, which enabled many planters to exploit him to the utmost limit." The Polish Consul in Sao Paulo was of the opinion that the planters had to treat Italians and Brazilians fairly, because they were volatile workers, able to demand their rights and if need be resort to force; with Poles, that was not the case.[13] A similar opinion was expressed about Polish workers in Buenos Aires. The phenomenon had nothing to do with the Slavic temperament but was a result of the socio-economic system existing in the Polish countryside at the end of the nineteenth century which had shaped the Polish peasant's attitudes.

Nevertheless, in a different socio-economic system, such as that of Brazil, the Polish peasant's disposition started to change. Observers stated many times the transformation of the submissive attitude of Polish emigrants into the rebellious one. "Here, the Polish settler, being free, economically independent, rises as a human being and develops self-respect," Dmowski noted. Michał Pankiewicz, who knew the emigrants well and was considered an expert on Polish emigration to South America, noticed "the disappearance of the spirit of serfdom and slavery" among Parana peasants.[14]

The Role of Assimilation

In discussing the problem of assimilation we know most about Brazilian Polonia. In the light of current research we have a picture of a Polish Brazilian community at the end of the interwar period which was no longer Polish but was not yet Brazilian. It was a community that was evolving according to its own dynamics. The changes occurred most quickly where there was an economic or social necessity; therefore the speed of change was more marked in the realm of everyday behaviour in material culture and social life, than in the sphere of consciousness. Due to the disappearance of the tradition of patrimony and to the earlier emancipation of children, the institution of the peasant family underwent changes. Religion started to perform a new function, playing a central role in the maintenance of a Polish ethnic identity. From the point of view of a peasant, especially one settled in the interior of the country, Polonia societies were a new phenomenon. For the conflict between mansion and village, common in Poland, was substituted the antagonism between peasant and intellectual in the new world. In southern Brazil, the development of Polonia communities, representing something more than a statistical set of individuals who had arrived from the Polish homeland, meant the development of a new supra-regional identification, unknown before. Certain aspects of cultivation, the contact with the market not through the fair but through a store and a merchant, the way of building a house, elements of clothing and food—all these were new. The possession and use of firearms was also a totally new phenomenon. Ritual life was simplified because the Polonia community did not possess institutional support larger than the family.

The dynamics of the Polish Brazilian community was still more specific, as the links with the old country weakened much earlier and more radically than in the case of North American Polonia. A subject of a separate study would be to ascertain how strong were these ties at the end of the interwar period. Investigations by

M.A. Ignatowicz in the late seventies in north Mazowsze/Masuria (i.e., on the territories from which once mass emigration to Brazil had started) revealed an absence of even a folk memory of the emigration to Brazil from this area.

Almost nothing is known about the course of assimilation among representatives of national minorities, where social adaptation and the evolution of national identification could be more multi-dimensional than in the case of emigrants of Polish origin. For example, in Misiones, Ukrainians from Poland sometimes became Polonized and sometimes strengthened their Ukrainian identification.

Relatively little is known about the course of assimilation after 1939. Even for earlier periods there is a lack of information on the factors which accelerated or hindered the process of assimilation. It seems that the Polish peasant was not predestined to assimilate easily. His traditionalism, his attachment to his own concept of the mother country, his desire to reproduce Poland on the antipodes—all factors that had worked before the decision to emigrate was made—did not facilitate assimilation. Living in foreign surroundings and liberated from the feudal conditions of the homeland, in Latin America, the peasant felt that he was a Pole to a much higher degree than when he lived close to Rypin or Lipno. The fact that the Polish state has not existed prior to 1918 probably strengthened emigrants' attachment to Polishness, and made them consider the land they had left as only abandoned temporarily. Because the state had not existed, even clearly isolationist ideas became more understandable. For example, *Gazeta Polska w Brazylii* (The Polish Gazette in Brazil) advised Poles not to get involved in the uprising that broke out in Rio Grande do Sul in 1893 and it gave a very characteristic explanation: "Our time has not approached, yet. To sacrifice one's own life aimlessly on a foreign land would be unwise. Our duty is to work, save, educate ourselves and future generations, to be able to hasten to our own mother-country's help when the star of hope for freedom flares up."

Assimilation was also hindered by the attitude of Polonia towards the host society, an attitude which also gave rise to the isolationist tendencies. Obviously, in the history of Polish emigration to Latin America, examples of enthusiasm for the new country can be found. Domeyko, Gombrowicz and Tuwim, for example, proved in their works that the world around them attracted them very strongly.[15] J.H. Retinger, who had excellent knowledge of Mexican life in the interwar period, wrote of his profound knowledge and favourable attitude towards this country.[16] Polish peasants were also enchanted by Brazil and at least at the beginning had a positive attitude towards it. One of them, probably naively, but frankly, wrote: "People are very good here, polite and characterized by tractability and the same refers to Black people, the government is very good and keeps order."[17]

That was not the only attitude, however. Most Poles exhibited a contemptuous attitude towards Latin America societies and states. Many of them still retained the sense of civilizing mission, European conceit, specific xenophobia and the stereotyped image of a lazy Black and a dirty native. They behaved as if their own country over the centuries had been an oasis of honesty, industry, stability and peace, had never experienced strife and social unrest many times.

A logical complement to the emigrants' sense of superiority was the opinion that the "natives" were inferior beings. Even at the end of the interwar period, the General Consul of the Polish Republic in Curitiba could state that emigrants and their offsprings were in no hurry to accept Portuguese culture and language as "this would cause their civilization and economic degradation."[18] Some children were not taught the Portuguese language because their parents did not wish to have "savages" at home.

It was not, unfortunately, as Jan Parandowski wished it to be, that the Polish tradition "never talked about 'savages' but always about people worthy of respect and friendship."[19] In the autobiographical novel about the fate of Polish refugees of the war in one of the Latin American countries, Michał Choromański put in one of his protagonists' mouths the following sentence about the hosts: "It was difficult to expect their sympathy, since we had just said about them that 'they jumped into their cars straight from a palm-tree'."[20] Although in a different literary convention, Gombrowicz wrote in a similar way:

> In the comprehension of a Pole who came after the war from England or France, Argentina is something totally primitive, not worthy of reflection and which should be deprecated. It does not matter that at every step he sees prosperity, standard of living, neatness, good manners, he never dreamt of, in Poland. It does not matter that the number of cars in Buenos Aires only, surpasses several times the number of cars in whole Poland. It does not matter that the subway here is better than the one in Paris, that houses are more modern, that many sky-scrapers have tens of storeys and that a several storeys' house with no lift is unthinkable. In spite of all this, a Pole would treat them from the summit of his "Europeanness."[21]

There were various reasons for the development of this attitude elements of which appeared in different times and in different social circles, and which can be found even among people who in general sympathized with Latin American civilization. It was not specifically Polish; it was found in the attitudes of many immigrants. At the end of the nineteenth century, one of Poland's natural historians, Jan Sztolcman, wrote:

> Every emigrant in Peru considers himself infinitely superior compared to the native inhabitant, whether he has or has not the right

> to do so. Very often, people who are scum of the European society, dregs of various countries, fugitives from their fatherlands to which the law forbids them to return, in the other hemisphere, wish to play and often do play the role of very important persons, they deride the natives and treat them superiorily.[22]

The fact that this attitude was common suggests that its origins should be sought in more general phenomena of social psychology. In the case of Polish immigrants the attitude of superiority they brought with them could have been reinforced by the ethnocentrism growing among peasants in Poland, by the idea that the possession of cultivated land gave added prestige and by the policy of the Polish government in the interwar years justifying its territorial ambitions. Peasants who came at the end of the nineteenth century were surprised by the primitiveness of Brazilian agriculture. They did not notice that not all of Brazil consisted of backwoods, that Sao Paulo was already a big industrial centre in the course of development, that the coffee-producing states were experiencing a boom. They did not notice that although they thought they acted independently, in fact they were the instruments of Brazilian groups in their drive toward the development and modernization of the country. Polish emigrants informed their families that the lands they obtained were not sufficiently cultivated, that "when they start to work everything will be different,"[23] and that they considered themselves the better. "The standard of living of Brazilians with whom our settler was in contact is too low to impress; on the contrary, it raises generally contempt and scoff," Dmowski noted, after he had visited Parana.[24]

In the interwar period, Polish agencies supported this attitude among the emigrants. The Polish diplomatic service in Brazil behaved in a way that it would never have done in France, England, the United States or any other country for which it had respect. But Polish emissaries did not hesitate to develop the irredentist activity in Latin America. There, at the confluence of Brazilian, Argentinian and Paraguayan borders, the dangerous visionaries of the Warsaw Ministry of Foreign Affairs planned in the late thirties to create a centre of Polish settlement which could function as a stepping-stone for the development of a Polish colony. The plan was an impossible fantasy. Brazilians just as much as Poles were aware of the strategic and economic significance of this region. In the course of time it became evident that the Brazilian police knew all about this plan. There were no chances for its success, but the fact that it had developed illustrates the attitude of lesser Polish functionaries towards Brazil.

The policy of Polish authorities on emigration to Latin America in the period preceding the outbreak of World War Two was unrealistic. Putting aside the question of the political viability of developing projects in Latin America, Poland was "too poor to cover the costs of mass settlers' emigration and too weak to fight for the improvement of her refugees' life and work conditions abroad."[25] The attempts to create colonies of Polish emigrant-farmers in Latin America proved abortive and caused severe hardships for these people. Polish emigration doctrine was based on nineteenth-century colonial doctrines, but it only came to be put into effect at a time when transatlantic emigration had begun to subside.

This colonization thrust was not only impractical, it was also detrimental to Polonia communities in Latin America. The picture of heroic Poland ("Polonia heroica") which had been created in the period of partitions and had functioned in educated circles in many Latin American countries, was transformed, in the inter-war period, into a vision of a state similar, as regards its aspirations, to totalitarian states. The power of this vision became evident during the campaign organized in Brazil in the late thirties. In August 1938, Manuel Ribas, the representative of the Brazilian federal government in Parana, conjectured that the "joint German, Polish and Italian navy will invade our coasts."[26] In the late thirties fears of an aggressive Poland, similar to Germany, Japan and Italy, spread among many Latin American countries. It only served to reinforce the negative stereotype of Poles, which was already widely held.

To the same extent as Polonia had a low opinion of the receiving societies, these societies returned it in kind. Latin Americans had a very high opinion of West European nations, the English being at the top, and a very low one of Asian and African nations (with some nuances as regards the Japanese). Central European nations occupied a middle position on this scale. In 1936 in Columbia this scale received, in a way, a legal expression; for immigrants from Bulgaria, China, Egypt, Estonia, Greece, India, Latvia, Libya, Lithuania, Morocco, Palestine, Poland, Romania, Russia, Syria and Turkey, higher immigration securities were demanded.[27] In the same year in Costa Rica, a kind of selective population census for Poles, Chinese and Blacks was organized. Although in the Argentine and Brazil ethnic quotas did not receive legal force, in many cases discrimination in this respect was evident. In the late twenties the Polish Consul in Sao Paulo wrote:

> Brazilians who know the names of outstanding Poles from history or the press, have to make an effort to realize that they are members of the same nation as poor Polish emigrants treated here with contempt. It happens sometimes that if Brazilians meet a well-mannered and educated Pole, they are not able to hide their surprise, that he is of Polish nationality.[28]

Wańkowicz observed that in Cuba the word "Pole" became a "contemptuous label" for every foreigner and that it denoted "all seven mortal sins."[29] Obviously, a negative stereotype of other Polish national groups was also developed. Emigrants of Jewish origin especially were a convenient target for attacks, as they concentrated in trade. There were more Polish Jews in the cities than Polish Catholics and therefore the Latin American opinion had the tendency to identify them all as Polish emigrants; thus the negative stereotype of everybody who came from the Vistula River became still stronger. Contradictory opinions were attached to Jews: they were represented as exploiters and, simultaneously, as communists.

After World War Two there was some improvement in the attitude towards Polonia. Gombrowicz observed: "Today in Argentina, the influx of large numbers of Polish intelligentsia who gradually feather their nests, contributes to a significant improvement of Polish quotations on labour market."[30] The Brazilian sociologist Octavio Ianni, however, has found a strongly negative stereotype of a Pole in the southern part of his country.[31] Stereotypes are hard to eradicate; they endure even if the position of a group of immigrants or of their mother country, which probably underlaid the development of these stereotypes, is not that low any more. They serve the satisfaction of certain needs, exactly as the idea of the civilizing mission of the Poles in Latin America compensated them for their actual lack of economic potential.

The process of assimilation of Latin American Polonia was determined however not only by factors dependent on the will or attitude of groups involved in it, but also, and probably mainly, by objective factors. It can be supposed that the low status of the group was not conducive to quick assimilation. A similar negative influence on assimilation had to have strong occupational specialization of the group, especially in agriculture; in general, communities having the repertoire of professional roles similar to the one of the global society, as well as urban groups, assimilate more quickly. The situation was summed up by an emigrant activist, K. Warchalowski, at the beginning of the century:

> Our emigrants have created here, in trackless forests, homogeneous agricultural colonies.... Open to foreign influences on a very small scale, even new generations of our settlers, born here, do not denationalize.... The Polish element here has the chances not only for the preservation of its national language and features, but also for the development of new forms of the Polish life.[32]

The slow economic advancement of the emigrants, partly due to their own attitudes, partly to external conditions, was also not conducive to assimilation. The government in the state of Sao Paulo also had some influence on this process, since it allowed separate centres of settlement to develop. J. Siemiradzki, the Polish geologist, geographer and expert in emigration who had visited Brazil at the height of the mass immigration, stated that the Sao Paulo state gradually became "New Italy," Santa Catarina "New Germany" and Parana "New Poland."[33] Although there was undoubtedly some exaggeration in this statement, coherent ethnic centres did develop in Brazil. Other organizations, such as the army, the schools, which in a modern state can exercise considerable pressure for assimilation, had very little influence in Brazil. We do not mean here assimilative pressures but a pervasive influence on all groups in society, similar to that to which the aboriginal population of the country is exposed. In the late thirties, the Brazilian government acted to integrate their ethnic groups. President Getulio Vargas issued several decrees opposing the maintenance of immigrants' systems of education, organizations, the development of their national culture. The decrees were followed by a flood of spontaneous chauvinism which washed over practically the whole of Latin America. Undoubtedly, President Vargas' action suppressed most of the external manifestations of ethnic group identity, but its true effect on the process of assimilation is still being discussed. It is probable that the Argentine policy based on the development of the system of education and the exacting of obligatory school attendance of emigrants' children were more favourable for assimilation than coercion. Sociologists commonly assume that the process of assimilation develops more quickly when its course is natural and not subject to pressures.

In spite of all the obstacles, assimilation, or at least integration of Polonia groups in Latin America, was progressing. The way Polonia acted in dramatic moments can be viewed as a good test of this process. When Poland regained its independence, Polonia, although it had waited for this moment, did not return to the mother country, even though there were by this time few financial barriers to doing so. The attempt to recruit members of Brazilian Polonia to the army of General Haller failed; only just over one hundred volunteers went.[34] Similarly, the action organized by General Sikorski's deputies to recruit emigrants to the Polish armed forces during World War Two brought a much smaller response than was expected by the Commander-in-Chief. The few people who joined up, in general, were not representative of the masses of peasant settlers. In Argentina the answer of Polonia was similar. Integration, if not yet extensive assimilation of Polonia to the countries of settlement, was already well advanced. The change of the socio-economic system in Poland after 1945, the reduction of contacts between Polonia and Poland in the early part of the fifties, the improvement of Polonia economic status, could only accelerate this process.

Undoubtedly, today, a great majority of immigrants' descendants consider themselves a part of Latin American nations where they live. The fact that the word "Brasileiro" was included in the title of the magazine *Anais da comunidade Brasileiro-Polonesa* (Yearbooks of the Brazilian-Polish Community), preceding the word "Polish," symbolizes the feeling of the young historians who founded this magazine, for the country of their ancestors and their interest in their own past do not mean a loss of identification with their adopted land. One of them, Ruy Christovan Wachowicz, a professor of the Federal University in Curitiba, during the Eleventh General Meeting of Polish Historians (Toruń, 1974), discussed the decision of his parents at his very Polish family home in Brazil to teach him Portuguese. "And they were right," he concluded.

Conclusion

Polonia communities in Latin America in the long course of their history occupied low positions on the ladder of wealth, social prestige and power. It seems that the Polish group in North America surpassed them in every way. If it is true that the point of departure of both groups was similar, then one should admit that the developed capitalistic system—urbanization, industry, commercialized agriculture, the organizations of the modern state, all characteristic of North America—was more favourable for the social rise and assimilation of the Polonias than the underdeveloped structure of Latin American countries.

Notes

1. This paper is based on my work *Polonia brazylijska* [Brazilian Polonia] (Warsaw: Ludowa Spółdzielnia Wydawnicza), and on a collective work, which as an editor I am preparing now for print, *Dzieje Polonii w Ameryce Łacińskiej* [The History of Polonia in Latin America]. In the latter work a broad bibliography is included.
2. General Consulate of the Polish Republic to the Ministry of Foreign Affairs, Sept. 23, 1936, Archiwum Akt Nowych [Archives of New Records] (Warsaw (cited below as ANF), zespół Swiatowego Związku Polaków z Zagranicy [World Union of Poles Abroad collection]), 272, pp. 30-31.
3. Antoni Hempel, *Polacy w Brazylii* [Poles in Brazil] (Lvov, 1893), p. 55.
4. A report of the General Consulate of the Polish Republic in New York from 1924, ANF, the set collection of the Polish Embassy in Washington, 967, pp. 6-7.
5. Melchior Wańkowicz, *W kościołach Meksyku* [In Mexico's Churches] (Warsaw, 1927), p. 33.
6. Quoted from Ryszard Stemplowski, "Rekrutacja w Brazylii do oddziałów Sikorskiego" ["The Recruitment in Brazil to Sikorski's Detachments"], *Przęglad Polonijny,* no. 1 (1976), p. 77.
7. From the text of J. Kozakiewicz in the Central Archives of the Central Committee of Polish United Workers' Party, Warsaw, Polish Socialist Party collection, AM 1190 [4].

8. Jan Hempel, *Tomek. Opowiadanie z życia osadników polskich w Paranie* [Tomek. A Story about the Life of Polish Settlers in Parana] (Lublin: *Kurier*, July 2-Aug. 4, 1909).
9. Witôld Kula, Nina Assorodobraj-Kula, and Marcin Kula, eds., *Listy emigrantów z Brazylii i Stanów Zjednoczonych. 1890-1891* [Emigrants' Letters from Brazil and the United States. 1890-1891] (Warsaw: Ludowa Spółdzielnia Wydawnicza, 1973), letter 77.
10. W. Dean, *The Industrialization of Sao Paulo. 1880-1945* (Austin: Texas University Press, 1969), p. 51.
11. M. Swirski, *Polacy w Sao Paulo,* 1929, ANF, Ministry of Foreign Affairs collection (cited below as MFA), 10372, p. 28.
12. Roman Dmowski, "Z Parany" ["From Parana"], *Przęglad Wszechpolski* (1900), nos. 2, 3, 6.
13. M. Swirski, *Perspektywy rozwoju emigracji polskiej w stanie Sao Paulo* [Perspectives for the Development of Polish Emigration in Sao Paulo State] 1929, ANF, MFA, 9639, pp. 158, 166.
14. Quoted after Izabela Klarner-[Kosińska], *Emigracja z Królestwa Polskiego do Brazylii w latach 1890-1914* [Emigration from the Polish Kingdom to Brazil in the years 1890-1914] (Warsaw, 1975), p. 152.
15. Ignacy Domeyko, *Moje podróże. Pamiętniki wygnańca. 1831-1888* [My Trips: Memoirs of an Exile, 1831-1888] (Wrocław: Ossolineum, 1962); Witold Gombrowicz, *Dziennik* [Journal] 1953-1956 (Paris: Instytut Literacki, 1957); the same author, *Dziennik* [Journal] 1957-1961 (Paris: Instytut Literacki, 1962). Parts of the *Journal* referring to the stay in Argentina were published in Buenos Aires in 1968 as "Diario Argentino"; by the same author, *Wędrówki po Argentynie* [Wandering around Argentina], in *Dzieła Zebrane* [Collected Works] XI (Paris: Instytut Literacki, 1977); Julian Tuwim, *Kwiaty Polskie* [Polish Flowers], many editions.
16. Józef H. Retinger, *Morones of Mexico. A History of the Labour Movement in that Country* (London, 1926); the same author, *Tierra Mexicana. A History of Land and Agriculture in Ancient and Modern Mexico* (London, 1926 (?)). Compare an episode about Mexico in this author's memoir in *Memoirs of an Eminence Grise,* ed. J. Pomian (Sussex: University Press, 1972).
17. *Listy emigrantów,* letter 68.
18. J. Gieburowski to MFA, Curitiba, Jan. 30, 1938, ANF, MFA, 10026, p. 5.
19. In the introduction to Mieczysław B. Lepecki, *Pan Jakobus Sobieski* [Mr. Jakobus Sobieski] (Warsaw, 1970), p. 1.
20. Michał Choromański, *Głownictwo, moglitwa i praktykarze* 2 (Poznan, 1971), pp. 5-6.
21. Gombrowicz, *Wędrówki po Argentynie,* pp. 195-96.
22. Jan Sztolcman, *Peru. Wspomnienia z podróży* [Peru. Reminiscences of a Voyage] 1 (Warsaw-Cracow, 1912).
23. *Listy emigrantów,* letter 77.
24. Dmowski, "Z Parany."

25. E. Kołodziej, "Wychodźstwo zarobkowe z Polski w latach 1918-1939. Studia nad polityką emigracyjną II Rzeczypospolitej" ["Economic Emigration from Poland in the Years 1918-1939. Studies on the Emigration Policy of the Second Republic"] (Ph.D. dissertation, Wrocław University, 1978), p. 311 of the typescript.

26. B. Lepecki, Vice-consul of the Polish Republic in Curitiba to the Legation of the Polish Republic in Rio de Janeiro, Aug. 25, 1938, ANF, MFA, 10386, p. 83.

27. K. Smolana, "Sobre a genese do estereótipo do Polones na America Latina (caso brasileiro)," *Estudios Latinoamericanos* V (Wrocław, 1979).

28. Swirski, *Polacy w Sao Paulo,* pp. 31-32.

29. Melchior Wańkowicz, "Polska emigracja na Kubie" ["Polish Emigration in Cuba"], in *Kurier Warszawski,* 3 Nov. 1926.

30. Gombrowicz, *Wędrówki po Argentynie,* p. 186.

31. O. Ianni, *Racas e classes sociais no Brasil* (Rio de Janeiro, 1966), chapter 6.

32. Text with no title and date, ANF, the collection of J. K. Warchałowski, 19, p. 7.

33. Józef Siemiradzki, *La Nouvelle Pologne. Etat de Parana (Bresil)* (Brussels, 1899), p. 11.

34. M. A. Ignatowicz, "Postawa Polonii brazylijskiej wobec odzyskania niepodległości Polski w 1918" ["The Attitude of Brazilian Polonia Towards the Recovery of Polish Independence in 1918"], in *Polonia wobec niepodległości Polski w czasie l wojny światowej* [The Attitude of Polonia Towards Polish Independence During World War I], eds. Halina Florkowska-Francic, Mirosław Francic, Hieronion Kubiak (Wrocław: Ossolineum, 1979).

Religion and Culture

The Pilgrimage from *Gemeinschaft* to *Gesellschaft:* Sociological Functions of Religion in the Polish American Community

Leonard F. Chrobot

It is difficult to exaggerate the radical change which took place in the consciousness of the Polish peasant who emigrated to the United States at the turn of the nineteenth century. So traumatic a transition was possible because one institution served as a "decompression chamber" in the movement from the traditional culture of eastern Europe (*Gemeinschaft*) to a modern, urban and technological culture of America (*Gesellschaft*). The concern of this paper is the role of the Polish American parish as a sociological creation of the Polish peasant to accomplish this transition.

In order to grasp the implications of this phenomenon I will comment upon the role that religion has traditionally played in Polish history, indicate some of the characteristics of the traditional culture which they brought with them and demonstrate how this was diametrically opposed to the new culture in which they found themselves. I will show how some of these attitudes affected one institution–marriage. Further, I will review some of the universal functions of religion in all societies, showing how some of these functions were achieved in the institution of the parish, and how the structure of the parish changed in its adaptation to American society. The approach of the paper is sociological, not theological, attempting to analyse phenomenon as it occurred, without making any judgment about it, with the hope of gaining some insights not only into what happened in the past, but what is happening in the present.

The Role of Religion in Polish History

Religion has played a vital role in the self-definition of the Polish nation throughout history. Positively, it served as a vehicle of unification of the various Slavic tribes. It baptized the primitive religious sentiment of paganism and brought it into the mainstream of western Roman culture. Serving as a bridge between eastern Orthodoxy and western Protestantism, Poland's religious culture has motivated great heroism and endurance, creating a romantic culture which permeated all society, from the lowliest peasant to the highest aristocracy. Never a Sunday-only affair, religion became part and parcel of a unified culture, with little sense of separation between the sacred and the secular. Whereas American culture distinguishes between holy days and holidays, linguistically Polish allows only for the former (*święto*). It reinforced a sense of the sacred in all aspects of life, institutionalizing this in custom and tradition which persist to this day.

Negatively, however, it also provided an opportunity for the development of a negative identity. Poles knew who they were because they were not Orthodox or Protestant, not German or Russian. It sustained a type of fatalism, acceptance of the status quo, with rigid subjection to authority, especially the privileged position of the clergy who spoke with the authority of the divine. Class distinctions were often made sacred in a hierarchical arrangement of society. Religion resisted the breakdown of the feudal system because of its suspicion of upward mobility and its predominantly rural and agricultural ritual. There was little official emphasis within the Polish Catholic church on social action to make people economically freer until after the great emigration overseas had well begun. Excesses in the sense of the sacred sometimes confused mystery with superstition, granting inordinate power to the priest who was looked upon as the keeper of the sacred rites mediating between God and man. Correct performance of the ritual sometimes became more important than communication of the sense of mystery. The role of the pastor often became absolute, not subject to criticism, reinforcing an excessive deference of the laity to him.

It was this combination of positive and negative characteristics of religion which the Polish peasant brought with him as he plunged into a society with few of these attitudes. American culture was progressively becoming more secular; there was separation of church and state; there were pluralistic identities, both ethnic and religious; the dominant cultural ethos was white, Anglo-Saxon and Protestant; the dominant philosophical position was that of pragmatism in which people acted, then tested, the validity of their action by the relative success of the results. For the first time the peasant became totally subject to the clock, the division of time into quantifiable segments, not the natural cycles of day and night and the progression of spring, summer, fall and winter. He was forced to work inside with or on machines. His hands no longer worked with the soil. He became subject to impersonal economic forces, with cycles of "boom or bust," over which he had no control. He was exploited by the "captains of industry," whose own philosophical position was bolstered by the Social Darwinist philosophy of the late nineteenth century. The map of his universe had been torn to bits, the familiar bulwarks of his security shattered. In a world of increasing complexity and confusion, he no longer had any force to pray to, and his traditional morality, based upon precepts of humility, justice and cooperation, was of small use in a world in which survival was accorded only to the strong and predatory. The culture shock which the Polish peasant experienced would have reverberations for many generations to come.

Characteristics of Traditional and Modern Culture

There is a cluster of values and attitudes which formed the world view of the Polish peasant (and most people from any more traditional culture) which are still recognizable today. It is important to note that they are listed in terms of Max Weber's concept of "ideal types,"—in other words, they do not exist in any one person in pure form. On a continuum between the extremes of traditional and modern culture, people can be found holding views which are either more traditional or more modern. Some of these characteristics include:

Stability—There was an eternal quality to traditional society, for nothing changed. There was a sense of continuity because there was no upward mobility, no sense of striving, no competition; people were content to "get by" rather than "get ahead." Information on farming, child-rearing, religion was passed on from one generation to the next. The wisdom of experience became crystallized in countless folk sayings, for example, 'Nie ma złego co by na dobro nie wyszło' ('Nothing bad happens to us that some good cannot come from it'), which became the memorized recordings by which reality was processed for a lifetime.

Surveillance and Social Control—In traditional society, where most people knew one another by name, everyone knew everything about everybody. Gossip became a very effective means of keeping social control and limiting deviance. Protection of the good name of a family was far more important than individual wants or needs.

Scarcity of Material Goods—When there was insufficient food, clothing and shelter, people were forced to cooperate in order to survive. Individualism was virtually impossible because the group was more important for survival. People were simply not aware of themselves as individuals, but only as members of a group. The solidarity of the group, in all of its aspects, became the dominant force.

The Family as an Economic Unit—The extended family, consisting of parents, grandparents, children and close relatives, functioned as an economic unit, with each member's role clearly established. Numerous children in such a traditional society were considered a blessing from God, because they provided free farm labour and assured the social welfare of the group and the security of the older members. The roles of mother and father were clearly defined, with clear expectations which were administered by the community. There was no such concept as time off; there were no vacations or weekends. Children did not play, they worked at tasks appropriate to their age to contribute to the survival of the group.

Hierarchical Structure—Society was based on a clearly defined father-son, king-peasant relationship. Father or king punished bad behaviour and rewarded good. Most people viewed God in precisely the same manner. Fear was the dominant force. Authority enforced the norms of society with little or no consideration for the wants or needs of the individual.

Male Domination—Because brawn was more necessary for survival than brains, men dominated, with women being relegated to the reproductive and survival aspects of the family. All authority was vested in men.

Sexuality was Mysterious and Sacred—Because sexuality participated in the life-giving function of God, it was mysterious and sacred; it was *res tremenda,* holding both fascination and fear. It was never separated from the family context. It was a "duty" to be "performed" for survival of the family and the community. The norm of marriage was not romantic love, but respect for the mutual obligations of the roles to be performed. Marriages were arranged by the families, not the individuals, and both families had a stake, even economically, in the survival of the bond.

Nature was Power—People in traditional societies were overwhelmed by the power of nature, over which they had little control. They were subject to it, hence they learned to live in harmony with it. They lived in the cycle of the days and nights, the cycle of seasons. They worked in and with nature, as part of its system, never against it.

Veneration of the Aged—In the absence of change, knowledge was accumulated through the ages, and the old were held in veneration because they knew the ways of survival.

Fatalism—Because things did not change, people learned to accept the world the way it was. There was little desire to alter roles, structures, systems. There was little expectation of the way things will be. An absence of future orientation made the postponement of gratification to achieve some distant goal as senseless. The future simply tended to be an extension of the present, and the present a re-enactment of the past.

This is the world from which the Polish peasant came. He entered a world that was gradually becoming characterized by the exact opposite of these values and attitudes, a world moving toward rapid industrialization, urbanization and technology. This world was characterized by:

Change—Modern society is characterized by constant change; there is little of the eternal quality of the past, little sense of continuity, with much emphasis on upward mobility and striving. People seldom live in the same home all their lives, and few keep the same jobs. Some do not even keep the same spouses. Wisdom is characterized by the newest information, which can now be processed by computers. Americans, as Harvey Cox says, have an active prejudice against the past.

Anonymity—Few people know each other by name, hence people can lose themselves in the crowd. Social control must come from outside agencies, the police, the courts, etc. Deviance has little to control it. Individual wants and needs now become individual rights, often to the detriment of the community.

Affluence—When people no longer need simply to survive, their needs become more complex. Self-fulfilment and self-actualization become important because people become aware of themselves as individuals. Many children in America today assume that they have a right to their own bedroom, their own telephone, their own television sets or stereos. We are no longer worried about food for survival, we are concerned about gourmet dishes and caloric content. Clothing no longer functions to keep us warm, it is a symbol of upward mobility and fashion. The home is no longer the symbol of the stability of the family, it is an investment opportunity, a status symbol.

The Nuclear Family—The model of the family becomes husband and wife and two children. The traditional structures of fidelity and permanence begin to break down. Children are often viewed as an intrusion into the self-fulfilment desires of the parents. They must be fed and clothed and sheltered and educated for some twenty years, at an estimated cost of some $85,000 only to leave the home and the parents afterwards. With luck, they may visit at Thanksgiving, Christmas and Easter. The survival and protection function of the large family is now performed by specialized institutions, such as insurance agencies or government. The roles of mother and father have become blurred, and there is little community consenus about them. "Living" is relegated to time off from work. There is no economic expectation of children. Adolescence is now prolonged childhood. If work is performed, it is solely for the individual and personal needs of the adolescent, not the family.

Democratic Equality—Emphasis on individual or personal development is accompanied by a decline in parental authority (as well as the divine and clerical authority on which it is modelled). The wants and needs of each individual begin to assume equal weight and to weigh more heavily than the demands of social units such as the family or parish.

Female Emergence—Since brawn is now replaced by machinery, brains become important, and women are rediscovering their potential to contribute beyond the structures of the home and family to society at large. Social movements to equalize the rights of the sexes are common. Careers which before were always limited to men are now available to women. The reproductive function is now something freely chosen.

Liberalization of Sexual Mores—As the procreative and social functions of marriage decline in importance, deviation from traditional sexual role requirements becomes more acceptable. Romantic love, in which individuals find fulfilment through mutual affection and regard, is the norm of a sexual relationship.

Human Environment—Once nature is tamed, man begins to live in a man-made world, and when something goes wrong, man is to blame. Technology becomes the means of control, hence it takes on an almost religious quality. Automatic lights and heat and coolness control the cycles of day and night and of the seasons.

Veneration of the Young—The young are more readily adaptable to constant change, hence there is a veneration of the young. The old represent the past, and the past has little utility for the future.

Hope in the Future—With constant change, there is always the hope that things will be better in the future. The world can never be accepted the way it is. There is constant tampering with roles, structures, systems. We constantly create scenarios of the way things will be and are subject to frequent disappointment when our expectations are not fulfilled. The postponement of gratification makes us unable to experience the present moment.

I have purposely drawn the dichotomy to extremes. American culture at the time of the mass immigration had not yet achieved such a degree of modernization, but the process had begun. The descendants of these immigrants, in the second, third, and fourth generation, are the ones who experience the change more dramatically. We cannot overestimate, however, the importance of the confrontation of the two world views as it took place in the everyday life of the Polish peasant. When they came to America they faced a tremendous, radical change in all they felt, thought and did.

As Thomas and Znaniecki have pointed out in *The Polish Peasant in Europe and America,* the peasant had adapted himself to the life of a permanent agricultural community, which had been settled for many hundreds of years in the same locality, changing so slowly that each generation simply repeated the patterns of the previous one.[1] He was unaccustomed to expect unfamiliar happenings, and if they came, he relied on the group for assistance to regain his mental balance and recover the feeling that life was normal. He drew all of his social stimulations, checks and suggestions from direct social contact with his milieu. The principle of solidarity of the community was uppermost in his world, and this became so much a part of his unified culture that any small change in any part of it threatened his entire world view. He had been a member of a politically and culturally passive class, never having participated consciously in any impersonal institutions existing in his own country.

In the face of the disorganization of traditional society, the group tried to defend itself by methods consciously tending to strengthen the influence of the traditional rules of behaviour. This could have been effective as long as outside contacts remained limited, but it simply was not possible in the interaction which took place in the Polish American community. The community either sought to suppress many of the new attitudes (hence the conservative function of the Polish American parish), or it sought to institutionalize the new for socially productive purposes. Often a church or a pastor became the focus of this conflict, as illustrated in Daniel Buczek's *Immigrant Pastor,* an account of the life and work of Monsignor Łucjan Bójnowski in New Britain, Connecticut.

The family disorganization which began with the first generation was well documented by Thomas and Znaniecki. They did indeed "photograph" the Polish family just at that point when the immigration trauma was having its most dramatic effects, as Andrew Greeley points out.[2] The Polish family survived, however. It focused its energies, called up its resources; it created ecclesiastical, political and fraternal structures to serve precisely as the "decompression chamber" in the pilgrimage from *Gemeinschaft* to *Gesellschaft.* Barbara Les, of the Polonia Research Institute, Jagiellonian University, has suggested that the process of assimilation differed among Polish Baptists, Polish Nationals and Polish Roman Catholics.[3] She maintains that the change occurred the fastest among the Polish Baptists. Although small in number, they became urbanized more quickly and lost the values of the traditional order. Polish Nationals would represent an intermediate speed, while the slowest to urbanize were the Polish Roman Catholics. This may account for what Andrew Greeley sees as the survival of a strong, vigorous and tenacious family life among Polish Americans who, even in the third and fourth generation, managed in some way to balance the identity-producing stability of the traditional order with the creature comforts of the modern world.[4] Some sociologists see the emergence of the ethnic parish as the principal cause for the fidelity of the working class to the church in American society, a situation quite different in many western European countries.[5] Ewa Morawska, elsewhere in this collection, has described the drive of the Polish immigrant for upward mobility and achievement within and in terms of the values of his family and community.

Changes in the Institution of Marriage

Social disorganization is defined as the decrease in the influence of existing social rules of behaviour upon individual members of a group. It arises when group norms, sanctions, status and role expectations are absent or so severely disrupted that individual behaviour is no longer effectively controlled. It is the cause of increased deviance and crime. The Polish American family and the institution of marriage experienced this phenomenon dramatically as it found itself in the new world of American society.

In Poland marriage was a social institution, a part of the wider family institution, a part of the economic life organization of the society. As Thomas and Znaniecki have pointed out, the large families of both the husband and the wife had a stake in preserving the marriage bond. The marriage was "their work," not that of the individuals. A break in the bond had undesirable effects, both social and economic, on both families. Each family enforced the traditional rules of behaviour and were ready to defend any break in the rules, no matter by whom. When the families failed to enforce the rules, the larger community exercised its right. The traditional system was sanctioned by the entire social milieu, the village, the church and the state. It was simply "the way things were done." In the assimilation process in American society, however, the Polish family gradually discovered that the large family gradually ceased to be a real social body. There are often few concrete interests among its members, who become increasingly geographically scattered. The community loses its tradition. Communities become voluntary. If the pressures of a community become uncomfortable for the individual, he or she can readily move. Even the church becomes a free-will congregation, to whose sanctions one must give voluntary consent. Marriage depends increasingly on the desire for personal fulfilment and the mutual affection of the partners; goals which may also be realized outside of traditional marriage. Even the old compulsions of economics are no longer effective bonds, since individuals in a marriage can survive separately.

Thomas and Znaniecki have pointed out some of the factors causing the decay of the traditional institution of marriage:

> *Temperamental Misadaptation*—Temperament differences, psychological or physiological, can become the occasion for arguments often for objectively trivial reasons. This can cause the husband and/or wife to search for comfort and intimacy outside of the existing institution of marriage. In the more traditional system, the social milieu kept such expressions to a minimum. Spouses, seeing no escape from the pressure of their families and the community would simply put up with differences and learn to adjust to each other. In the more modern system, however, spouses know that they can escape from unpleasant situations. If the burden of marriage becomes too heavy, they can simply reject it. Often the break of the bond emerges as the *only* answer.
>
> *Sexual Interests*—Sexuality today assumes a different role from the one it played in traditional society. Violations of the sexual code then were not matters of morality as much as violations of the social order. Rules were not abstract moral principles but addressed concrete issues of survival. Infidelity was anti-social, because it weakened the family, and that weakened the very social organization. If there was infidelity, there was more concern for

counteracting any bad consequences to the family rather than concern for hurt feelings. Sexual indulgence was not so much "wicked," as disruptive of the family structure. Marriage was a form of economic cooperation and a system for raising children; sexual infidelity was purely a private affair. In modern society, sexual satisfaction assumes greater importance. The wife is defined not only as a homemaker and mother, but as a lover. In this light, marriage ceases to be an indissoluble institution, and divorce becomes socially acceptable.

Economic Pressures—Whereas in traditional society it was economically efficient to maintain the marriage bond, today, when the partnership becomes economically inefficient, it is revised or dissolved. The shifting demands of the American economic system—the necessities of frequent occupational change, geographical mobility, and cyclical unemployment—can produce feelings of powerlessness and encourage privatism. Resentments may arise toward the limitations imposed by marriage, its demands for stability, regularity and order. Since marriage is arranged by individuals, not by families, its dissolution is not penalized by a loss of economic security or social prestige.

Interferences of the State—Detectives, police or judges in modern society seldom strengthen the bond of marriage. They tend to arbitrate between husband and wife, to encourage each to get the best of each other, not to support the solidarity. They look at individuals, not the family. In the older system, the individual was made to feel that he or she sinned against the sacredness of marriage, not that he or she was wronged. The role of the community was not to step in between husband and wife to arbitrate between personal and individual claims, but to uphold the unity of the marriage. The normal connection between individuals in modern society is the contract, a free association which is dissoluble at will. The law treats the husband and the wife as isolated individuals.

It was in the meeting of these two radically different views of the nature of society that the Polish American parish emerged as a functional adaptation to bridge the gap.

The Functions and Dysfunctions of Religion

Religion, always and everywhere, performs certain functions within a society which are necessary for survival. In more traditional societies, obviously the role of religion plays a more important part, since because of centuries of interaction with the culture, it tends to become more closely intertwined with the very warp and woof of the structures of that society. This is certainly true of Polish culture. Just as the Polish language became a vehicle of the expression of the identity of the nation, especially during the *Kulturkampf* of Prussia and the Russification of the tsars in the nineteenth century, religion, in its Roman Catholic tradition in Poland, became truly an expression of the identity of the nation. For many to be Polish meant to be Catholic. In more modern societies with their inevitable move toward secularization, many of the functions of religion become increasingly performed by private and/or state institutions. This is especially evident in communist countries, where most of these functions of religion are taken over by the state.

The Polish priest in America, strongly supported by his peasant congregation, made ready use of the functions of religion in constructing the vast network of over eight hundred parishes and schools throughout the north and east to meet the needs of a burgeoning mass of people streaming into a rapidly urbanizing America. In the following section I will briefly describe each of these functions and show how the Polish American community adapted these functions to meet their needs of constructing the "decompression chamber" in this society.

The Priestly Function

The Polish American parish adapted the priestly functions to its own structural needs.[6] Unlike some of the Protestant churches in America, which often sanctified the value system of expansionist and exploitative American capitalism, the Polish American parish made the norms of the more traditional Polish culture sacred even in an American setting. It stood, in fact, against many of the values of a dominant Protestant culture, creating the atmosphere of a transplanted village in an urban and industrialized society. To leave the church was to sell out to the enemy, to be unfaithful to the heritage of their ancestors, to deny their traditions. Intermarriage with non-Poles, public education, leaving the neighbourhood, going to an "Irish" parish—all of these were condemned from the pulpit as "sins" against the solidarity of the community. Individual goals of upward mobility into the mainstreams of American society were roundly condemned, while group goals of bettering the lot of the parish family were strongly supported. Positively such an approach maintained the solidarity of the group, but often at the cost of the individual. It caused the formation of parallel institutions alongside American ones, to meet the needs of the group, but often prevented the possibility of real influence on American institutions through the integration of Polish cultural values into mainstream American life.

The Prophetic Function

One of the basic themes of Polish literature of the nineteenth century was that of Messianism, the idea that Poland must suffer to redeem the sins of mankind. This, coupled with the Slavic, perhaps more Russian, belief that salvation would not come from an elite but from the masses, created a distinctly Polish American attitude of accepting the sufferings brought on by the exploitation of American capitalism with the hope that honesty in work, dedication to the American system, an almost religious obligation to vote, fidelity to family and neighbourhood, cleanliness that sometimes verged on the compulsive, loyalty to the parish and its pastor, humility before representatives of mainstream American culture—all of these created an attitude which would ultimately conquer all. It also created a somewhat docile group who often embodied traditional values, but limited the achievement of its more progressive members.

The Self-Identity Function

Although there was much in the feudal system of nineteenth century Europe which could have produced a Polish *lumpenproletariat*—a group of dispossessed and uprooted individuals cut off from the economic and social class with which they might normally be identified, the Polish parish gave to the peasant a sense of limited dignity in the face of extremely dehumanizing structures of society. The village church in rural Poland may have served a purpose similar to churches among blacks in the American South in the nineteenth century. Both preserved a fraction of individual self-worth amid a degrading social system. Both offered a chance for autonomous social development: for blacks, when slavery was abolished; for Poles, when they emigrated overseas.

Although the Polish peasant knew his place in the church of the village, in ultimate analysis when it came to the reception of the sacraments, he was the equal of the lord of the manor. Eucharist given to the delicate and finest arrayed *dama* of aristocracy was of no greater importance than that given to the roughhewn, weather-beaten face of the poorest peasant. The Protestant work ethic, which viewed wealth as a sign of God's favour, was not part of the tradition of the Polish American. Poverty was not a curse from God, it was the way things were. One could be poor but decent. Poverty was not the fault of the system, the establishment, the "man," and Polish Americans did not expect much from government to alleviate their plight. Positively, it created an ethnic group with a distinctive type of dignity. Negatively, by American standards of competitiveness and upward mobility, it restricted their full realization of the American dream of rags to riches. The under-representation of Polish Catholic in white-collar jobs would indicate this.[7]

The Buttress Function

Of all of the functions of religion, the buttress function is perhaps best seen in the role that the Polish American parish played in the transition from traditional to modern culture. In comparison to the other large Catholic ethnic groups, notably the Irish and the German, Polish Americans had greater obstacles to overcome in the assimilation process. German Catholics arrived earlier than most other groups; they came with education and skills and with the experience of being a minority religion in the old country.

Irish Catholics came in vast numbers only a little earlier than the Poles, but they came speaking English, and with a well-developed experience of dealing with English hegemony. Both groups easily came to dominate the American church hierarchy. The vast majority of Poles who came had little education and could not speak English. Their experience of fighting for their identity centred on the preservation of their language. The establishment of voluntary ghettoes and parish structures that were almost total in taking care of their needs was their response to the conditions of America. One such example cited by Thomas and Znaniecki was St. Stanislaus Kostka parish in Chicago, with over two hundred separate organizations to meet almost any kind of need of the parishioners.[8]

In a 1963-64 study by the National Opinion Research Center, Harold Abramson shows that the Irish, the French Canadians and the Germans are the most frequently involved in the formal religious and educational requirements of the church.[9] The Poles and eastern Europeans, although relatively high in their association, do not emerge with the same consistent intensity of involvement that characterizes the first three groups. The Italians, the Mexicans and the Puerto Ricans all display the least amount of association. It is unfortunate that such cross-cultural statistics are not available for turn of the century comparison.

The association of the Polish Americans with their parish structure in the buttress functions certainly allowed the "decompression" to take place. On the other hand, the parish structures did take a tremendous amount of time, energy and money to maintain. Whether those resources could have been applied to other areas of life in America is a moot point. Eugene Kusielewicz has repeatedly raised the difficult question of whether the resources poured into the parish structure by Polish Americans could have not better served them if they had been spent on higher education of the succeeding generations.[10]

The Explanation Function

The heart of the religious belief system of the Polish peasant is animistic in nature, attributing conscious life to nature and all natural objects. The relationship of man to nature is such that man is a being of the same class as any natural object, although men understand one another better and are more closely connected with one another than with the animals or plants. As Sula Benet indicates in *Song, Dance, and Customs of Peasant Poland,* emphasis is not on points of doctrine, or on any mystical content, but on concrete observance.[11] The peasants are devout, but their piety is practical rather than theoretical. They are concerned with the deity and the saints as living beings who can help or harm, not as the embodiment of abstract principles. Because of this there have been few dissident sects in Polish Catholicism.

This "explanation function" of religion becomes manifested in the countless customs and traditions, rituals and songs, holy days and special celebrations, processions and devotions which are the hallmark of Polish Catholicism. In the absence of a distinction between the sacred and the secular, all of society, all of its activities became sacralized. Blessed food, at the Christmas *wigilia* and the Easter *święconka,* are typical examples. Even the days of the month are given the names of saints, rather than numerical designation.

This unique approach to religion for the Polish peasant differed significantly from the western European tradition of rationalism and credal formulae which so influenced the Protestant tradition in America and much of western Roman Catholicism. This created a unique type of Polish American Catholicism which sustained several generations of Polish Americans. Many of the customs have been handed down to successive generations, containing as they do a Montessori-type catechesis, with emphasis on doing concrete things rather than on rational dogma. Many of the customs have even become adopted by non-Polish parishes (e.g., *święconka,* or the blessing of Easter food).[12]

Nevertheless, societies undergoing modernization have a progressive de-emphasis on local groupings and loyalties in favour of more universal, trans-national and humanistic loyalties. Geographic and social mobility tends to reduce the strong religious sentiments of traditional groups. Emile Durkheim points out that mobility, especially when combined with "liberal" education, works to weaken customary religious beliefs and commitments. This is especially true when religion is based on animism. Many younger Polish Americans do not appreciate the apparent excesses of devotionalism, the Baroque architecture of the older churches, the traditional authority role of the clergy. This, coupled with the flight to the suburbs, with their territorial parishes based on non-Polish models of Catholicism, has created tension between the generations. The additional modernization of the Catholic church which occurred as a result of the Second Vatican Council has created some further challenges. In many areas, however, the Polish American parish still functions with many of the traditional attitudes and feelings.

Functions of the Polish American Parish

In order to understand how the parish functioned in America, it is necessary to understand how it functioned first in Poland. In Poland the most important events of life, of the individual, of the family, and of the community were celebrated in the parish. Any changes in the parish or the community were first sanctioned by the parish. It was the source of moral education, the centre and symbol of the unity of the community and its unity with previous generations. Through the practice of collective religion, it underscored the consciousness of the collectivity, the unity of the people. It caused them to react in the same way, forming the public opinion of the group.

It is with this background of the experience of the parish that the Polish peasant set about the task of constructing new parish structures in America. The needs and circumstances of the times modified the structure significantly. In America the parish possessed a special kind of power, much greater than even the most conservative peasant community in Poland. In a unique way it became the old primary community reorganized and concentrated. In addition to its usual ritual function, it served as a bridge between local community activity and the larger society. The American parish already had an established history and form for the training of community leadership. This function was expanded to include the activity of various organizations and fraternals designed to maintain a national culture through music and song, and to support people incapable of work. The decoration of the church building became an aesthetic expression of the entire community, more important than the comfort and beauty of the family home. In some cities people even mortgaged their homes for the building and decoration of cathedral-type churches as an expression of their solidarity with the community and as a symbol to the larger community of their achievement. The attachment they felt to the parish was also important because it was an institution over which they had some control, founded by their free association. The parish, in its turn, provided them with encouragement for the common activities, prestige for their accomplishments, personal recognition and satisfaction of their social instinct.

An integral part of the parish was the school. It functioned to continue the religious, linguistic and cultural traditions of the group and gave continuity to successive generations. Participation of the parents in the activities of the school fostered community involvement, strengthened the bond between the older generation and the new, and prevented estrangement from parents by acquainting the children with the religion, language and national history of the parents, while inculcating respect for traditional values. It also functioned to create new community among the young. Finally, it was a necessary expression of the tendency of the immigrant community to self-preservation and self-development.

Notes

1. William Thomas and Florian Znaniecki, *The Polish Peasant in Europe and America* II (New York: Dover, 1958), pp. 1824-27.

2. Andrew Greeley, "Catholicism in America: Two Hundred Years and Counting," *The Critic* (Summer 1976), p. 20.
3. Barbara Les, "The Dynamics of the Character and Functions of the Parish of the Polish National Catholic Church in the United States: A Study of the All Saints Cathedral Parish in Chicago," paper delivered at the Conference of the Polish National Catholic Church, Scranton, Pennsylvania, April 12-13, 1980.
4. Greeley, "Catholicism in America," p. 21.
5. Gibson Winter, *The Suburban Captivity of the Churches* (New York: Macmillan, 1962), p. 125.
6. The description of the functions of religion are taken from Ronald Smith and Frederick Preston, *Sociology, An Introduction* (New York: St. Martin Press, 1977), p. 208-14.
7. Harold Abramson, *Ethnic Diversity in Catholic America* (New York: Wiley, 1973), p. 41.
8. Thomas and Znaniecki, *Polish Peasant in Europe and America,* p. 1624.
9. Abramson, *Ethnic Diversity,* pp. 117-18.
10. Eugene Kusielewicz, *Reflections on the Polish American Community* (New York: Kosciuszko Foundation, 1970).
11. Sula Benet, *Song, Dance, and Customs of Peasant Poland* (New York: AMS Press, 1979), p. 25.
12. Theresita Polzin, *The Polish Americans: Whence and Whither* (Pulaski: Franciscan Publishers, 1973).

Wenceslaus Kruszka and the Origins of Polish Roman Catholic Separatism in the United States*

Anthony J. Kuzniewski

Vexatious is, perhaps, the most appropriate word to describe the historical relationship between Polish immigrants and Roman Catholic leaders in the United States. At least, scholarly accounts suggest that conclusion. Historians and sociologists have produced one-sided accounts which either extol the Polish newcomers for sacrifice and generosity in the face of Irish- and German-Catholic insensitivity to their leadership aspirations or condemn Poles for being a clannish, ethnocentric drag on the development of American Catholicism. Nowhere, it seems, can consensus be found on the meaning of the religious experience of Polish Americans. They are depicted as either exclusive or excluded.

On the Polish side, for instance, Eugene Kusielewicz has cited the relatively low number of his countrymen in hierarchical office as proof that the American church is "one, holy, Irish, and apostolic."[1] Knowledgeable Catholics of all backgrounds admit the existence in many dioceses of a closed-off "Polish circuit" which has limited the Polish clergy to working exclusively within their own ethnic group. Sociologist Helena Lopata attributes Polish American social insularity inside and outside the church at least partly to their awareness of the prejudice held against them by non-Poles.[2] On the other side, writers like Thomas McAvoy have chosen to ignore Polish Americans in histories of Catholicism in America.[3] Robert Leckie, writing in 1970, lamented that Poles were "not malleable"—persons whose attachment to the language of their ancestors helped constitute the "dark side" of Catholic history in the United States.[4] John Tracy Ellis's principal statement about them focused on the Polish schism which rent American Catholicism at the turn of the century.[5] Even Philip Gleason,

* This is a revised version of a paper presented to the American Catholic Studies Seminar at Notre Dame University in 1977.

in a carefully nuanced article on Americanization in the contemporary church, denigrated the resistance of people like the Poles to the crusade for open housing.[6] The sole point of agreement among all these scholars seems to be that Polish Americans have occupied a distinct and largely separate position in the life of their church. The argument begins with the explanations.

Ultimately, the controversy is related to one of the clearest and most perplexing features of the life of Polish American Catholics: their failure to achieve leadership positions in proportion to their numbers. About two million Poles migrated to the United States where, by 1920, they accounted for 15 to 20 per cent of the total number of Catholics.[7] They built churches, formed religious associations, entered seminaries and convents, established educational and charitable institutions, and supported the Catholic press. Yet their presence in hierarchical circles was slight. One Polish American, Paul Rhode of Green Bay, occupied an American see in 1920, and appointments in subsequent years were consistently rare. Apparently restricted to the lower echelons of the institutional church, Polish leaders developed a sense of isolation which came to be regarded as the norm of their participation. The situation reinforced itself until few could imagine that these people had ever responded to broader ecclesiastical structures in any other way.

The apparent simplicity of the pattern, however, conceals a complicated development. The reaction of Polish immigrants to the American church was not uniformly segregationist, nor does the record show a consistent refusal to come to terms with life in the new world in ways which might have indicated a more integrated development. Rather, as Daniel Buczek has pointed out, the leadership aspirations of Polish Catholics originally fell into three distinct channels, ranging from total independence to submission and separation within the church.[8] One option, explored by Rev. Wenceslaus Kruszka of Wisconsin, pressed for a greater role for Poles in church leadership. For a time it nearly succeeded. But by 1918 external forces and pressures within the Polish community had helped to determine that the separatistic channel would be main. Once that development came to be accepted as necessary or unavoidable, its vexatious character was assured.

The most familiar pattern of Polish American religious life centred on the national parish, where the language and religious traditions of the old country could encounter American influence at a slow, measured pace.[9] Outstanding proponents of this approach were Chicago's Resurrectionists, the Franciscans of Pulaski, Wisconsin, and pastors like Lucjan Bójnowski of New Britain, Connecticut. Such leaders did not aggressively oppose the exclusively non-Polish character of American church leadership. Rather, they served as intermediaries between the bishops and their Polish constituents. Often figures of considerable prestige among their people, they concentrated on Polish American affairs, local and national. Sometimes they and their allies were able to organize virtually autonomous ethnic communities. Bójnowski's parish, for instance, included schools, an orphanage, a newspaper, a bank, an old age home, a cemetery, and various recreational facilities for children and adults.[10] Such Poles lived mostly at peace with the other Catholics, but at the cost of virtual isolation within the communion of believers. Consigned *de facto* to a relatively minor role in the larger church, they engaged in activities only at those levels at which the church was really theirs. Many even assumed that the few Polish American bishops would operate within this essentially isolated Polish and Catholic community.

Other Polish American Christians adopted a belligerent stance towards the Catholic church, declared independence of Rome, and eventually coalesced as the Polish National Catholic Church under the leadership of Francis Hodur of Scranton. The movement erupted spontaneously in Chicago, Buffalo, Detroit and Scranton. The issues were similar: on the surface, lay trusteeism and control of property; below the surface, national pride and a frustrated feeling that generosity was being taken for granted by unsympathetic ecclesiastical leaders.[11] The bottom line was clear in the policies of the new church. The mass was celebrated in Polish; clergy were forbidden to receive a salary larger than the median of the parish; lay persons participated in church government.[12] The presence of the Independents implicitly challenged loyal Poles to justify their continued allegiance to Rome. "Why is it that you are not allowed to have at least one bishop of your own nationality to represent you in the Church?" the Hodurites would ask. "Why is it that the Holy Ghost never deigns to come down on any of your good and zealous priests? Why? Because the Irish and German bishops object to it, because they consider the Poles unfit for such a dignity." Influenced by the arguments, a significant number of Poles broke with their bishops. By 1901 the Independents were claiming 50,000 adherents.[13] Their history has been described by competent scholars, including Laurence Orzell in this volume. But adding this tale of withdrawal and independence to the account of Polish Catholic insularity does not complete the understanding of the Polish immigrants' role in American church history.

For there was a third group of Polish Americans, small and of indeterminate number, which attempted for a time to steer a middle course. Led by the Kruszka brothers of Milwaukee and Father Casimir Sztuczko of Chicago, they probed for ways to gain "equality" for Polish American Catholics and recognition of the legitimacy in America of Polish approaches to the faith without resorting to independence or isolation. Unlike the Bójnowski-

Resurrectionist element, they sought involvement at all levels of church life. And, in distinction from the schismatics, they maintained the Roman ties. They concentrated on obtaining bishops of Polish ancestry, and influenced the entire ethnic group in the years before the First World War. Then, as now, the movement could only be understood in connection with its principal advocate, Wenceslaus Kruszka—priest, historian, and journalist in the archdiocese of Milwaukee.[14]

It was not entirely surprising that Kruszka should have worked from a Wisconsin base. Despite Chicago's numerical and cultural importance in Polish America, Wisconsin's community developed earlier and matured more rapidly. These settlers arrived early in the movement of Poles, mostly before 1890. By the turn of the century they numbered well over 100,000, about half of whom lived in Milwaukee County. Nearly three-quarters were from the German Partition.[15] For them, the experience of the *Kulturkampf* was a unifying characteristic and helped to account for a relatively acute sense of national consciousness which included sensitivity to the uses of religion for denationalization.[16] Early arrival in the economic life of the state also assured the Poles a level of prosperity which heightened their interest in public affairs and accustomed them to a certain amount of participation and recognition in politics.

Michael Kruszka, an older half-brother of Wenceslaus, led the way. In 1888, three years after his arrival in Milwaukee, he founded the *Kuryer Polski* (Polish Courier), the first successful Polish daily in the United States. Two years later he was elected to the state assembly; and in 1892 he became a state senator, the highest elective office achieved by a Polish immigrant to that time. Although Michael eventually gave up his political career, he and his associates learned from experience that they could, without prejudice, assume responsibilities in the common life of their adopted land.[17] None of them, apparently, had difficulty in reconciling feelings for Poland with allegiance to America.

Wenceslaus Kruszka was born in 1868. In his autobiography he disclosed that many of his earliest memories were connected with the *Kulturkampf.* Even the family dog was named Bismarck in a good-humoured effort to vent some frustration. Wenceslaus entered the Society of Jesus in Galicia in 1883 and remained in the order for ten years. During his formative years with the Jesuits, he developed academic abilities and an inner tenacity which remained long after misunderstandings led to his dismissal. In 1893 he followed Michael to Milwaukee, where he completed training for the priesthood in the diocesan seminary. There, he began to exhibit his flair for leadership and journalism. He wrote regularly for the *Kuryer* and was elected president of the association of Polish seminarians. Shortly after his ordination in 1895, he was assigned to the farm town of Ripon, where he headed the smallest Polish parish in the archdiocese and found time for literary efforts.

The greatest of those efforts resulted from his discovery, in 1899, that one of the pioneer Polish priests in Wisconsin was buried in an unmarked grave close to Ripon. Struck by the fact that the story of Polish immigrants was already being forgotten, Kruszka resolved to write a history before all the early traces of the movement had disappeared. He advertised in the *Kuryer* for information on each Polish colony. He corresponded with old settlers and scanned secondary sources for additional information. He also used his periodic travels, particularly in the east, to gather data. It was a project which, by virtue of his skills, training and free time, he was well equipped to undertake. It also acquainted him with the wide extent and rapid growth of Polish immigration and provided easy access to leaders and files of organizations and institutions.[18] When *The Polish History in America* finally appeared in print between 1905 and 1908, it filled thirteen volumes, totalling over two thousand pages.

While he was preparing his history, Kruszka was certainly aware of the growing momentum for the appointment of a Polish bishop. Cardinal Gibbons provided an early hint in 1892 when he toured Milwaukee's Polish South Side on a visit to the city: "... if, up to this time, you have not been sufficiently recognized, it was probably because we didn't know. The Apostolic Capitol will hear about this [successful community] and you will be blessed."[19] By 1893, the *Kuryer Poznański* (Poznan Courier) was telling Poles in Europe that suffragan bishops of Polish extraction ought to be appointed in such centres of Polish settlement as Chicago and Milwaukee. The Polish American press periodically echoed the theme and repeated rumours that first one and then another pastor would shortly receive the mitre. Also heartening was the fact that the Congregation for the Propagation of the Faith at the Vatican was headed after 1892 by Mieczysław Ledóchowski, a religious and national hero who, as primate of Poland, had been imprisoned for defying Bismarck. Now, it seemed, with sympathetic cardinals in Rome and Baltimore, Polish Americans would begin to enjoy in the church a measure of recognition and responsibility comparable to that which they were enjoying in the civil sphere.[20]

The fulfilment of that expectation, however, was long in coming, and it was not easy to know what to do about the delay. The influx of eastern and southern Europeans, the debate over Cahenslyism and periodic outbursts of anti-Catholic nativism were challenging the best Catholic minds at a time when Anglo-conformity functioned as the commonest norm of Americanization. Neither the German nor the Irish Catholic leaders won complete vindication during their crisis at the end of the nineteenth century, but a truce did emerge. Unfortunately, it left little place for

Polish aspirations. Irish prelates were still concerned about demonstrating the compatibility between Catholicism and patriotic Americanism. Germans still defended the tie between religion and language, but scrupulously avoided advocacy of national dioceses. Neither position was wholly unbiased nor free from the assumptions and interests of the particular group.

In the short run, the chief beneficiary of the lack of Polish American bishops was the National Church movement among the Poles. Although independent churches had occasionally challenged loyal Polish Catholics since 1870, the movements took root and organized just before 1900. Concerned by the defections from their ranks, Polish Roman Catholics met in a series of congresses to consider a common response. The first, held in Buffalo in 1896, was hosted by Jan Pitass, pastor of the large (thirty thousand members) St. Stanislaus parish and publisher of *Polak w Ameryce* (The Pole in America). The 318 clerical and lay delegates compromised their efforts by failing to provide a means for follow-through on their resolutions. Thus, by 1901, a second congress was needed.[21] By then, Wenceslaus Kruszka was ready to participate.

Kruszka had become the object of wide interest and attention because of his work on the history. It received trial publication in the weekly edition of the *Kuryer* between 1901 and 1904 so that readers could submit corrections. The most heavily criticized section of the serialized version was Kruszka's description of the Polish American identity. In it, the young historian rejected the then popular idea that Polish Americans constituted a Fourth Partition of Poland in America and the concept that they should be islands of Polish life in the new world. He viewed those options as unacceptable because they rejected too much the new circumstances of American life. Instead, he defined the ethnic community in terms of common descent and feeling. The object was not to constitute a segment of Poland on American soil but to maintain feelings of love for the fatherland and of respect for the achievements of forebears in America and Poland. Kruszka advocated an evolving, pluralistic society as the best way of actualizing the motto of his adopted land. It was to resemble a beautiful forest containing different types of trees. Resurrectionists and others protested that Kruszka was not tying language closely enough with nationality. He was risking the faith, which depended on the language. But Kruszka was firm: nationality was to be a matter of inner awareness and not of outward form. Polish immigrants were to enter American life as they found it.[22]
outward form. Polish immigrants were to enter American life as they found it.[22]

Kruszka's integrationist position became more evident in 1900 and 1901 when he wrote a number of articles in response to the language decrees of Bishops Frederick Eis of Marquette and Sebastian Messmer of Green Bay. The directives ordered English sermons to be given at least twice monthly in each parish of the dioceses. The *Kuryer* protested, as did the Polish Roman Catholic Union. But Kruszka defended the bishops, arguing that the intent of the orders was to assure that all Catholics would be able to receive religious instruction in languages they could understand.[23] The issuance of *Testem Benevolentiae* (the Pope's admonition to American Catholic leaders on the potential dangers of a liberal, "americanist" representation of Catholicism) also prodded his thinking. In a commentary on the papal letter, Kruszka explained that the Pope was not insisting that faith be divorced from national custom. The real issue, as he understood it, was that the faith was not to be altered to make it more acceptable in a given context. Thus, the Pope was safeguarding the unity of faith—a faith which Kruszka likened to one sun shining on many nations. In America, he concluded, the unity of faith was being preserved through the use of the various languages of the faithful. This practice followed both the letter and the spirit of the Pope's instruction.[24]

Kruszka's earnest belief that the American church ought to be a mixture of its immigrant nationalities was challenged during the summer of 1901 in an editorial carried by the Resurrectionist *Dziennik Chicagoski* (The Chicago Daily News). The writer claimed that Polish bishops were needed in the United States to found a "Poland in America." Kruszka rejected that stand because it argued the matter from a purely national point of view. The Vatican, he noted, was concerned with upholding the faith and not with nations. Therefore, the correct approach was to stress the essential office of the bishop as pastor and teacher. To fulfill those functions, a bishop had to communicate the word of God to his people in languages they could understand. Any other relationship between prelate and people was scripturally and historically abnormal. The young priest developed these points in a letter to the *Kuryer* which concluded that it was not national separatism which furnished the justification for the demand for Polish prelates, but the office of the bishop itself. Kruszka did not envision some form of Poland-in-America as the goal of the campaign but the communication of the gospel. And those best equipped to carry out that responsibility towards the Poles in America, he argued, were the community's own members.[25]

The perilous last step in the development of Kruszka's rationale for Polish bishops followed quickly. In August 1901 he published an English article, "Polyglot Bishops for Polyglot Dioceses," in New York's *Freeman's Journal.* The statement, which filled seven columns when reprinted in the *Kuryer* on September 21, praised the idea of unity in the cultural diversity of the Catholic church. Because of immigration, Kruszka argued, the American church resembled the universal church; it was unified without being uniform. And, whatever the future held with regard to the use of English in the United States, the fact was that many newly arrived Catholics did not speak English even as a second language. That fact did not jeopardize institutional unity, in Kruszka's view, but it did promote misunderstandings and communication difficulties between the "one-tongued American prelates" and many of their people. The situation was inconvenient on all sides. Yet, the responsibility for accommodation in the matter of language lay with the prelate because the bishop is created to serve the needs of the diocese. To argue the reverse would be to hold wrongly that the diocese exists for the convenience of the bishop. "Therefore," he concluded, "if the diocese is polyglot, the bishop must be polyglot, too."

Kruszka was convinced that more was at stake than an unrealistic plea for bishops with uncommon linguistic abilities. It was a matter crucial for the faith of millions who, even after learning English, continued to pray and make their confessions in the mother tongue. Religious truths, the young pastor asserted, require a special and difficult terminology. Even the most advanced newcomers were thus hindered in comprehending the word of God in English sermons. The Pentecost miracle was an indication of God's own concern that native languages be used to communicate the gospel. To justify his assertions, Kruszka turned to scripture, supporting his position from John 10:4-5: it is essential for Christians to understand the voice of the Shepherd. And in each diocese, he maintained, the "pastor proper" is the bishop. For these reasons, Kruszka advanced his most dramatic assertion:

> I do affirm with certainty . . . that nowadays in the United States, whosoever [a candidate] dares to assume the duties of a bishop in a polyglot diocese, without being a polyglot himself, takes duties upon himself which he knows he is unable to perform, and therefore commits a mortal sin.

The article concluded with a statistical review of the growing importance of the Slavic elements in the American church. Their needs, Kruszka said, had not been recognized. Instead, certain American prelates had vowed that there would never be bishops of the Polish nationality in the United States. The article ended with a plea not to take Poland's historic loyalty to the Holy See for granted and not to imagine that, in asking for bishops, the Poles were looking for privileges which were not accorded to others: ". . . we Poles in America do not ask for any special privilege, we only ask for just and EQUAL treatment in the ecclesiastical hierarchy."

Reactions to the article were mixed. One of the harshest appeared in Cleveland's *Catholic Universe,* which pleaded for a priesthood "thoroughly Catholic and American." Kruszka replied that he shared the same hope, but that the Cleveland editors were actually more interested in an Irish American church.[26] By 1902, according to his memoirs, he was already regarding Cahensly's plan for national dioceses as "a completely healthy and normal movement for the development of the Catholic Church in America," the best way to care adequately for the immigrants. In Kruszka's view, the supernatural order within the church would be safeguarded, not destroyed, by the "natural order of nationality." The failure of the proposal for national dioceses he attributed to the "almighty Irish episcopacy" which had destroyed the idea and then claimed Rome had done so. Kruszka was apparently unaware that Cahensly's proposals had posed the threat of foreign interference in American Catholic affairs and had been rejected for that reason even by most German American Catholics.[27] Nevertheless, there was a certain logic in his position. Few bishops could realistically know or learn the languages of all the members of their dioceses during the immigrant era. In effect, each was limited to serving personally only those people whom he could understand and to whom he could preach the word of God. Essentially, then, the United States already had national dioceses, but only for English- and German-speaking Catholics. *De facto,* others were accorded unequal consideration from the point of view of episcopal ministry.[28]

If nothing else, Kruszka's writings assured him a prominent position at the second Polish American Congress which met a week after the appearance of the "Polyglot Bishops" article. The delegates gave priority to devising a means for securing bishops. The result was a direct appeal to the American hierarchy to be followed, if necessary, by petitioning the Pope in a delegation to consist of Pitass and Kruszka. An executive committee was established to oversee the work of the delegates and of commissions designated to handle other problems.

The bishops received the petition at their meeting in Washington in November 1901. Strictly withheld from the press, the document described the success of the independent Polish churches, attributing their rapid growth in part to their arguments that Poles were being denied appropriate recognition in the Roman Catholic Church and that priests loyal to the Pope were traitors to the Polish nationality and "ignoble slaves of the foreign-born Hierarchy." As a remedy, the congress asked not for Polish dioceses but for Polish auxiliary bishops in those areas where they could be effectively employed.[29] The document ignored Kruszka's arguments from the pastoral nature of the episcopal office and his private convictions on the double standard regarding national dioceses. Perhaps the petitioners chose this course because they were aware of the position of many bishops that an English-language approach to religion was the only way to meet the proselytizing priorities of the church in the United States. In any event, they adopted a practical tone designed to appeal to the prelates' interest in averting further losses among Polish Catholics.

Bishop John Keane's reply for the group acknowledged the importance of the issue, but cautioned that the matter was for each bishop to determine locally.[30] The executive committee then appealed to Frederick Katzer, the American prelate known to be most sympathetic to the Polish cause. In January 1902 Katzer wrote personally to Cardinal Ledóchowski to request a Polish auxiliary for Milwaukee. Ledóchowski refused. The appointment would not be opportune, he said, expressing the hope that the movement for a bishop would soon subside because of the example of the Polish priests in providing a model of ecclesiastical discipline.[31] Unwilling to abandon the effort, Katzer journeyed to Rome with Rev. Hyacinth Gulski, the acknowledged leader of Polish Catholics in the Milwaukee archdiocese. Speculation rose that Gulski would return a bishop. When the archbishop returned empty-handed to Milwaukee six months later, he admitted that he had attempted to see Ledóchowski on the Polish matter. But the aged cardinal had been suffering from a terminal illness at that time and the meeting never took place.[32]

At this point, the executive committee authorized the delegates to depart for Rome. Although Pitass was unable to go, he enlisted the help of Rowland Mahany, a Republican politician who was then Collector of the Port of Buffalo. Since Mahany was a friend of President Roosevelt, Pitass reasoned, his participation would serve to allay Vatican fears that Washington was hostile to the project. After their arrival in Rome, Kruszka prepared a written memorial, fifty pages in length, which rehearsed the arguments for bishops and included a summary of the statistical information he had collected for his history. The delegates secured the help of Mgr. Joseph Antonucci; under his guidance they visited the sixteen cardinals who comprised the Propaganda. Leo XIII died before they could speak with him, but his successor, Pius X, received Kruszka, Mahany and Antonucci in a private audience in September 1903, about five weeks after his election. He told them that he was acquainted with their cause and that the matter was already under consideration by the cardinals of the Propaganda. He promised to do what he could to help.

In the months that followed, opposition to the effort began to build in the United States. Cardinal Gibbons and others stated publicly that they opposed the selection of bishops for nationalistic reasons and alleged that Kruszka's appeal was jeopardizing the standard procedures for episcopal appointments. Kruszka, who found these attacks hypocritical, observed that "Catholicism and nationality... are mutually fulfilling like body and soul." The executive committee, however, was worried about the adverse reaction and cautioned Kruszka to be explicit that his request was for bishops to work within the diocesan structures and not for bishops to work exclusively with Poles. Kruszka responded by appealing from Rome to each of the American bishops for support. Except for an encouraging letter from John Lancaster Spalding, the reaction was disappointing. The harshest critics did not even reply. The soundest advice came from James Trobec of St. Cloud who urged Kruszka to be realistic in his hopes: "There are great difficulties in the way as long as the present mode of obtaining bishops for the United States obtains." By now it was clear that American bishops were not likely to assent to the Polish wishes spontaneously and that they would oppose appeals made over their heads. Prospects seemed dim.

Finally, on April 15, 1904, Pius X summoned Kruszka to receive his reply to the petition. The answer was positive but indefinite: "Tell the Poles in America that the decision will be made as soon as possible, and it will be made according to your wishes." Outside, Kruszka recited the *Te Deum* with a friend and sent a jubilant cable to America: "Rome has spoken, the matter is closed.... I believe strongly, and the faith is not to be shaken, that the pope's words... would be fulfilled soon, that we would shortly have Polish bishops in America, just as we have wished." Kruszka made triumphal stops at Polish settlements between New York and Wisconsin to repeat the promise and administer the papal blessing. When he arrived in Ripon, the small depot was overflowing, and the crowd escorted him to his rectory with shouts of "Hurrah!" and "Long may he live!"[33]

Not everyone, however, was enthusiastic about the Roman accomplishment. Mgr. Kelly, writing from Rome for English-language Catholic journals in America under the pseudonym "Vox Urbis," questioned the significance of the Pope's endorsement of the Polish appeal. Probably, Kelly asserted, the Pope was only promising to remedy the matter "if there is evil in the situation." Sebastian Messmer, who had succeeded to the Milwaukee archdiocese during Kruszka's absence, also warned against undue enthusiasm. He attributed the agitation for a bishop to ambitious Polish priests, since, in his opinion, the Polish people did not really desire bishops of their own nationality. Messmer himself was in a delicate position. He was certainly aware of the tumult between Irish and German interests which had surrounded the succession of his two predecessors. Although the press in Milwaukee was speculating that a Pole would now succeed Messmer in Green Bay, the archbishop was determined not to arouse a new controversy. In the end, Joseph Fox was appointed, continuing for the moment the totally Germanic composition of Wisconsin Catholic leadership.[34]

In 1905 the arrival of Archbishop Francis Albin Symon of Plock advanced the Polish cause again. Symon was sent by the Vatican to investigate the circumstances of the Polish Catholics. In preparation for his coming, his secretary exchanged a series of letters with Kruszka about the visit. Evidently the Pope wished Symon's mission to have an official nature, but Cardinal Gotti of the Propaganda had prevented it because of the hostility of a number of American bishops to any action which might appear to interfere with their jurisdictional authority. As a compromise Symon was delegated to visit the Polish settlements unofficially and to report his findings to the Pope and the Propaganda. Even at this level, the undertaking evoked the opposition of the Irish interests in the United States. William J. D. Croke, Roman correspondent for a number of American Catholic papers, denied that the mission was even an unofficial tour of inspection, for that would be to slur the American hierarchy. "There is nothing in the affair," he concluded, "but gracious concession and paternal indulgence for the Poles and the Polish descendants."[35]

Obviously, Symon disagreed. He told a group in Buffalo that he had come "with the knowledge, desire, and blessing of the Holy Father," and admitted that his task was to study the situation of the Poles within their church. Symon visited the papal delegate and Cardinal Gibbons. He met with President Roosevelt, who told him: "If the official relationship between church and state did not forbid it, I would tell the pope that it would be good for the Polish people in America to have its clergy represented in the ecclesiastical hierarchy in America." Although Symon visited Wisconsin twice during his American journey, he did not go to Ripon. The omission cannot be explained simply as antagonism towards Kruszka's increasingly belligerent stance on the bishop issue, since the visitor granted a long interview to the *Kuryer,* where Michael Kruszka was, if anything, more hostile to the American hierarchy than his brother. It was probably a tactical decision. With a mission as suspect and presumably even as unwelcome in many places as Symon's, the bishop may have decided to avoid the grounds for further antagonism by keeping his distance from the very person whose actions had been responsible for the tour. Kruszka has had his say, the action implied; it is time to hear from the others.

When he returned to Rome, Symon's reports stressed the warm reception he had received in America, praised the progress of the Poles, and affirmed that Polish American priests were "locked out" of the hierarchy. His secretary continued to correspond with Kruszka, convincing the Ripon pastor that Rome was still favourably disposed towards the cause.[36] This private information led Kruszka to conclude that the causes of the delay were to be found among the American prelates. In this he was substantially correct. Messmer himself wrote to Gibbons that the Poles were not ready for a bishop because such an appointment would attract the allegiance of all the American Poles to that one man. And the archbishop told Kruszka again that the high-reaching Polish clergy were the source of the discontent.[37]

Kruszka's response, based to a large extent on his knowledge of differences between the American and Roman responses, reflected his growing frustration. He vented his feelings in a biweekly column for the *Kuryer,* beginning in December 1905. The articles contained little that was new; the issue was generally couched in terms of justice for the Poles. Without contradicting his earlier plea for bishops because of the nature of the office, Kruszka was beginning to evoke national pride and to insist that the circumstances warranted national dioceses as the only practical solution. The intransigence of the American bishops was leading him to conclude that their treatment of Polish Americans was pastorally destructive. During 1906 thc year in which Messmer collaborated with most of his Polish priests to found the *Nowiny Polskie* (The Polish News) in opposition to the *Kuryer,* Kruszka became increasingly anti-German. He invoked memories of the *Kulturkampf* to brand Sebastian Messmer and Henry Moeller of Cincinnati as modern-day Teutonic Knights. The tone of the newspaper war sank steadily and even spilled over occasionally into the English-language press. Messmer first requested, then commanded, Kruszka to discontinue the columns. With a characteristically dramatic final column, Kruszka complied.[38] Thirteen months later, in April 1908, the archbishop assured Kruszka privately of his determination to ask for a Polish auxiliary.[39]

But before that could happen, Archbishop James Quigley of Chicago received authorization to appoint a Polish auxiliary and took the unusual step of allowing the Polish priests of the archdiocese to elect one of their number. Their nearly unanimous choice, Paul Peter Rhode, was consecrated in 1908 amidst protestations of affection between Polish Americans and the hierarchy.[40] But neither the fact of the appointment nor Rhode's unofficial status as bishop for all the Poles in America stilled the discontent.

In Wisconsin Kruszka filed a canonical suit to still the personal attacks carried in the *Nowiny.* After Rhode pressured him to withdraw it, Messmer finally transferred him to the Milwaukee pastorate to which he had long been entitled under the seniority system.[41] This more central location enabled Kruszka to engage in speaking, one of the outlets still open to him. He addressed patriotic meetings, always reiterating the Pope's promise and seeking to explain why the hopes were so difficult to achieve. In 1910 he wrote two articles for the Chicago publication, *Polonia,* distinguishing between theoretical and practical descent from the apostles. Only priests and bishops characterized by love of God and neighbour, he maintained, were true successors.[42] Under the circumstances, the point was hard to miss.

By 1911 the battle had grown so emotional that it was almost inevitable that the fight for recognition would lead to segregation. In October Michael Kruszka announced the formation of the Federation of Polish Catholic Laymen which began to challenge bishops for control of Polish schools and properties. In the same month, the Chancery office in Milwaukee announced the appointment of a Polish-speaking Czech American, Joseph Koudelka, as auxiliary. Unexpectedly, twenty-four Polish priests, Kruszka among them, rejected the appointment as unsatisfactory for easing the tensions. Instead they asked "humbly but emphatically" for the appointment of a Pole. In this way many of Kruszka's harshest critics within the Polish community joined with him in resisting the archbishop on national grounds. By December Kruszka was carrying the movement one step further: according to newspaper reports, he told a Kenosha audience that a non-Polish bishop would enter his church over his dead body.[43]

The situation reached a turning point in early 1912. The bishops of the Wisconsin province issued a pastoral letter to impose the ban on the *Kuryer Polski* and forbid membership in the Federation of Polish Catholic Laymen.[44] Kruszka was summoned to the Chancery to explain his Kenosha address. Although Messmer suggested that "it would be better if you broke openly with the Church," Kruszka declined. After ascertaining that an appeal to the papal delegate would be futile, he signed and read publicly a retraction which affirmed that he would "receive with due respect and honor any and every Catholic bishop of whatever nationality . . . who may come to my . . . church vested with lawful ecclesiastical authority." Kruszka maintained that he had been misquoted; he denied disloyalty to the archbishop. But few really believed him.[45] Thus Wenceslaus Kruszka remained in the church, but with little support. He was denied faculties in the other dioceses of the state and expelled from the convention of Polish priests which met in Detroit in February. Shunned even by those who shared his desire for Polish bishops, Kruszka clung to the promise.

The hope was not in vain. In the summer of 1913, the hapless Koudelka was reassigned to the vacant see of Superior. His successor, announced in October, was Edward Kozlowski, a Polish-born priest from Michigan. Although Messmer was careful to assert that the selection had followed normal channels, it was no ordinary appointment. Kozlowski's installation became the occasion of a great show of unity between the Polish clergy and the archbishop. And when the new bishop announced that he had been given "extensive authority" by Messmer to deal with Polish parishes and affairs, even Wenceslaus Kruszka expressed his satisfaction.[46] Significantly, Kozlowski viewed his episcopal role in terms of delaying Americanization so that the faith would be preserved. He advocated the use of the Polish language and the promotion of special societies to foster the distinctiveness of Polish Americans. He described the priest as "not only a servant of God, but also a high priest of love of country."[47] Thus, both the circumstances of his appointment and his actions helped to assure the separated position of Polish Catholics and to demonstrate that the designation of Polish American bishops would not be a means of integration into the broader life of the Catholic church.

Kozlowski's premature death in August 1915 ended the presence of a Polish auxiliary in Milwaukee. But by then Polish Catholics in the state had another leader in Paul Rhode who, a month before Kozlowski's death, had been selected to succeed Bishop Fox in Green Bay. There, Rhode filled a special role for the state's Poles since Messmer authorized the Polish pastors of his archdiocese to invite Rhode to their parishes for confirmation and other activities exactly as if he were their own ordinary.[48] At one level, then, Wenceslaus Kruszka's campaign had succeeded in his home state. Between 1911 and 1914, three Slavic bishops were appointed in Wisconsin in the effort to recognize the aspirations of the Poles. But ironically, the appointments only emphasized the isolation of the Polish Catholics. In the thick of a long battle, Kruszka's plan for Polish equality and integration had been displaced.

After World War One, nothing was quite the same. Messmer, who in 1914 condemned Belgium for its "treacherous conduct" against Germany and told a friend he was praying for "the victory of the just cause of Austria and Germany,"[49] later became fully persuaded of the advantages of full Americanism. By 1924 he was writing that the Poles were clannish, and that he had appointed Kozlowski not from principle but out of urgency in defending the authority of the church. "When poor Bishop Kozlowski died in 1915 it was felt like a relief by all, and no one wished for another Polish auxiliary."[50] The point was exaggerated, but it reflected the increased unwillingness within the hierarchy to favour the aspirations of Poles until they became more "Americanized." Paradoxically, experience had taught the Poles that they could advance in the Church only if they were clannish. Isolation became the mode of their participation.

There are several lessons to be learned from Wenceslaus Kruszka's efforts to obtain bishops. The first is that in Wisconsin, where the potential for misunderstanding was greater than between Poles and Irish American bishops elsewhere, widespread schism was averted. In the end Katzer and Messmer allowed battles over the meaning of universality and ethnic interest to be fought out within the church. In allowing that to happen, and in choosing bishops openly on the basis of their nationality, they demonstrated that, even after the turn of the century, the decisions of the 1890s were open to interpretation. Leadership on both sides proved to be imaginative and flexible enough to let this happen. As a consequence, most of Wisconsin's Poles were able to fulfill the more crucial of their aspirations within the limits of Catholic discipline. Some Poles in other parts of the country were led to establish independent churches to accomplish approximately the same end.

The second lesson touches on the lingering image of the early generations of Polish Catholics as an unassimilated, inward-looking element in American Catholic life. At the beginning of the campaign for bishops, two different theories were advanced within the church. The dominant one focused almost exclusively on the Polish subcommunity, an ethnic enclave which harboured the old language and the Polish expression of Catholicism. Within this model the work of bishops was to be largely confined to a distinctively Polish American setting. The second option was upheld by Wenceslaus Kruszka and might have succeeded in the well-established Polish areas. Its definition of Polish-ness was more open-ended and it came to terms with the church as a whole. Bluntly stated, Kruszka and his supporters sought bishops on the basis of pastoral needs in a pluralistic church. Where the first group saw Polish bishops as a means of aiding distinctiveness, Kruszka favoured them because their distinctiveness represented a substantial element within the church and because their appointment would signal the ecclesiastical integration and acceptance of Poles. A whole set of circumstances, including the papal promise, the delayed response and the situation of the American church helped the first group. Quigley and Messmer also supported them in the end because their less confrontational attitude seemed to pose fewer problems for church unity and authority. In the process they unwittingly became the accomplices of Polish American separatism.

Perhaps the end of that first round in the campaign for Polish bishops was implicit in its beginnings. Certainly the cultural, educational, occupational and linguistic qualities which distinguished Polish immigrants from more established Americans also operated within the church. Certainly aggressive claims for recognition and equality raised legitimate questions about institutional unity. And certainly the presence of Polish nationalism in the immigrant community generated momentum for the separatistic approach. But the phenomenon of Polish clannishness and the virtual exclusion of Polish priests from ecclesiastical leadership in the first generation of life in America cannot be fully explained by the newcomers' attitudes, experience and behaviour. For, from the moment they began to interact with their co-religionists in the United States, Poles encountered factors beyond their control. The Cahensly and Americanist disputes had left scars without, as it turned out, satisfactorily addressing the issues raised by newer Catholic immigrants seeking access to leadership.

At stake was the status of the various Catholic traditions in the new world. After all, the bishop's office had symbolic as well as pastoral importance in a highly structured, hierarchical church. It was not surprising, therefore, that episcopal appointments were construed by almost everybody as a test of acceptance. At that level, power and responsibility were shared. Nor could the battle, once engaged, be lightly broken off. The campaign threatened the tenuous stability of the turn-of-the-century American church and challenged the assumptions of its leaders. Fear and one-sidedness affected good judgment in this encounter with the unfamiliar; for the Polish crusade was new, unanticipated, and to a large extent unwelcome. Under the circumstances, counsels of patience from bishops of German and Irish background were not likely to be well received by the Poles.

It was not easy to sort out the issues of responsibility and power, to maintain unity while promoting diversity, or to resolve the conflict between pastoral and proselytizing priorities. Church leaders had to struggle with a situation and solutions which were, admittedly, less than ideal. In these perplexing circumstances, Wenceslaus Kruszka's plea for integration in a pluralistic church evolved into a shrill cry for national bishops. That his best plan failed was at least as much a result of the church's policies as their cause. In the end, Poles developed whatever clannishness they possessed partly because it was the only way they could participate in the leadership of the church. And the pattern, once in existence, generated a life of its own.

Notes

1. Kusielewicz, *Reflections on the Cultural Condition of the Polish American Community* (New York, 1969), p. 12.
2. Lopata, *Polish Americans: Status Competition in an Ethnic Community* (Englewood Cliffs, New Jersey, 1976), pp. 86-87.
3. McAvoy, *A History of the Catholic Church in the United States* (Notre Dame, 1969).
4. Leckie, *American and Catholic* (New York, 1970), pp. 235-36, 266-67.
5. *American Catholicism* (2d ed., revised; Chicago, 1969), pp. 129-30.
6. "The Crisis of Americanization," in Gleason (ed.), *Contemporary Catholicism in the United States* (Notre Dame, 1969), p. 8.
7. McAvoy, in *Catholic Church,* pp. 371-72, estimated a total of 17 million Catholics in the United States in 1917. There were at least 2.5 million first- and second-generation Polish Americans in 1920. Frank Renkiewicz (ed.), *The Poles in America* (Dobbs Ferry, New York, 1973), p. 21.
8. Buczek, *Immigrant Pastor* (Waterbury, 1974), pp. 143-50.
9. Milton Gordon, *Assimilation in American Life* (New York, 1964), pp. 216-17.
10. On the Resurrectionists, see John Iwicki, *The First One Hundred Years* (Rome, 1966). Buczek's *Immigrant Pastor* treats Bojnowski.

On the Pulaski Franciscans, see Dacian Bluma and Theophilus Chowaniec, *A History of the Province of the Assumption of the Blessed Virgin Mary* (Pulaski, 1967), and parish histories by Constantine Klukowski.

11. Jan Piekoszewski describes the Irish-American bishops' treatment of Poles as "unjust persecution." "Kościół i Polonia w Stanach Zjednoczonych Ameryki" ["The Church and Polonia in the United States of America"], in *Stan i Potrzeby Badań nad Zbiorwościami Polonijnymi* [The State and Needs of Research on Polonian Communities], edited by Hieronim Kubiak and Andrzej Pilch (Wrocław, 1976), p. 386. Victor Greene disagrees. "For God and Country: The Origins of Slavic Catholic Self-Consciousness in America," in *Church History* 35 (1966), pp. 456-67.
12. The best source on the PNCC is Hieronim Kubiak, *Polski Narodowy Kościół Katolicki w Stanach Zjednoczonych Ameryki w Latach 1897-1965* [The Polish National Catholic Church in the United States of America in 1897-1965] (Wrocław, 1970).
13. Petition of the Second Polish-American Congress to the American Archbishops, November 10, 1901, in Milwaukee Archdiocesan Archives [hereafter MAA], "Kurjer Polski" file.
14. On Wenceslaus Kruszka, see Victor Greene, *For God and Country* (Madison, 1975); Daniel S. Buczek, "Polish Americans and the Roman Catholic Church," in *The Polish Review* 21 (1976), pp. 39-62; Andrzej Brożek, *Polonia Amerykańska, 1854-1939* [The Polish American Community, 1854-1939] (Warsaw, 1977); and Anthony J. Kuzniewski, *Faith and Fatherland: The Polish Church War in Wisconsin* (Notre Dame, 1980).
15. Kuzniewski, *Faith and Fatherland,* p. 19.
16. Łucja Borodziej, *Pruska polityka oświatowa na ziemach polskich w okresie Kulturkampfu* [Prussian Educational Politics in the Polish Lands in the Period of the Culture Struggle] (Warsaw, 1972), pp. 227-28; Lech Trzeciakowski, *Kulturkampf w zaborze pruskim* [The Culture Struggle in the Prussian Sector] (Poznań, 1970), pp. 274-78.
17. Kuzniewski, *Faith and Fatherland,* pp. 29-35, 39.
18. Wenceslaus Kruszka, *Siedm Siedmioleci czyli Pół Wieku Życia: Pamiętnik i Przyczynek do Historji Polskiej w Ameryce* [Seven Times Seven or a Half Century of Life: Recollections and Contributions to Polish History in America] I (2 vols.; Poznań, 1924), pp. 36-195, 228-52, 267-68, 335-40.
19. *Kuryer Polski* [Polish Courier], 18 September 1891.
20. Kuzniewski, *Faith and Fatherland,* pp. 15, 32-33.
21. W. Kruszka, *Historya Polska w Ameryce* [History of Poland in America] 2 (13 vols.; Milwaukee, 1905-08), pp. 35-42.
22. Ibid., 1, pp. 26-47; Kruszka, *Siedm* 1, pp. 375-78, 477-84.
23. Kruszka, *Siedm* 1, pp. 350-53.
24. Ibid., 1, pp. 329-34.
25. Ibid., 1, pp. 385-89.
26. Ibid., 1, pp. 402-04.

27. Ibid., 1, pp. 548-50; Colman J. Barry, *The Catholic Church and German Americans* (Milwaukee, 1953), pp. 131-82.
28. The Council of Trent stated that "the preaching of the Gospel is . . . the chief duty of the bishops." Prelates were required to designate competent replacements to fill these responsibilities when "hindered by a legitimate impediment." Sess. V, chap. 2 de ref. and Sess. XXIV, chaps. 4 and 7 de ref., in *Canons and Decrees of the Council of Trent,* translated by H.J. Schroeder (St. Louis, 1941), pp. 26-27, 195-98. Obviously, interpretations could vary, but Kruszka was raising issues connected with the spirit of the Tridentine decrees.
29. Executive Committee of the Polish Catholic Congress to American Catholic Archbishops, 10 November 1901. On the first two congresses, see Kruszka, *Historya* 2, pp. 39-46.
30. Kruszka reprinted the letter in *Siedm* 1, p. 445.
31. The letter was dated 22 March 1902. MAA, 55.
32. *Kuryer Polski,* 5 April 1902; *The Free Press* (Milwaukee), 10 October 1902.
33. Kruszka's description of the mission is in *Siedm* 1, pp. 550-816; 2, pp. 7-15. The *Kuryer* reported it between April 1903 and May 1904.
34. For the Kelly column, see Kruszka, *Siedm* 2, pp. 19-22. Kruszka also described Messmer's reaction. Ibid., 2, p. 61. Speculation on a Polish successor to Messmer in Green Bay is in *Siedm* 1, pp. 759, 781-82, 785-86, and in *Kuryer,* 21 August, 24-26 November 1903.
35. The correspondence is in *Siedm* 2, pp. 87-88.
36. Kruszka offered his view of the Symon mission in *Siedm* 2, pp. 31-199 passim. See also Kuzniewski, *Faith and Fatherland,* pp. 56-58.
37. The letter to Gibbons was dated 19 January 1904. Archives of the Archdiocese of Baltimore, 102-A, in Barry, *German Americans,* p. 275. Messmer's letter to Kruszka on the bishop issue, 31 October 1905, is in *Siedm* 2, p. 177.
38. Kruszka reprinted the entire set of articles. *Siedm* 2, pp. 206-577.
39. The letter was dated 22 April 1908. *Siedm* 2, p. 623.
40. Greene, *God and Country,* pp. 141-42.
41. Kruszka, *Siedm* 2, pp. 603-08, 614-23, 626-27, 638-58, 672.
42. Kruszka reprinted the second article in *Siedm* 2, pp. 658-61.
43. Kuzniewski, *Faith and Fatherland,* pp. 85-86. The document of the priests rejecting Koudelka's appointment is in MAA, untitled file.
44. A copy of the letter is in MAA, "Kurjer Polski" file.
45. Kruszka described the episode in *Siedm* 2, pp. 723-33, 773-76. His MS explanation, "Sketch of what and why I spoke at Kenosha, Wis., Dec. 10th, 1911," dated at Milwaukee, 27 January 1912, is in MAA, untitled file. The retraction, dated 4 March 1912, is in MAA, Messmer Correspondence.
46. *Nowiny Polskie,* 13 October 1913 and 15 January 1914. The text of Kozlowski's inaugural sermon was printed in *Nowiny,* 17 January 1914. See also Kruszka, *Siedm* 2, pp. 799-801.

47. Edward Kozlowski, "Postulaty Naszego Spoleczeństwa pod Względem Zachowania Wiary Św. Naszego Ludu," in *Przegląd Kościelny* [Church Review] 2 (March-April 1915), pp. 157-59.
48. *Miesięcznik Franciszkański* [Franciscan Monthly] 8 (August 1915), pp. 701-03; Messmer to "A.D.," Milwaukee, 9 May 1924, MAA, Messmer Correspondence.
49. *The Catholic Citizen* (Milwaukee), 3 October 1914.
50. Messmer to "A.D.," 9 May 1924.

The "National Catholic" Response: Franciszek Hodur and his Followers, 1897-1907

Laurence J. Orzell

The first decade of the Polish National Catholic Church (PNCC), organized by Rev. Franciszek Hodur (1866-1953) of Scranton, Pennsylvania, saw the emergence of a viable ecclesiastical alternative for immigrant Poles in North America. While conflicts among the immigrants, their pastors and the non-Polish hierarchy led to the establishment of several Independent parishes in the United States and Canada, the National Church achieved a greater degree of success than did similar, rival organizations. Now in its ninth decade of existence, the PNCC numbers approximately 140 parishes in North America.[1]

This success stemmed in large measure from the skill of Hodur, who articulated and acted upon the perceived economic, social and religious needs of numerous immigrant Poles. During this initial period the PNCC, formed originally in response to disputes over parish properties and selection of pastors, engaged in a wide-ranging quest for self-identity. The somewhat amorphous goal of being or becoming *Kościół Narodowy*—"Catholic" and "Polish" but neither "Roman" nor "Independent"—coloured the fledgling denomination's activities. The progressive components of this idea emerged in efforts to raise the Poles' political and national consciousness. Yet the attendant anti-clericalism and criticism of alleged Roman Catholic abuses did not result in a general departure from Catholic faith and practice. Hodur's consecration as bishop in 1907 by the European Old Catholics did not remove all obstacles to the PNCC's growth, but it did supply a legitimate institutional basis on which to seek the unification of those Poles who did not find it possible or desirable to remain within the Roman Catholic fold. This paper will examine the principal policies formulated by Hodur and his followers in response to the religious and social conditions existing among Polish immigrants at the turn of the century.

Religious dissent among Polish immigrants antedated the emergence of the PNCC by several years. A shortage of competent Polish priests; dictatorial pastors such as Chicago's Wincenty Barzyński and Buffalo's Jan Pitass; the US hierarchy's desire to "Americanize" the immigrants; and problems of adjustment to a foreign environment all helped to foster discontent among the Poles. In general, this discontent involved the ownership of church properties, parish administration and the laity's role in pastoral appointments. Because the immigrants usually built and maintained their parishes, many Poles claimed a role in church management. Such ambitions collided with American Roman Catholic practice, according to which the diocesan ordinary held title to parish properties; moreover, pastors not infrequently carried out their duties without consulting their flocks. Under the circumstances, open dissent became all but inevitable.[2]

Chicago and Buffalo constituted two major centres of dissension and schism. Fr. Antoni Kozłowski established an independent parish in Chicago in 1895. He and his followers believed that "church properties should belong to the parish which purchased them and not to one person, the bishop" and that "all church finances should be in the hands of a committee elected" by the parishioners.[3] Kozłowski's movement spread and eventually included about twenty parishes. In 1897 he was consecrated bishop by European Old Catholics. The Polish prelate did not, however, emphasize his break with Rome or his Old Catholic ties; instead he styled himself "Bishop of the Independent Catholic Diocese of Chicago" and told his flock: "...you neither intended to form a new religion or new creeds, nor to reject the faith, which was transmitted to you by your fathers."[4] Similar events occurred at Buffalo in 1895; three years later the dissident leader there, Fr. Stefan Kamiński, received the episcopate from Joseph Rene Vilatte, an eccentric *episcopus vagans* whose peregrinations in America and Europe led to the establishment of numerous pseudo-Old Catholic sects.[5] Like his confrère at Chicago, Kamiński did not make clear his break with Rome, and this ambiguity constituted a characteristic of these Independent congregations, whose members in effect were Roman Catholics outside the Roman church.

The events in autumn 1896 that gave rise to the organization of the PNCC at Scranton, in the midst of northeastern Pennsylvania's anthracite fields, reflected many of the traits inherent in the earlier Independent movements. The parishioners at Scranton's Sacred Hearts of Jesus and Mary Polish Church, dissatisfied with their pastor, Richard Aust, demanded lay supervision of parish finances. Aust's refusal, which enjoyed the support of his bishop, William O'Hara, stimulated yet greater opposition. Two leftist newspaper editors, Zygmunt Łopatyner of the Wilkes-Barre *Górnik* and Dangel (or Dangiel) Langowski of the more ephemeral *Tygodnik Pensylwański*, counselled resistance on the part of the immigrants. A series of scuffles outside Sacred Hearts Church led to a small-scale riot on 6 September 1896. O'Hara thereupon replaced Aust with Fr. Bronisław Dembiński of Hazleton, but a sizable minority refused to accept this arrangement. They proceeded to build another parish church and made no secret of the fact that they wished to have as their pastor Fr. Hodur, who had served previously as Aust's assistant and who at that time was stationed in nearby Nanticoke.[6] Later that year the county court granted a charter to the new "Saint Stanislaus Polish Roman Catholic Church," and its parish committee, who retained the deeds to the property, subsequently requested O'Hara to bless the structure. He referred the Poles to his coadjutor, Michael Hoban, who refused their request in order to set "an example" of the way in which the diocese dealt with such rebellious behaviour.[7]

The dissidents did not yield. In March 1897 they formally requested Hodur, who had done nothing to discourage them, to assume the new pastorate at St. Stanislaus. Hodur subsequently wrote that Satan appeared to him in an attempt to dissuade him from assuming the new charge, but he rejected this infernal advice and threw in his lot with the dissidents. At a congregational meeting on March 14, 1897, Hodur heard his new flock pledge that they would "never surrender" their deeds to the bishop. Bishop O'Hara suspended the contumacious cleric the following day, but the dissidents proceeded to formulate a constitution that provided for greater participation by the laity "in matters of administration"; however, the pastor "governs in matters of faith. . . ."[8]

Thus far, the Scranton schism differed little from those at Chicago and Buffalo. But it gradually became apparent that the Scranton group would blaze new trails. Hodur himself was a progressive and a nationalist. His concerns and those of his immediate co-workers extended beyond the establishment of Independent parishes and aimed at the creation of *Kościół Narodowy* ("National Church"), a body that would organize Polish immigrants in North America and cultivate a sense of national consciousness. As he explained in his weekly paper, *Straż,* founded in April 1897, Hodur believed that American freedoms would enable Poles to liberate themselves from "foreign" domination in the religious, economic and political spheres. He called upon the Polish clergy to put the good of the people above their own allegedly selfish and pecuniary interests. Initially, Hodur believed that the Poles could obtain "socio-administrative reforms" and "self-government" within the Roman church. He clearly perceived that the immigrants faced denationalization and resolved to resist this through two related means: an "elevation of the sense of human dignity" among Polish workers, and the establishment of a National Church to preserve their "national character." The lines of battle as laid out in the pages of *Straż* were clear-cut and rather simplistically drawn: on the one side were the poor Polish miners and factory workers confronted by economic exploitation and cultural denationalization; on the other were the "Irish" and "German" bishops aided by their Polish clerical collaborators.[9]

These theoretical considerations provided the foundation for the formulation of four basic *desiderata* by Scranton's dissidents: (1) Polish immigrants should be the legal "owners" of church properties; (2) the administrative "rights" of ownership should be exercised through elected parish committees; (3) bishops should name as pastors only those whom the people approved; and (4) priests and laity should "appoint and choose" Polish bishops, subject to papal confirmation. Hodur's efforts gained support, and congregations that adhered to his program emerged in nearby Priceburg (now Dickson City) and Philadelphia.[10]

Two other traits of the Scranton dissidents emerged at this time and, apart from some periodical policy shifts, these generally characterized the emergent National Church: hostility to their Independent compatriots at Chicago and Buffalo, and leftist political leanings. *Straż* asserted that neither Kozłowski nor Kamiński cared for "progress" or for the people but only for their mitres. Kamiński's connection with Vilatte, who engaged in dealings with the Orthodox Russians, and Kozłowski's ties to the Germanic Old Catholics, linked them in Hodur's mind to Poland's mortal enemies.[11] And Jan Szlupas, a Polish-Lithuanian socialist physician who supported Hodur, used the occasion of the Lattimer massacre in September 1897 to expostulate on the need for a workers' party to combat "today's unjust capitalist economic system." *Straż* also commented favourably on Eugene Debs, and while the paper formally eschewed the endorsement of candidates, its leftist sympathies became even more transparent as Langowski assumed a role of increasing prominence on the paper's staff.[12]

The year 1898 witnessed the further development of trends established in the Scranton movement. In an effort to gain the Vatican's ear, Hodur in January 1898 left for Rome, where he submitted a memorandum based on the dissidents' demands. Upon his return he set about to collect signed petitions that would substantiate the degree of discontent among the immigrants. Hodur hoped for approximately ten thousand signatures, but the collection proved slow, due no doubt to Polish Roman Catholic resistance to his radical program. By June his supporters had garnered "a few thousand" signatures, and in September *Straż* announced that 6,230 had been collected. The tardiness and the less than overwhelming support did not help Hodur's case at Rome. His hand strengthened by the Vatican's silence on the petitions and by Leo XIII's excommunication of Kozłowski in April, Bishop Hoban called upon Hodur in early September to submit to his authority. The latter replied that he would do so only if the prelate agreed to the dissidents' demands concerning parish ownership and administration. Hoban responded with the issuance of a decree of excommunication effective September 29, 1898.[13]

Hodur's excommunication marked a major stage in the formation of the PNCC. In response, the rebellious priest asserted that the problem did not really involve a conflict between him and his bishop but concerned "the domination of the Irish over the Poles." The pages of *Straż* reeked with anti-clerical and anti-Roman invective. Even before Hodur's excommunication, his journal opined that the clergy sought to keep the masses uneducated and moribund; this explained why only a minority of Poles thus far supported his program of "radical reform." Hodur declared that the "exploitation and degradation" of the Poles would persist "so long as the clergy delude the people and persuade them that the Lord God wishes some to possess billions, palaces, carriages and slaves . . . and others to work fourteen or more hours and earn only enough so that they will not die of starvation. . . . " This animus extended to Rome as well. Infallibility did not constitute one of the pope's prerogatives. Moreover, *Straż* asserted, "history teaches us that Rome has contributed much to the corruption of our nation. . . . "[14]

Along with this went attempts to consolidate the Poles politically under socialistic tenets. *Straż* claimed that neither the Republicans nor the Democrats served Polish interests. The immigrants thus should band together in a workers' party that would resist capitalist "exploitation." In a series of meetings and programs, Łopatyner, Langowski and Szlupas all sought to disseminate these ideas among the dissidents. Hodur for the most part kept busy with less political and more pastoral concerns. Through plays, patriotic rallies and promotion of self-education, he sought to inculcate the immigrants with a sense of national pride. By the end of 1898 his fledgling National Church had added congregations in Fall River, Massachusetts, and Plymouth, Pennsylvania.[15]

Straż's radical rhetoric did not mean, however, that either Hodur or the bulk of his adherents intended to break with Catholic faith and practice. The Scranton clergyman and the few ex-Roman Catholic and ex-Independent priests who joined his ranks continued to celebrate mass in Latin, observe Marian devotions and generally to hold to a Catholicism purged of alleged Roman errors and "medieval" superstitions, particularly those propagated by monastic orders. True, Hodur departed from the late nineteenth-century understanding of hell—probably because his opponents invariably consigned him and his followers there in the next life—but he claimed that he had not diverged from a genuinely Catholic position on this question. And despite his virulent anti-clericalism, Hodur clearly rejected lay domination or "chłopokracja," particularly if it threatened to impinge upon the clergy's purely religious prerogatives. Nor did his socialist sympathies rest on materialistic foundations. He said that socialism should seek improvements "in the name of God" and should not deprive workers of their "faith in God and in His love for mankind."[16] This attitude, along with his prevailing nationalism, would ensure that the National Church would not become a tool of the socialists.

Thus, despite his radicalism, Hodur believed he could preserve Catholicism outside the Roman fold. He did not question the necessity of episcopal government in the church or the need for Apostolic Succession, largely because the latter was a prerequisite for the valid ordination of clergy to spread his movement. The Scranton priest's attitude towards his Independent colleagues nonetheless continued unabated. While he criticized Kozłowski's episcopal ambitions and their satisfaction by the Old Catholics,[17] Hodur himself proved eager to obtain a mitre of his own from Old Catholic hands. In January 1899 he dispatched a priest, W. E. Błażowski, on a mission to the Netherlands. Błażowski was to acquaint the Dutch Old Catholics with the religious situation of Poles in America. Hodur also forwarded a letter to the Old Catholics in which he affirmed his group's loyalty to Catholicism and requested consecration; notarized petitions from his congregations accompanied this missive.[18]

Hodur's request went unfulfilled. The Old Catholics did not believe that the situation in America warranted the consecration of a second bishop, especially because relations between Hodur and Kozłowski were far less than cordial. During mid-March 1899 the Scranton pastor sent another epistle. Once again no definite action followed. Hodur then reached the conclusion that the road to Utrecht lay through Chicago. Never averse to tactical volte faces, he made peace with Kozłowski and returned to the charge in early 1900. Now supported by his erstwhile foe, Hodur again requested consecration, and his parishes sent new petitions in which they pledged loyalty to the Gospel, Apostolic Tradition and all ecumenical councils save Vatican I. In February 1900 *Straż* began to praise Kozłowski and spoke of union with him but maintained a prudent silence about overtures to Utrecht. Yet the Old Catholics did not honour the Scranton priest's request, largely because not all of Kozłowski's adherents agreed to bury the hatchet with Hodur.[19]

While efforts to establish closer links with the Chicago Independents as a prelude to Hodur's consecration continued throughout 1900,[20] the activist and radical components of the National Catholic movement remained much in evidence. Local officials of the United Mine Workers endorsed *Straż* "as a paper that has at all times expressed sympathy for the working man." The paper advised all workers to unionize and consistently supported strikes at area mines: scabs, *Straż* warned, were like Judas and worse than Cain. In effect, Hodur and Langowski, who as "Stanisław

Dangel" would become *Straż* editor and publisher in September 1900, considered the National Church and organized labour as two aspects of the same cause: the liberation of Polish workers. And while *Straż* continued to advocate socialistic ideas, the paper linked this to Christianity and condemned violence in favour of peaceful, constitutional change. Socialism based solely on the notion of class struggle could not succeed; it had to accord due weight to legitimate national aspirations.[21]

Not surprisingly, therefore, this support for socialism waned whenever Polish candidates appeared on other parties' tickets. *Straż* continued to avoid direct endorsements but did not conceal its support for Jan Sliwiński, a member of Priceburg's National Catholic congregation who ran as Republican candidate for justice of the peace in 1900. And though the paper periodically condemned the Republican platform as one of "militarism and capitalism," Dangel published a special "political edition" that all but endorsed William McKinley in the 1900 elections. But this appears less a question of fundamental political convictions than of opposition to the Democrats, who were identified with the Irish oppressors.[22]

Hodur, who did not openly engage in secular politics, concentrated upon attempts to encourage Poles "to come to our Polish Catholic Church." He claimed that the PNCC adhered to "the truths contained in holy scripture . . . , interpreted and explained at the first universal councils." As he travelled about the northeastern United States, he criticized the Pope for his alleged obeisance to "emperors and kings," the bishops for their pecuniary concerns, and what he termed the "Polish-Irish" clergy who promoted this dreadful situation. Thus, the Poles should throw off the Roman yoke because the bishops desired "to Americanize and to denationalize them."[23]

Yet by the close of 1900, only about ten congregations in Pennsylvania, New Jersey and Massachusetts affiliated themselves in varying degrees with the National Church. Hodur admitted that "some people" among his Scranton flock desired rapprochement with the local diocese. His attempts to secure consecration frustrated, and not inclined to join with either of the Independent prelates, Hodur in December 1900 approached Archbishop Sebastiano Martinelli, the Apostolic Delegate, and Bishop Hoban, who had succeeded Bishop O'Hara upon the latter's death in 1899, with a view towards reconciliation. Martinelli gave Hodur no succour, and Hoban demanded capitulation on the questions of lay ownership and administration. At a congregational meeting in St. Stanislaus Church on December 16, 1900, Hodur's parishioners discussed Hoban's high-handed treatment of their case and vowed that they would "never again" ask for reconciliation and would "never submit" to Hoban's demands because they could "recognize only a Polish bishop."[24]

Given this vote of confidence, Hodur continued to promote the PNCC as the "only anchor against the anglicization of our emigrants and in future the only sure defense of the people against bad priests and bishops." He noted Polish Roman Catholic attempts to request the appointment of Polish prelates in the United States but remarked that a few bishops would do no good, particularly if chosen from the allegedly rotten ranks of Polish Roman clergy. In June 1901 he advised the organizers of the Second Polish Catholic Congress to emulate his separatist example. And though he professed to see some good arise out of the congress, which convened in September and which called for the nomination of Polish suffragans, he subsequently made light of the whole affair and doubted whether it would achieve its goal. Attacks on Kozłowski and Kamiński meanwhile reappeared in *Straż*. Clearly, Hodur believed that he alone could lead the Poles out of their latter-day Babylonian captivity.[25]

But Hodur accurately perceived that he had to go beyond negative rhetoric and no doubt believed that if the congress' attempts succeeded, his movement would find itself in trouble. In November 1901 *Straż* indicated Hodur's intention to substitute Polish for Latin in the liturgy, a radical break with Roman Catholic tradition that the Independents had not seen fit to adopt. Hodur announced that he would celebrate a Polish mass in St. Stanislaus Church at 10:30 A.M. on Christmas Day, 1901. He cited both "religious" and "national" reasons for this step. In one of his several moves that anticipated changes in the church which excommunicated him, Hodur said that liturgy should draw people closer to God, and vernacular rites could achieve this better than those in a foreign tongue. Moreover, cognizant of Prussian attempts to ban the use of Polish by school children in Września, Poland, a vernacular mass would indicate that the Polish language continued to live despite attempts to quash it by the partitioners in Europe and by foreign hierarchs in America.[26]

Hodur's introduction of a Polish liturgy did much to consolidate his movement and promote its future growth. Over the next two and a half years the PNCC grew slowly. By September 1904 twelve congregations with over ten thousand adherents under ten priests had formally affiliated themselves with Hodur. The latter perceived that a lack of clergy hindered the National Church's development, and he made several unsuccessful attempts to establish a seminary. Not all of his priests remained loyal; for example, Józef Bohdan returned to the Roman church, and Fr. Błażowski, Hodur's envoy extraordinary to Holland, wound up for a time in Canada as pastor of an Independent congregation. A trip by Hodur and Dangel to Poland during 1902 did not result in any great influx of clergy from the homeland. Nor did Hodur's approach that year to an Armenian prelate in Massachusetts for episcopal consecration produce any results.[27]

What the PNCC may have lacked in size, however, it more than compensated for by sheer activity. In early 1902 Hodur began a campaign to build a "Polish Work Home and Refuge" named in honour of the Polish hero Bartosz Głowacki. Sliwiński tried in 1903 to organize a Polish cooperative trade society. The fact that these projects did not achieve any great degree of success did not dampen Hodur's ardour. He criticized what he termed the Poles' "softness of character" and "weak will" and enumerated their faults: "lack of sufficient national consciousness and national solidarity"; "drunkenness"; "blind faith" in the clergy; and "laziness of spirit." The PNCC, in Hodur's opinion, constituted the best means to combat these faults. Patriotic plays and programs continued. *Straż* advocated the establishment of Polish political clubs. Szlupas, who would move to Philadelphia later in 1902, still called for the creation of a workers' party, but the paper alternated such appeals with pro-Republican and anti-Democrat sentiments. *Straż* continued to espouse socialist ideas but periodically ran afoul of the Socialist paper *Robotnik,* largely on the question of nationalism. As one *Straż* reader wrote in 1904, "...we are not only workers but also Poles." And during the anthracite strike of 1902 *Straż* consistently followed the United Mine Workers' line and enjoyed the support of most Polish strikers.[28]

In the more purely ecclesiastical sphere Hodur and his followers still distanced themselves from the Independents. Hodur taunted them for their reluctance to break more clearly with Roman Catholicism. Yet he characterized Kozłowski's attempts in 1902 to establish intercommunion with the Protestant Episcopal Church as "humbug" and as a sell-out of the Poles for material gain. Kozłowski, no doubt disturbed by his rival's radical rhetoric, washed his hands of Hodur and unsuccessfully promoted the consecration of his vicar-general, a Bohemian named Jan Francis Tichy, at an Old Catholic synod in Switzerland during 1904.[29]

Nor did Hodur think very highly of those Polish Roman Catholics who sought to ameliorate the immigrants' plight by remaining within the Roman church. *Straż*'s comments on the visit of Fr. Wacław Kruszka to Rome during 1903 in connection with the Polish Catholic Congress' petition for the consecration of Polish bishops reflected Hodur's accurate belief that the Vatican was not overly concerned at the Poles' plight. Hodur admired the courage of the "young but defiant" pastor from Ripon, Wisconsin, yet the National Catholic leader considered Kruszka somewhat "crazy." Rome would never overrule the American hierarchy, which supposedly kept the Pope well funded. And even if the Vatican yielded, of what help would a Polish bishop be, particularly if he were of the calibre of Jan Pitass? When the failure of Kruszka's mission became all the more apparent the following year, *Straż* scoffed, "Poor Fr. Kruszka!! He prayed..., displayed himself in the anterooms of Vatican prelates, bought masses and even gave the pope a fifteen-pound candle," yet received nothing for his troubles.[30]

The failure of the Kruszka mission could not, however, mask the still rather modest achievements of the National Catholic movement. Always favourable to the Polish National Alliance as a potent force against clericalism, Hodur and his followers nonetheless did not enjoy the fraternal organization's formal support, even though several Alliance lodges consisted by and large of the dissidents. Moreover, *Straż* occasionally criticized the Alliance's organ, *Zgoda,* for what the former considered its increasingly pro-clerical and anti-Hodur leanings. Hodur's appearance at the 1903 Alliance Sejm in Wilkes-Barre did not alter this state of affairs. In an effort to consolidate his movement, refute Roman Catholic claims that it was disintegrating and formulate a more coherent program of activities, Hodur announced in July 1904 that the "First Synod of the Polish National Catholic Church" would convene in Scranton the following September.[31]

The synodal summons also signalled a change in policy towards the Independents. In a characteristic tactical shift, Hodur extended an olive branch to both Kamiński and Kozłowski when he suggested that they also send representatives to the Scranton assembly. Kozłowski, whose efforts to enter into intercommunion with the Episcopalians had come to nought, apparently proved amenable, and two of his clergy appeared at Scranton in September. But when *Straż* announced that the synod would be like councils in the primitive church that dealt with matters of doctrine and elected bishops, it became clear that Hodur desired unity only on his terms and under his leadership as bishop. Kamiński, for his part, kept his distance from Scranton.[32]

The synod met on September 6-8, 1904, at St. Stanislaus Church and consisted of 131 lay and 15 clerical delegates who represented twelve National Catholic parishes; one non-aligned Independent church in Passaic, New Jersey; fourteen Alliance lodges; six other Polish organizations; and the Kozłowski group. The participants adopted a constitution which established a quinquennial general synod as the highest authority in matters of ecclesiastical administration. While parishes would enjoy considerable autonomy, they owed "respect and obedience" to a bishop elected for life by the synod "in questions of faith, morals and discipline." The bishop, however, would administer the church in consultation with a Grand Council of six priests and six laymen. Moreover, the synod sanctioned the establishment of a seminary, declared *Straż* to be the official church organ and roundly rejected papal infallibility as "a blasphemy against God." To no one's surprise, Hodur was elected bishop and the delegates went on record in support of union with Kozłowski's group.[33]

To follow up on these developments, Hodur, who now assumed the title of bishop, journeyed to Chicago and apparently met a favourable reception. Kozłowski, whose financial picture at that time was not the brightest, agreed to present a plan of union based upon the concept of a joint synod and common Grand Council to an assembly of his followers in December.[34] Meanwhile, Hodur approached Gerard Gul, Old Catholic Archbishop of Utrecht, through the medium of one Fr. Kamiński, an Old Catholic cleric in Baden, Germany. The bishop-elect told of his visit to Chicago and appealed for assistance, but stopped short of a direct appeal for consecration. Instead, contrary to his publicly expressed position, he asserted that Kruszka's previous efforts might yet bear fruit. If Rome adopted a policy of "tractability" on the questions of ecclesiastical properties and Polish bishops, all the dissidents' efforts would "collapse within five years." The Poles and the Old Catholics therefore must go further than either Kozłowski or Kamiński and promote a thoroughgoing reform of the church grounded in scripture and tradition. Finally, he suggested that one or more of the Old Catholic prelates themselves might visit America to assess the situation.[35]

The Old Catholics did not extend the desired helping hand, nor did they offer to confer the episcopal dignity that Hodur sought so assiduously, largely because the promising alliance with Chicago, which received approval at Kozłowski's December assembly, remained a dead letter. Utrecht subsequently claimed that "the obscure relationship between Kozłowski and Hodur" which continued beyond 1904 prevented any positive response to the Scranton bishop-elect's overtures.[36] Why the rapprochement collapsed remains unclear, but one may surmise that the two dissident leaders could not easily forget years of feuding and that Hodur's radical rhetoric could not but disturb the more staid Chicago hierarch. While *Straż* did not openly criticize Kozłowski up to the time of his death in January 1907, the paper did suggest that his concerns lay more in good relations with the Episcopalians and Orthodox than with ties to his countrymen at Scranton.[37] Moreover, Kozłowski's midwestern clergy may not have taken kindly to the prospect of affiliation with, and eventual submission to, a prelate in Pennsylvania. In any event, Hodur had problems of his own closer to home.

The years 1905 and 1906 witnessed a slow growth of the PNCC, but they also saw several serious challenges to Hodur. The fiery priest claimed that his movement hung like "the sword of Damocles" over the Polish Roman Catholic clergy. Yet it became apparent that threats–internal and external–loomed over the National Church as well. The arrival in the United States during May 1905 of Archbishop Francis Albin Symon on an unofficial investigative mission and his subsequent stay among the Poles appeared to indicate that Rome was not as unconcerned about the immigrants as Hodur had asserted. *Straż* initially greeted the prelate of Polish origin as a fellow countryman, invited him to

Scranton and expressed the hope that he would study the PNCC, not condemn it. When it became obvious that Symon's attitude towards the dissidents was less than conciliatory, *Straż* condemned the "Vatican's delegate to Polish pockets." Hodur reminded him that Rome's rule caused the "moral and political death" of Poland. For good measure Hodur added a challenge to a public debate, but the visiting dignitary did not see fit to honour the bishop-elect's request. Efforts to establish a National Catholic parish at Newark, New Jersey, in mid-1905 constituted for Hodur "the reply of enlightened people to the anathemas and attacks of Archbishop Symon."[38]

Symon's visit was not the only problem with which Hodur had to contend. Rebellion periodically reared its head within his own ranks. Józef Dawidowski, pastor of the National Catholic congregation at Plymouth, acted too independently for his superior's liking and found himself suspended. Apparently befriended by the Baptists, Dawidowski engaged in an unedifying controversy with Hodur that eventually wound up in the courts. Other examples of clergy who rebelled about this time were Wincenty Łagan of Webster, Massachusetts, and Jan Radziszewski, who had represented his congregation in Perth Amboy, New Jersey, at the 1904 synod. Hodur admitted his difficulties when in July 1905 he summoned a National Church conference "to study the weak aspects of our cause, to censure disloyalty and to find means of assistance."[39] The pressure of the Symon visit, the failure of his approaches to Utrecht and clerical misbehaviour apparently persuaded Hodur to take desperate measures to save his movement. In a clear break with Catholic tradition, he "ordained" two men, Franciszek Laszkiewicz and Józef Zielonka, to the priesthood during July and November 1905, respectively.[40]

Dissension also manifested itself in the administration of *Straż*. Under Dangel's editorship the paper continued to be pro-labour and increasingly pro-Republican in tone; largely due to this the socialists attacked both him and Hodur. Yet Dangel became disenchanted and began to criticize what he considered the National Church's lack of progress. In June 1905 he denied that *Straż* constituted the church's organ and asserted the paper's independence. During March 1906 he announced that he would turn the paper over to Hodur if the latter would "unfrock himself and . . . work for the good of all our people, not restricted by religious sectarianism." This served as the proverbial last straw. In July the less flamboyant justice of the peace from Priceburg, Jan Sliwiński, replaced Dangel, who repaired to Buffalo.[41]

These difficulties nonetheless did not prevent efforts to establish new parishes at places such as Shamokin, Pennsylvania, and Adams, Massachusetts. In June 1906 Hodur announced the convocation of a "Special Synod" for the following August to consolidate his movement and carry out the still unimplemented programs adopted two years earlier, such as construction of a seminary. His presynodal announcements affirmed the PNCC's loyalty to Catholic principles, defended the validity of its priests' sacramental administrations and specifically mentioned Apostolic Succession; nonetheless he did not directly address the question of his previous "ordinations" of priests. And in an interesting shift, he decried the efforts of enemies to present his followers as "opponents of assimilation and capitalism."[42]

Seventeen parishes in the National Catholic fold dispatched delegates to the "Special Synod" which met at Scranton on August 21-23. The assembly focused on administrative and disciplinary matters. For instance, the synod empowered Hodur to excommunicate contumacious clergy; assessed members for construction of a seminary; sanctioned the establishment of a new publication, *Trybuna,* as the official Church organ; and instituted two new ecclesiastical feasts, those of "Poor Shepherds" and "Brotherly Love and Unity of the Polish Nation." Efforts to abolish mandatory clerical celibacy surfaced, but the majority of delegates resisted any change in discipline. And the synod also reaffirmed the PNCC's "Catholic" nature, in that the movement "acknowledges Jesus Christ and uses those means which he instituted for our sanctification and salvation."[43]

Despite the high degree of unity manifested at the Scranton assembly and continued efforts to establish new parishes, Hodur undoubtedly knew he could not make good his claim to spiritual leadership of the Polish dissidents without valid episcopal consecration. When Kozłowski died at Chicago on January 14, 1907, the situation changed. The prelate did not leave any formally designated and accepted successor. Moreover, by April 1907 only eight parishes with six priests remained within the Chicago-based dissident movement, and these suffered from internal dissension and financial problems. One of the late bishop's clergy, Kazimierz Rosicki, became an administrator of the vacant see. The Czech, Fr. Tichy, who at one time had enjoyed the late bishop's support as a candidate for the episcopate, also assumed the rank of administrator in Cleveland. He now set out to claim the coveted episcopal prize for himself and planned to attend the Old Catholic Congress at The Hague in September for this purpose. Word of these moves reached Hodur, who not surprisingly considered Tichy unsuitable as a successor to Kozłowski. And if the Old Catholics did not know what to make of the situation in America, their confusion could only have increased when in February 1907 Fr. Łagan, suspended by Hodur, advised them to consecrate no one, ostensibly because the Poles were anti-German and did not consider themselves Old Catholics. Fr. Radziszewski, who also had been excluded from Hodur's ranks, reported to Utrecht in March of his own missionary work in Alberta and Manitoba, but he failed to indicate whose jurisdiction he recognized.[44]

Hodur, for his part, now demonstrated a rather ambivalent attitude towards the Old Catholics, even though he no doubt knew that he could hardly remain passive in view of his Czech competitor's activities. Rebuffed on three earlier occasions, he prudently refrained from any direct approach to Utrecht until he could claim the support of what was left of Kozłowski's shepherdless flock. This support did not come easily; as late as June 1907 Hodur publicly denied any links to Rosicki or to the Old Catholics. But Chicago's dissident *locum tenens* and some other clergy eventually decided to throw in their lot with Hodur. Perhaps the possibility of a Czech, not Polish, successor to Kozłowski did not appeal to them. Of equal if not greater weight in this decision was the Old Catholics' view that the Poles "must be reconciled" because their "disagreements are a scandal." On July 25, Rosicki, four other priests and three laymen met at Chicago and formally selected Hodur as Kozłowski's successor. When he conveyed this decision to Archbishop Gul in early August, Rosicki cited the small size of the Chicago-based movement as the principal reason for their action. On August 7, Rosicki and Fr. Józef Plaga of the Chicago group joined Hodur and four of the latter's clergy at the St. Denis Hotel in New York City, where a union of the hitherto separate dissident camps at long last was consummated.[45]

Whether Hodur expected the Old Catholics to recognize this union and consecrate him remained uncertain, for at the same time he also found it necessary to "ordain" one Stanisław Ciećkiewicz to the priesthood. Nonetheless, his case as strong as he could reasonably expect, Hodur wrote on August 22 to Archbishop Gul requesting consecration and closer ties to the Old Catholics. The end of August found him on board the *Caronia* bound for Liverpool, and he arrived at The Hague for the Old Catholic Congress in early September.[46]

Now so close to his goal, one major obstacle remained in Hodur's path: Tichy. The Czech priest had not been idle after Kozłowski's death, and he too appeared at the Old Catholic assembly with a request for consecration. The Old Catholic prelates had an open mind as to the merits of the two supplicants and gave each candidate an opportunity to present his case. Tichy claimed that he represented over twenty Polish, Czech and Slovak parishes. Hodur in turn denied that the Czech represented any Poles and eloquently held forth on the dire consequences which would supposedly follow in the wake of Tichy's consecration. The Scranton priest's argument carried the day in practice if not in theory. After some deliberation the Old Catholic bishops announced that they would consecrate Hodur. If the latter satisfied himself as to the need for a second diocese in America he in turn could consecrate Tichy, who was to enter into communion with Hodur. The Czech reportedly received this verdict with something less than good grace. Bishop Hodur subsequently recalled that the ex-vicar general "sprang up from his place, seized his top hat from the table, threw it on the ground, stamped his foot in the greatest anger and left the hall." Despite this final unpleasantness, however, Hodur had at long last attained his goal. He signed the Declaration of Utrecht, an Old Catholic creedal statement, on September 5, and on September 29—the ninth anniversary of his excommunication by Scranton diocesan officials—he received the episcopate in St. Gertrude's Cathedral, Utrecht, at the hands of Archbishop Gul and two other Dutch prelates.[47]

The newly consecrated bishop received a regal welcome after his return to America on board the *Teutonic* in October. The seal of Apostolic Succession now appeared on the PNCC, which during 1907 had added congregations in Rhode Island, Minnesota and Connecticut, in addition to the several Chicago-group parishes that had joined with Hodur. The National Catholic movement now numbered twenty parishes with nearly fifteen thousand souls. *Straż,* which previously had maintained a prudent silence about approaches to Utrecht, now exulted in the PNCC's "triumph," though it eschewed use of the term "Old Catholic" in favour of the more familiar and less objectionable words "National Catholic" in its description of events in the Netherlands. The paper, which by now ceased to express strong socialistic sentiments, viewed the consecration as an endorsement of Hodur's resistance to Roman centralization and alleged denigration of Polish nationalism. Now possessed of their own bishop, all Poles in America once and for all should throw off the Irish yoke hitherto fastened by ecclesiastical laws on church properties and by policies of denationalization. Hodur reminded the immigrants that had the Poles been united in the revolutions of 1831 and 1863 they could have liberated themselves from foreign oppression; the opportunity for religious liberation now beckoned and he invited them to unite under his banner.[48]

Only a minority within the Polish immigrant minority eventually would answer Bishop Hodur's summons to battle. Even though a good number resented what they considered unfair treatment by both their own clergy and the non-Polish hierarchy, the majority regarded separation from Rome as too radical a remedy for their problems. But by 1907 Hodur's PNCC clearly had demonstrated its viability as an ecclesiastical alternative for those daring immigrants who concluded that the preservation of their language and culture in the North American environment, as well as the exercise of their socio-economic "rights," was not possible within the Roman Catholic communion. The wide-ranging and not invariably consistent program developed by Hodur and his followers during the period 1897-1907 aimed at the creation of a "Polish" and "Catholic" church free from alleged "Irish" and "Roman" domination in the religious, economic, political and cultural spheres. Unlike other Polish dissident movements, Hodur's progressive yet pragmatic National Church successfully fostered and benefitted from the immigrants' frustration at their perceived inferiority in each of these spheres. Even so, the religious and political radicalism which manifested itself in the PNCC mellowed by 1907. Hodur no doubt knew that such radicalism, if unchecked, would discredit his efforts both in the eyes of his countrymen and in those of the broader, non-Polish North American society. He therefore sought and obtained episcopal consecration from a reputable source—an action which clearly demonstrated a desire to maintain a claim to Catholicity. And the movement's leftist leanings, always tempered by nationalism, gradually evolved into more moderate socio-political views. By 1907, therefore, Hodur and his followers had set the stage as best they could for the further development of the Polish National Catholic Church, an ethno-religious phenomenon that consequently has persisted to this day.

Notes

1. No definitive history of the PNCC exists. Works favourable to the PNCC include Stephen Włodarski, *The Origin and Growth of the Polish National Catholic Church* (Scranton: PNCC, 1974); Theodore Andrews, *The Polish National Catholic Church in America and Poland* (London: S. P. C. K., 1953); and Paul Fox, *The Polish National Catholic Church* (Scranton: School of Christian Living, n.d.). For a Roman Catholic view of the PNCC's origins, see John P. Gallagher, *A Century of History: The Diocese of Scranton, 1868-1968* (Scranton: Diocese of Scranton, 1968). Hieronim Kubiak, *Polski Narodowy Kościół Katolicki w Stanach Zjednoczonych Ameryki w latach 1897-1965* [The Polish National Catholic Church in the United States of America in 1897-1965] (Wrocław: Polish Academy of Sciences, 1970) presents a contemporary Polish sociological study of the denomination. The PNCC established itself in Poland and still functions there as an autonomous body called the "Polish Catholic Church."
2. Laurence Orzell, "A Minority within a Minority: The Polish National Catholic Church, 1896-1907," *Polish American Studies* 36, no. 1 (1979), pp. 7-9. The present paper utilizes source materials not previously accessible and develops themes not given detailed treatment in my previous essay.
3. Secretary's Minute Book, All Saints Church, Chicago, 11 Nov. 1895, p. 61. These minutes form part of the archives at All Saints PNCC Cathedral, Chicago.
4. "Pastoral Letter of the Right Reverend Anthony Kozlowski, Bishop of the Indep. Catholic Diocese of Chicago," 19 Dec. 1897. This printed manifesto is located in the archives of the Christian Catholic (Old Catholic) Church in Bern, Switzerland.

5. See "Recent Schismatical Movements Among Catholics of the United States," *American Ecclesiastical Review* 1 (July 1899), pp. 1-13. Kozłowski and Kamiński did not join forces, as each claimed to lead the Independent movement.
6. Hodur arrived in the U.S. during 1893, and Bishop William O'Hara of the Scranton diocese ordained him in August of that year. See Włodarski, pp. 37-42.
7. Gallagher, pp. 220-21.
8. "Chwila z przed dziesięciu lat" ["A Moment since Ten Years Ago"], *Trybuna* [Tribune] (Scranton), March 1907, pp. 27-29. Parish Committee Meeting Minutes, St. Stanislaus Church, 14 and 20 Mar. 1897, pp. 7-12. These minutes are located at St. Stanislaus PNCC Cathedral, Scranton.
9. *Straż* [The Guard] 14 Apr., 8, 15 May, 5, 12 June, 28 Aug., 5 Dec. 1897.
10. Orzell, p. 16.
11. *Straż,* 29 May, 4 Sept., 20 Nov., 31 Dec. 1897.
12. Ibid., 26 June, 25 Sept., 2, 23, 30 Oct. 1897.
13. Ibid., 12 Feb., 19 Mar., 14 May, 2 July, 10, 24 Sept. 1898; *The Diocesan Record* (Scranton), 22 Oct. 1898.
14. *Straż,* 16 Apr., 27 Aug., 17, 24 Sept., 15 Oct. 1898.
15. Ibid., 22 Dec. 1897; 12 Mar., 28 May, 25 June, 10 Sept., 22 Oct., 19 Nov. 1898. Łopatyner ceased to edit *Górnik* [The Miner] in 1899 and thereafter did not play any active role in dissident affairs.
16. Ibid., 14 May, 3, 10 Sept., 19 Nov. 1898.
17. Ibid., 18 June 1898. The Old Catholics maintained ecumenical contacts with the Russian Orthodox, and this provided grist for Hodur's anti-Kozłowski mill.
18. Hodur to [Gerard Gul, Archbishop of Utrecht], 19 Jan. 1899; same to [same], 19 Jan. 1899, both in the private papers of the Archbishops of Utrecht, Utrecht, The Netherlands, file "Noord Amerika, Fr. Hodur I (1899-1908): Verkiering en Wijding, 14/9." Hereafter abbreviated PPAU, 14/9. The addresses of letters are not always clearly indicated. The petitions are also in PPAU, 14/9. I wish to express my thanks to Mgr. Marinus Kok, Archbishop of Utrecht, for permission to examine these papers.
19. Hodur to [Gul], 15 Mar. 1899; Hodur to [Gul or Edouard Herzog, Christian Catholic Bishop in Switzerland], 9 Feb. 1900; Theodor Weber, Old Catholic Bishop in Germany, to Gul, 11 July 1900, all in PPAU, 14/9. An undated memorandum in PPAU, 14/9 discusses a letter Hodur sent to Herzog about this time and the opinion of one Dr. Paul Pollack, an associate of Kozłowski. Pollack counselled reserve on the part of the Old Catholics towards Hodur's request. Hodur visited Chicago in March 1900 for Forty Hours' Devotions. See *Straż,* 24 Feb., 31 Mar. 1900.
20. For these efforts, see *Straż,* 29 Sept. 1900 and *Wiarus* [The Veteran] (Winona, Minn.) 12 April 1900.

21. *Straż,* 20 Jan., 17 Feb., 17, 24 Mar., 3 Aug., 15 Sept., 6 Oct. 1900; 16 Feb., 3 Aug. 1901.
22. Ibid., 10 Feb., 7 Apr., 25 Oct., 3 Nov. 1900.
23. Ibid., 21, 28 Apr., 9 June, 14 July, 1 Dec. 1900.
24. Parish Committee Meeting Minutes, St. Stanislaus Church, 16 Dec. 1900, pp. 79-81. See also *Straż,* 5 Jan. 1901. According to the undated memorandum in PPAU, 14/9 cited above, Hodur claimed congregations in Scranton, Priceburg, Plymouth, Duryea, Nanticoke and Smithville (Pa.); Jersey City and Passaic (N.J.); and Fall River and Chicopee (Mass.).
25. *Straż,* 5 Jan., 8 June, 5, 12, 19 Oct., 2 Nov. 1901. *Nowe Drogi* [New Way] (1901; rpt. Scranton: Bishop Hodur Biography Commission, 1972), written by Hodur under the pseudonym W. Waręga, called the Independent prelates "crafty" men, "not conspicuous for their learning, virtue or eloquence" (p. 11).
26. *Straż,* 30 Nov., 21 Dec. 1901. Earlier that year Hodur introduced Polish into certain parts of the Corpus Christi service. See *Straż,* 8 June 1901.
27. Ibid., 23 Feb., 17 Aug. 1901; 15 Mar., 6, 27 Sept., 1 Nov. 1902; 5 Dec. 1903; 13, 20 Feb. 1904; 5 Aug. 1905. See also Gallagher, p. 238.
28. *Straż,* 4 Jan., n.d. (Easter issue), 19 July, 30 Aug. 1902; 3 Jan., 14 Feb., 7, 14 Nov., 19 Dec. 1903; 23 Jan., 25 June 1904.
29. Ibid., 4 Jan., 3 May, 11 Oct., 1 Nov. 1902; "Berichten: Amerika," *De Oud-Katholiek,* March 1907, pp. 31-32. I should like here to thank officials at the Old Catholic seminary in Amersfoort, The Netherlands, for permission to consult their library. *De Oud-Katholiek* is the official organ of the Dutch Old Catholics.
30. *Straż,* 13, 20 June, 5, 26 Sept., 14 Nov. 1903; 15 Oct. 1904.
31. Ibid., 24 May, 2 Aug. 1902; 10, 31 Oct. 1903; 9, 16 July 1904. Both Dangel and Sliwiński were extremely active in Alliance affairs, and the Sejm's local organizing committee requested Hodur to offer a mass for the intention of the assembly. To counter the effects of this, Polish Roman Catholics held a mass of their own for the Sejm. See *Straż,* 19, 26 Sept. 1903. *Straż* criticized *Zgoda* [Harmony] for the latter's refusal to print Hodur's synodal summons. See *Straż,* 27 Aug. 1904.
32. Ibid., 23 July, 20 Aug. 1904.
33. Ibid., 3, 17 Sept. 1904; "Ustawy Kościoła Polsko-Narodowego w Ameryce," *Trybuna,* March 1907, pp. 8-12. See also Robert Janowski, ed., *The Growth of a Church: A Historical Documentary* (Scranton: n.p., 1965), pp. 30-34.
34. *Straż,* 22 Oct. 1904; "Oud-Katholieken in Amerika," *De Oud-Katholiek,* Nov. 1907, p. 127.
35. Hodur to Kamiński, 28 Oct. 1904; Kamiński to Gul, 14 Nov. 1904, both in PPAU, 14/9.
36. *Straż,* n.d. (Christmas issue), 1904; "Oud-Katholieken in Amerika," *De Oud-Katholiek,* Nov. 1907, p. 127.

37. *Straż,* 31 Mar., 9 June 1906.

38. Ibid., 14 Jan., 13, 20 May, 1 July, 5 Aug., 16 Sept. 1905.

39. Ibid., 29 July, 5 Aug., 16, 30 Sept., 7, 21 Oct. 1905; 6, 27 Jan., 10 Feb. 1906. The Dawidowski matter dragged on throughout the first half of 1906 but eventually was resolved in Hodur's favour.

40. Ibid., 22 July, 18 Nov. 1905. My recent research on this subject necessitates a revision of my earlier supposition that such "ordinations" did not in fact occur. See my *Rome and the Validity of Orders in the Polish National Catholic Church* (Scranton: Savonarola Theological Seminary Alumni Association, 1977), pp. 19-20. This stemmed from the lack of evidence and gross overgeneralization in Roman Catholic polemical works which assume their existence. See, for example, Joseph Przudzik, "Schism in America," *The Homiletic and Pastoral Review* 47 (September 1947), pp. 986-87. Nonetheless, the historical fact of these few ordinations does not in itself prove that Hodur did not possess the requisite sacramental intention at his own consecration in 1907 or at his subsequent ordinations of priests and bishops.

41. *Straż,* 3 June, 15 July, 21 Oct. 1905; 10, 24 Mar., 30 June, 7 July 1906.

42. Ibid., 16 June 1906.

43. Ibid., 25 Aug. 1906; Parish Committee Meeting Minutes, St. Stanislaus Church, 30 Aug. 1906, pp. 191-93; *Trybuna,* March 1907, pp. 20-21.

44. "Oud-Katholieken in Amerika," *De Oud-Katholiek,* Nov. 1907, p. 127. Hodur subsequently wrote two accounts of events leading up to his consecration in *Rola Boża,* which became the PNCC's official organ in 1923: "Jeszcze kilka słów o tak zwanych niezależnych 'starokatolickich' biskupach i księżach w Ameryce" ["Still More Words about the So-Called Independent 'Old Catholic' Bishops and Priests in America"], 31 Oct. 1925 (pp. 341-42) and "33–Trzydzieści Trzy Lata Temu–33" ["33–Thirty-three Years Ago–33"], 12 Oct. 1940, pp. 322-26. Łagan to Gul, 26 Feb. 1907; Radziszewski to Gul, 23 Mar. 1907, both in PPAU, 14/9.

45. *Straż,* 1 June 1907; "Oud-Katholieken in Amerika," *De Oud-Katholiek,* Nov. 1907, p. 127; Rosicki to Gul, 15 Aug. 1907, PPAU, 14/9. The Bishop Hodur Biography Commission collection at Good Shepherd PNCC Parish, Plymouth, Pa., contains a copy of an agreed memorandum produced at the New York meeting.

46. *Straż,* 10, 31 Aug. 1907; Hodur to Gul, 22 Aug. 1907, PPAU, 14/9.

47. "Oud-Katholieken in Amerika," *De Oud-Katholiek,* Nov. 1907, pp. 127-28; "Jeszcze kilka słów," *Rola Boża,* 31 Oct. 1925, pp. 341-42; "Trzydzieści Trzy Lata Temu," ibid., 12 Oct. 1940, pp. 324-26.

48. *Straż,* 19, 26 Oct., 2, 9 Nov. 1907.

Family

Beyond Ethnicity: Polish Generations in Industrial America

John Bodnar

Scholars have not been reluctant to generalize about the behaviour of Polish immigrant families in industrial America. The classic work of William Thomas and Florian Znaniecki painted a widely accepted portrait of communal disintegration and familial breakdown, punctuated with accounts of physical abuse, intergenerational conflict, and youth gangs as evidence of the debilitating effects of urban-industrial life.[1] Subsequent studies eroded this view and found enduring religious and familial ties among Poles which originated in the traditional culture of their homeland.[2] Continuity of tradition was emphasized in recent works such as those of Victor Greene and Helena Lopata. Greene found Poles in Chicago pursuing traditional objectives, while Lopata argued that their behaviour was influenced chiefly by a longstanding system of status competition. In a contemporary analysis of Detroit, Paul Wrobel took a somewhat different stance by revealing that while families did remain intact, serious ambiguities pervaded Polish life. Specifically, he found Polish parents attempting to direct their children into lives significantly different from their own; fathers wanted sons to escape the blue-collar world for the rewards of the professional middle class.[3] In one half-century, in other words, Polish immigrant families have moved from victimized families, to enduring families, to the troubled families of modern-day Detroit.

Scholarly descriptions of Polish American familial behaviour have generally been the result of investigations by sociologists and anthropologists more interested in formulating sweeping patterns of behaviour than in studying a specific society at a particular moment. This somewhat historical emphasis on social theory at the expense of time and place has resulted in assumptions that all Polish family behaviour was ethnically based and therefore different from other immigrant groups, that all Poles acted alike, and that Poles were acting out of cultural imperatives independently of the industrial economy which surrounded them in America.

But for most Polish newcomers the time was the late nineteenth and early twentieth century, when the forces of expanding capitalism were dislodging Polish families and their traditional ties to the land, small town crafts, and the cottage industry and were forcing them into routinized, industrial jobs. And the place was usually the urban neighbourhoods, mill towns and mining districts of America, where a fluctuating industrial economy could demand specific types of behaviour without necessarily destroying familial life. This essay, then, hopes to redirect the study of Polish American families by suggesting specific examples of how Poles, by interacting with an economy, were neither unique among working-class immigrant families nor simply victimized by the pressures of the urban milieu or their cultural past. Moreover, all Poles did not act in concert, and significant behavioural differences characterized the component groups of the Polish community. Beyond generalizations of the Poles as an ethnic group were specific people confronting the challenges of an expanding industrial economy in both the old country and the new.

In delving into the behaviour of Poles in historical time, two divergent lines of inquiry will be pursued. First, oral interviews with working-class immigrant families in industrial Pennsylvania will be analysed for suggestions they might offer on the workings of the Polish family before World War Two. Secondly, quantitative data extracted from the United States Manuscript Census for 1900 will be searched for two urban communities, Scranton and Philadelphia, for indications of how significant differences in behaviour may have existed *within* the Polish community—differences which would take us beyond the ethnic group itself as an analytical framework.

Generations in the Family

When Paul Wrobel found that Polish parents in contemporary Detroit were attempting to push their children out of the traditional, working-class community into the sweep of American upwardly mobile culture, he also discovered a curious reaction on the part of the children: they were reluctant to listen. Polish youth was fearful of leaving familiar neighbourhoods and skeptical of continued education. In 1970, nearly three-fourths of those between the ages of 20 and 21 were not enrolled in school and one in five between the ages 16 and 21 never finished high school.[4] Although neither Wrobel nor the Detroit Poles were probably aware of it, this posture was a familiar remnant of the necessity for all members to contribute to the immigrant family's economy —a pattern nurtured during the initial encounter of Polish peasants with industrial America.

The Polish immigrant family during the half-century of settlement following the 1880s had its share of problems and tensions. Wladimier K., for instance, emigrated to Pittsburgh in 1913 from Russian Poland, became blind while mixing lime at a steel mill, and became "highly nervous" when he had to terminate work and remain at home. He became convinced that he had lost his family's affection. When his wife admitted to him that she went out with other men he felt like an outcast in his own family.[5] But familial disorder did not characterize the vast majority of immigrant homes. While not tension-free, the Polish family could certainly be described as an effective agent in assisting newcomers move to America, acquire jobs and meet the realities of a capitalistic system.

Immigration itself relied heavily on kinship networks and ties. Poles, like all immigrant groups, followed kin to specific American cities rather than randomly jumping into the new land. These networks served as the basis not only for urban communities but also for occupational clusters in selected industries. Thus, Poles concentrated in Chicago meat-packing plants, Pittsburgh steel mills and Philadelphia tanneries because of the operation of familial ties. Regional groups of German or Russian Poles followed others from the same region into specific neighbourhoods and jobs. Russian and Prussian Poles concentrated on Detroit's East Side whereas Galicians settled largely on the West Side. In Scranton, Russian Poles were much more likely to be found in coal-mining, for instance, than Poles from the Prussian areas.[6]

Because kinship networks became so vital in initially integrating newcomers into an industrial economy, the family itself, which Thomas and Znaniecki had suggested was slowly withering in land-scarce Poland by the late nineteenth century,[7] found important new functions in industrial society and was reinvigorated. Whereas Poles had found it difficult to pass on land in the homeland, they could now offer access to jobs in America. The result was the beginning of a system whereby family networks, which became the key to job acquisition, became crucial to maintain.[8]

Inside the immigrant family the overriding preoccupation was not with social organization, status competition, traditional culture, religion, or mobility, but with income maintenance. It was not that those other concerns were ignored; but first and foremost, the immigrant family had to meet the reality of making a living. It was just that industrial capitalism, while offering wages superior to peasant Poland, guaranteed neither steady work, sustained prosperity nor freedom from crippling injury. Evidence from interviews with Polish families from industrial regions suggests exactly how the Polish family confronted the demands of the American economy to maintain a steady income.

Generally, a father's or a household head's income was insufficient for family sustenance and had to be supplemented. Sometimes, especially in the early years of immigration, this could be done by taking in boarders. But after World War One, this source of income dwindled as immigration was restricted; the burden of supplemental income had to be transferred to the children.

In Nanticoke and Plymouth, two towns in Pennsylvania's anthracite district, Polish families frequently opened small grocery stores which could be operated by kin while a father worked or by men who were no longer able to work in mining. Arlene G., who was raised in Nanticoke by Polish parents, left school early so she could work in the family store and kill and clean chickens for sale. Family income was increased additionally by living only in the upstairs portion of their home because the downstairs was worth three dollars more in monthly rent. This arrangement was maintained in spite of the fact that her mother found it painful to climb a long row of steps. In Plymouth, Frances B. and her sisters left school after the eighth grade in order to make dresses at home until they married, as their mother had done before them. The one exception was a sister who worked in a cigar factory to earn extra wages.[9]

Even when attending school, Polish children were spending their after-school hours on minor tasks. Typical was Steve M. who began working part-time in a Monessen grocery store at the age of 11 cleaning the fruit stand after school and scrubbing meat cases on Saturday. At thirteen he would get up at 3:30 A.M. to deliver milk. Similar experiences were related in the Lawrenceville section of Pittsburgh and Bethlehem's south side. Girls also cleaned at home and regularly assisted in laundry work. By caring for younger brothers and sisters, older children freed mothers to care for boarders, run stores and cook meals. In mining areas children tended livestock and fed chickens.[10]

A combination of forces hastened the departure of young Poles from the classroom and thrust them into roles of family maintenance. Given the choices involved, immigrant parents in industrial regions more often than not ignored any pretentions toward mobility and took their children out of school in order to put them to work. Polish families sought to teach behavioural traits such as obedience, sharing and hard work—qualities that would ensure their survival in American society later in life. Young Poles were regularly sent to work and asked to relinquish all wages to parents, usually the mother, for use by the entire household. Many recalled scenes where the family would gather periodically and place their pay envelopes on the kitchen table. Prolonged schooling could only delay participation in such a ritual.[11]

This imposition of parental wishes was bound to generate intergenerational tensions despite the fact that parents seemed genuinely concerned for their children's welfare in adulthood. A number of Polish women in Nanticoke confessed that they eagerly sought a marriage partner in order to escape from their families and the employment burdens they endured. In several instances when a child attempted to defy a parent and remain in school an older brother or sister would object. This was so in the case of Stella K. In 1930 she had an opportunity to leave Nanticoke and live with a wealthy family on Long Island. The arrangement was such that she would have been allowed to simultaneously perform domestic service and complete her high school education. The plan was abandoned, however, when her brother bitterly complained because he had been forced to leave high school early and enter the mines.[12]

While internal disagreements over work and school existed, an impression that they were common would be misleading. More typical was the immigrant youth who not only abided by parental persuasion but actually initiated the idea to leave school early. And not all parents minimized the potential value of extended schooling. In a small number of homes children were urged to acquire as much education as possible even if the loss of their earnings caused tremendous economic sacrifices on the part of the parents. Even in these homes children were likely to display a deep obligation to ease the financial burdens by leaving school and earning wages which could increase the income of the entire family. Antoinette W. was one of five children raised in a Polish family in Wilkes-Barre. At the age of 14 she decided to work in a silk mill. Although her mother was opposed, Antoinette explained that she was unable to concentrate on school when money was needed so badly at home. A Monessen steelworker left school early and delayed his marriage until he was 31 in order to remain at home and assist his parents. Eleanor D. decided to quit after one year of high school. Her mother recalled, "She was sixteen years old and she just wanted to leave and help in our store." Eleanor's husband left school at 14 to work with her uncle in a butcher shop despite parental objections. Tom L. returned to Cokesburg from Detroit in the 1930s because his father became unemployed and his brother was still too young to work; he felt an obligation to support his family. Virginia V. felt ambivalent about getting married and leaving her mother, and was only persuaded to do so because two sisters remained at home to provide support. The overall attitude was summarized by Lillian N. As a young girl she thought of being a nurse but decided instead to leave school and go to work in a Nanticoke silk mill. She carefully detailed her reasoning:

> I figured I would leave school in the first year of high school. I couldn't go away to be a nurse because I was needed at home much more than anything else because I helped with the children

> and all. We had to bathe the children, dress them and put them to sleep. My mother had enough to do with just cooking.[13]

This brief glimpse of the Polish immigrant family suggests that previous explanations of behaviour based on cultural persistence, or even inner turmoil among generations, have failed to appreciate the impact of an industrial economy and do not take into account how adroitly Poles fabricated particular strategies to deal with that economy. The Polish family economy, indeed, was a case of innovation within a traditional framework. Wrobel's Poles, in fact, were carrying out a tradition of innovation when they asked their children to redirect their socioeconomic priorities to areas where steady employment seemed more attainable. That Wrobel's third-generation sample seemed reluctant to abandon their parental world was also quite characteristic of Polish-American children before them. Even more importantly, this behaviour was similar to that of Slovaks, Serbs, Croatians, Hungarians and other Eastern European newcomers who responded to the demands of an industrial structure by creating similar familial-based economics.

Generations Within the Community

If generations within the Polish family found a common ground on which to act in some degree of harmony, generations within the larger Polish community exhibited marked differences. Generalizations about ethnic behaviour weaken considerably when the age-structure and geographical origins of Polish newcomers are identified. Such analysis suggests that both the age at which industrialization dislocated an individual from his homeland and pulled him into a new economic structure and also his regional background played an important part, regardless of his Polish ethnicity.[14]

Examination of demographic data from the United States Manuscript Census for 1900 in two Polish settlements, Scranton and Philadelphia, offer evidence that all Poles did not behave in a similar manner. Consider the results of Table 1, where a sample of Polish household heads drawn from both cities was arranged by the decade of their birth. It is clear that industrial and social dislocations in Europe forced those born in the 1850s to migrate at a later age than those born in later decades. In fact, they were forced to leave around the age of 30 while those born in the 1870s could leave at around 20. This 1850 cohort also emigrated much later after marriage and at a later age. The 1860 and 1870 cohort, for instance, tended to migrate before they married, but those dislocated by the time they were 30 had already been married for about five years.

Table 1: Polish Household Heads by Birth Cohort, Philadelphia and Scranton, 1900

	Born 1851-60	Born 1861-70	Born 1871-80
N	492	1,824	1,213
Age married	25.8	23.4	23.7
Age emigrated	30.9	24.6	20.1
Years in U.S.	12.2	6.0	7.6
Persistence, 1900-10	37%	19%	19%
Nuclear households	63.3%	50.9%	52.4%
Own home	46.9%	30.0%	22.0%
% unskilled	74%	62%	67%

NOTE: All statistical data in this study is based upon samples drawn from the U.S. Manuscript Census, 1900 for Philadelphia and Scranton, Pennsylvania. A 5 per cent sample was taken for both cities.

It would seem logical that the older, more established an individual, the less reluctant he would be to move continuously. True to form, the 1850 cohort tended to persist in their new home towns at twice the rate (37 per cent to 19 per cent) of those born in later decades who migrated at a younger age. They also tended to live more often in nuclear families and own their own homes, an indication that they were intent on reconstituting in America the families they had already established in Europe. The younger migrants, conversely, tended to be more transient and less likely to settle in traditional family settings.

In Scranton, as Table 2 reveals, Poles born in the 1850s were leaving for America at a later age, were more likely to be married, between 1900 and 1910 remained in the city at a greater rate, and owned their own homes more frequently than those who emigrated earlier in life. The oldest at the time of emigration were Russian Poles in the 1850s (31.9); in the first decade of this century German Poles of the same generation were highest in persistence (41 per cent) and home ownership (45 per cent). By contrast Russian Poles born in the 1870s had persistence and ownership rates of about 10 per cent.

Regional differences were also evident among Poles in Scranton. German Poles exceeded other regional groups in their inclination to remain and sink roots. In every birth cohort they were the leading homeowners (45 per cent) and the greatest persisters (41 per cent). Homeownership rates for German Poles born in the 1860s were nearly six times the rates for Austrian Poles born in the same decade. They quadrupled the ownership rate of Russian Poles in the 1870 cohort. Of course, it might be inferred that higher ownership rates were simply the result of being in America

Table 2: Polish Heads of Households by Birth Cohort, Scranton, 1900

	1851-60	1861-70	1871-80
		Austrian Poles	
Age married	24.6	25.2	23
Age emigrated	30.5	23.6	21.1
Persistence	16%	9%	11%
Home owners	15.7%	4%	14.2%
Years here	11.8	10.2	5
		Russian Poles	
Age married	27.2	20.8	22.1
Age emigrated	31.9	26.7	19.7
Persistence	37%	10%	10%
Home owners	39%	18.5%	10.7%
Years here	11.0	10.4	7
		German Poles	
Age married	26.3	24.8	23.5
Age emigrated	30.3	22.2	15.5
Persistence	41.0%	42%	24%
Home owners	45.0%	24.2%	40%
Years here	14.7	13	10.1

longer. But a simple correlation between the length of residence in this country and ownership is just not supported by the data. Younger groups, such as the 1860s cohort of Russian Poles, owned homes at a higher ratio than Austrian Poles in all cohorts. In the case of German Poles born in the 1870s, it appears that they generally arrived in America with their parents at the age of 15, spent about eight years in their new city before marriage, and probably could count on some parental assistance in acquiring property.

A glance at the statistics of Polish household heads in Philadelphia gives further weight to the argument that regional background and the life-stage of an immigrant transcended ethnic culture as a determinant of immigrant behaviour. In every birth cohort German Poles, as Table 3 reveals, tended to remain in the city and purchase homes at a higher ratio than other regional groups. Among German Poles born in the 1850s, over 42 per cent were able to purchase homes by 1900 compared to a complete absence of owners among Russian Poles of the same cohort. It is important to note, moreover, that such attainments were not simply a function of longevity in America, since this sample of Russian Poles has been in America only 2.7 years less than newcomers from Prussia born in the same decade. German Poles born in the 1860s exhibited an ownership rate of 30.4 per cent despite being here only a few months longer on the average than the early Russian Polish cohort. In Philadelphia, as in Scranton, German Poles born in the 1870s were among the youngest at time

Table 3: Polish Household Heads by Birth Cohort, Philadelphia, 1900

	1851-60	1861-70	1871-80
		Austrian Poles	
Age married	(insufficient data)	26.2	25.7
Age emigrated		29.0	27.7
Persistence		12.0%	0%
Home owners		28.5%	0%
Years here		7.8	5.0
		Russian Poles	
Age married	22.5	26.4	24.8
Age emigrated	30.3	23.6	21.6
Persistence	13.3%	13.5%	21.4%
Home owners	0%	12.5%	7.6%
Years here	10.2	8.4	7.4
		German Poles	
Age married	26.2	23.5	26.7
Age emigrated	31.6	24.5	17.5
Persistence	17.6%	30%	42.8%
Home owners	42.2%	30.4%	37.5%
Years here	12.9	10.8	12.5

of arrival and probably came with parents around the age of 17. Not surprisingly, they showed the highest persistence rate (42.8 per cent) of any group and relatively high (37.5 per cent) rates of proprietorship since their entry into adulthood was facilitated by the presence of parents already here.

A substantial number of Poles (as Tables 2 and 3 suggest) left their homeland as married rather than single males. Because they left later in life, the 1850s cohort tended to migrate after a family had been relatively well established. For instance, emigration of Russian Poles born in the 1850s usually occurred about eight years after marriage, for German Poles of the same cohort it was five years. As in Scranton, younger Poles tended to marry after arrival. This was especially true of Philadelphia German Poles born in the 1870s who arrived before they were 18 years old and remained single for nearly nine more years. But Russian Poles of the 1870s generation also married about three years after arrival.

Finally, Poles in Philadelphia resembled working-class residents of many American cities in the early twentieth century in that they were highly transient. With the exception of German Poles, persistence rates for these newcomers between 1900 and 1910 were characteristically low, as Table 4 illustrates. Only 12 per cent of the Austrian Poles born in the 1860s were found in the city a decade after 1900 and none were found persisting from the 1870 cohort. Russian Polish persistence rates were equally low. Comparisons with other studies reveal that even the rela-

Table 4: Persistence in Selected Cities

Years	Community/Group	Percentage persisting
1900-10	Scranton (German Poles born in 1850s)	41
1900-10	Scranton (German Poles born in 1860s)	42
1900-10	Scranton (Russian Poles born in 1860s)	10
1900-10	Philadelphia (German Poles born in 1860s)	30
1900-10	Philadelphia (Russian Poles born in 1860s)	13.5
1900-10	Philadelphia (Russian Poles born in 1870s)	21.4
1900-05	Pittsburgh (German Poles)	27.1
1900-05	Pittsburgh (Russian Poles)	15
1900-05	Pittsburgh (Italians)	14.1
1900-15	Steelton (Slavs-Italians)	32
1900-10	Omaha (entire city)	44
1910-20	Boston (entire city)	41

NOTE: The Pittsburgh data are drawn from John Bodnar, Michael Weber, and Roger Simon, *Lives of their Own: Blacks, Italians and Poles in Pittsburgh* (Urbana, Ill., 1981), Chapter 5. Steelton data are from Bodnar, *Immigration and Industrialization: Ethnicity in an American Mill Town* (Pittsburgh, 1977), p. 58; Omaha data are from Howard Chudacoff, *Mobile Americans: Residential and Social Mobility in Omaha 1880-1930* (New York, 1972). Boston data are from Stephen Thernstrom, *The Other Bostonians: Poverty and Progress in the American Metropolis, 1880-1970* (Cambridge, 1973), p. 222. Scranton and Philadelphia figures are from 1900 census, sample data.

tively high German Polish figures, while always the highest among Polish immigrants, were only average when compared to the population as a whole. For example, persistence for the general population of Omaha and Boston in the early twentieth century matched the early German Poles in Scranton and Philadelphia—usually around 41 per cent. Poles from other regions, however, persisted at rates somewhere below 25 per cent, which was lower than rates for the general population but comparable to patterns displayed by immigrants in other urban-industrial settings.

In 1900 Russian Polish families had the lowest number of nuclear households regardless of age cohort. That is to say, they were more likely than Poles from other regions to have boarders or relatives in their households besides the basic unit of parents and children. Among every cohort, on the other hand, German Poles always had the highest percentage of nuclear households, an indication of the way they generally migrated in family units. It should also be stressed that German Polish migration was terminating by the end of the century while Russian Polish movement accelerated. It would, therefore, be expected that Russian Poles would continue to assist friends and relatives who were still arriving in Scranton by boarding them.

Among most Polish families in Scranton, moreover, households became more nuclear over time. The sample households were divided into early stages, which were those with children under 14 years of age, and intermediate homes, with children over 14 who were eligible for work. A prevailing pattern emerged in which Polish families stopped boarding friends and relatives as they reached the intermediate stage. Abundant oral history data from Pennsylvania have suggested that this was due to the increased earnings of Polish children who were systematically turning over their wages to their parents as they entered adolescence, thus removing much of the need to keep boarders in the first place. In Scranton, for instance, the percentage of German Polish families in the 1860s cohort increased from 63 to 100 while Russian Polish families in the same cohort rose from 41.2 per cent to 64 per cent nuclear between the early and intermediate family stage.

A glaring exception existed to the prevailing pattern. Austrian Poles were less likely to be nuclear in the intermediate than early family stages. Young families generally needed boarders to provide income before children were able to work but the Austrian Poles in Scranton either were not receiving support from their children or found it difficult to obtain work which allowed the family to be self-sufficient. As a result they were forced to take in more boarders as they entered the intermediate stage rather than less.

Table 5: Percentage of Polish Nuclear Families by Region and Cohort, Scranton

	Austrian Poles	Russian Poles	German Poles
	1850s		
Total group	61	59	73.9
Early stage	41.6	—	66.3
Intermediate stage	37.5	59	73.6
	1860s		
Total group	60.8	50	76.6
Early stage	68.7	42.2	63.2
Intermediate stage	20	64	100
	1870s		
Total group	71.4	50	83.3
Early stage	71.4	42	83.3
Intermediate stage	—	64	—

In looking at the shape of household structure in Philadelphia's Polish households, a striking difference is noticeable in the overall level of nuclear families (see total figure in Table 6). The traditional parent-children structure was much less characteristic of Philadelphia than Scranton Poles. This is somewhat surprising in

Table 6: Percentage of Polish Nuclear Families by Region and Cohort, Philadelphia, 1900

	Austrian Poles	Russian Poles	German Poles
	1850s		
Total	Too Small	60	61.6
Early		33.3	100
Intermediate		72.8	53.8
	1860s		
Total	14.2	38.0	41.7
Early	14.2	12.3	35
Intermediate	—	68	75
	1870s		
Total	25	37.8	66.6
Early	25	36.8	66.6
Intermediate	—	—	—

that Philadelphia was known as the city of homes, and individual proprietorship was relatively accessible. For instance, with the exception of Russian Polish households headed by individuals born in the 1850s, Philadelphia Poles were considerably less nuclear in the arrangements in every single category. Even among German Poles, traditionally the most nuclear, Philadelphia's group trailed behind Scranton. In the 1860s cohort the difference was clear with 76.6 per cent of the German Poles in Scranton residing in nuclear households compared to 41.7 per cent of the German Poles in Philadelphia. The figures of 14.2 per cent and 25 per cent for nuclear families among Austrian Poles from the 1860 cohort in Philadelphia were also unusually low even during periods of heavy immigration.

Some patterns, of course, remained the same. Philadelphia Poles, like those in Scranton, in general continued to discard boarders and relatives between the early and intermediate stages as children entered the workplace. And German Poles, despite the overall lower rates in the city, continued to be more nuclear than other regional groups.

Finally it comes as no surprise to see that Poles in both cities were clustered largely in less skilled occupations regardless of geographic origin. Most immigrants to industrial America were employed in such jobs. But it is significant that Poles in Philadelphia found greater opportunities in semi-skilled pursuits than in Scranton. Some 34 per cent of Polish newcomers from the Austrian and Russian regions were in semi-skilled operations in Philadelphia while only 10 per cent of the Austrial Poles and 22 per cent of the Russian Poles secured such tasks in Scranton, suggesting that urban structure could influence job patterns more than ethnic background. Philadelphia simply offered a greater variety of jobs which demanded more skills. Poles designated as labourers in Philadelphia, for instance, toiled in shipyards, chemical factories, brickyards, and on numerous construction tasks. Those performing operations requiring slightly more skill worked as tanners and finishers in leather factories or spring-makers in furniture factories. Poles also found jobs as bookbinders, chairmakers, machinists, carpenters and shoemakers. Clearly, Philadelphia offered more potential than Scranton, where few opportunities existed above the unskilled level other than contract miner, carpenter or shoemaker. Most Poles found themselves working as miner's helpers, or as labourers for iron mills and the railroad.[15]

Table 7: Occupational Distribution of Polish Heads by Region of Origin, Scranton and Philadelphia, 1900

Occupational classification	Austrian Poles	Russian Poles	German Poles
	Scranton		
Unskilled	78%	73%	69%
Semiskilled	10	22	15
Skilled	6	4	9
Small businessmen	6	1	7
	Philadelphia		
Unskilled	59	59	63
Semiskilled	34	34	22
Skilled	6	4	12
Small businessmen	1	3	3

Conclusion

Inside both the Polish household and community, significant behavioural patterns existed which transcend many previous characterizations of Polish immigrant family life. Ethnic culture did not exist as a broad blanket which covered all of Polonia and forced it to act in a completely uniform or unique way. Certainly it comes as no surprise that its traditional aspects were not destroyed. But to cling to traditional culture—or any other variable—as an all-encompassing determinant only promises to obscure the importance of time and space, of particular Poles carefully working out life strategies in particular circumstances using whatever resources were available to them—including their traditions.

This essay has sought to point out two broad areas where ethnic culture proved to be an insufficient explanation for interpreting Polish familial behaviour. First, Poles operated a functional family economy which combined a traditional reliance on kinship with pragmatic responses to the demands of industrial capitalism. This familial-based system represented neither cultural continuity nor disintegration but was simply an adjustment to working-class life.[16] Moreover, it was similar to the family system employed by Slovaks, Ukrainians, Italians, Serbs and many other Europeans at the same time.

Secondly, in the larger Polish community, variables of regional background, age at time of emigration, and even local occupational structures, divided Poles into categories of behaviour which could not be explained in terms of ethnicity. Thus, those who emigrated latest in life, for instance, were generally more likely to be married, persisters in their new homes, homeowners, and unskilled than fellow Poles who migrated at a younger age and who could afford to be more highly mobile. In fact, the temporary, wage-earning sojourner model which has been employed to characterize many Poles may apply only to younger emigrants and not the entire mass of newcomers.

Beyond ethnicity and other earlier generalizations of Polish behaviour, then, resides the historical complexities of working-class individuals attempting to deal with their cultural inheritance, and the time and space in which they were living. Only when this historical pragmatism supplants the abundance of theoretical constructs will the full story of the Polish immigrant family emerge.

Notes

1. William I. Thomas and Florian Znaniecki, *The Polish Peasant in Europe and America* (5 vols.; Boston, 1920), I, pp. 89-104; II, pp. 1143-63; Frederic M. Thrasher, *The Gang* (Chicago, 1927), p. 218; Sophonisba P. Breckenridge and Edith Abbott, *The Delinquent Child and the Home* (New York, 1917), pp. 289-304.
2. See W. Lloyd Warner, *The Social System of a Modern Community* (New Haven, 1942), *passim.;* Chester A. Jurczak, "Ethnicity, Status, and Generational Positioning, A Study of Health Practices Among Polonians in Five Ethnic Islands," (Ph.D. diss., Univ. of Pittsburgh, 1964); Elizabeth Rooney, "Polish Americans and Family Disorganization," *American Catholic Sociological Review* (March 1957), pp. 48-49; Andrew Greeley, *Ethnicity in the United States, A Preliminary Reconnaissance,* (New York, 1974), pp. 157-76; Edward Wakin and Joseph Shover, *The De-Romanization of the American Catholic Church* (New York, 1966) emphasized the persistence of Polish family life.

3. Victor Greene, *For God and Country, The Rise of Polish and Lithuanian Ethnic Consciousness in America* (Madison, Wisconsin, 1975), p. 27; Helena Znaniecki Lopata, *Polish Americans: Status Competition in an Ethnic Community* (Englewood Cliffs, N.J., 1976), pp. 106-07; Paul Wrobel, *Our Way, Family, Parish, and Neighborhood in a Polish-American Community* (Notre Dame, Ind., 1979), pp. 77-79.

4. Wrobel, *Our Way*, pp. 82-84, 181.

5. American Service Institute Files, file 4, drawer 1, Case 4826, Archives of Industrial Society, University of Pittsburgh.

6. See John Bodnar, "Immigration, Kinship, and the Rise of Working-Class Realism in Industrial America," *Journal of Social History*, (Fall 1980); Sister M. Remigia, *The Polish Immigrant in Detroit to 1914* (Chicago: Polish Roman Catholic Union, 1946), pp. 25-30. U.S. Manuscript Census, 1900, for Scranton revealed 79 per cent of the Russian Poles in coal mining, 48 per cent of the German Poles and 48 per cent of the Austrian Poles.

7. Thomas and Znaniecki, *The Polish Peasant* IV, *passim.*

8. See Bodnar, Michael Weber, and Roger Simon, *Lives of Their Own: Blacks, Italians, and Poles in Pittsburgh, 1900-1960* (Urbana, Ill., 1981), chapters 3 and 4.

9. Interviews with Helen G., Nanticoke, Aug. 3, 1977; Arlene G., Nanticoke, Dec. 11, 1977; Frances B., Plymouth, Sept. 12, 1977. Tapes used in this study are on file at the Pennsylvania Historical and Museum Commission.

10. Interviews with Frances B., Plymouth, Sept. 12, 1977; Lillian N., Nanticoke, July 13, 1977; Rose P., Monessen, March 3, 1977. Steve M., Monessen. See also John Bodnar, "Immigration and Modernization: The Case of Slavic Peasants in Industrial America," *Journal of Social History* 10 (Fall 1976), 44 ff.

11. H. Barry, Irvin Child, and Margaret Bacon, "Relationship of Child Training to Subsistence Economy," *American Anthropologist* 67 (Feb. 1969), pp. 51-63.

12. Interviews with Arlene G., Nanticoke, Dec. 11, 1977; Stella K., Benton Twp., Aug. 17, 1977. Winifred Bolin, "The Economies of Middle-Income Family Life; Working Women During the Great Depression," *Journal of American History* 65 (June 1978), pp. 72-73 suggested that only 15 per cent of all married women worked by 1940 because of the cultural stigma against a working wife. It is possible, however, that marriage seemed a preferable alternative to the drudgery working-class women experienced during adolescence in silk mills and cigar factories.

13. Interview with Lillian N., Nanticoke, July 13, 1977.

14. See Stefan Kieniewicz, *The Emancipation of the Polish Peasantry* (Chicago, 1969), pp. 58-65, 190-94. Prussian areas such as Silesia which were already industrialized supplied almost no immigrants by 1900 partially because surplus labour could be absorbed.

15. See Allen F. Davis and Mark H. Haller, eds., *The Peoples of Philadelphia, A History of Ethnic Groups and Lower-Class Life, 1790-1940* (Philadelphia, 1973); Carolyn Golab, *Immigrant Destination* (Philadelphia, 1977).

16. Interestingly in Scranton, Russian Poles were clustered in mining to a greater extent than Poles from other regions. A full 79 per cent of the Russian Poles were in mining either as contract miners or labourers compared to 48 per cent for the Austrian Poles and 48 per cent for the German Poles. This was probably due to the impact of kinship networks in bringing individuals from Poland into specific, industrial jobs.

The "Serdeczna Matko" of the Sweatshops: Marital and Family Crises of Immigrant Working-Class Women in Late Nineteenth-Century Chicago

Joseph John Parot

"Serdeczna Matko" (Beloved Mother) is certainly one of the most beautiful, moving and cherished of Polish hymns. Sung to the same melody as the religious version of Poland's national anthem ("Boże Coś Polskę"), the hymn has reinforced traditional peasant beliefs as to the natural rhythms of life: all are born of the womb; all must toil for their existence and survival; all must eventually die. Life on this earth, aside from a few moments of true joy, is filled with anguish and grief. The cradle of Bethlehem gives way to the workshop in Nazareth which in turn leads to the road to Jerusalem and inevitably the hill of Calvary. Birth, life, work and death—no one escapes these basic elements of existence. Not even the "Serdeczna Matko" is spared the pain of childbirth, or the humble station of being a carpenter's wife, or the final anguish of witnessing the death, by crucifixion, of her only Son. Thus the heart of the "Serdeczna Matko" is "always open to all," bringing "solace in distress to all her children"; and her undying love, in the end, "triumphs over all grief," leading all "to eternal rest."[1]

In Chicago Polonia, as in Polish settlements throughout the old and new world, the spirit of "Serdeczna Matko" remained at the heart of numerous Marian devotions and continued to inspire thousands of working-class mothers who could easily identify with the mood and theme of the hymn. The *Zbiór Pieśni Nabożnych Katolickich,* a late nineteenth-century collection of religious devotions and songs (published only a few doors away from Chicago's oldest Polish Catholic parish), confirms that "Serdeczna Matko" was a premier Marian hymn.[2] And nearly a century later, when the Roman Catholic Archdiocese of Chicago celebrated the millenium of Polish Christianity, 75,000 communicants at Soldier Field joined in the singing of "Serdeczna Matko" during a dramatic night-time procession in a fitting climax to ceremonies in honour of Our Lady of Czestochowa. The universality of the hymn's appeal and message appeared in every way to correspond to the life experiences of the thousands of women present, many of whom had already lived through, sometimes several times over, the basic life-pattern undergone by their "Serdeczna Matko." From the pangs of childbirth, to the seemingly never ending trials and sorrows associated with lower working-class, urban ghetto life, to the premature death of their children—the women singing this sombre hymn knew deep in their hearts that they were daily assuming the role of a "Serdeczna Matko" in the lives of their families.[3]

Such was especially the case in 1900 Chicago Polonia. It was here, in the sweatshop district adjoining St. Stanislaus Kostka and Holy Trinity parishes, known to inhabitants as "Stanisławowo-Trójcowo," that the role of "Serdeczna Matko" was assumed, in one way or another, by virtually every married woman. It was here where young Polish girls were seldom given the opportunity to finish even a grammar-school education; it was here where young Polish girls, out of cultural background or sheer economic necessity, were hustled into any one of several dozen sweatshops located in the environs of the Milwaukee, Ashland and Division Street "triangle"; it was here where most Polish women "escaped" the exploitation of the shops by settling into rigidly endogamous marriages which, under the best of circumstances, did little to improve material living standards; it was here, in one of the most degrading tenement districts in all of Chicago, that the Polish working-class female experienced the highest fertility rate of any major ethnic group in the city; and it was here where the mortality rate of children born to Polish women exceeded that of any other ethnic group—despite the fact that Chicago had witnessed a declining mortality rate throughout the 1890s and had maintained one of the lowest mortality rates for large cities in the United States in 1900.[4]

Much of the quantitative data and lines of argument in this paper should prove to be of interest to those currently working in the specific genre of women's and/or family history; generally, the evidence presented should serve as a backdrop for the study of a deeply religious community (at least in the institutional sense) as well as for the comparative study of immigrant groups in cities at the turn of the century. The paper draws on variations of current methodology in the field dealing with the complex interrelationship of marital fertility, child mortality, ethnicity, occupation and geographic location in city life. Numerous other variables—household size, educational attainment, marital endogamy and occupational mobility—will be introduced to illustrate the basic life-pattern experienced by Polish women as compared to their ethnic counterparts in Chicago in 1900.[5] Moreover, the evidence, which is based on a comprehensive examination of 5,784 households listed in the manuscript schedules of the twelfth federal census (2,761 Polish households and 3,023 from an "ethnic aggregate" of Italian, Bohemian, Jewish, German and Irish households), will most probably invite the social historian of immigration to re-examine the historiographical shift which has taken place between the time of Handlin's *The Uprooted* (1951) and the views expressed since then by advocates of the so-called New Ethnicity or New Pluralism.[6]

Requirements of space do not permit an in-depth analysis of either the methodology or the final selection of the sample areas which form the foundation of this paper. I have already done this elsewhere.[7] However, I do refer the reader to Maps 1 and 2 and Appendix 1 which pinpoint the geographic and census sample areas. Generally, the geographic area containing the 2,761 Polish households closely and deliberately approximates the target areas selected by pioneer social reformers of the Chicago School at the turn of the century. One such study was the well-publicized City Homes Association Report on *Tenement Conditions in Chicago* (1901); another was a series of articles on immigrant housing conditions compiled by Sophonisba Breckinridge and Edith Abbott and published in the *American Journal of Sociology,* subsequently reissued under the title *The Housing Problem in Chicago* (1910-1915). Both these reports constituted what for that time were the most comprehensive and significant statistical studies on immigrant ghettoes in Chicago. The ten block area (see Map 2), which researchers for both reports felt was most representative of living conditions for Polish immigrants at the time, was located in the heart of Stanisławowo-Trójcowo. Known as the "Polish Downtown" to later Polish settlers in the 1920s, the target area was bounded by Ashland (previously Reuben) Street to the west, Division Street to the south, Noble Street to the east and Blanche Street to the north. The target area was then situated on the east end of the 16th ward in a community area now known as West Town. The City Homes Association Report claimed that this particular Polish settlement was the most densely populated in all Chicago, and perhaps one of the most densely populated urban areas in the United States. In Stanisławowo, house-to-house enumerators placed the average population density at 339.8 persons per acre; in fact, one city block registered 457 persons per acre, which was one of the highest in the city at the time. In order to enable the present-day reader to comprehend the quality of life which would have existed in such congested quarters, the following hypothetical calculation is offered: assuming that the average population density of Stanisławowo were extended over the entire city of Chicago (122,450 acres in the year 1900), the total population of Chicago would have been approximately 41.5 million. In other words, more than the entire population of post-World War

Map 1: Major Sample Areas

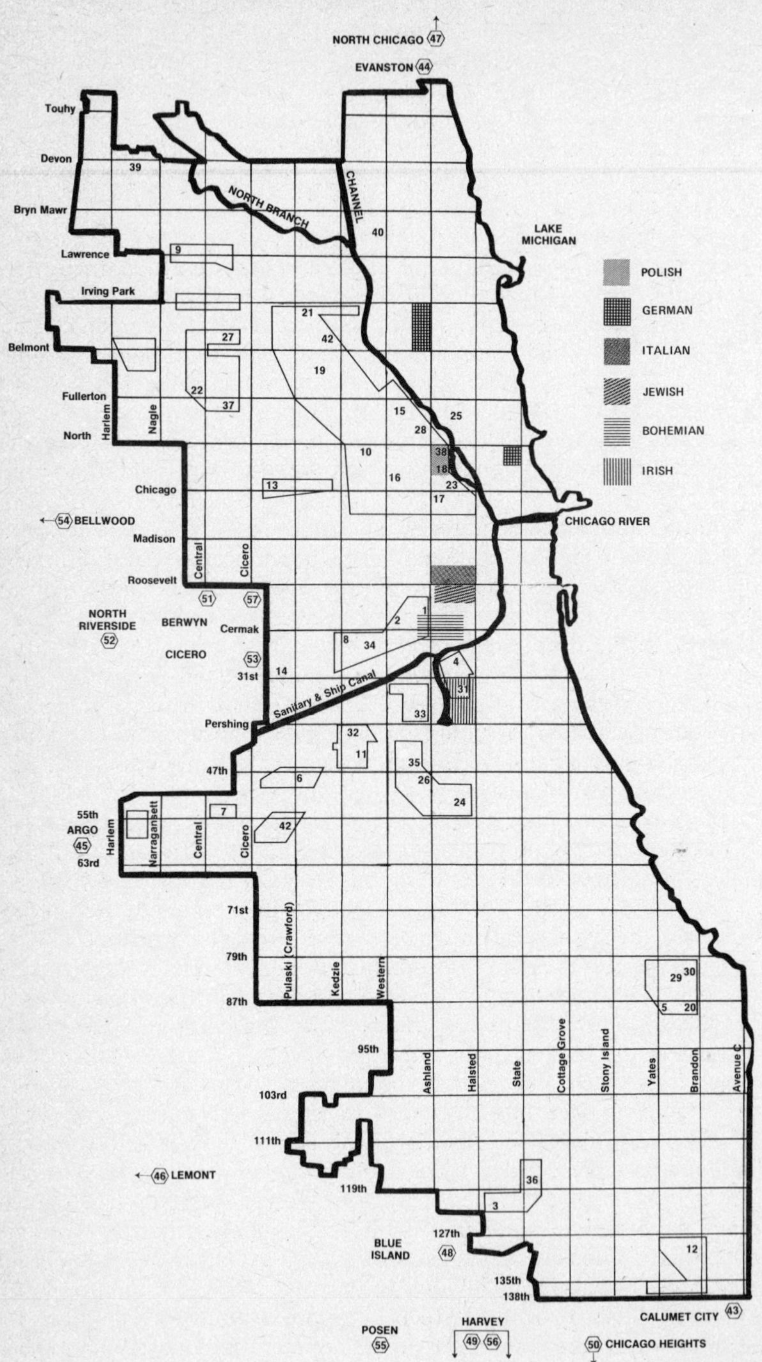

Map 2: Chicago Polonia: Census Sample Area including Ten Block Polish District Canvassed in City Homes Association Report

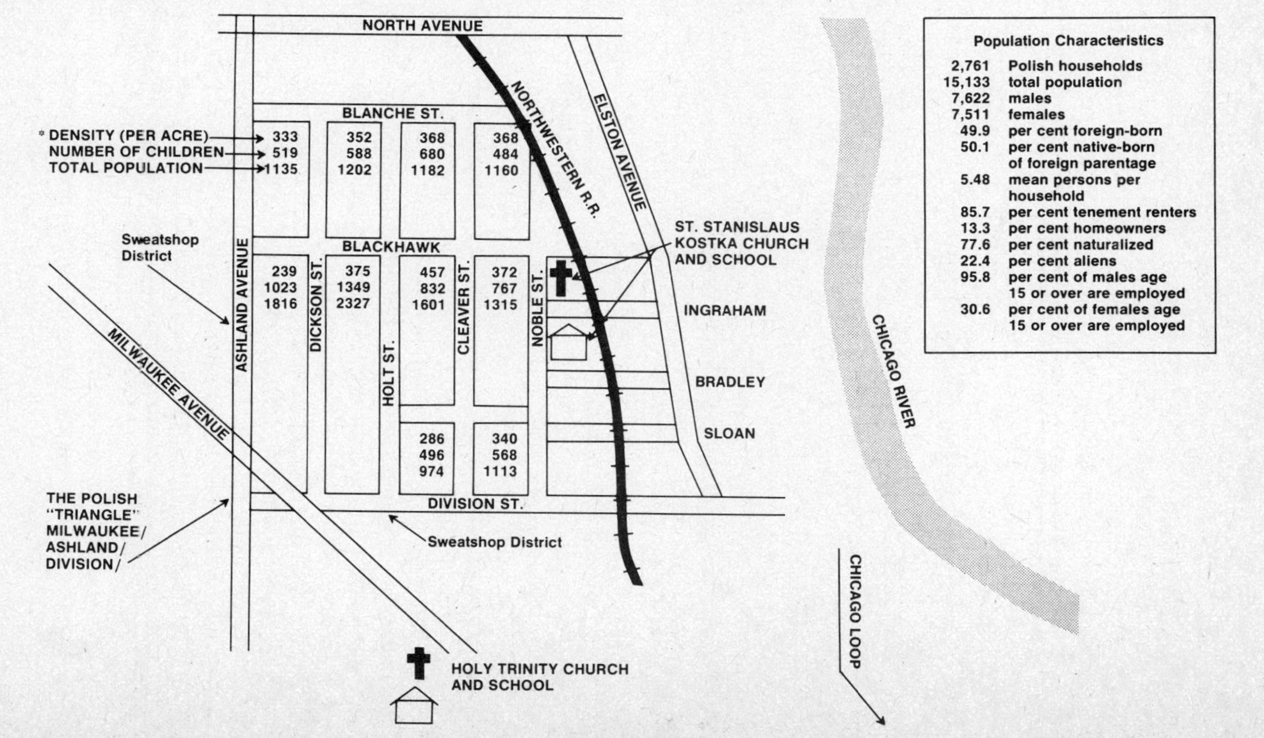

* These three designations also apply (in the same sequence) to all columns of numbers appearing on this map.

Two Poland would had to have been packed into the city limits of 1900 Chicago to equal the density in Stanisławowo![8]

The remaining target areas in the sample include the following (see Appendix 1): the Jewish settlement in the Maxwell Street/Hull House area in Ward 8 of the West Side community area; the "Little Italy" area in Ward 19 immediately adjacent to the Jewish settlement; the Bohemian neighbourhood known as Pilsen in Ward 9 of the Lower West Side community area; the Irish settlement in Ward 6 of the Bridgeport community area; and, finally, the German community in Lakeview in Ward 26 on the city's far north side.[9]

From Childhood to the Sweatshop

The evidence for Polish female participation in the garment trades and in the sweating system in Chicago at the turn of the century is conclusive. On a city-wide basis, 7,258 (or 38.7 per cent of all Polish females who were employed) worked in the garment trades as tailoresses, seamstresses, dressmakers or glovemakers. Moreover, another 527 (7.3 per cent) worked as laundresses and laundry workers, many of them living close by the sweatshops. If one includes all other auxiliary garment trade occupations or functions (e.g., laundry workers, finishers, pressers), nearly half of the Polish female workforce in 1900 Chicago can be included under the overall occupational rubric known as the garment trades. Of the remaining half of the Polish female workforce, 927 were employed in domestic service, 449 in tobacco and cigar work, 319 in sales work, 202 in common labour, 147 in clerical work, 113 in meat or fruit packing, and 102 in miscellaneous packing. Only 1.7 per cent could be classified as "professionals": census enumerators tabulated 94 teachers (most of whom were teaching nuns), 19 "musicians" and 12 "miscellaneous professionals." All told, in addition to the fledgling professional class, 58.9 per cent were employed in manufacturing (a category which included the sizable garment trades category); 25.2 per cent were engaged in the domestic services; 11.7 per cent in trade and transportation; and 2.5 per cent in miscellaneous occupations.[10] In the 2,761 household target sample area in Stanisławowo, the total "employable" female population (ages 15 to 69 in this study) came to 3,918; of this number, 1,198 women (or 23.2 per cent) were actually employed, 712 of them in the garment trades. Thus the evidence clearly indicates that for Polish female workers the garment trade was the major source of employment, and that the trade was centred in the sweatshop district of Stanisławowo-Trójcowo.[11]

A reliable contemporary study of the sweating system in Chicago pinpointed the location of at least sixteen sweatshops along

Division and Dickson Streets, where Polish females were employed: eight of these shops manufactured coats; six manufactured pants; and two produced cloaks and suits. Footpower was used in all but three of the shops (two had steam and one had gas-powered equipment). The sixteen shops employed at least 150 "adult" females and 37 girls under sixteen years of age; nearly all of the workers were paid by the piece. Wages for operators ranged between $3.14 to $5.73 per week; handworkers averaged $2.05 per week; pressers as high as $4.88 per week; and home finishers (who were in the majority), only $1.63 per week. The overall weekly wage for Polish females came to $3.14 per week (a fifty-hour week of five ten-hour days), or approximately 6.2 cents per hour (four of the sixteen shops required the women to work more than ten hours per day). Working conditions in the shops were hardly conducive to high morale, good health or even moderate productivity. Two of the shops were quartered in basements, three were reported to be "near stables," and one "deserved no better name than a barn, and that not a neat or sweet-smelling one." Lighting in the shops was generally poor, conditions were on the whole described as "filthy," and ventilation, especially in the winter, was "dreadful," because windows were kept tightly closed to conserve heat and firewood.[12] The report also noted that Polish women were paid significantly less than neighbouring Jewish, Bohemian and Swedish counterparts, who were averaging $3.75, $3.82 and $4.46 per week respectively. This differential between Polish and Swedish wages in the sweatshops—amounting to about $65.00 per year—was in 1900 dollars equivalent to ten months' rent on the average apartment dwelling in Stanisławowo. But investigators for the report blamed the Polish girls for this wage differential: "They were afraid to go away from home," and hence were "at the mercy of the nearest competitor." Furthermore, the report stated that the Polish girl was "held fast in the fetters of her religion and her ignorance."[13]

An examination of school attendance figures listed in the census manuscript schedules (see Table 1) demonstrates clearly the correlation between inadequate schooling for Polish females, especially in the lower primary grade years, and their subsequent occupational immobility:

Table 1: School Attendance for Polish and Other Ethnic Females Ages 5-19 in Chicago, 1900

Age group	Total females		Total attending school		Per cent attending	
	Polish	Ethnic	Polish	Ethnic	Polish	Ethnic
5-9	1187	1109	311	454	26.2	40.9
10-14	997	793	683	524	68.5	66.1
15-19	818	695	73	68	8.9	9.8
Total	3002	2597	1067	1046	35.5	40.3

This evidence suggests that Polish girls were "late starters" in the educational process (three out of every four girls were not even attending school in the kindergarten/grade three levels); that when Polish girls finally did enter school, at roughly age nine or ten, they were in all probability only beginning in first grade; and that very few went on to high school (which was also true for girls from other ethnic groups as well). Moreover, only 35.5 per cent of all Polish females in 1900 were even attending school, less than the percentage attending in 1870 or 1880 (43.1 per cent and 41.4 per cent, respectively).[14] The data on school attendance, then, are in inverse proportion to the number of Polish females entering the sweating system. Without the basic rudiments of literacy taught in the elementary school years and lacking some of the more advanced clerical skills taught in secondary schools at the time, young Polish girls, as the report claimed, were forced "to stay close to home" and risk exploitation in the shops.[15]

The census aggregates for Stanisławowo-Trójcowo and the other five immigrant communities in our sample also reveal that virtually the entire female immigrant workforce was made up of unmarried women. The only significant exception to this generalization has to do with the higher proportion of married women in the Bohemian community in Pilsen who were engaged in the domestic services. The data in Table 2 are, of course, subject to various other interpretations. However, it is likely that marriage may indeed have been used as an avenue of escape from the squalor, exploitation and boredom of the sweatshop. Moreover, when one correlates this "escape factor" to the high fertility rate in Polonia (discussed later), one might even hazard the interpreta-

Table 2: Breakdown of Married and Unmarried Females Employed in Chicago by Nationality, 1900

Category	Polish	Italian	Jewish	Bohemian	German	Irish
Total no. wives	2450	722	456	456	615	548
Total wives employed	46	0	3	42	4	5
Per cent employed	1.9	0.0	0.6	9.2*	0.6	0.9
Per cent unemployed	98.1	100.0	99.4	91.8	99.4	99.1
Total female work-force (ages 15-69)	3918	744	756	746	869	1016
Unmarried females (age 15 and over)	1553	28	308	306	254	468
Unmarried females age 15+ employed	1152	21	178	262	132	250
Per cent unmarried females employed	74.2	75.0	57.8	85.6	52.0	53.4
Per cent unmarried females unemployed	25.8	25.0	42.2	14.4	48.0	46.4

*Figure includes housekeepers; 2.0 per cent excluding housekeepers.

tion that Polish women viewed each pregnancy as some sort of "guarantee" against ever again returning to the sweatshops.[16] After all, when one observes that a sweatshop force of 712 women contained only 23 married women (3.2 per cent of the total), one is forced to accept at least one conclusion: Polish women, for whatever reasons, once married did not return to the sweatshops.

Endogamous Dating and Marriage in Polonia

Ever since Ruby Jo Reeves Kennedy published her study of marital endogamy and the "triple melting pot" process on New Haven (1953), the subject has remained of some interest to sociologists and social historians, perhaps because of prevailing theories that endogamous marriages are related to family stability and low divorce rates.[17] In any event, the evidence—quantitative and otherwise—points to the fact that marital endogamy was not only a prized ideal in Chicago Polonia but was also universally realized. In a contemporary editorial on the subject, the *Dziennik Chicagoski* went so far as to list *twenty* "Precautions for Catholics Who Wish To Marry A Person Of Another Nationality." The twenty "commandments," which some scholars today might view with a certain amount of humour and charm, were by 1900 standards intended in all seriousness. The editor-publishers of the *Dziennik Chicagoski* (most of whom were priests belonging to the Congregation of the Resurrection) immediately made it clear to all engaged couples in Polonia that endogamy not only meant marrying within one's nationality group but also within one's religion and socio-economic class. Young couples were told to marry within the Catholic faith because "God will not recognize you without your religion." Another command stipulated that one "ought choose a person from his or her own class," and that it was far better "to choose a person rather poor but energetic rather than a rich person who is lazy; rather a faithful person than an elegant brute; rather a sober workman than a drunken master." Polonia's young ladies were also warned "not to seek earthly pleasures, but to strive for eternal and lasting joy," for "the rearing of children was the true path to heaven." Other admonitions cautioned against choosing a mate "while drinking or dancing" or "marrying for money." On the other hand, all young men were advised "to stay away from widows or divorcees."[18] The *Naród Polski,* official newspaper of the Polish Roman Catholic Union, was even more crude regarding the subject of endogamy. The paper lashed out at young Polish girls who "went strolling around the city, lingering at hotels of questionable character, and frequenting all kinds of Venetian gardens in the company of the worst type, young Jews, Greeks and other underworld scum."[19] The *Naród Polski* also waged war against attendance at the cinema, for movies were said to be "ruinous of good morals," and against dancing, which the paper claimed brought about "tireless exertion, quite often injurious to health ... especially to young girls squeezed tightly into corsets" which caused "the blood to become overheated, the heart to beat faster, and the lungs to expand." This was said to be the cause "of common fainting spells and even sudden death of tightly laced dancers."[20] To anxious parents concerned about the physical and moral health of dating couples, the advice of the *Naród Polski* was clear and simple: "Teenagers should be at home at 8 p.m. at the latest, either reading or doing something useful."[21]

The Polish press never tired in its campaign to uphold traditional old world values during the courtship years. Maintaining that endogamous dating and marriage was not only good common sense but also a preserver of good morals, the Polish press invariably would draw comparisons between "American" and good "Polish" girls: if "American girls" were "intelligent and businesslike," they were also said to be "too flirtateous" and prone to "overly-long engagements"; by contrast, "Polish girls" were described as "modest and bashful, clean, industrious, guardians of the home and having few divorces."[22] The Polish Catholic community-parish network in Chicago, so as to assist in safeguarding the moral character of working-class girls, even made several attempts to institutionalize what was commonly thought to be a unique and superior value system (at least from the Polish community's standpoint). At St. Stanislaus Kostka parish, for example, the Society of the Virgins of the Holy Rosary was organized in the early years of that parish so that the virtue of chastity before marriage received its due emphasis. The Holy Rosary Society evolved into a model for more than three dozen subsequent Polish parishes in the archdiocese of Chicago. Moreover, the Sisters of the Holy Family of Nazareth established a home on West Division Street, not far from the parish church, so as to assist young working girls during the traumatic adolescent years, who could be found on tenement street corners everywhere in overpopulated Chicago Polonia.[23]

As Table 3 indicates, the campaign for endogamy, at least in the 1900 census year, was overwhelmingly successful. The strong endogamous character of Polish marriages and family life is statistically evident and did indeed contribute to an almost nonexistent divorce rate. But then the same could be said for surrounding white-ethnic groups in nearby areas, who may have achieved the same results without trying as hard.

Birth, Life and Death in Polonia

In none of the census variables introduced in this study was there greater and more significant variance between the Poles and other immigrant groups in Chicago than in the differing fertility and mortality rates and in the composition and size of immigrant

Table 3: Selected Marriage and Family Characteristics, Polish Group and Combined Ethnic Group Samples

Category	Polish Sample	Combined Ethnic Sample
Total households	2761	3023
Households headed by member of said nationality	2753	2912
Per cent households headed by member of said nationality	99.7	96.3
Total marriages*	2450	2797
Endogamous marriages	2438	2641
Per cent endogamous	99.5	94.4
Mean years married	14.68	13.77
Total no. widowed	346	449
Total no. divorced	4	7
Distribution married (%)	87.5	86.0
– widowed	12.4	13.8
– divorced	0.1	0.2

* Excludes married couples in which one spouse resided in the United States and the other in the mother country.

households. It is the study of these particular factors that leads us to contend that virtually every married woman in Chicago Polonia assumed the role of "Serdeczna Matko."

The methodology for computing fertility rates and women-to-children ratios is varied and complex. Each method had its particular advantages and drawbacks. Several scholars in recent studies have utilized the method of determining the number of children per household in attempts to explain differing fertility rates; others have fallen back on the method which computes the total number of children per 1,000 women reporting (to census enumerators). Yasukichi Yasuba, in his study of birth rates among the white population of the United States between 1800 and 1860, devised an index based on the number of children under ten years of age per 1,000 women ages 16-44 (as well as per 1,000 adult white population) to determine fertility. But of the several techniques at the disposal of social historians and demographers today, the most adequate method is the one devised by Grabill, and further refined by Harevan and Vinovskis, which utilizes as a base the number of children under age five per 1,000 women ages 20-49.[24]

For our purposes here, we will use variations of the Yasuba-Grabill-Harevan methodology by calculating the number of children under age five, under ten and under fifteen per 1,000 women ages 20-49 in each of our sample areas. Finally, we will also compute the total number of children ever born per 1,000 married women reporting. By offering statistical data via each of these respectable methods, it is believed that more accurate generalizations and comparisons as to the fertility rates of Polish, Italian, Jewish, Bohemian, German and Irish women will have been presented.[25]

An examination of the data in Table 4 shows that the Polish women maintained the highest fertility rate, followed in descending order by Italian, Jewish, Bohemian, German and Irish women. With the single (and slight) exception via the Grabill method, whereby Italian women recorded a greater number of children under five, the Polish women of Stanisławowo-Trójcowo registered what was most probably the highest fertility rate in Chicago at the turn of the century. Not only that, when the index which computes the total number of children *ever born* per 1,000 married women is introduced (see Tables 4 and 5), the Polish women are by far the highest of our six sample ethnic groups;[26] furthermore, the overall distribution of large Polish families and households (with six or more children) is significantly greater than for all the other ethnic groups (see Tables 5 and 6). And even more surprising is the fact that Polish mothers in four out of every five households were forced to care for these large families without any support outside the nulcear family (Table 7). On the other hand, the alleged "lodger problem"—with all its potential for disruption of "normal" Polish family life—may have been vastly overstated, at least by sources contemporary to 1900 Chicago Polonia.[27]

On the whole, this study, given its scope and limitations, does indeed support several findings of Harevan and Vinovskis in their study of immigrant family life in South Boston in the late nineteenth century. For one, the data for Chicago demonstrate that ethnicity was a prominent factor in the determination of fertility rates, and that high fertility rates, as Harevan and Vinovskis have concluded, was due to the "persistence of premigration customs and values," both among first-generation immigrants and native-born women of foreign parentage. Secondly, women whose husbands were engaged in the upper-middle class professional occupations in 1900 tended toward lower fertility than women whose husbands worked in the garment trades or as common labourers (correlations of marital, family and occupational characteristics for Chicago Polonia clearly show that the most common form of marriage was that between an unskilled male and a female working in the sweating system). Thirdly, age and the foreign-born character of the Polish were also significant factors: the mean age of Polish women in Stanisławowo-Trójcowo was only 15.4 as against the five-group sample of 18.1; moreover, 81.4 per cent of the Polish sample arrived in the United States after 1880, and in 1900, 49.7 per cent of the Polish population was still foreign-born. Thus a younger female population which retained strong premigration values would tend toward higher fertility.[28]

Finally, although space does not permit in-depth analysis of the matter, it must be remembered that the practice of birth

Table 4: Comparative Fertility Rates for Women from Selected Ethnic Groups in Chicago (1900 census fertility indexes)

	Polish (N=2634)*	Italian (N=560)	Jewish (N=503)	German (N=637)	Bohemian (N=511)	Irish (N=730)
No. of children under 5 years per 1,000 women 20-49 (adjusted)	1003	1065	911	721	717	596
	Polish (N=2634)	Italian (N=560)	Jewish (N=503)	German (N=637)	Bohemian (N=511)	Irish (N=730)
No. of children under 10 years per 1,000 women 20-49 (adjusted)	1891	1883	1769	1451	1482	1192
	Polish (N=3190)	Italian (N=650)	Jewish (N=588)	German (N=764)	Bohemian (N=603)	Irish (N=861)
No. of children under 15 years per 1,000 women 20 and over (adjusted)	2167	2028	2020	1700	1813	1423
	Polish (N=2714)	Italian (N=660)	Jewish (N=513)	German (N=654)	Bohemian (N=487)	Irish (N=623)
No. of children ever born per 1,000 married women (adjusted)	5811	4066	4709	3920	3780	4059

*N refers to the total number of women or married women in the table, not the total number of children.

Table 5: Children Born to All Married Women in Selected Sample Areas Reporting to Census Enumerators in Chicago, 1900

Number of Children	Mothers/Married Women–Aggregate				Mothers/Married Women–Per cent		
	Polish (N=2714)	Ethnic Total (N=2927)	Sample Total (N=5641)		Polish (N=2714)	Ethnic (N=2927)	Sample (N=5641)
0 Children	128	267	395		4.72	9.12	7.00
1	250	374	624		9.21	12.78	11.06
2	222	412	634		8.18	14.07	11.24
3	236	348	584		8.70	11.89	10.35
4	263	372	635		9.69	12.71	11.26
5	238	268	506		8.77	9.16	8.97
6	224	259	483		8.25	8.85	8.56
7	234	177	411		8.62	6.05	7.29
8	247	168	415		9.10	5.74	7.36
9	232	98	330		8.55	3.35	5.85
10	148	81	229		5.45	2.77	4.06
11	99	41	140		3.65	1.40	2.48
12	96	33	129		3.54	1.13	2.29
13	46	14	60		1.69	0.47	1.06
14	29	9	38		1.07	0.31	0.67
15	15	2	17		0.55	0.07	0.30
16+	7	4	11		0.26	0.13	0.20
Total children	15,772	12,148	27,920	Mean	5.81	4.15	4.95
				Median	5.09	3.17	3.92

NOTE: The ethnic total includes the Italian, Jewish, Bohemian, German and Irish mothers/married women. The sample total combines the Ethnic and Polish totals.

Table 6: Household Size of Ethnic Groups in Chicago, 1900 Census

Household Size	Polish Aggregate	Polish %	Ethnic Aggregate	Ethnic %	Sample Aggregate	Sample %
Households – 1 person	59	2.14	59	1.95	118	2.04
Households – 2 persons	275	9.96	355	11.74	630	10.89
Households – 3 persons	341	12.35	471	15.58	812	14.04
Households – 4 persons	383	13.87	535	17.70	918	15.87
Households – 5 persons	413	14.96	481	15.91	894	15.46
Households – 6 persons	386	13.98	422	13.96	808	13.97
Households – 7 persons	336	12.17	283	9.36	619	10.70
Households – 8 persons	249	9.02	210	6.95	459	7.94
Households – 9 persons	152	5.51	106	3.51	258	4.46
Households – 10 persons	100	3.62	55	1.82	155	2.68
Households – 11 persons	42	1.52	26	0.86	68	1.18
Households – 12 persons	16	0.58	10	0.33	26	0.44
Households – 13 persons	3	0.11	6	0.20	9	0.15
Households – 14 persons	2	0.07	2	0.07	4	0.07
Households – 15 persons	0	0.00	1	0.03	1	0.02
Households – 16 + persons	4*	0.14	1†	0.03	5	0.09
Total households	2,761	100.00	3,023	100.00	5,784	100.00
Persons per household-mean	5.48		4.89		5.20	
Persons per household-median	4.78		4.19		4.47	

* Four Polish households over 16 persons include 2 convents, 1 school and 1 rectory.
†One Irish household over 16 persons includes 1 convent.

Table 7: Composition and Distribution of Extended Families for Selected Ethnic Groups in Chicago, 1900

Ethnic group	Total households	Total families/ marriages	Families/with mother or mother-in-law	Families/with father or father-in-law	Families/with brother or sister	Families/with in-laws or other relatives	Families/with boarders, lodgers, non-family members
Polish	2761	2450	118	33	90	149	416
Italian	649	722	26	11	49	97	233
Jewish	510	456	15	5	14	31	101
Bohemian	531	456	3	1	3	28 (est.)	70
German	663	615	30	11	11	60	95
Irish	670	548	16	12	62	81	118

Ethnic group	Number of nuclear/ extended families		% total families extended	% total households extended	% extended families with kin	% extended household/ non-kin
	Nuclear	Extended				
Polish	1909	541	19.6	22.1	48.4	51.6
Italian	509	213	29.5	32.8	44.0	56.0
Jewish	358	98	21.5	19.2	39.2	60.8
Bohemian	378	78	17.1	14.7	33.3	66.7
German	488	127	20.7	19.2	54.1	45.9
Irish	388	160	29.2	23.9	59.2	40.8

NOTE: The total number of persons, kinfolk and otherwise, exceeds the total number of extended families since many households/families contained more than one individual beyond the nuclear family. In this regard, the mean number of persons beyond the immediate nuclear family in the respective extended families by ethnic group was as follows: POLISH–1.49; ITALIAN–1.95; JEWISH–1.69; BOHEMIAN–1.35; GERMAN–1.63; IRISH–1.81. In other words, the Italian, Irish and Jewish households contained larger extended families than the German, Polish or Bohemian. As for lodgers and/or non-family boarders, the ratio of lodgers to total households was highest in the Italian sample (35.9:100), followed by the Jewish (19.8:100); Irish (17.6:100); Polish (15.1:100); German (14.3:100) and Bohemian households (13.2:100).

control and abortion among Polish and other immigrant Catholics was universally condemned as morally reprehensible. The *Dziennik Zjednoczenia* was perhaps speaking for the entire Polish Catholic community when in its editorial pages it attacked proponents of birth control as spreading "murderous propaganda." The same paper argued that birth control "was the talk of fools" and proved "the idiotism of Socialist doctrine." Artificial methods were said "to ruin the health of both individuals, above all the woman's," and the paper concluded that "women who live the longest are those having a natural number of children."[29]

But the most startling finding of this study, and the one that most lends itself to the theme of "Serdeczna Matko," has to do with widely varying mortality rates in the respective sample areas. One might even conclude that the same variables affecting high fertility—ethnicity, occupation, socio-economic class, foreign-born composition, and location in the city—were also powerful determinants as to the death of children. For when one computes the number of children who died (children here does not necessarily mean *young* children) for every 1,000 women, the death rate in the Polish district was by far the highest, followed in descending order by the mortality rate in the Italian, German, Irish, Jewish and Bohemian families (see Table 8 and corresponding graph). Finally, Table 9 shows the mortality rate for age-specific categories of Polish women.

The abnormally high mortality rate in Chicago Polonia at the turn of the century, of course, calls for some explanation. After all, the city of Chicago had one of the lowest mortality rates for large cities in 1900. Equally disturbing is the fact that the mortality rate in Chicago had been steadily declining in each successive year between 1891 and 1901, while at the same time the death rate in Stanisławowo was rising to nearly three times the city-wide average.

Table 8: Child Mortality Rates for Selected Ethnic Groups in Sample Areas in Chicago (1900 census)

Ethnic group	Children ever born	Children alive, 1900	Total deaths	Total women reporting	Deaths per 1,000 women
Polish	15,772	10,003	5,769	2,714	2,128
Italian	2,684	1,741	943	660	1,428
German	2,566	1,858	708	654	1,082
Irish	2,521	1,897	624	623	1,001
Jewish	2,416	1,903	513	513	1,000
Bohemian	1,841	1,559	282	487	579
Total including Polish	27,800	18,960	8,840	5,681	1,557
Total excluding Polish	12,028	8,958	3,070	2,967	1,034

Table 9: Death Rate of Children of Polish and Polish American Mothers

Age-specific category (age of mother)	Number of children who died: 0	1	2	3	4	5	6	7	8	9	10	11	12	More than 12
15-19	18	2	1	—	—	—	—	—	—	—	—	—	—	—
20-29	352	189	78	29	9	1	—	—	1	—	—	—	—	—
30-39	216	195	161	126	62	32	23	6	13	3	—	1	1	—
40-49	70	88	119	82	76	55	40	26	17	8	3	2	—	4
50-59	40	24	44	26	35	29	15	17	7	3	6	1	3	1
60-69	33	15	18	25	21	20	10	10	8	2	1	4	—	—
70+	23	1	7	6	8	6	4	5	3	5	—	2	—	—
	752	514	428	294	211	143	92	64	49	21	10	10	4	5

Age category	Total mothers	Mothers losing no children	Mothers losing one or more children	Total no. children who died	Mean no. of children dead per mother
15-19	21 (100.0)	18 (85.7)	3 (14.3)	4	1.33
20-29	659 (100.0)	352 (53.4)	307 (46.6)	481	1.57
30-39	839 (100.0)	216 (25.7)	623 (74.3)	1637	2.63
40-49	590 (100.0)	70 (11.9)	520 (88.1)	1890	3.63
50-59	251 (100.0)	40 (15.9)	211 (84.1)	891	4.22
60-69	167 (100.0)	33 (19.8)	134 (80.2)	576	4.30
70+	70 (100.0)	23 (32.9)	47 (67.1)	245	5.21
Total	2707 (100.0)	752 (29.0)	1845 (71.0)	5724*	3.12

* Forty-five deaths were unaccounted for in the total sample due to difficulties in deciphering census manuscript schedules.

Fertility/Mortality Rates* for Selected Immigrant Groups in Chicago, 1900

Per cent ever born who died	Polish	Italian	German	Irish	Jewish	Bohemian	Mean (excl. Poles)	Mean (incl. Poles)
	36.6	35.1	27.6	24.7	21.2	15.6	25.3	31.7

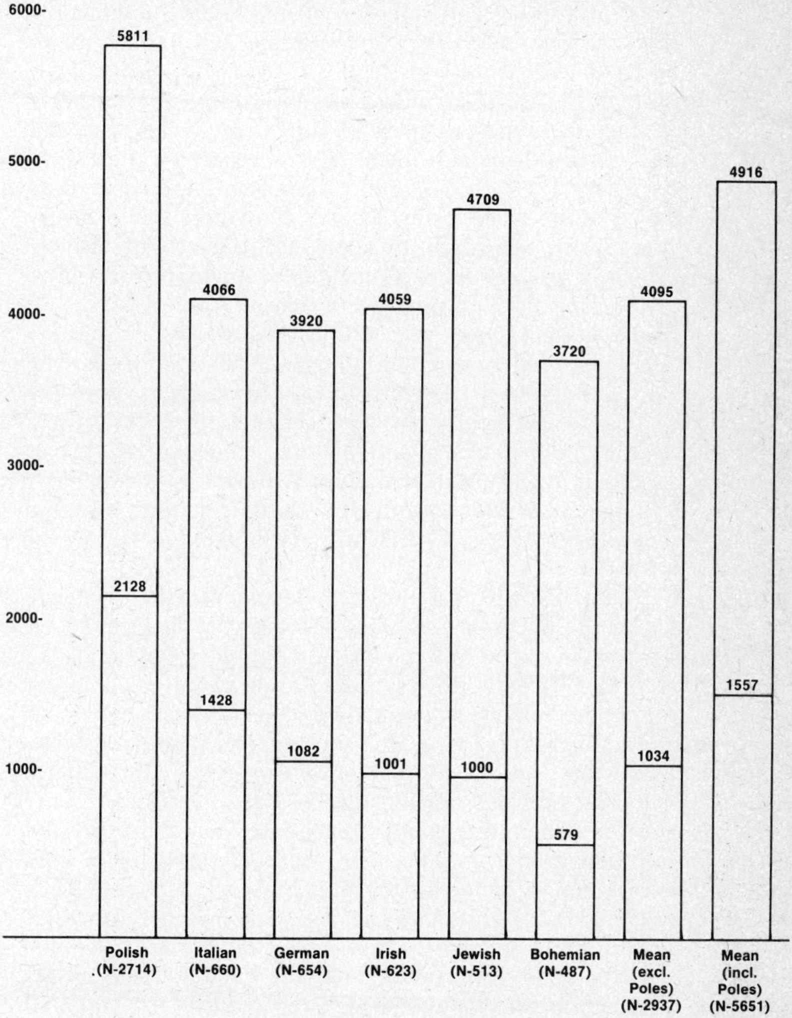

* Fertility Rate (higher figure): Number of children ever born per 1,000 mothers reporting.
Mortality Rate (lower figure): Number of children who died per 1,000 mothers reporting.

Several scientific studies done during this period offer the social historian reliable evidence for the widely varying child mortality rates in cities (or in different sections of the same city). One extensive symposium on the subject, published in 1908, concluded that the quality of milk available in cities was a significant factor; more numerous inspection of milk dairies, milk containers and the methods of milking and shipping of milk were subsequently called for.[30] A year later, *The Survey* published another major study—based on the causes of death of 44,226 infants in New York, Boston, Philadelphia and Chicago—which offered additional evidence in support of the bad milk theory. The study did note, however, that "where artificial food is concerned, ignorance and carelessness are no doubt more important influences than bad milk." This investigation concluded that three out of every four infant deaths were due to acute gastro-intestinal disease, acute respiratory disease and congenital or premature debility; but bad nutrition and high population density were also thought to be of greater significance than was earlier believed.[31] A study of working class mothers in London in the 1880-1914 period (the peak years of southern and eastern European immigration to the United States) also supports the view that infant mortality was directly related to high density urban life; inadequate forms of sewage disposal; artificial rather than breast-feeding; the employment of pregnant women during the third trimester; and the alleged general ignorance of working-class mothers in matters of child care.[32]

As for Stanisławowo, the most convincing primary evidence which speaks to the issue of child mortality is the report on *Tenement Conditions in Chicago* (1901), mentioned earlier. In the ten-block area of the northwest side Polish ghetto then under investigation, the matter of population density was singled out among numerous other causes for the high mortality rate. The report stated that the density in Stanisławowo was "three times that of the most crowded portions of Tokyo, Calcutta and many Asian cities." Enumerators going from house to house expressed their astonishment and bewilderment when they tabulated a total of 7,306 children in the ten-block area; in fact, one city block alone contained 1,349 children. The persistent practice of subdividing already small apartments into even smaller ones (from 400 square feet back to 250 square feet was commonplace) only served to increase the population density as well as compound any number of sanitation problems. Fresh air, lighting, and sewage and toilet facilities were found to be totally inadequate. Moreover, the dependence upon outdoor privy vaults for toilets and upon streetside manure boxes (which could be easily opened by any child) for storage of human and animal waste was directly related to various impure water and sewage-related diseases (Stanisławowo had an *average* of twenty manure boxes per city block!). And summer downpours backed up an already dilapidated sewer system which forced up raw sewage into the 556 basement apartments in the area. Investigators also noted that some of the transplanted rural-to-urban Polish peasants housed cattle *indoors.* Not only that, the haphazard schedule of garbage pick-up in the area also forced tenement dwellers to store garbage in the narrow causeways between buildings, which, of course, became breeding grounds for rats. On the whole, the City Homes Association Report of 1901 was not only a severe indictment of immigrant housing conditions but also one of the most significant contemporary explanations of the high mortality rate in Chicago Polonia.[33]

Conclusion

A substantial body of literature has evolved in scholarly journals as to the unhappy conclusions and predictions made by Thomas and Znaniecki in their classic study of the Polish peasant and Polish family life in America.[34] Those of us who have followed this long debate already know that the predicted breakdown of the Polish family in the second generation did not occur. Instead, even during the crisis years of the Great Depression, Polish family life was known for its remarkable overall stability, low divorce rate, and low delinquency and crime rates. On the other hand, despite the fact that the second-generation Polish family rose from the socio-economic ashes of the 1930s, the evidence presented here indeed leads one to believe that the original predictions made by Thomas and Znaniecki were based on a firm foundation. But due to the incredible tenacity, courage and spirit of thousands of unknown "Beloved Mothers" in Polonia—who in birth, work, life and death enabled their families to survive a most traumatic immigrant period—massive social deterioration never did occur. In the face of every conceivable social, economic and psychological adversity in 1900 Chicago—occupational exploitation; a skyrocketing birth rate; horrendously poor living conditions in the home, even for the slums of that era; and with death staring in the face of every woman who conceived—the "Serdeczna Matko of the Sweatshops" defied the odds and all social prognostications by somehow managing to persevere, even when there was precious little hope for the present or the future. At this point, the social historian must lay down his statistical tables and search for an entirely different brand of evidence to supply answers to questions of a largely religious nature. Immediately he will come to note that of the 144 parish societies founded at St. Stanislaus Kostka and Holy Trinity parishes between 1867 and 1918, at least 44 were specifically designed to meet the spiritual and emotional needs of immigrant women. The study of these Polish immigrant women's organizations may tell us the rest of the story.[35]

Notes

1. The hymn "Serdeczna Matko" is eight stanzas, four lines each, in length. The quotations come from my translation of various phrases in the song. For a complete text, see *Zbiór Pieśni Nabożnych Katolickich Do Użytku Kościelnego i Domowego* [Collection of Catholic Hymns for Church and Home Use] (Chicago: Polish American Publishing Company, n.d. but with imprimatur dated July 13, 1868), *Pieśn I* under section *O Niepokalanem Sercu Najśw. Maryi Panny* [Song Number I dedicated to the Immaculate Heart of the Virgin Mary], pp. 556-57.
2. See Ibid.
3. Program Souvenir entitled *Poland's Millenium of Christianity; Chicagoland Observance, Soldier Field, August 28, 1966* (Chicago: Roman Catholic Archdiocese of Chicago, 1966). The souvenir pamphlet (34 pp.) contains the entire program for the evening celebration. Also see the *Chicago Tribune,* August 29, 1966, pp. 1-2, for an account of the festivities and attendance at the solemn high mass.
4. These were some of the preliminary conclusions I reached in a paper entitled "Immigrant Labor and the Paradox of Pluralism in American Urban Society, 1860-1930: A Comparative Study and Census Analysis of Polish, German, Irish, Bohemian, Italian and Jewish Workers in Chicago," pp. 1-75, submitted to the Congress of Scholars of Polish Descent at the Jagiellonian University, Kracow, Poland, July 21-24, 1979. See Appendix 1 of this paper for a detailed breakdown of the census sample for census enumeration districts, ward numbers, community area designations from the Chicago Community Area Inventory, and roll numbers and pagination for the respective Polish, Irish, German, Bohemian, Italian and Jewish tracts as derived from the United States Census Bureau, *Federal Population Census Manuscript Schedules, Twelfth U.S. Census, 1900: Illinois, City of Chicago.* Hereafter cited as *FPCMS, Chicago, 1900.*
5. For example, see Tamara K. Harevan and Maris A. Vinovskis, "Marital Fertility, Ethnicity, and Occupation in Urban Families: An Analysis of South Boston and the South End in 1880," *Journal of Urban History* I (1975), pp. 293-315, for a detailed analysis of recent methodology having to do with fertility rates in the nineteenth century. For work on the nuclear and extended family, see Myfanwy Morgan and Hilda H. Golden, "Immigrant Families in an Industrial City: A Study of Households in Holyoke, 1880," *Journal of Family History* 4 (Spring 1979), pp. 59-68.
6. For a fuller treatment of this debate, see the bibliographic essay by Rudolph J. Vecoli, "European Americans: From Immigrants to Ethnics," in William H. Cartwright and Richard L. Watson (eds.), *The Reinterpretation of American History and Culture* (Washington, D.C.: National Council for the Social Studies, 1973), pp. 81-112. And for a sharper delineation of the debate between the New Pluralism and Handlin's Uprooted thesis, see Rudolph J. Vecoli, "Contadini in Chicago: A Critique of The Uprooted," *Journal of American History* 51 (December 1964), pp. 404-17.
7. Parot, "Immigrant Labor," pp. 28-37, 66-75, based on *FPCMS, Chicago, 1900.*

8. Robert Hunter, *Tenement Conditions in Chicago. Report by the Investigating Committee of the City Homes Association* (Chicago: City Homes Association, 1901), especially pp. 53-58, 195-96. Also see, Sophonisba Breckinridge and Edith Abbott, *The Housing Problem in Chicago* (Chicago, 1910-1915), a collection of reprints of previous studies published in the *American Journal of Sociology*. Note, too, that Edith Abbott, later in her career, published a follow-up study to these two previous efforts. See Edith Abbott, *The Tenements of Chicago, 1908-1935* (Chicago: University of Chicago Press, 1936). For a thorough discussion of the tenement reform movement, see Thomas Lee Philpott, *The Slum and the Ghetto; Neighborhood Deterioration and Middle Class Reform, Chicago, 1880-1930* (New York: Oxford University Press, 1978), especially pp. 6-42. For an analysis of the Polish ghetto in Stanisławowo see Joseph J. Parot, "Ethnic Versus Black Metropolis: The Origins of Polish-Black Housing Tensions in Chicago," *Polish American Studies* 29 (Spring-Autumn 1972), pp. 5-34.
9. For an excellent contemporary view of the Bohemian, Jewish and Italian colonies adjacent to Hull House, see Residents of Hull House, *Hull House Maps and Papers: A Presentation of Nationalities and Wages in a Congested District of Chicago* (New York: Crowell, 1895). There is as yet no standard history of the Bridgeport Irish in Chicago, nor is there any definitive study of any kind on the Germans in Chicago.
10. Department of Commerce and Labor, Bureau of the Census, Special Reports. *Occupations at the Twelfth Census* (Washington, D.C.: Government Printing Office, 1904), pp. 517-23.
11. Parot, "Immigrant Labor," p. 75, based on tabulations from the *FPCMS, Chicago, 1900,* Ward 16, Enumeration Districts 526, 527, 528, 529, 530, 531, 532, Roll Number 267.
12. Nellie Mason Auten, "Some Phases of the Sweating System in the Garment Trades in Chicago," *American Journal of Sociology* 6 (March 1901), pp. 602-45. The quotation is given on p. 612; tables on working conditions and wages are on pp. 615-16, 628. Note that Polish wages, however, were still "slightly higher" than wages paid to Italian workers. See, for example, Ninth Special Report of the Commissioner of Labor, *The Italians in Chicago; A Social and Economic Study* (Prepared under the direction of Carroll D. Wright, Commissioner of Labor; Washington, D.C.: Government Printing Office, 1897), especially pp. 376-80. Also, for comparisons, see Carroll D. Wright, "Influence of Trade Unions on Immigrants," *Bulletin of the Bureau of Labor* 10, no. 56 (January 1905), pp. 1-8; Frank J. Sheridan, "Italian, Slavic and Hungarian Unskilled Laborers in the United States," *Bulletin of the Bureau of Labor* 15, no. 72 (September 1907), pp. 403-86; United States Immigration Commission, *Immigrants in Cities: A Study of the Population of Selected Districts in New York, Chicago, Philadelphia, Boston, Cleveland and Milwaukee,* 2 vols. (Washington, D.C.: Government Printing Office, 1911).
13. Auten, "Some Phases of the Sweating System," pp. 612, 618. Note that Auten's wage chart gives figures for two-week periods; so as to avoid confusion with previous remarks in the paper and so as to maintain continuity, I have adjusted to wage rates to show dollar amounts on a weekly basis.

14. Based on a comprehensive study of all Poles in Chicago in 1870, I found that only 43.1 per cent of all females, ages 5-14, were attending school for that census year. Based on a sample study of 2,612 Poles in Stanisławowo-Trójcowo in 1880, I found that 41.4 per cent of all females, ages 5-14, were attending school. See Parot, "Immigrant Labor," Appendix Two, p. 59; Appendix Three, p. 62, based on *FPCMS, Chicago, 1870,* all wards, and *FPCMS, Chicago, 1880,* Ward 14, ED 140; 147; 148.

15. I base these conclusions on my comprehensive study of Poles in Chicago in 1870, based on tabulations from *FPCMS, Chicago, 1870* (all wards). Of the 274 women ages 15 and older in Chicago's Polish population in 1870, the manuscript schedules report that 100 could neither read nor write and that another 14 could not write. In other words, 41.6 per cent of Polish women in Chicago in that census year were either illiterate or semi-illiterate.

16. See, for example, Virginia Yans McLaughlin, "Patterns of Work and Family Organization: Buffalo's Italians," *Journal of Interdisciplinary History* 2 (Autumn 1971), pp. 299-314. Professor McLaughlin, basing her observations on Elizabeth Beardsley Butler, "The Working Women of Pittsburgh," *The Survey* 23 (1910), p. 573, and on Elias Tobenkin, "The Immigrant Girl in Chicago," *The Survey* 23 (1909), p. 190, argues that Polish women continued working after marriage.

17. Ruby Jo Reeves Kennedy, "Single or Triple Melting Pot: Intermarriage in New Haven," *American Journal of Sociology* 58 (1952), pp. 55-66. Also see Helena Znaniecki Lopata, "The Polish American Family," in Charles H. Mindel and Robert W. Habenstein, eds., *Ethnic Families in America* (New York: Elsevier, 1976), pp. 15-40 for an updated treatment of these related topics.

18. "Precautions for Catholics Who Wish to Marry a Person of Another Nationality," *Dziennik Chicagoski,* October 18, 1906.

19. "Let's Get a Couple of 'Pollack' Girls Tonight," editorial in *Naród Polski,* January 19, 1921.

20. *Naród Polski,* July 6, 1904. Note that the *Dziennik Chicagoski* was especially opposed to dancing during the Lenten season. The Resurrectionist priests frequently used the paper's editorial space to sermonize on this and other related "moral" issues. For example, see the *Dziennik Chicagoski,* February 19, 1907. Very often, the positions taken by the Resurrectionist clergy were adopted by the laity, who might make known their views in letters to the paper. See, for example, the letters to the editor, *Dziennik Chicagoski,* January 11, 1907.

21. *Naród Polski,* February 21, 1900.

22. "American Girls and Polish Girls," *Naród Polski,* February 8, 1908.

23. *Album Pamiątkowy Z Okazyi Złotego Jubileuszu Parafii Świętego Stanisława Kostki* [Memorial Album on the occasion of the Golden Jubilee of St. Stanislaus Kostka Parish] (Chicago: St. Stanislaus Kostka Parish, 1917), p. 100. Also see the letter of Superior General Mother Maureen Lauretta of the Holy Family of Nazareth Sisters to *The New World,* February 15, 1902.

24. For a detailed analysis of the strengths and weaknesses of each method, see Harevan and Vinovskis, "Marital Fertility, Ethnicity and Occupation," pp. 70-75. Harevan and Vinovskis also discuss standard statistical models appropriate to each. Note, however, that I have not introduced age-specific fertility ratios over a period of time, as was utilized by Harevan and Vinovskis.

    Also see Yasukichi Yasuba, *Birth Rates of the White Population in the United States, 1800-1860: An Economic Study* (The Johns Hopkins University Studies in Historical and Political Science 79, no. 2, Baltimore: Johns Hopkins, 1962); Wilson H. Grabill, Clyde V. Kiser and Pascal K. Whelpton, *The Fertility of American Women* (For the Social Science and Research Council in cooperation with the U.S. Department of Commerce, Bureau of the Census, New York: John Wiley and Sons, 1958); Clyde V. Kiser, Wilson H. Grabill and Arthur A. Campbell, *Trends and Variations in Fertility in the United States* (Cambridge: Harvard University Press, 1968).

25. For a study of fertility rates in Chicago, comparing Native Whites, Foreign Whites and Negroes, see Evelyn M. Kitagawa, "Differential Fertility in Chicago, 1920-1940," *American Journal of Sociology* 58 (March 1953), pp. 481-92.

26. I was surprised to discover that the rate of 5.81 children per 1,000 Polish women remained *exactly the same* for the 1910 census. The Census Bureau calculated a 5.868 birth rate per 1,000 Polish women that year; Italian mothers maintained a birth rate of 5.454; Mexican women, 5.298; Russian (Jewish?), 5.349; German, 4.020; Irish, 3.341; English and Welsh, 3.269; all others, 3.821. Thus the high fertility rate pattern of Polish, Italian and Jewish women appears to have been maintained nation-wide in 1910 as well. See U.S. Department of Commerce. Bureau of the Census. Current Population Reports, Series P. 20, No. 226, *Population Characteristics: Fertility Variations by Ethnic Origin* (Washington, D.C.: G.P.O., 1971), p. 28.

    Also note that the number of children ever born per women ever married, ages 45-74, was highest for the Polish group in 1910 as well. The rate was 7,422 per 1,000 Polish women ever married; followed by French Canadian women with 7,382 per 1,000; Russian women, 7,156 per 1,000; Mexican women, 6,507 per 1,000; women from Austria-Hungary, 6,044 per 1,000; Italian women, 5,942 per 1,000; German women, 5,785 per 1,000; and Irish women, 5,428 per 1,000. See Grabill, Kiser, Whelpton, *Fertility,* p. 108.

    Finally, note the unusually high fertility rate of women in Poland in the post-World War II period. See S. J. Behrman, Leslie Corsa, Jr., and Ronald Freedman (eds.), *Fertility and Family Planning; A World View* (Ann Arbor: University of Michigan Press, 1969), p. 32.

27. For instance, see M. B. Hunt, "Housing Non-Family Men in Chicago," *American Journal of Sociology* 16 (September 1910), pp. 145-70.

28. Parot, "Immigrant Labor," Appendix Four, pp. 66, 70 and *passim.*

29. "Murderous Propaganda," *Dziennik Zjedoczenia* 26, no. 8 (January 11, 1922).

30. "Infant Mortality Rates in Cities," compiled by G. B. Mangold for a symposium published in *The Annals of the American Academy of Political and Social Science* 31 (March 1908), pp. 184-94.

31. Edward T. Devine, "The Waste of Infant Life," *The Survey* 23 (December 4, 1909), pp. 314-20. For another view, see "The Most Important Factor in Infant Mortality," *American Monthly Review of Reviews* 36 (July 1907), pp. 116-17.

32. Carole Dyhouse, "Working Class Mothers and Infant Mortality in England, 1895-1914," *Journal of Social History* 12 (Winter 1978), pp. 248-67.

33. Hunter, *Tenement Conditions,* pp. 41-87, 129-34 and *passim.* For a comparison on congestion in Polish districts elsewhere, see *Hull House Maps and Papers;* also Abbott, *Tenements of Chicago, passim.*

34. William I. Thomas and Florian Znaniecki, *The Polish Peasant in Europe and America* 2 vols. (New York: Knopf, 1927), pp. 1703-1827. The literature dealing with the opposition to the methodology and findings of Thomas and Znaniecki is too vast to summarize here. But special note should be taken of Herbert Blumer, *Critiques of Research in the Social Sciences: I; An Appraisal of Thomas and Znaniecki's "The Polish Peasant in Europe and America"* (New York, 1949). For a more recent summary of the Polish family, see Lopata, "The Polish Family," pp. 24-31.

35. *Album Pamiątkowy . . . Św. Stanisława Kostki,* pp. 95-134; and compare with such parish albums as the *Pamietnik Parafii Święti Trójcy w Chicago, Illinois* [Memorial of Holy Trinity Parish in Chicago, Illinois] (Chicago: Holy Trinity Parish, 1918) and the *Książka Jubileuszowa Parafii Św. Trójcy, 1893-1943* [Jubilee Book of Holy Trinity Parish 1893-1943] (Chicago: Holy Trinity Parish, 1943). These commemorative parish albums are a mine of information on the early organization and development of Polish women's parish sodalities.

APPENDIX 1
Table of Census Enumeration Districts for Sample Areas: Chicago, 1900

POLISH SAMPLE: Ward 16, Microfilm Roll Number 267 (West Town Community Area, otherwise known as *Stanisławowo-Trójcowo* as well as the "Polish Downtown"), Enumeration District (ED) 526, pp. 1-22 (city blocks for Dickson, Blackhawk, Ashland and Milwaukee); ED 527, pp. 1-28a (Noble, Cleaver, Division and Holt); ED 528, pp. 1-26 (Noble, Cleaver, Division and Holt); ED 529, pp. 1-33 (Noble, Blackhawk, Cleaver and Holt); ED 530, pp. 1-32 (Noble, Ingraham, Bradley, Sloan, Division and Elston); ED 531 (part), pp. 1-2; 21-25 (Noble, Blackhawk); ED 532, pp. 1-29 (Noble, Cleaver, Blackhawk and Holt).

ITALIAN SAMPLE: Ward 19, Microfilm Roll Number 269 (near West Side Community Area, otherwise known as the Hull House settlement), ED 598, pp. 10-17; ED 599, pp. 1-23a; ED 600, pp. 1-18 (the more prominent city streets covered are Forquer, Ewing and Polk, among others).

BOHEMIAN SAMPLE: Ward 9, Roll Number 254 (lower West Side Community Area, otherwise known as "Pilsen"), ED 237, pp. 1-29 (West 18th and West 19th Sts., Throop, Loomis, Blue Island); ED 238, pp. 3-12 (Blue Island only).

GERMAN SAMPLE: Ward 26, Roll Numbers 276 and 277 (Lakeview Community Area), ED 793, pp. 1-22a (Western, Oakley, Leavitt, Hoyne, Roscoe and others); ED 803 (part), pp. 2-6 (Ashland, Hermitage, Paulina, Marshfield); ED 816, pp. 1-15a (Clark, Ridge, Rosehill, Winchester, Paulina and others). Note that there is some slight overlap into the North Center Community Area.

IRISH SAMPLE: Ward 6, Roll Number 250 (Bridgeport Community Area, also known as South Township on Manuscript Schedules), ED 157, pp. 1-15a (Wallace, Lowe, Union, 36th Street and others); ED 158, pp. 1-14a (Wallace, Parnell, 37th Street and others); ED 159, pp. 1-18a (Wallace, Lowe, 37th Street and others).

JEWISH SAMPLE: Ward 8, Roll Numbers 252 and 270 (West Side Community Area, otherwise known as the Hull House or Maxwell Street Settlements), ED 196, pp. 1-24 (Maxwell Street and nearby vicinity); ED 616, pp. 1-20 (Bunker, DesPlaines, Wentworth, Canal, 12th Street and others).

NOTE: Throughout the sampling, all names not belonging to said nationality or ethnic group were deleted. E.g. All non-Irish names were deleted from the Bridgeport sample. For this reason, my total population sample totals do not correspond to total population totals listed by enumerators for given enumeration districts.

SOURCE: United States Census Bureau, *Federal Population Census Manuscript Schedules, Twelfth U.S. Census, 1900: Illinois, City of Chicago.*

The Post-Immigrant Generation

Polish American or American? The Polish Parishes in the 1920s

Daniel Buczek

The period between the two world wars is sometimes wistfully referred to as the "golden age" of the Polish ethnic parishes and of the Polonia communities that grew up around them. On the surface, these communities seemed to be culturally vibrant, with an extensive network of parochial schools filled to capacity, newspapers of various persuasions carrying on a lively polemic about the future of the immigrant community, and a number of prosperous nation-wide fraternal organizations, Polish homes and Falcon Clubs, and political, social and religious organizations of various purposes, most of them the creations of the immigrant newcomers prior to World War One.[1]

As one surveys these parish-communities between the end of World War One and the beginning of the Great Depression in 1929, the optimistic picture of growth, confidence in the future and increasing maturity becomes blurred by the pall that began to settle on them in that crucial decade of their development. Indeed, it may be said that the Polish immigrant parish-communities of the 1920s faced an agonizing choice between the maintenance of a semblance of their Polish identity on the one hand and surrender to nativist demands to melt into an "Anglo conformist" pot and to the beguiling beckoning of America's burgeoning material civilization on the other hand. It is the most fundamental of all the issues that confront immigrant groups seeking to acculturate into an unfamiliar culture.

What made this choice especially painful for the Polish immigrant parishes was the fact that the educated social leadership or intelligentsia of the parish-communities were overwhelmingly priests of a church regarded as foreign, suspect and "un-American" by the wielders of power and influence in America. Because these priests were under the ecclesiastical discipline of bishops who overwhelmingly chose to mitigate the conflict with the Protestant majority by accommodating the Roman Church to that essentially Protestant culture, the Polish clergy as the intellectual leaders of their immigrant communities were faced with pressures from both nativists and bishops. How they were able to meet the challenge of these two external pressures must be seen in relation to certain internal pressures which confronted them in the so-called "roaring, fitful twenties" when an aura of prosperity superficially took hold of much of America.

Ironically, when the Polish immigrant communities had reason to rejoice at the end of the war in Europe and the consequent resurrection of their motherland, the Polish immigrant clergy were presented with an ominous and disquieting piece of legislation in the promulgation of a new codex of canon law on May 18, 1918. Article 216, paragraph 4 of the new codex clearly states that territorial parishes are the only truly canonical parishes and that henceforth no national parishes may be founded without permission of the Holy See except as affiliations or missions of established territorial parishes.[2] Such legislation seemed like a retrogressive step to the Polish clergy as the Church had in the past, as a practical and pastoral matter, recognized the need of separate non-territorial parishes based on language.

The future of the Polish parishes, so it seemed, was at stake and their fate aroused sufficient attention to warrant being placed high on the agenda of the third Convention of the Association of Polish Priests in America in Chicago on February 6-7, 1918.[3] Rev. Boleslaus Goral of Milwaukee sought to allay the fears of his fellow priests by pointing out that the canon could be interpreted in a literal sense, thus forbidding the establishment of any more ethnic parishes, or it could be interpreted in a looser sense, permitting the ethnic parishes to be established when an obvious need for such parishes existed.[4] The statistics bear out his contention, as 14 per cent of the Polish parishes were founded in the interwar period, and only the Archdiocese of Chicago held firm to the literal interpretation of the canon, that no Polish parishes, canonically recognized as such, were henceforth to be founded in that huge and pivotal archdiocese.[5] Nevertheless, in spite of Father Goral's analysis, and in spite of the good sense of most of the American hierarchy in interpreting the canon rather loosely, the new codex hovered like an albatross over the ethnic parishes, contributing to a feeling of insecurity.[6]

This feeling of insecurity among the clergy was reflected in their decision to return to the struggles of an earlier day, the campaign for *rownouprawnienie* or equal rights of representation for the Polish clergy within the Church. The Polish clergy placed great emphasis on this campaign in the five years following the end of the war for obvious reasons. Their failure to achieve a significant breakthrough in the number of Polish representatives in the American hierarchy before the war had resulted in the growth of independent congregations which coalesced into the Polish National Catholic Church. The presence of these schismatic congregations in their midst was a constant reminder to them of the importance of achieving an influential voice in the highest echelons of Church government. Such an end would still the criticism of the independents that the Polish clergy were being treated as second-class members of the Church's clerical order.

The Polish clergy were faced in the 1920s with a serious challenge. The campaign for *rownouprawnienie* was, by its very nature, an internal clerical affair which involved the laity minimally. In spite of a relative lack of success in achieving their goals, the Polish clergy were able to maintain their dominance over their parish-communities against the challenge of a number of anticlerical movements, such as the socialist-oriented Committee of National Defense, popularly known as KON, or more significantly the leadership of the large Polish National Alliance. For the most part, the prewar struggle for dominance was really a struggle between a clerical and an anti-clerical intelligentsia, both with roots in the soil of old Polish culture, both *deraciné,* feeling themselves unappreciated by their English-speaking American compatriots. Indeed, as one pursues the contest between them before the war in the Polish-language press, it is clear that both sides joined in the bold condemnation of American culture as immature, crude, crass, garish, serving mammon with a vengeance.[7] Polish culture, on the other hand, was presented in the most positive terms so that the issue of the acculturation of the immigrant to his new home had to await the rise to prominence of a new intelligentsia which would not suffer the constricting effects of deracination.

It is obvious that intellectual leaders such as Father Goral of Milwaukee, Smogor of Steubenville, Ohio, Pitass of Buffalo and Bojanowski of Worcester, Massachusetts were unable to grasp the meaning and significance of the new intelligentsia of Polish American business and professional leaders who arose after World War One either to take their place alongside the clergy or to come into open conflict with them. Although they were a second generation of immigrant priests, therefore extending their activity into the transitional 1920s, by birth and education they were still traditionally European, Polish and Roman, culturally apart from the native Polish American leadership whose knowledge of and interest in the culture and politics of Poland was confined to an occasional patriotic rally.

Basically two perceptions and two mentalities clashed. There was the traditional priest, European-bred or educated, whose experience with an industrial society was confined to his own American city and parish, and whose anti-materialist mentality perceived that society to be full of enemies and moral snares. He could easily accept the tradition of American democratic government because that tradition had provided an opportunity for the free exercise of religion without government interference. He was not so impractical that he did not concede to immigrants the necessity of learning the dominant, official language for their economic well-being, but the process stopped there. However, there was no answer to the obvious question: If the necessity of learning the English language is conceded, does this not lay the immigrant open to the wiles and snares of a materialist culture?

On the other hand, the rising young American business and professional class of Polish ancestry, born, bred and educated in America, with only an imperfect, often naive, knowledge of the traditional culture of Catholic Poland, was separated from the clergy by a profound cultural barrier. Much of the constant sermonizing in the churches and parochial schools against American materialism had some effect on young students and some of it was carried beyond the classroom into the practical world of American business and industry.[8] However, a point is reached at which the purported "superiority of Polish culture" would have to be demonstrated in a tangible, practical way, which, in the absence of direct contact with the motherland of the culture, would mean exposure to the kind of traditional humanistic education to which the clerical intelligentsia themselves had been exposed.[9]

As we reflect upon that generational conflict in the 1920s, what is striking is the emphasis on the first line of defence: the preservation of the language. For those priests who continued to insist on the preservation of the language while conceding the necessity of learning English, the answer to the future of their parishes was the hyphenated bilingual, bicultural community which could only be achieved by cooperation between the traditionalist priest and the business-oriented lay intelligentsia. At what point could this cooperation be achieved? The native-bred intelligentsia considered that the first practical measure was to press for the introduction of English sermons into the church.[10] But at the risk of driving away some of the younger parishioners, the pastor had to stand his ground; for here he was bound by a commandment, *salus animarum suprema lex*—the salvation of souls is the supreme law—and the number of immigrant parents who were comfortable only in the Polish language was still much larger than the number of "young Turks" who were at least operationally bilingual. But cooperation between the two groups was not always forthcoming. It is difficult to understand why the parish of the Assumption of the Blessed Virgin Mary, founded in 1909 by Polish immigrants in the small village of Iron River, Michigan, was transformed in 1924 into an English-language parish with but the slightest protest, whereas the Rev. Michael Wenta, pastor of St. Hedwig's parish in Milwaukee, faced a withering fire of criticism in 1925 for daring to introduce a five-minute sermon in English at one mass in his increasingly ethnically-mixed parish.[11]

Wherever the generational conflict erupted into open disagreement and even where that disagreement was kept from the front pages of the local newspapers, the focus of the disenchantment was the parochial school which, as its opponents charged, was both educationally inferior to the public schools, and was unable, because of its emphasis on the Polish language and religion, to prepare young people for life in an American environment. Such charges heralded changes in emphasis. The Polish parochial school was clearly declining, as the editor of the *Przegląd Kościelny* (Church Review) admitted in an editorial in 1921.[12] And Father Wenta in Milwaukee in 1925 concluded that the Americanization of the Polish parishes was an inevitable process which had already begun because there were now more Polish children attending public schools than the parochial schools in Milwaukee. Thus, Father Wenta uttered the unpalatable: the Polish language cannot be saved, but let us at least save the "Polish heart" even though we must use another language to do so.[13]

That year, 1924, the Association of Polish Priests met in triennial convention in Philadelphia. The attendance at that gathering indicated the depth of the inroads made by the generational conflict in the ranks of the clergy themselves. Although there were approximately 1,200 Polish priests in the country attached to approximately 800 Polish parishes, only some 200 came to the convention.[14] The diminishing number of Polish priests who remained active in the Association and who considered the defence of traditional *Polskość* (Polishness) to be a high priority for the Polish parishes had evidently fallen sharply.

It is difficult to assess the causes of this sharp decline of interest in the Polish parish-communities. However, the mood, bordering on despair, seems to have been pervasive. The Philadelphia convention met with the vivid memory of an innocent and unintended attack on the Polish parochial schools by the bishops of Buffalo and Brooklyn who reminded school principals that instruction during official hours in New York State was to be exclusively in English. The storm of protest in the Buffalo area quickly receded when it was pointed out that the bishops had merely reminded the schools of a New York State education statute to that effect.[15] These reactions were indicative of the mood of despair, convulsively passing from aggressiveness to apathy.[16]

The Philadelphia convention, like the more general Polonian Congress in Detroit the following year, became an exercise in frustration and futility. Its agenda reveals the mood: the highest priority was assigned to the question of *rownouprawnienie,* followed by the defence of the Polish language, the education of Polish youth, and the protection of the national interests of the Poles.[17] As the *Nowiny Polskie* of Milwaukee expressed it succinctly: we try to get Polish bishops but we do not think seriously about preparing a field for their work. Of what value is it to get Polish bishops if they will not be able to speak to anyone in Polish?[18]

The reality of declining interest and competence in the Polish language created greater interest in the remarks of the Rev. Dr. Alexander Pitass of Buffalo than in those of the keynote speaker, the fiery Chicago priest-consultor, Rev. Ludwik Grudzinski. Father Grudzinski's impassioned rhetoric, full of invective against these twin enemies of the past, the American nativists such as the Ku Klux Klan, and the intransigent American Catholic hierarchy for having insisted on the denationalization of the immigrants, was in marked contrast to the calm, reasoned and practical address of Father Pitass who followed him.[19] Father Pitass provided the practical corollary to the disturbing question of *Nowiny Polskie.* He did not question the value or the effectiveness of the Polish parochial school. But, he asked, what happens to the Polish youth once they have left the parochial school? They are thrown into the public high school or the world of business and industry where the results of the parochial school's religious, moral and linguistic education are quickly undone. Therefore, as a concession to American reality, and borrowing the tactics of non-Catholic opponents such as the YMCA, every Polish Catholic pastor, still mindful of the traditional Christian motto, *salus animarum suprema lex,* must seek to bind the youth to his parish beyond the parochial school years by a network of clubs and societies in which religious consciousness would be tied to "fun and games." Thus, through the 1920s and 1930s, the Polish Catholic parishes became veritable beehives of club activity, with new religious-social or religious-athletic orientations the rule. Typical of the first type were the Holy Name Societies; of the second were the parish baseball or bowling teams.

These new parochial clubs for a time exacerbated the generational conflict between the older, immigrant-founded societies and the younger, American-born generation. The success of this experiment in cultural hyphenation depended on a variety of factors and local conditions. These clubs sought, above all, to preserve the Catholic commitment of the children of the Polish immigration; in this sense they were undoubtedly successful. At the same time, even though they managed, with somewhat less success, to maintain the consciousness of being Polish, they failed to improve the declining linguistic competence of their members. Meetings were in Polish, but as one reads the minutes of these societies in the 1920s, the language is a steadily corrupted patois.

The *Catholic Leader* of New Britain, Connecticut—the journal of Rev. Lucyan Bójnowski, the patriarch of New England's Polish Catholic clergy—perhaps foreshadowed Father Pitass' change of emphasis when it editorialized that "if we cannot preserve our language, then at least we can preserve the Polish spirit in our youth."[20] Applying Milton M. Gordon's distinction between "cultural pluralism" and "structural pluralism," the Polish parishes were beginning the transition from the hyphenated cultural world the Polonia communities had experienced in the first two decades of the twentieth century toward "structural pluralism," or the retention of at least the spirit and institutions of the Polish past, while de-emphasizing both language and formal ties to the motherland of Polish culture.[21] The debate, chiefly between the older immigrant pastors and the younger American-born curates and pastors, continued throughout the last fifteen years prior to American entry into World War Two. The issue in these years was formulated in a different way: no longer was there any doubt that the Polonian parish and community was not "the fourth part of Poland," as pre-World War One journalists were fond of referring to it; the question was whether the Polish parish should retain the language and traditions of its Polish origins or proceed with deliberate speed toward a complete merging with mainline American Catholicism.[22]

The five years between the Philadelphia convention and the beginning of the Great Depression saw some interesting changes, even the faint beginnings of convergence, of a sincere attempt to understand the position of the other side. The editor of the *American Ecclesiastical Review* confessed in 1928 that "perhaps nothing in our Catholic history is so inexplicable as our neglect of the immigrant.... The work of this Bureau [of Immigration of N.C.W.C.] since its inception exalts and depresses: it exalts because it reveals what can be done...; depresses, because one thinks of how many we have lost and how even now we have not reached below the surface of the problem."[23] The public confessions of bishops Schrembs of Cleveland, Gallagher of Detroit and Walsh of Newark that the American hierarchy had been mistaken in its past insistence on the Americanization of the immigrant indicated a gradual shift from intransigence toward understanding, whereas, in the same years, the Polish-language press, though still pressing for *rownouprawnienie,* became less hostile to American culture.[24]

There were other harbingers of the gradual change in mentality—a process which continues to the present day—which lie beyond the scope of this paper.[25] However, one final note: the editor of the *American Ecclesiastical Review,* house organ of the American ecclesiastical establishment, predicted in 1924 that the process of Americanization of the immigrant parishes would, by the end of this century, make the national parish unnecessary. We do not know what will happen in the next two decades, but at least all the signs present today make him look like a better prognosticator than a historian.[26]

Notes

1. Stanisław Targosz, *Polonja Katolicka w Stanach Zjednoczonych w przekroju* [Catholic Polonia in the United States in Cross-Section] (Detroit, 1943), p. 6 claimed that the number of Polish parishes in the American Catholic Church in 1942 was 831.
2. T. Lincoln Bouscaren, S.J., Adam C. Lewis, S.J. and Francis N. Korth, S.J., *Canon Law: A Text and Commentary*, 4th ed. (Milwaukee, 1943), p. 154; Stanislaus Woywod, O.F.M., *A Practical Commentary on the Code of Canon Law*, rev. ed. (New York, 1957), p. 97; Joseph E. Ciesluk, J.C.L., *National Parishes in the United States* (Washington, D.C., 1944), pp. 54-59.
3. The contents of the new codex of canon law had been known before its formal proclamation and was widely discussed. See A. B. Meehan, "The New Code of Canon Law," *American Ecclesiastical Review* 57 (1917), pp. 357-70.
4. Bolesław Góral, "Nowy kodeks prawa kanonicznego jako środek zaradczy przeciw szerzeniu sie niedowiarstwa między Polakami w Ameryce" ["The New Code of Canon Law as the Central Remedy against the Spread of Unbelief among Poles in America"], *Przegląd Kościelny* [Church Review] 5 (1918), pp. 126-31, 218-35.
5. *National Catholic Directory* (New York, 1918-39).
6. Rev. Tomasz Misicki, a well-travelled, highly respected pastor and author from Williamsport, Pennsylvania, complained editorially that American bishops refused to create enough Polish parishes because they were intent on making Americans of all Poles. See *Polak w Ameryce* [The Pole in America] (Buffalo, N.Y.), February 20, 1920, p. 2.
7. John Bodnar, "Immigration and Modernization: The Case of Slavic Peasants in Industrial America," in *American Workingclass Culture; Explorations in American Labor and Social History*, ed. Milton Cantor (Westport, Ct., 1979), p. 336, confirms this "non-capitalist" mentality among Poles and other Slavic groups. I use the terms "clerical" and "anticlerical" broadly. An anticlerical may be a churchgoer but one who opposes clerical domination in the life of Polonia. I base the distinction on a reading of contemporary newspapers. It is my conviction that ultimately it was the role of the church and its priests that was central to the issue of what Polonia would become. No secondary work yet deals adequately with the subject, but see Victor Greene, *For God and Country: the Rise of Polish and Lithuanian Ethnic Consciousness in America, 1860-1910* (Madison, Wis.: State Historical Society of Wisconsin, 1975).
8. One must agree, at least, with the conclusion of the sociologist Theresita Polzin, *The Polish Americans: Whence and Whither?* (Pulaski, Wis., 1973), p. 207, that "it was the religious value system . . . of the Poles that preserved their family system in America. . . . "
9. *Dziennik Nowoyorski* [New York Daily News] 27 May 1921, p. 2 editorialized pessimistically that the second generation, because it has no cultural roots to Poland, moves away from "Polishness" into a cultural no-man's land.

10. *Gazeta Polska* [The Polish Gazette] (Chicago, Ill.), 11 January 1912, p. 4, reported that a number of Franciscan-conducted parishes in the midwest had already introduced the reading of the Gospel in English.
11. *Kuryer Polski* [Polish Courier] (Milwaukee, Wis.), 25 February 1925, p. 4; 14 March 1925, p. 4; 9 April 1925, p. 4.
12. *Przegląd Kościelny* 8 (1921), p. 204.
13. *Nowiny Polskie* [Polish News] (Milwaukee, Wis.), 9 April 1924, p. 5.
14. *Philadelphia Inquirer,* 27 February 1924, p. 6, reported 400 in attendance; *Catholic Standard and Times* (Philadelphia, Pa.), 1 March 1924, p. 1, counted 300 in attendance.
15. D. Szopinski, "Zamach władzy duchowej na język polski w amerykańskich szkolach parafialnych" ["Attempts of Authority on the Polish Language in American Parochial Schools"], *Przeglad Kościelny* 10 (1923), pp. 568-86. The order of the Bishop of Buffalo is included verbatim on pp. 568-70.
16. The pressure of the Americanizing nativists was most insistent in the five years prior to the passage of the Johnson-Reed Immigration Act of 1924. A good example of this type of literature at that time was published by Brand Blanshard, *The Church and the Polish Immigrant* (no imprint, 1920). Mr. Blanshard, at that time a young graduate student at Columbia University, later Sterling Professor of Philosophy at Yale University, conducted a "study" of Philadelphia's Polish parishes for a Protestant mission society. His conclusions, dressed in scholarly apparatus, repeated the stock nativist charges that, because the Polish immigrant was Roman Catholic, it would be very difficult to Americanize him.
17. *Przegląd Kościelny* 11 (1924), p. 17.
18. *Nowiny Polskie,* 9 October 1924, p. 4.
19. *Przegląd Kościelny* 11 (1924), pp. 192-207 for Father Grudziński's paper; pp. 207-19 for Father Pitass' paper.
20. *Przewodnik Katolicki* [Catholic Leader] (New Britain, Ct.), 14 March 1924, p. 26. The same idea was expressed by *Nowiny Polskie,* 9 April 1924, p. 5.
21. Milton M. Gordon, *Assimilation in American Life; the role of race, religion and national origin* (New York, 1964), p. 159.
22. The exodus of parishioners from the Polish parishes toward the territorial parishes began to alarm some pastors in the 1920s. See *Kuryer Polski,* 10 August 1925, p. 7.
23. *American Ecclesiastical Review* 79 (1928), p. 348.
24. On Bishop Schrembs, *Nowiny Polski,* 11 April 1925; on Bishop Gallagher, *Nowiny Polskie,* 9 June 1924, p. 1; on Bishop Walsh, *Przegląd Katolicki* 4 (1929), p. 172.
25. Among these was the increasing emphasis in the press of the late 1920s on the involvement of Poles in politics, education and labour unions. See, for instance, *Kuryer Polski,* 7 April and 29 May 1925.
26. *American Ecclesiastical Review* 72 (1925), p. 85.

Ethnic Conflict and the Polish Americans of Detroit, 1921-42

Thaddeus C. Radzialowski

Ethnic identity in the industrialized world, like class or national identity, is a modern phenomenon. It sometimes developed in conjunction with those other identities and at other times and places in opposition or reaction to them. Ethnicity replaced older local and status identities which lost meaning and relevance on the journey from the village to the city. Among European immigrants to the United States, ethnicity became a complex of identities organized around the notion of membership in a certain national group in America. The component identities of ethnicity, such as class or occupational identification, ties to region of origin, local parochial or civic loyalties in the United States and religious affiliation existed in a dynamic tension with each other. The saliency of each, alone or in combination, for a group or individual, changed with time, place and circumstance.

Periodically, events crystallized a particular combination of loyalties and characteristics into a pattern that for a time defined the boundaries of a group's ethnicity. In the process some elements were sloughed off and others were added. In the Polish community several such junctures can be identified. Victor Greene has analysed the importance of the struggle among elite elements over the nature of the community and its relationship to the American Catholic church at the end of the nineteenth and the beginning of the twentieth century in shaping Polish American consciousness. The First World War and the battle for Polish independence created another period of critical re-examination in the Polish American community.[1] I would suggest that the experience of Polish Americans in the depression and the struggle to unionize industrial workers during the 1930s constituted still another set of events that had a decisive impact on the self-definition and world view of the community.

The effect of these events on Polish Americans has never been closely studied. Yet the depression and unionization were the central external events that affected them just as the various Polonias were making the transition from immigrant community to ethnic community. The depression hit Polish Americans harder than most other groups in American society, set them back in their struggle to achieve a minimum level of economic security and, in fact, for a time seemed to jeopardize almost all of their gains. The New Deal Coalition and the drive to unionize the industries in which they worked mobilized them on an unprecedented scale. It emphasized and gave new meaning to their awareness of themselves as a working-class group.

By the hundreds of thousands they poured into the ranks of the new unions in the short space of a few years. In those industries in which the CIO effort was concentrated—steel, auto, coal mining, meat packing and agricultural machinery—Polish Americans formed the largest single group. It is clear that without their support the new industrial unions would have been crippled or defeated. We have begun to understand the effect of their ethnicity on their actions during this period but we still have little sense of how their participation in these events transformed their ethnicity.[2]

These large questions are beyond the scope of a short paper. However, I would here like to look at one important aspect of that crucial era: the way the events of this period shaped the reaction of Detroit's Poles to the growing Black community.

Detroit's Polonia was founded shortly after the Civil War by skilled artisans from Prussian Poland. They were followed by peasant migrants who came in a moderate stream to take jobs as field hands for the Ferry Seed Company and as labourers in the city's foundries, stove factories, railroad shops and cigarette factories. By 1900 the Polish community in Detroit numbered 50,000. The stream became a flood after the turn of the century as new Polish immigrants joined thousands of fellow countrymen who had earlier found work in the upper Michigan copper mines and the Pennsylvania coalfields to flock into the booming auto factories. By the time the First World War cut off immigration the Polish community in Detroit had more than doubled to over 110,000. Fifteen years later when the Great Depression struck it had almost doubled again to well over 200,000 people.[3]

Prior to the thirties, the history of Detroit's Polonia was not marked by any violent struggle for jobs with the city's Blacks. Although Detroit Poles were no doubt aware that such battles had taken place elsewhere, there was no Lemont Massacre, Pullman or Packinghouse strike in their experience. The competition for work between the two groups was initially confined to a small number of jobs on the docks and for the custom in a few trades such as whitewashing. Detroit's Black community numbered only

4,000 at the turn of the century—about one-twelfth of the size of the city's Polonia. As a result, there was also little competition for housing. In a few older areas of the city Blacks and Poles shared the same very poor neighbourhoods without friction. For the most part, however, the incoming Poles did not move wholesale into old neighbourhoods abandoned by earlier immigrants but created new ones around their new churches in farmland on the eastern and western edges of the rapidly expanding city.

About a decade after the Poles, Black immigrants in large numbers began to arrive in the city. Escaping the poverty and oppression of the South and lured by a hope for steady work and better pay, Blacks came north to fill the demand for labour that had been created by the halt to immigration caused first by the war and then later by immigration restriction. By the depression the number of Blacks in Detroit had risen dramatically to about 120,000—one-half the size of the Polish population. The depression cruelly extinguished their prospects and crushed their hopes for a better life. The stage was set for a deadly competition between the two groups at the bottom of Detroit's society for work and space.[4]

Both groups brought with them into the competition a strong sense of oppression, a feeling that they were victims of profound historic injustice and of brutal persecution. For Polish Americans this sense was a product of the historic national consciousness they distilled out of the brooding, romantic tragedy of the partitions and the poverty and discrimination they suffered in America and Europe. The two sources reinforced and fed one another and each received additional impetus as the events of the twentieth century unfolded.[5]

Several historians, including myself, have pointed out that the class and ethnic prejudice directed against the Polish community in Detroit was perhaps more intense and persistent than elsewhere and that fact markedly affected the Poles' attitude toward their Black rivals. Robert Shogan and Thomas Craig note, for example, that "The Poles, looked down upon by the more established groups in Detroit, took out their resentment against Negroes, whom they regarded as a threat to the economic gains they were struggling to make."[6]

It is worth noting that some Black leaders in Detroit clearly recognized the importance of anti-Polish discrimination and prejudice and the resultant feelings of anger and alienation in poisoning relations between the two groups. In 1942 during the Sojourner Truth incident (to be discussed below), Rev. Charles Hill, a leading Black spokesman, in an appeal to the Polish community for cooperation assured the Poles that unlike others who disliked them in Detroit, Blacks did not believe that "Polish people are stupid, uncouth and unfit for anything except manual work."[7]

A consciousness of historic injustices and a knowledge that

they were the victims of discrimination increased the intensity of the confrontation between the two groups when it came, but the real cause of the contention was rooted in the poverty and difficulties each faced and the scarcity of the resources for which they struggled. The problems of the Black community prior to the depression are well described elsewhere and are not within the scope of this paper. They were heavy indeed. The Polish community, however, was only a little better off in the twenties. The wartime boom notwithstanding, the Poles in Detroit found themselves economically and socially near the bottom as the postwar depression inaugurated the twenties. The community struggled in these difficult conditions to absorb a large number of recent immigrants, many of them young single men, and to stabilize itself at a time when other Polish communities were already moving into a more mature stage of development. The 1922 Detroit Welfare report described the problems faced by Polish immigrants in the city:

> Detroit [in 1921 and early 1922] . . . was faced with a situation more serious than that which confronted other large cities. Unemployment extended over a longer period in Detroit and affected largely a recent population who had not yet been able to achieve that degree of economic security which comes with thrift exercised over a long period of time.[8]

A more detailed and personal account of the plight of many people in Polonia came from the pen of Helen Wendell, a writer and social reformer, who visited Hamtramck in 1921. Even allowing for exaggeration, it is a grim description. She writes:

> Please believe me when I assert that there lies within our very gates tragedy and privation and sorrow and these deplorable conditions have called forth no flood of commiseration, no deluge of merciful aid.
>
> In Hamtramck, starvation is the slow kind because the destitute contrive by some means or other to obtain a little food now and then and by this uncertain sustenance to keep going, their undernourished condition offering less resistence, day by day . . . to lurking disease germs which finally attack it. It is unbelievable on what little they can subsist.[9]

Helen Wendell's examples are pitiful: lack of basic sanitation measures by the city, intense overcrowding, rampant tuberculosis, unemployment, cruel treatment of sick and injured employees by the auto companies, hunger and poverty. She wonders that Detroiters committed to the cause of "famished China" or "starving Poland" should be so ignorant or indifferent to their own "starving Poland" in Hamtramck. The plight of Hamtramck's poor, she writes, was aggravated by the depletion of the relief funds because the demand for aid was so great.[10]

Even when economic conditions improved during the 1920s, a substantial segment of the Polish American population remained in difficult straits. During the entire decade the percentage of welfare recipients in Wayne County (Detroit) who were members of families headed by parents born in Poland remained constant: 14.8 per cent in 1922, 15 per cent in 1926, 14.9 per cent in 1927, 16 per cent in 1929.[11] In 1929, the last year before the Great Depression, the number of Polish Americans served by the Welfare Agency exceeded all others (including the hard-pressed Blacks) with the sole exception of native-born whites.[12]

The 1929 Annual Report of Public Welfare for Detroit offers a detailed picture of indigence in the city—the only report in the inter-war period that does so. Because it lists the recipients of welfare by place of birth and also indicates the cause that led them to seek aid, it gives us some idea of the problems faced by the poorer elements of Detroit's Polonia. The numbers of Polish Americans served by relief agencies exceeded that of *all* other groups except "Native Whites" in cases arising out of alcoholism, death in the family, handicaps, injury at work, marital incompatibility, child neglect, non-support, sickness, widow or widowerhood and imprisonment. In cases of illegitimacy they were also second in the city, this time exceeding native-born whites but second to Blacks. They were the third-largest group of clients in the city, behind Blacks and native-born Whites, in cases of desertion, divorce or separation, insufficient income, insanity or feeblemindedness and unemployment. In only one category, cases arising out of problems of old age, reflecting the youth of the Polish population, were they not among the top three groups.[13]

Several observations should be made about those statistics. First, the percentage of Poles on welfare is approximately equal to their percentage in the city population. Secondly, it must be noted that welfare services were on a small scale and offered only in cases of dire necessity. The absolute number of those served was small by modern standards; about 5,700 Poles were on the rolls. Thirdly, the report clearly understates the problems of the Polish community. Polish immigrants were likely to resort to social service agencies only in extremity and as a last resort when family, church and neighbourhood resources had been exhausted, were unavailable for some reason, or were non-existent. Also, by 1929 there was already a significant number of families headed by second-generation Polish Americans. If they turned to the public agencies for support, they would be enumerated among native-born whites. Lastly, because the report lists all ethnic groups in the city, it is a good indicator of the problems of the Polish community relative to those of all other groups in the population.

If a significant minority in Detroit's Polonia were in difficulty during the relatively prosperous twenties, the thirties saw a majority of the community driven to extremity. An immigrant group still in the first stages of a boot-strap operation had its progress stopped and the basis on which it hoped to build its security severely undermined. The Great Depression attacked two of the most important pillars of Polish American working-class life; a secure job and homestead. In their urban forms, these transformed village values provided the fabric of respectability, pride and dignity which held the community together. Unemployment, poverty, foreclosure, led Polish Americans to reaffirm them with considerable force and in this new emphasis change their meaning. The threat to jobs and housing was so severe that the struggle to maintain them took on tones of desperate defensiveness rarely encountered prior to the depression.

The collapse of auto production made the 1930s particularly grim for Polish Americans in the Detroit area. Unemployment at the height of the depression in 1932 was close to 50 per cent in the Polish community. In Hamtramck more than half of the 11,000 families were on public relief. All those families in the city with less than three children were removed from the welfare rolls in a desperate effort to conserve resources and get aid to the neediest. In Detroit, where Polish Americans were one of the largest groups on welfare, public assistance fell to fifteen cents per person per day before running out entirely. Those few who worked suffered intolerable conditions, low pay, incessant demands for the speed up of production and the constant threat of being fired. The speed up at the Dodge Main plant with its predominantly Polish American work force was one of the worst in the industry in the mid-thirties.[14] A recent history of Detroit notes that after each annual model changeover,

> older men used shoe polish to darken their hair when they reapplied for work, fearful the foremen would pass over them and hire younger workers. Men left baskets of food and liquor at the gatehouse for the foremen in the hope that they could buy their way back into the plant. Women were forced to give sexual favors if they wanted to get and keep jobs.[15]

The situation for Polish Americans in housing was as unsettling and insecure as their employment prospects. By 1932 as many as 4,500 families a month were being evicted in the Detroit area.[16] Polish Americans who lived through that period remember the anguish when they, or their friends and relatives were evicted or lost homes they had struggled to buy. Those who lost homes or were forced to move often took up residence with relatives. Three or even four families in a single home were not rare occurrences in Detroit's Polish neighbourhoods. Many who did not lose their homes still recall vividly how close they came to that catastrophe. The struggle to hold on to the family home is often the central memory of the depression period. In Hamtramck, candidates for constable hoped to win the homeowners' and renters' votes with promises to conduct evictions and foreclosures in a dignified and humane manner.[17]

Ownership of a house and a bit of land was of prime importance to Polish Americans in Detroit as elsewhere. At the beginning of the century their desire to acquire their own homes led them to become the leading group in Detroit's "informal" housing market, as the recent work by Olivier Zunz has pointed out. Rather than wait to accumulate the relatively large sums necessary to buy an existing house or one built for them by a professional builder, they often built their own small inexpensive houses with the aid of friends and neighbours.

Detroit's Poles, like Stephen Thernstrom's Newberrysport Irish, chose a mobility strategy that centred on property rather than education or the accumulation of capital for entrepreneurial activity. In the traditional world that shaped their values, land was the only sure guarantee of status, position and respect. But land did more than confer status. Its possession was also essential to survival. In traditional societies such as rural Poland, all property was considered as a productive asset and Polish immigrants brought that notion with them to the city. Polish workers used their small plots, even in densely settled industrial areas, to grow vegetables and raise animals in order to supplement the family's earnings. House and land therefore, not only gave Polish American families a place in the physical and social universe but, in their minds, was also essential to economic survival.

One of the indicators of the gradual recovery from the depression by Detroit's Poles was the slow but steady increase in the homeownership rate in Polish neighbourhoods. In Hamtramck, it rose from 38.9 per cent in 1936 to 42 per cent in 1945. In the areas adjacent to the Polish churches—in which almost all the residents were Polish—the concentration of homeowners comprised 48 to 57 per cent of the total number of residents in 1940. Yet it is an indication of the lingering poverty that most of the homes were classified as substandard during the 1940 census. For example, on the area closest to St. Florian Church on the west, 100 out of 143 housing units were classified as in need of major repair or a private bath.[18]

Average monthly rent is a good index of the relative economic level of an area. In spite of distortions caused by scarcity or abundance of housing, transportation facilities or distances from work, it is also a fair indicator of family income. It is instructive to compare the rents in Hamtramck and the Polish areas of Detroit with other areas of the city. The average monthly rent in Detroit in 1940 was $35.88, ranging from a low of $18.00 in the poorest areas to $120.00 in the wealthiest. The average rent in Hamtramck was $23.97 a month, with a low of $18.26 in the poorest section—an area almost 30 per cent Black—to $26.45 in the areas nearest St. Florian and St. Ladislaus churches. In the other heavily Polish areas the rents were in the $20.00 to $29.00 average range.[19]

Other data from the period give additional indications of the problems and marginal condition of the Polish American population of Detroit as it emerged out of the depression. The tuberculosis death rate in the Polish neighbourhoods south of Hamtramck was 40 to 79 per 100,000, a rate exceeded only in some of the poor Black and southern White areas of the city. The infant death rate in east side and west side Polish neighbourhoods was one of the highest in the city in 1939/40, ranging from 40 to over 60 per 1,000 live births. Finally, the juvenile delinquency complaints in the Polish areas of the city centre between 1936 and 1939 showed rates considerably above the city averages. In some sections in the heart of the Polish east side it ranged as high as .40 to .74 complaints per 100 children of school age, according to court records.[20]

It is against this background of poverty, discrimination and a severe threat to jobs and housing that the first major struggle between the Polish community and Detroit's Blacks developed. With the Poles beginning to move in large numbers into the union movement by 1936, they found Blacks the largest and certainly the most prominent group among those recruited to break their strikes. Employers exploited the poverty and catastrophic unemployment in the Black community to recruit workers to replace the immigrants and their sons when they struck. At Dodge Main in Hamtramck, for example, when the predominantly Polish American work force struck in 1939 for relief from a murderous speed up and the sympathetic and largely Polish city police force closed the Hamtramck gates to the plant, Detroit Police held open the Detroit exits for the more than two hundred Blacks brought in to try to smash the strike.[21] The bitterness of the confrontation even erupted at times in violence. During the attempt to organize the Ford Motor Company in 1941, street battles between armed Black men supporting the company and the UAW pickets took place before the gates of the huge Rouge plant, as hundreds of Black and Polish Americans fought each other for precious jobs.[22]

The housing competition began to develop considerably later than the job competition. In the 1920s the burgeoning Black population began crowding into housing on the edges of Polish neighbourhoods but not seriously challenging them.[23] The depression halted the search for more and better housing by both groups. As Detroit began to repair some of the ravages of the depression, however, the competition over housing between the two groups became intense. In little over a decade from 1930 to 1942 the number of families in the city increased by 120,000 while the number of dwelling units increased only by 55,000.[24] As the two largest and poorest ethnic groups in the city, Poles and Blacks found themselves pitted against each other in the neighbourhoods as in the work place. By 1940 frequent violent scuffles between gangs of young Poles and Blacks heralded the beginning of intense and bitter conflict between the two groups. In the fall of 1941 an argument over control of what became the Sojourner Truth housing project led to the first major housing battle marked by violence. The conflict brought to the surface all of the fears and insecurity of the Polish community born out of longstanding marginal status and the community's recent experience during the Great Depression.

The crises developed when the city of Detroit with federal assistance decided to build desperately needed housing for Black working-class families. The site chosen for the project was next to the newest Polish neighbourhood in Detroit, an area adjacent to three Polish parishes. The intention of the planners has never been revealed but the result of the site choice was clear. It put the undesirable Blacks away from the higher prestige groups in the city and next to the only slightly less desirable Poles. The Poles in the area immediately began to lobby and agitate at municipal, state and federal levels for the transfer of the housing to White occupation. Control of the project shifted back and forth between the groups throughout the autumn and winter as the construction neared completion. The final decision in January 1942 was in favour of the Blacks. As the first Black residents began to move in at the end of February, violence broke out between the newcomers and the neighbourhood people. Outside groups with an interest in racial strife, such as the Ku Klux Klan, rushed into the fray with incendiary leaflets and a burning cross. Finally, in late March 1942, under police protection, the Black families moved in.[25]

The time of the riot was a particularly difficult period in Detroit. The United States had just declared war and the country was beginning full-scale mobilization of its industries. In Detroit this meant the end of resources for the production of civilian automobiles and the changeover to war production. To effect the changeover more than 250,000 workers were laid off and many of them faced the prospect of finding new work because their jobs had been eliminated for the duration of the war. Some corporations were laying off employees in Detroit and gearing up for war production elsewhere. It was unclear in early 1942 just how many jobs would be permanently lost in Detroit. The unemployment of so many of its members agitated the Polish community. The economic news and plight of the unemployed dominated the front pages of the Polish newspaper. John Dingell, the Polish American congressman from Detroit, led the struggle in the U.S. Congress for a special $300 million appropriation to aid Detroit unemployed.[26]

The reaction of the Polish American community to the Sojourner Truth affair is recorded in the reports of the meetings of various concerned groups. The most common complaint at these meetings was that as a result of the building project "disorderly people" would be introduced into the community.[27] A speaker at one meeting summed up clearly the anxiety of the Poles:

> The neighbourhood is a new one and the residents of the neighbourhood are primarily workers who laboured hard for the money they invested in their homes. The movement of Negroes into this neighbourhood would lower the value of the possessions of these poor workers after which will come impoverishment.[28]

The deprivation of the depression clearly echoes in that speech.

The February 21 meeting of the Henryk Sienkiewicz Society, Group 2049 of the Polish National Alliance, highlighted sharply the tie between job anxiety and the status and housing fears of the Polish American community. The agenda of this crowded meeting contained two main items for discussion: how to obtain more government assistance to aid the many unemployed in the Polish community, and the issue of Blacks moving into the Fenelon-Nevada (Sojourner Truth) housing project. The assembly passed resolutions petitioning their elected representatives for redress in both cases.[29]

The most thorough analysis of the Sojourner Truth affair was made in a series of secret memoranda by the U.S. government Office of Facts and Figures (OFF). The study was done in order to assess the impact of racial tension on war production. The first report completed on March 5, 1942 concluded that

> The conflict dramatizes all of the insecurity and displaced aggression of the immigrant in northern cities. . . . The conflict could better be called a Polish-Negro conflict . . . than a Black-White conflict.[30]

The first report was followed by a memorandum from Rensis Likert, head of the Surveys Division of OFF, to R. Keith Kane, head of the OFF Bureau of Intelligence. Likert's analysis which underlined clearly the tie between jobs and the housing struggle, is worth quoting at length:

> In Detroit, the Poles are the biggest cultural minority and the Negroes the second. . . . During the past depression and to a certain extent even during the lush pre-war boom, and now again . . . there have never been enough jobs to go around.
>
> The immigrant class is a working class. The Negro class is a working class. Due to a competitive set up they both compete with each other for jobs. Due to the many things both groups have suffered, both tend to look for substitute targets for their aggression and feelings of resentment against injustice and oppression, because they are afraid to make a direct attack upon the authors of their misery, or because they haven't the education or the patience under strain to sit down and figure out by social analysis why their living standards are low and why they must compete against each other for jobs.

> Under such a condition one always wonders why he does not get a job when someone else does and begins to devise rationalizations why he should have a job and the other fellow not.
>
> The important facts in this case are that immigrants say white men should have jobs before Negroes and Negroes say that people who have been in this country the longest should have jobs first.[31]

The Sojourner Truth riot was one of the first and in many ways the prototype of the postwar confrontations over housing that masked accumulated anger over an incessant job rivalry in a condition of always looming unemployment. It was also the product of aggression born of long years of contempt and discrimination by the dominant groups in the United States. The Poles and Blacks living in the same areas and working at the same jobs found each other the handiest and safest targets for venting frustration.

Notes

1. Victor Greene, *For God and Country* (Madison, Wis.: State Historical Society, 1975). See also his article "Slavic American Nationalism, 1870-1919" in Anna Cienciala (ed.), *American Contributions to the Seventh International Congress of Slavists* III: *History* (The Hague: Mouton, 1973), pp. 197-215.
2. Peter Friedlander, *The Emergence of a UAW Local 1936-1939* (Pittsburgh: Univ. of Pittsburgh, 1975). Stanisław Nowak, "Udział Polaków w Organizowaniu Związku Zawodowego Robotników Automobilowych w USA," [The Place of Poles in the Organization of the United Automobile Workers Union in the USA"], *Problemy Polonii Zagranicznej* [Problems of Poles Abroad] 6-8 (1971), pp. 165-89.
3. T. Radzialowski with D. Binkowski, "Polish Americans in Detroit Politics" in A. Pienkos (ed.), *Ethnic Politics in Urban America* (Chicago: Polish American Historical Assn., 1978), pp. 40-65.
4. Ibid.
5. T. Radzialowski, "View from a Polish Ghetto," *Ethnicity* I, no. 2 (1974), pp. 125-50.
6. Robert Shogan and Tom Craig, *The Detroit Race Riot* (Philadelphia: Chelton, 1964), p. 19.
7. Sojourner Truth Citizen's Committee, "To Loyal and Patriotic Polish Americans Living near Sojourner Truth Homes," copy of leaflet in Reference File "Housing" in Albert J. Zak Memorial Library, Hamtramck, Michigan.
8. City of Detroit, *Annual Report of the Department of Public Welfare for Calendar Year 1922.* On file Burton Collection, Detroit Public Library.
9. Helen Wendell, "Conditions in Hamtramck," *Pipps Weekly* 2, no. 23 (September 24, 1921), pp. 10-11.

10. Ibid.
11. City of Detroit, *Annual Reports of the Departments of Public Welfare, 1922, 1926, 1927, 1929.* On file Burton Collection, Detroit Public Library.
12. City of Detroit, *Annual Reports of the Department of Public Welfare 1929,* pp. 14-18. The 1929 report is the only report to make this breakdown. The department published no further reports until it issued a summary in 1937.
13. Ibid.
14. Caroline Bird, *The Invisible Scar* (New York: David McKay, 1966), p. 33. Workers Education Local 189, *Union Town* (Detroit: Labor History Task Force, 1980), pp. 4-5.
15. *Union Town,* p. 5.
16. R. Conot, *American Odyssey* (New York: Quadrangle, 1974), p. 285.
17. Field notes, interview with Stephen Morawski, Hamtramck, Michigan, August 8, 1980. Field notes, interview with Genevieve O. Radzialowski, Hamtramck, Michigan, August 9, 1980.
18. "Housing, Hamtramck" Reference File, Albert J. Zak Memorial Library, Hamtramck, Michigan.
19. Sixteenth Census of the United States (1940). U.S. Department of Commerce, *Housing Bulletin for Michigan. Hamtramck Block Statistics.* Prepared under supervision of Leon E. Truesdell (Washington, D.C.: U.S. Gov't Printing Office, 1942), pp. 5-8.
20. City of Detroit, City Plan Commission, *Master Plan Reports: The People of Detroit* (Detroit, 1946), pp. 33-34.
21. *Union Town,* pp. 20-21.
22. B. J. Widick, *Detroit: City of Race and Class Violence* (Chicago: Quadrangle, 1972), pp. 30-31.
23. J. Parot sees the housing struggle (like the job competition) in Chicago developing somewhat earlier. He dates the beginning of the attempt by Poles and other ethnics to "hold the line" to the aftermath of the race riot of 1919. J. Parot, "Ethnic versus Black Metropolis: The Origins of Polish-Black Housing Tensions in Chicago," *Polish American Studies* 29, nos. 1-2 (Spring-Autumn 1972), pp. 5-33.
24. Earl Brown, *Lessons from Detroit,* Public Affairs Pamphlet No. 87 (New York: Public Affairs Co., 1944), p. 4.
25. Alfred McClung Lee and Norman Humphrey, *Race Riot* (New York: Octagon Books, 1968), pp. 31-32.
26. On unemployment and the Dingell Bill see, for example, *Dziennik Polski* [Polish Daily News] (Detroit), 5 February 1942.
27. See the report of the meeting of the Pulaski Democratic Club in *Dziennik Polski,* 5 February 1942.
28. See "Kom. Obywateli Przecziw Przeznaniu Mieszkan przy Fenelon Murzynom," ["Meeting of the Citizens Committee Against the Assigning of the Fenelon Ave. Homes to Negroes"] *Dziennik Polski,* 21 February 1942.

29. *Dziennik Polski,* 21 February 1942.
30. The reports were never released. They were leaked to a New York newspaper during the 1943 Detroit race riot and published as an exposé of government inaction in the face of what it knew for over a year to be a volatile situation. See *P.M.,* (New York), 27 June 1943.
31. Ibid.

Ethnicity in Post-Industrial Society, 1940-80

Work

Occupational Trends in the Polish Canadian Community 1941-71

Rudolf K. Kogler

The purpose of this paper is to describe changes in the occupational composition which occurred within the Polish community in Canada between 1941 and 1971. Parallel comparisons will also be provided with changes that occurred in the Canadian labour force as a whole and within selected ethnic communities. Unfortunately, there are no available statistical data on the ethnic labour force prior to 1941. However, 1941 is a convenient starting point since it summarizes the occupational structure of immigrants who arrived in Canada at any time prior to 1939 and thus will provide a useful reference point for comparisons of the occupational structure of the post-1941 community which is composed both of immigrants and persons born in Canada of Polish parents.

At the outset I feel that a caveat is necessary: a *strict* historical comparison of data shown for each decennial interval is not possible, since the definition of the term "occupation" tends to change at each census. It was not until the 1971 census that an attempt was made to employ a standardized occupational classification system. This is the classification which will be used in this paper.

However, despite these difficulties, a long-run analysis can be conducted at the broad level of occupational categories, exposing changes which occurred in the occupational structure both in the national context or within a specific community.

For this study I have used the 1971 census classification of occupations composed of 22 major groups. In order to make the comparisons easier, I have aggregated eleven of the major groups, whose affinity is close enough, into four larger classes.[1]

Table 2 indicates a gradual change in the composition of the Polish labour force. This change reflects the evolution which took place in the Canadian society in the educational, social, economic and technological context. It was also influenced by shifts in the occupational mix of immigrants during the period under observation. In addition, some immigrants tend to upgrade their skills and transfer to different occupational groups than those reported at the time of entry or reported at a previous census.

Before we embark on the discussion of the occupational structure of the Polish ethnic group in Canada a brief outline of the growth of the community is necessary.

Historians of the Polish community in Canada trace the presence of Poles in this country back at least two hundred years. Most of the immigrants arriving before 1851 were political refugees seeking asylum from the oppressive governments of the three powers which partitioned Poland at the close of the eighteenth century: Russia, Prussia and Austria. These people were well educated, intelligent and politically oriented, some of whom left a lasting impact upon the political and cultural life of Canada. However, being but a handful in number and settled across this vast land, they were easily assimilated by the larger English and French communities. They were not instrumental to any degree in the formation of the Polish Canadian community as it exists today.

The actual history of the Polish community starts with the arrival of the first settlers to the Ottawa River Valley in 1858. This initial group consisted of some 77 immigrants from the Kaszuby region in the northwest of Poland, who were joined shortly by other families, and by 1864 the number of Poles in Renfrew County, in the Wilno area, increased to about 500.

Another group, also from German-occupied Poland, settled in Waterloo County around 1860. The railway construction boom and other major projects of the 1850s and 1860s attracted Polish labourers from the northern United States, some of whom later acquired land either by purchase or through the Dominion Act of 1872. On the whole, however, the size of the Polish community was small and dispersed throughout the country.

The significant growth of the community began with the initiation of a vigorous immigration policy by Sir Clifford Sifton, who as Minister of the Interior in the Laurier administration started a recruitment campaign in central and eastern Europe. As a result of this policy, during the period from 1896 to 1914, about 115,000 Polish immigrants settled in Canada. It is worth mentioning that these immigrants hailed from the poorest social strata for whom migration was the only available way to improve their lot. For the most part they were landless farm labourers or poor farmers who tried to acquire or increase their holdings through savings earned abroad. The majority of Polish immigrants intended to return home. Some managed to do that but in the end the majority decided to stay although the decision might have been forced upon them by the outbreak of hostilities in Europe in 1914 or later by the Great Depression of the 1930s.

Soon after the armistice of 1918 migration from Poland resumed, and during the interwar period some 62,000 Poles settled in Canada. During the war years from 1939 to 1945, Polish immigration slowed to a trickle when only 800 arrived. Among this group were about 500 engineers and technicians who were recruited by the Canadian government to fill vacancies in the armament industries. This group later played a significant role in the development of the Polish community.

Since the end of World War Two some 110,000 Polish immigrants arrived in Canada. In contrast to the pre-1939 period, the postwar immigrants represented all social strata, including a large group of professionally trained people, such as engineers, lawyers, teachers and scientists.

An analysis of available statistics can establish the fact that between 1896 and 1971 about 285,000 Polish immigrants settled in Canada. Some 115,000 should be added as a result of natural increase (births minus deaths). The 1971 census of Canada shows only 316,000 people declaring their ethnic background to be Polish. The discrepancy amounts to 84,000 persons. Some of them migrated to the United States, and a fair proportion returned to Poland during the interwar period. This is a rough estimate, since exact vital statistics by ethnicity are not available which would confirm the above-mentioned trends.[2]

Before discussing the changing structure of ethnic occupations in Canada, it would be advisable to provide a brief overview of the general economic conditions in Canada since 1921; these conditions predicate the immigration levels as well as the level of employment.

Economic conditions in Canada during the 1920s were generally good, if not booming, until the stock exchange crash in the autumn of 1929 ushered in a decade of depression which reached bottom in 1933 with almost 20.0 per cent of the labour force unemployed. After 1933 the economy slowly started to improve. The year 1941 was one of tremendous recovery as the Canadian economy began to gear for war production. Unemployment dropped to almost 4.0 per cent of the labour force and by 1944 reached its lowest level of 1.4 per cent.

The period after the conclusion of World War Two could be characterized as a period of some economic hesitation during which the unemployment levels oscillated between 2 and 4 per cent of the labour force. There was a surge of economic activity in the early 1950s induced by the outbreak of hostilities in Korea. Unemployment rates were generally low. In the second part of the 1950s there again ensued a period of economic hesitation reaching the lowest point of activity in 1961 with an unemployment level of 7 per cent. During the 1960s economic conditions were generally good with unemployment levels oscillating around the 4 per cent mark.

The Polish labour force in Canada grew from 65,000 in 1941 to 148,000 in 1971, an increase of 126.4 per cent, a slightly faster rate than the growth of the Polish community at large, which grew by 117.5 per cent during the thirty-year period. In comparison, the Canadian labour force grew by 105.6 per cent, from 4,196,000 in 1941 to 8,627,000 in 1971.

A comparison of participation rates[3] between 1941 and 1971 may be at this stage useful:

	1941		1971		Difference: 1941-71	
Ethnic Group	Male	Female	Male	Female	Male	Female
British	74.9	21.1	76.3	39.9	+ 1.4	+ 18.8
French	81.7	21.7	69.4	33.2	− 12.3	+ 11.5
German	92.1	19.3	82.2	42.7	− 9.9	+ 23.4
Italian	82.7	22.3	82.3	42.4	− 0.4	+ 20.1
Polish	**84.5**	**19.9**	**77.4**	**45.2**	**− 7.1**	**+ 25.3**
Ukrainian	85.3	15.8	76.9	44.6	− 8.4	+ 28.8
Total Labour Force	78.6	20.7	75.1	38.7	− 3.5	+ 18.0

The increased participation rates for women are a widely known phenomenon. They are the result of many factors—higher educational levels and changing attitudes toward women working, the wish to provide more amenities for the family, the rising rate of breakdown of marriages and the growth of the service sector of the economy where women have traditionally found employment, especially of a temporary or part-time nature. The lower readings of male participation rates in 1971 than those shown for 1941 could be explained by the fact that at the lower age categories, 15-24, a larger proportion of males tend to stay at school longer, thus postponing the start of economic activity.

It is interesting to note that in 1971 the highest participation rates were recorded among German and Italian males, 82.2 and 82.3 per cent respectively, and among Polish and Ukrainian women, 45.2 and 44.6 per cent respectively.

During the thirty-year period under our scrutiny, 1941-71, there was a significant transformation of the Canadian labour force. The work force doubled from 4,196,000 in 1941 to 8,627,000 in 1971, an increase of 105.6 per cent. There was a dramatic increase in the female labour force, from 833,000 in 1941 to 2,961,000 in 1971 (255.5 per cent). In comparison the male labour force increased by only 68.5 per cent, from 3,363,000 to 5,666,000. In addition there occurred a considerable amount of occupational shifting, so that it is not quite appropriate to compare the 1971 occupational structure with that of 1941.

Perhaps the most striking example of the effect of distributional change is that of the agricultural occupations. In 1941 the employment in this sector amounted to 1,084,000, whereas in 1971 there were only 512,000 people engaged in farming, a drop of 53.0 per cent. On the other hand, employment in the service sector–clerical, sales and services–increased from 992,000, for both sexes, in 1941 to 3,159,000 in 1971.

While the transformation of the occupational structure of the labour force between 1941 and 1971 has greatly increased the service sector jobs and dramatically reduced the importance of farming, the shifting pattern had very little effect on the relative size of employment in blue collar or manual occupations, whose relative strength in the labour force remained static, at around 33 per cent during the whole period.

The net increase in the professional job category (managerial, administrative, teaching, etc.) amounted to 946,100, from 519,200 in 1941 to 1,465,100 in 1971 (182.2 per cent). The number of males in professional occupations grew by 515,000 (140.7 per cent) and that of females by 431,100 (281.3 per cent). The net increase stemmed primarily from a change in labour force composition between those two dates when a wide range of new professional jobs were created. Although the absolute and relative increases in the female component of professional occupations is very impressive, one should remember that these increases were concentrated mainly in teaching and nursing and to a lesser degree in the area of science and engineering. All these trends in the occupational distribution of the Canadian labour force also applied to ethnic groups, but they did not necessarily emerge in tandem. In order to facilitate the measurement of the magnitude and direction of change which occurred among the various ethnic labour forces one has to adopt a summary index. The easiest one to use seems to be the Index of Dissimilarity which is based on the absolute differences between the relative distributions. In this study the index measures the difference between the respective ethnic labour force composition and that of the national labour force. The lower the index the less is the difference.

The following table provides an insight into the magnitude of differences in the occupational structures, by sex, for selected ethnic groups in 1941 and 1971:

Index of Dissimilarity, Selected Ethnic Groups, 1941 and 1971

	1941		1971	
Ethnic Group	Male	Female	Male	Female
British	5.7	4.2	4.1	5.5
French	4.4	8.4	3.5	5.6
German	20.0	7.8	8.4	5.1
Italian	25.5	23.2	19.5	26.8
Polish	**13.7**	**12.4**	**6.7**	**5.2**
Ukrainian	21.7	14.0	5.9	7.8

The index is higher for Polish males in 1941 due to the fact that the proportion of Poles holding jobs in the primary sectors was about 7 per cent higher than the national average. At the same time they were under-represented by the same proportion in professional and service jobs. The index in 1971 is almost half the size of 1941, indicating that occupational distribution was closer to the national structure, but there was still a preponderance of those holding manufacturing jobs.

The index for Polish women in 1941 is also higher due to the fact that they were under-represented in professional occupations by 12 per cent and over-represented in manufacturing and services. In 1971 the occupational distribution is closer to the national average and similar to that of British, French and German women; Polish women are still rather under-represented in the professional group of occupations.

Scrutiny of the ethnic male labour forces in 1971 reveals some interesting observations regarding occupational preferences: the British are strongly represented in professional occupations, the French and Poles in the manufacturing sector, Ukrainians and Germans in agriculture and the Italians favour construction and manufacturing. On the other hand, Poles, Ukrainians, French and Italians are under-represented in the professions, Germans in services, and the British in manufacturing.

On the female side of the labour force, the 1941 distribution of occupations shows that Ukrainian, German and British women had a strong preference for service jobs; Polish, French and Italian women favoured manufacturing. By 1971 there occurred an interesting shift among Poles, Ukrainians and Germans towards farming, Italian women increased their preference for manufacturing, British women for service occupations, while the French did not express any particular preference. Polish, Ukrainian, German and Italian women were under-represented in professional occupations, French women in service occupations and the British in manufacturing.

A more detailed examination of occupational trends within the Polish community between 1941 and 1971 reveals some interesting observations, which the following tabulations bring out:

Growth of the Polish Labour Force, 1941-71

Year	Male	Female	Total	Per cent of Total Male	Per cent of Total Female
1941	54,800	10,600	65,400	83.8	16.2
1951	78,800	20,400	99,200	79.4	20.6
1961	96,100	34,900	131,000	73.4	26.6
1971	95,800	52,500	148,300	64.6	35.4

The overall Polish labour force during the thirty-year period grew by 82,900, or 126.8 per cent. Almost half of this growth was contributed by Polish women whose numerical size increased fivefold. The growth on the male side of the labour force amounts to only 75 per cent. At the beginning of the period the male component constitutes almost 84 per cent of the Polish labour force, whereas in 1971 the proportion of males dropped to 65 per cent. The female counterpart increased its contribution from 16 to 35 per cent.

The highest growth rate occurred in the professional group of occupations. The following tabulation will illustrate this trend in detail:

Polish Males in Selected Occupations, 1941 and 1971

Occupation	1941	1971	Net Difference	Per cent of National Employment 1941	1971
Managerial, Administrative	1,399	3,375	1,976	0.6	1.1
Occ. in Natural Science and Engineering	142	4,395	4,253	0.4	2.0
Occ. in Social Sciences	52	510	458	0.3	1.0
Teaching	149	1,805	1,656	0.6	1.3
University	6	300	294	0.2	1.4
Other	143	1,505	1,362	0.7	1.4
Occ. in Medicine					
Health	68	1,170	1,102	0.4	1.3
Doctors	41	415	374	0.3	1.2
Other	27	755	728	0.8	2.6
Artistic, Literary, etc.	82	795	716	0.5	1.4

The tabulation indicates great progress both in absolute and relative terms during the thirty-year period. However, this group as a whole was still 2.7 per cent below the national average in 1971; in 1941 the differential was 7.2 per cent. The data for 1971 include professionals who settled in Canada after 1939, as well as persons born and educated in Canada. The 1981 census will undoubtedly show further improvement, since a large number of young males have passed through the Canadian educational system since 1971.

Similar observation can be made regarding females in professional occupations, with some exceptions. The ratio of Polish women occupied in natural sciences and engineering, university teaching and those holding a doctor's diploma was higher than the national average in 1971. However, the group as a whole was still 4.5 per cent below the national average in 1971, although this is an improvement over the proportion of 12.3 per cent in 1941.

The following tabulation illustrates this more clearly:

Polish Women in Selected Occupations, 1941 and 1971

Occupation	1941	1971	Net Difference	Per cent of National Employment 1941	1971
Managerial, Administrative	100	750	650	0.6	1.3
Occ. in Natural Sciences or Engineering	3	425	422	0.7	2.5
Occ. in Social Sciences	34	380	346	0.5	1.3
Teaching	226	2,585	2,359	0.3	1.2
University	—	85	85	—	1.8
Other	226	2,500	2,274	0.3	1.2
Occ. in Medicine and Health	219	3,555	3,336	0.5	1.5
Doctors	2	80	78	0.4	1.9
Artistic, Literary, etc.	22	290	268	0.3	1.3

Conclusion

In order to trace the impact of Polish immigration on the postwar development of the Polish labour force in Canada, we have to compare the immigration statistics, published by the Department of Manpower and Immigration, with the occupational statistics shown in respective postwar population censuses. Between 1946 and 1971 some 108,000 Polish immigrants settled in Canada. As a group they are not homogeneous and they should be subdivided into at least two chronological groups: those who arrived between 1946 and 1955, and those who arrived after 1955. The first group of some 62,000 consisted mainly of ex-servicemen and displaced persons from various locations in western Europe. There were almost no immigrants from Poland among them, since the Polish government discouraged emigration.

The second group of some 46,000 consisted mostly of immigrants from Poland. The Polish government relaxed emigration somewhat, allowing relatives of previous immigrants to join them. The new regulations also permitted visits abroad. Most of the visitors to Canada decided to remain permanently in this country. The second group also included some immigrants from Britain and western Europe, but since the pool of potential migrants dried up (those who intended to migrate did so prior to 1955) their number was not too large.

There is a marked difference between these two groups. In the first group, 62 per cent were destined to join the labour market and 38 per cent were admitted as dependants. In the second group the proportions were reversed: 60 per cent were admitted as dependants, whereas 40 per cent were ready to join the labour force.

There is a marked difference in the occupational distribution of these two groups, as seen in the following table:

Occupational Distribution of Polish Immigrants, 1946-71
(in relative terms)

Occupation	Period of Immigration 1946-55 %	1956-71 %	Net Difference Percentage Points
Professional, Administrative	3.4	13.0	9.6
Service occupations	16.9	25.5	8.6
Primary occupations	45.5	11.0	-34.5
Manufacturing & construction	31.2	49.0	17.8
Not stated	3.0	1.5	-1.5
Total	100.0	100.0	0

At first glance we note a dramatic decline of 34.5 percentage points in the "primary" occupational category (agriculture and mining) among immigrants arriving after 1955 as compared to those who landed in Canada prior to 1955 and concomitantly an increase in the remaining occupational categories. In the first group we note a high proportion (45.5 per cent) of immigrants destined to join primary occupations. This unusual development was caused by pressure exerted by immigration officials on Polish veterans and refugees to take this kind of employment in order to alleviate the acute shortage of manpower in agriculture and mining. As a result 4,500 ex-servicemen were allowed to settle in Canada on condition that they sign a two-year contract as farm labourers. A large number of displaced persons were also so directed. Most of them left farming after the fulfillment of their contractual obligations.

A comparison of census data for 1951 and 1961 seems to indicate that a large proportion of immigrants who arrived between 1946 and 1955 and who were initially employed in farming and mining quit these occupations and moved later to service and manufacturing occupations. It is also evident that some professional people were masquerading for some time as farmers or labourers but later joined their professions. For example, the census of 1941 shows 2,700 Poles engaged in professional occupations. The same group is reported in the 1951 census to number 8,500. We may assume that part of the 5,800 increment of professionals within the Polish community during the decade was the product of the Canadian educational system. However, a community of some 150,000 Poles around 1941 could not have produced that number of graduates. The only explanation is that a sizable number of immigrants who arrived during 1946-55 switched after a short time from provisional jobs to their more regular occupations.

Also, due to the declining importance of farming as a source of employment, a large number of the original settlers (of the pre-1939 vintage) and postwar immigrants had to take up employment in other occupations, mainly in manufacturing and services. This is clearly evident from the scrutiny of census reports.

Every immigration report shows the proportion of immigrants who on arrival join the labour force and those who are admitted as dependants. A large proportion of dependants eventually enter the labour market. This is most certainly the case with children who upon achieving maturity must enter the labour market. This also applies to spouses. The dramatic growth, in absolute and relative terms, of Polish women in the labour force since 1941 is to some extent caused by the decision on their part to enter the labour market in order to speed up the realization of their families' economic goals.

In conclusion, one brief observation. The changes of the Polish occupational structure affected in turn the rural-urban residential dichotomy. In 1941, 51 per cent of the Polish community lived in a rural environment. By 1971 this proportion dropped to 20 per cent. In 1941 only one-third of the community lived in centres of 30,000 population or more. In 1971, 66 per cent did so. In short, within the span of thirty years the Polish community was transformed from a society with a strongly rural complexion to a predominantly urban society. Furthermore, the centre of gravity of the community shifted from the prairies to southern Ontario where over 50 per cent of the Polish community in Canada now live.

Notes

1. See Table 1 in the Appendix for details of this operation and the description of occupational skills contained in each of the fifteen major categories.
2. Ethnicity is established in Canadian censuses in response to the following question: "To what ethnic or cultural groups did you or your ancestor (on the male side) belong on coming to this continent?"
3. The participation rate is the portion of the population who are of working age 15-65, and who are part of the labour force of the economy, i.e., the economically active part of the population.

APPENDIX

Table 1: Occupational Composition of Poles in the Labour Force, 1941-71

	1971				1961				1951			
	MALE		FEMALE		MALE		FEMALE		MALE		FEMALE	
OCCUPATION	NO.	%	NO.	%	NO.	%	NO.	%	NO.	%	NO.	%
All occupations.	95,770	100.0	52,510	100.0	96,100	100.0	34,870	100.0	78,780	100.0	20,408	100.0
1. Managerial, administrative.	3,375	3.5	750	1.4	8,813	9.2	1,202	3.5	4,433	5.6	569	2.8
2. Occupations in natural sciences, engineering, mathematics, social sciences; religion; and artistic, literary, recreational.	5,880	6.1	1,135	2.2	4,890	5.1	664	1.9	1,608	2.0	244	1.2
3. Teaching.	1,805	1.9	2,585	4.9	776	0.8	1,156	3.3	307	0.4	442	2.2
(University)	(300)	(0.3)	(85)	(0.2)	(95)	(0.1)	(18)	(0.0)	(38)	(0.1)	(2)	(0.0)
(Other)	(1,505)	(1.6)	(2,500)	(4.7)	(681)	(0.7)	(1,138)	(3.3)	(269)	(0.3)	(440)	(2.2)
4. Occupations in medicine & health.	1,170	1.2	3,555	6.8	863	0.9	1,248	3.6	280	0.3	577	2.8
(Doctors)	(415)	(0.4)	(80)	(0.2)	(502)	(0.5)	(64)	(0.2)	(156)	(0.2)	(17)	(0.1)
(Nursing)	(425)	(0.4)	(2,775)	(5.3)	(69)	(0.1)	(931)	(2.7)	(8)	(0.0)	(485)	(2.4)
(Other)	(330)	(0.3)	(705)	(1.3)	(292)	(0.3)	(253)	(0.7)	(116)	(0.1)	(75)	(0.3)
5. Clerical occupations.	6,190	6.5	14,905	28.4	4,962	5.2	8,235	23.6	2,553	3.2	4,247	20.8
6. Sales occupations.	6,740	7.0	4,010	7.6	3,693	3.8	2,409	6.9	2,033	2.6	1,850	9.1
7. Service occupations.	8,955	9.3	10,385	19.8	6,971	7.3	9,442	27.1	4,314	5.5	5,653	27.7
8. Farming.	8,675	9.1	3,185	6.1	13,468	14.0	3,287	9.4	18,434	23.4	1,166	5.7
9. Fishing, forestry & mining.	2,385	2.5	35	0.0	3,423	3.6	6	0.0	4,342	5.5	3	0.0
10. Processing & machining.	11,565	12.1	1,580	3.0	13,919	14.5	2,245	6.4	10,085	12.8	1,482	7.3
11. Product fabricating.	9,830	10.3	3,310	6.3	8,184	8.5	2,787	8.0	6,268	8.0	2,941	14.4
12. Construction.	9,815	10.2	110	0.2	6,149	6.4	12	0.0	5,635	7.1	26	0.1
13. Transport.	4,105	4.3	110	0.2	4,276	4.4	25	0.1	5,403	6.9	30	0.1
14. Materials handling; other crafts & equipment operating; and occupations n.e.s.	7,735	8.1	1,610	3.1	13,018	13.5	1,114	3.2	12,252	15.6	961	4.7
15. Occupations not stated.	7,545	7.9	5,245	10.0	2,695	2.8	1,038	3.0	833	1.1	217	1.1
SUMMARY TABLE												
1-4 "White Collar" occupations.	12,230	12.8	8,025	15.3	15,342	16.0	4,270	12.3	6,628	8.4	1,832	9.0
5-7 Service occupations.	21,885	22.9	29,300	55.8	15,626	16.2	20,086	57.6	8,900	11.3	11,750	57.6
8-9 Primary occupations.	11,060	11.5	3,220	6.1	16,891	17.6	3,293	9.4	22,776	28.9	1,169	5.7
10-14 Manufacturing & construction.	43,050	45.0	6,720	12.8	45,546	47.4	6,183	17.7	39,643	50.3	5,440	26.6
15 Not specified.	7,545	7.8	5,245	10.0	2,695	2.8	1,038	3.0	833	1.1	217	1.1
Total	95,770	100.0	52,510	100.0	96,100	100.0	34,870	100.0	78,780	100.0	20,408	100.0
Population, age 15+.	123,700		116,265		117,736		101,767		89,743		73,335	
Participation rate.	77.4		45.2		81.6		34.3		87.8		27.8	
Canadian participation rate.	75.1		38.7		77.7		29.5		83.8		24.1	

Table 1 (cont'd.)

	1941			
	MALE		FEMALE	
OCCUPATION	NO.	%	NO.	%
All occupations.	54,846	100.0	10,631	100.0
1. Managerial, administrative.	1,399	2.5	100	0.9
2. Occupations in natural sciences, engineering, mathematics, social sciences; religion; and artistic, literary, recreational.	411	0.7	102	0.9
3. Teaching.	149	0.3	226	2.1
(University)	(6)	(0.0)	(-)	(-)
(Other)	(143)	(0.3)	(226)	(2.1)
4. Occupations in medicine & health.	68	0.1	219	2.1
(Doctors)	(41)	(0.1)	(2)	(0.0)
(Nursing)	(2)	(0.0)	(178)	(1.7)
(Other)	(25)	(0.0)	(39)	(0.4)
5. Clerical occupations.	864	1.6	739	7.0
6. Sales occupations.	1,075	2.0	743	7.0
7. Service occupations.	2,423	4.4	5,482	51.6
8. Farming.	20,547	37.5	433	4.0
9. Fishing, forestry & mining.	3,932	7.1	-	-
10. Processing & machining.	10,730	19.6	2,359	22.2
11. Product fabricating.				
12. Construction.	2,666	4.9	6	0.1
13. Transport.	3,737	6.8	45	0.4
14. Materials handling; other crafts & equipment operating; and occupations n.e.s.	6,690	12.2	160	1.5
15. Not specified.	155	0.3	17	0.2
SUMMARY TABLE				
1-4 "White Collar" occupations.	2,027	3.7	647	6.1
5-7 Service occupations.	4,362	8.0	6,964	65.5
8-9 Primary occupations.	24,479	44.6	433	4.1
10-14 Manufacturing & construction.	23,823	43.4	2,570	24.2
15 Not specified.	155	0.3	17	0.1
Total	54,846	100.0	10,631	100.0
Population, age 15+	64,924		53,443	
Participation rate.	84.5		19.9	
Canadian participation rate.	78.6		20.7	

Table 2: Number of Immigrants by Major Ethnic Group and Intended Occupation, 1946-55

Occupational Group	British	French	German	Italian	Polish	Ukrainian	Other	Total	Per cent of Total Labour Force
1. Professional	23,702	1,191	2,726	514	1,283	359	18,964	48,739	7.3
2. Clerical	30,413	1,126	2,833	380	579	129	11,328	46,788	7.0
3. Transportation & Communications	7,510	285	662	912	971	700	4,212	15,252	2.3
4. Commercial	13,105	526	992	257	286	43	10,048	25,257	3.8
5. Financial	301	11	6	2	4	–	150	474	0.1
6. Service	11,089	787	18,448	8,076	4,681	2,448	23,477	69,006	10.4
7. Agriculture	12,005	2,473	23,425	25,291	13,619	7,938	53,444	138,195	20.8
8. Fishing, Trapping & Mining	2,758	299	3,201	2,071	3,829	2,695	8,104	22,957	3.4
9. Manufacturing	63,289	4,801	28,645	15,831	7,880	4,151	58,067	182,664	27.5
10. Labourers	12,081	991	9,599	25,574	4,091	2,175	22,700	77,211	11.6
11. Not Stated	15,051	599	3,543	1,724	1,156	510	16,033	38,616	5.8
Total, Labour Force	191,304	13,089	94,080	80,632	38,379	21,148	226,527	665,159	100.0
Dependents	176,401	11,063	65,127	54,524	23,199	13,191	213,655	557,160	
Total	367,705	24,152	159,207	135,156	61,578	34,339	440,182	1,222,319	
Per cent	30.1	2.0	13.0	11.1	5.0	2.8	36.0	100.0	

SOURCE: Employment and Immigration Canada, 1946-55.

Table 3: Number of Immigrants by Major Ethnic Group and Intended Occupation, 1956-61

Occupational Group	British	French	German	Italian	Polish	Ukrainian	Other	Total	Per cent of Total Labour Force
1. Professional	30,246	1,341	2,552	821	774	69	23,926	59,729	13.3
2. Clerical	30,716	1,208	4,477	384	378	22	11,432	48,617	10.9
3. Transportation & Communications	5,676	352	744	732	144	30	3,856	11,534	2.6
4. Commercial	9,211	454	1,402	206	124	7	5,480	16,884	3.8
5. Financial	713	30	21	7	5	—	451	1,227	0.3
6. Service	12,046	1,493	11,939	12,824	1,111	109	28,413	67,935	15.2
7. Agriculture	4,737	609	3,189	5,763	668	93	20,977	36,036	8.0
8. Fishing, Trapping & Mining	2,238	89	766	369	149	26	2,411	6,048	1.3
9. Manufacturing	37,445	2,912	27,479	16,783	2,484	388	48,044	135,535	30.3
10. Labourers	5,220	455	5,367	30,059	1,096	197	19,351	61,745	13.8
11. Not Stated	698	78	215	121	121	11	1,027	2,271	0.5
Total, Labour Force	138,946	9,021	58,151	68,069	7,054	952	165,368	447,561	100.0
Dependents	105,332	7,802	40,083	82,504	10,788	1,154	159,376	407,039	
Total	244,278	16,823	98,234	150,573	17,842	2,106	324,744	854,600	
Per cent	28.6	2.0	11.5	7.6	2.1	0.2	38.0	100.0	

SOURCE: Employment and Immigration Canada, 1956-61.

Table 4: Number of Immigrants by Country of Last Permanent Residence and Intended Occupation, 1962-71

Occupational Group	Britain	France	Germany	Italy	Poland	Ukraine*	Other	Total	Per cent of Total Labour Force
1. Professional	62,162	8,015	6,599	3,382	823		136,855	217,836	29.0
2. Clerical	36,927	3,395	5,110	1,387	391		58,493	105,703	14.1
3. Transportation & Communications	3,917	311	477	630	133		5,119	10,587	1.4
4. Commercial	7,961	1,000	1,117	407	79		12,414	22,978	3.1
5. Financial	958	85	60	34	2		1,914	3,053	0.4
6. Service	12,951	4,473	5,194	10,401	772		44,099	77,890	10.4
7. Agriculture	2,753	1,060	1,141	2,172	501		17,382	25,009	3.3
8. Fishing, Trapping & Mining	1,013	311	479	227	32		2,052	4,114	0.5
9. Manufacturing	50,219	12,876	19,690	40,543	1,873		105,891	231,092	30.8
10. Labourers	2,667	478	1,897	23,506	566		14,461	43,575	5.8
11. Not Stated	1,084	316	213	1,004	67		6,027	8,711	1.2
Total, Labour Force	182,612	32,320	41,977	83,693	5,239		404,707	750,548	100.0
Dependents	164,255	22,793	27,590	96,230	8,717		389,705	709,290	
Total	346,867	55,113	69,567	179,923	13,956		794,412	1,459,838	
Per cent	23.8	3.8	4.8	12.3	0.9		54.4	100.0	

*No data.

SOURCE: Employment and Immigration Canada, 1962-71.

Table 5: Number of Immigrants by Country of Last Permanent Residence and Intended Occupation, 1972-78

Occupational Group	Britain	France	Germany	Italy	Poland	Ukraine*	Other	Total	Per cent of Total Labour Force
1. Professional	29,265	5,011	3,128	2,223	817		103,589	144,033	29.8
2. Clerical	15,834	1,475	860	596	307		51,788	70,860	14.7
3. Transportation & Communications	2,248	200	145	338	143		7,934	11,008	2.3
4. Commercial	3,761	469	304	297	59		14,118	19,008	3.9
5. Financial[1]	183	19	14	6	1		726	949	0.2
6. Service	7,150	2,260	893	1,207	474		38,099	50,083	10.4
7. Agriculture	924	271	267	270	164		10,759	12,655	2.6
8. Fishing, Trapping & Mining	343	79	54	40	19		1,329	1,864	0.4
9. Manufacturing	24,507	3,241	2,979	6,535	1,263		100,281	138,806	28.7
10. Labourers[1]	210	74	44	374	45		3,171	3,918	0.8
11. Not Stated	1,040	173	176	1,499	199		26,958	30,045	6.2
Total, Labour Force	85,465	13,272	8,864	13,385	3,491		358,752	483,229	100.0
Dependents	84,485	8,941	9,210	17,912	3,403		456,028	579,979	
Total	169,950	22,213	18,074	31,297	6,894		814,780	1,063,208	
Per cent	16.0	2.1	1.7	2.9	0.7		76.6	100.0	

* No data.

[1] No data since 1974.

SOURCE: Employment and Immigration Canada, 1972-78.

Occupational Mobility of Polish Americans in Selected U.S. Cities after World War Two

Grzegorz Babinski

Theories of cultural pluralism and ethnic revival have dominated American sociology in recent years. But in predictions of the future of American ethnic groups, particularly white European ethnic groups, two opposing kinds of statements can be found. The first is assimilationist and is based mostly on evidence provided by analyses of census data and other statistical materials. These data show an upward occupational mobility and a growing education of the members of minority groups and also their increasing movement from the inner cities to suburbs. The second prediction is revitalizationist and is based on the research of the political behaviour and growing cultural activities of various ethnic groups. According to this prediction, ethnic heritage and culture could last for a long time, despite structural assimilation. There are also arguments that full and effective structural assimilation never took place in American society. Minorities advanced in occupational and economic dimensions but they always remained within relatively homogeneous groups and were never able to penetrate the elite power structure.

I am not going to discuss in detail the arguments of both these theories. First of all I do not think they are contradictory. Structural (i.e., occupational, residential) assimilation certainly exists, at least to some extent. It is also true that ethnic culture and consciousness, reinforced by pluralistic ideology and common political and economic interests, could shape members of the immigrant communities into well-organized groups, despite the decreasing occupational, educational and spatial homogeneity of this group.

Occupational mobility of ethnic group members is considered by many sociologists as the most vital dimension of ethnic assimilation. Milton Gordon in his model of assimilation categorized structural assimilation as the most important element. However, Gordon's meaning of structural assimilation encompasses more than occupational mobility; full-scale entrance of ethnic group members into clubs, neighbourhoods and into the informal structure of the host society was also essential in the process of ethnic assimilation.[1] But such entrance into the full social structure can take place only after considerable achievement in occupational mobility.

Many empirical studies focused only on occupational mobility and on ethnic occupational stratification. Most of the analyses were concentrated either on nation-wide or on local community levels. Both levels of analysis are important and both could provide materials for a full analysis of occupational achievement of Polish Americans. But these two levels of analysis are often not comparable. There is a third level, a very important one, higher than the local community level, but not as high as the nation-wide level. The analysis done by E. Obidinski reveals important differences between the occupational position of Polish "foreign stock" (i.e., Polish-born or having at least one Polish-born parent) in different American cities. But Obidinski's analysis does not include any control variables. His data show only global occupational distribution of Polish Americans in selected metropolitan areas. They do not reveal the influences of such variables as age, sex or generation.

Structural assimilation of ethnic groups within the host society is a long, multidimensional process in which many historical, cultural and local factors and events play important roles. Nation-wide analysis and comparisons are important but only local (i.e., city, neighbourhood or community) level research can provide answers to questions on the interrelationships between many variables which produce this process.

Research on the occupational mobility of Polish Americans is slight. In a study done in 1950 by E. P. Hutchinson Poles scored low on occupational position scales.[2] Polish Americans were considerably under-represented in all higher and more prestigious social and occupational categories of American society. They were almost absent in the highest occupational groups—professionals—and heavily concentrated in the unskilled and semi-skilled categories. Hutchinson's findings are consistent with the earliest research done by L. Warner et al. in Yankee City.[3] Research done later shows a similar occupational position of Polish Americans, but a slow upward movement was detected. In the seventies two syntheses of the research on Polish Americans' social standing were made.[4]

Almost all research on this topic falls into four main categories. First, there are the publications in which authors used published, synthetic information about average occupational positions of all Polish Americans, plus such dimensions of social position as annual family income, median school years completed and so forth. Such information, essential on the initial stage of analysis, does not provide the more detailed knowledge that would advance the research. Secondly, some authors, for example, Hutchinson, rearranged or transformed census data, but did not use any control variables. Results of such analyses, though important, are also not sufficient for broader generalizations. Thirdly, there are surveys in which questions about the respondent's occupational and social status were included. But again, such research has seldom been representative enough to permit wider interpretations. Finally, occupational mobility and position of Polish American local communities have been the subject of some research. Much of it provides detailed information about individual or family occupational patterns but these data are usually not representative and are seldom comparable.[5]

In my analysis I will use only U.S. census data. But by statistical analysis, I hope to draw out from these statistics important new information. First, I am trying to show that there are many important control variables which must be taken into account. In this short paper only a small part of the broader, multidimensional analysis can be included. This research should not be applied in isolation; it should be connected with the analysis of the spatial movement of ethnic group members and with research on local ethnic community transformations. The results of this research presented here are, I think, more important as a methodological proposition than as a basis for theoretical generalizations and broader explanations.

Hypotheses and Assumptions

In much of the research on ethnic occupational mobility similar processes of upward movement were found. From Warner's to Lieberson's analysis[6] all ethnic groups advanced slowly but significantly in structural assimilation. Lieberson found important differences in ethnic occupational mobility in different American cities. These same patterns were visible in the 1970s.[7] But control variables were included in only a few of the research studies. In my research I try to show ethnic occupational differentiation in selected U.S. cities. My initial hypothesis is that the significant structural assimilation which took place in the sixties and seventies does not mean that all occupational differences between ethnic groups will soon disappear. There are differences in ethnic occupational stratification in major American cities. My second hypothesis is that there are some important control variables which, when held constant, reveal important regularities and peculiar ways of ethnic mobility. In this paper only three such variables were partly controlled, namely age, sex and ethnic generation. My third hypothesis is that occupational mobility is created to some extent by educational advancement of the ethnic group. Educational preference and large-scale entrance of the younger generations to colleges and universities will create large occupational upward mobility. Because of this I also took into account the educational mobility of Polish Americans.

Data and Methods

To make a proper analysis of occupational mobility, information about each individual is necessary. Such individual data were not available. Instead, data from the 1950, 1960 and 1970 censuses were re-analysed and recounted. Unfortunately, these data are not fully comparable. In standard U.S. census publications from 1960, information on Standard Metropolitan Statistical Areas (SMSA) levels was not available. Because of this main comparisons were made between 1950 and 1970. SMSA were chosen to compare ethnic patterns in some American cities. Only cities with a heavy Polish ethnic concentration were taken into account. And finally, I decided to exclude from the analysis two cities with many Americans of Polish descent, namely New York City and Boston. In both these cities the percentage of first and second generation Polish immigrants with a mother tongue other than Polish or English is so high that this breaks the ethnic homogeneousness of Polish foreign stock.

There are two statistical measures applied in these analyses. The first measure is average occupational position of foreign stock. It is computed as a mean of occupation group positions. For the U.S. Census of 1950 this mean ranges from 1–lowest positions–to 10–highest. For the 1970 census data this measure ranges from 1 to 12. There were simple rank order scores ascribed to each occupational category. The second measure is an index of occupational dissimilarity, which shows the percentage of the members of a particular ethnic group who have to change their occupational category to match occupational distribution of some other group.

Results

During twenty years, between 1950 and 1970, the occupational structure of American society as a whole has changed considerably. This change influenced the occupational structure of all American ethnic groups, among them Polish Americans. But the upward occupational and social mobility of many ethnic groups was more rapid during this same period than the change in occupational structure for Americans in general. Polish Americans, like other groups in the seventies, are much closer to middle and high social positions than they were in the fifties. Table 1 shows a decreasing gap between occupational distribution of Polish first and second generation immigrants and American society. Foreign-born, both men and women, were heavily concentrated in manual workers categories. In 1970 this concentration is still visible, but the category of high skilled craftsmen and foremen has become most numerous.

Table 1 compares the occupational distribution of Polish Americans in the 25-44 age group with those of native-born U.S. When age is held constant, the occupational distribution of Polish Americans is very close to the similar distribution of all native Americans. Unfortunately the census does not provide information about the third and fourth ethnic generations. But some research shows that each next generation is higher on the social occupational ladder.[8] This means that Polish Americans are to a great extent structurally assimilated into American society. But this general statement is only partly true. First, occupational assimilation does not mean full structural assimilation. Secondly, even if the members of ethnic groups are proportionately represented in the highest occupational categories, they seldom belong to the aristocracy and the narrow elite groups.[9] Polish Americans have entered higher positions but most of them still belong to the blue-collar categories. They are structurally assimilated not to the social structure of American society but to the local—city or neighbourhood—social structure.

Table 4 shows the occupational position and social advancement of Polish Americans in selected cities in 1970. In 1950 they were below the average occupational position of all employees in those cities but at the same levels as the German, Irish or Italian groups. In 1970 Polish Americans were closer to the average occupational position in all cities. There are significant differences in ethnic occupational stratification. In Buffalo all four subcategories of Polish foreign stock were significantly below not only total Buffalo population, but also all ethnic groups included in this analysis. Only Polish foreign-born were higher than Italian foreign-born. In Chicago the average occupational position of Polish Americans was higher than in Buffalo and closer to the occupational position of the whole population. Polish Americans in Chicago, who never gained political power in that city, are much better in occupational mobility than their compatriots from Buffalo. They are higher than Italian males. There is a similar situation in Cleveland, though in that city Polish Americans score lower on the occupational scale than Italians. Again in Detroit, Italians are higher, except foreign-born men. Milwaukee and Pittsburgh are the next two cities in which the average occupational position of Polish Americans is relatively low. The tables reveal important and significant differences of the subcategories of ethnic groups in American cities. Census data do not provide sufficient information for explanation of these differences, but some plausible hypothetical explanations could be suggested. First, there are peculiar local patterns and values which determine individual careers. It might be connected with the development of particular branches of industry or accessibility of jobs. Secondly, the speed and the pattern of emigration of ethnic group members to the suburbs and the decreasing cohesiveness of traditional ethnic neighbourhoods could affect occupational mobility. Thirdly, occupational advancement is to a great extent a product of previous or actual discrimination against ethnic groups.

Conclusion

In this short presentation I am not going to discuss all problems and questions connected with ethnic occupational mobility and its significance for the processes of assimilation. There is no doubt that the occupational advancement of Polish Americans is a much more complex process than is revealed by analysis of the U.S. census data. But even these data show many important regularities and significant subprocesses of ethnic occupational stratification. Comparative analysis of these same processes in a few American cities permits me to offer some generalizations.[10]

1) Structural assimilation of immigrants, measured by change in occupational position and occupational dissimilarity, is inevitable. But this assimilation is much more complicated and multidimensional than it seems to be, judging from the results of research done on higher levels of generalizations.
2) Despite the one-directional process of occupational mobility, each ethnic group shows unique specific patterns of occupational mobility. Differences between first and second generations and between men and women are particularly important.
3) Polish Americans in these cities move upward in average occupational position in a manner and rate similar to other ethnic groups. Changes of America's Polonia are neither slower nor different than changes of other groups.
4) There are similar patterns of the upward occupational mobility of Polish Americans in all cities examined, despite some local irregularities and the different levels of this advancement.
5) When age is held constant, the index of occupational dissimilarity between second-generation Polish Americans and all Americans of native, of foreign, or mixed parentage is low. This index also gives a low score for Polish second generation

compared with the American population as a whole. But one has to be aware that the scale of occupations used in the census is not very precise and distinguishes only the major occupational categories.

6) The next step in the research on ethnic occupational movement and the structural assimilation should be a more detailed analysis of subprocesses which take place within cities. It has not been possible to present the results of these analyses here, though they were already done. They reveal significant interrelationships between spatial and occupational mobility. The correlations between ethnic segregation, concentration and structural assimilation are also very important.

Notes

1. O.P. Duncan and P. Blau, *The American Occupational Structure* (New York, 1964).
2. E.P. Hutchinson, *Immigrants and Their Children 1850-1950* (New York, 1956).
3. L. Warner et al., *The Social Systems of American Ethnic Groups* (New York, 1945).
4. I. Sanders and E. Morawska, *Polish-American Community Life: a Survey of Research* (New York, 1975).
5. N. Sandberg, *Ethnic Identity and Assimilation: the Polish-American Community,* case study of Metropolitan Los Angeles (New York, 1974).
6. S. Lieberson, *Ethnic Patterns in American Cities* (New York, 1963); and Warner, *Social Systems of American Ethnic Groups.*
7. S.E. Bleda, "Intergenerational Differences and Patterns and Basis of Ethnic Residential Dissimilarity," *Ethnicity* 5, no. 2 (1978), pp. 91-107.
8. P. Chi and J. Zubrzycki, "Ethnic Origin and Social Status of the United States Population," *Ethnicity* 5, no. 4 (1978), pp. 312-27.
9. E.D. Baltzell, *The Protestant Establishment. Aristocracy and Caste in America* (New York, 1964).
10. G. Babinski, "Change in the Settlement and Occupational Mobility of Selected Ethnic Groups in the Greater Detroit Area after World War Two," paper presented at a conference at Wayne State University, May 1979.

Table 1: Occupational Distribution of Polish American and Native-born, 1950-70, Age Group 25-44 (percentage)

	Men				Women			
	1950		1970		1950		1970	
	U.S.	Polish	U.S.	Polish	U.S.	Polish	U.S.	Polish
Professional and technical	9.8	7.3	21.9	24.3	11.0	7.0	19.7	19.4
Managers and administrators	12.7	9.3	14.3	13.3	4.5	3.6	4.1	3.7
Sales workers			7.8	7.9			6.8	6.5
	15.1	12.8			40.5	30.7		
Clerical workers			7.6	8.2			41.1	42.1
Craftsmen	21.3	23.6	21.0	21.0	2.1	2.7	1.7	1.7
Operatives, except transport			10.0	11.7			11.8	14.4
	23.6	32.6			27.6	42.2		
Transport equipment operatives			5.1	4.5			0.5	0.4
Labourers, except farm	6.0	6.9	4.0	3.3	0.8	1.3	0.7	0.8
Farmers and farm managers	4.7	1.8	1.3	0.6	0.2	0.2	0.1	0.1
Farm labourers and farm foremen	1.5	0.8	0.8	0.2	1.5	0.7	0.4	0.1
Service workers, except domestic	4.7	4.3	6.2	5.1	8.8	9.2	12.2	10.4
Domestic workers	—	—	—	—	1.8	1.5	0.8	0.4
Index of occupational dissimilarity: U.S. versus Polish	12		5		16		3	

Table 2: Index of Occupational Dissimilarity between Subcategories of Polish, German, and Italian Foreign Stock in Selected U.S. Cities, 1970

	Buffalo	Chicago	Cleveland	Detroit	Milwaukee	Philadelphia	Pittsburgh
1. Polish versus German: native of foreign or mixed parentage, men	16	10	12	11	9	8	11
2. Polish versus German: native of foreign or mixed parentage, women	24	18	22	12	11	19	15
3. Polish versus German: foreign born, men	28	21	15	21	27	20	20
4. Polish versus German: foreign born, women	35	30	30	28	11	23	21
5. Polish versus Italian: native of foreign or mixed parentage, men	16	12	12	10	16	7	10
6. Polish versus Italian: native of foreign or mixed parentage, women	12	9	4	9	9	5	9
7. Polish versus Italian: foreign born men	15	15	14	17	19	20	17
8. Polish versus Italian: foreign born, women	10	14	19	15	30	23	19

Index of dissimilarity shows percentage of one group which has to change occupational category to achieve equal occupational distribution with another group. It varies from 0—complete similarity—to 100—complete dissimilarity.

Table 3: Median School Years Completed of Polish and the U.S. Foreign Stock, 1950, 1960 and 1970

	Native of Foreign or Mixed Parentage				Foreign-born			
	Men		Women		Men		Women	
	Total	Age 25-44	Total	Age 25-44	Total	Age 25-44	Total	Age 25-44
1950 United States	10.2	11.5	10.4	11.6	8.2	9.9	8.2	9.8
Polish foreign stock	10.2	10.5	10.0	10.1	6.5	9.0	5.4	8.8
1960 United States	10.9	12.2	11.1	12.2	8.4	11.6	8.5	11.6
Polish foreign stock	10.9	11.8	10.6	11.6	7.6	9.9	6.3	9.4
1970 United States	12.1	12.6	12.1	12.5	9.3	12.4	9.0	12.2
Polish foreign stock	11.8	12.7	11.3	12.5	8.4	12.1	7.8	11.3

Table 4: Average Occupational Position of the Subcategories of Polish and Some Other Ethnic Groups in Selected U.S. Cities, 1970

	Total native	Total U.S. foreign stock	Polish	German	Italian	Irish	Hungarian
Buffalo							
NFP	8.01	8.10	7.70	8.25	7.98	8.10	7.89
NFP / W /	7.90	7.80	7.11	7.85	7.75	8.91	7.80
FB / M /	8.14	7.96	7.32	8.20	6.97	7.50	8.33
FB / W /	8.16	7.26	6.32	6.07	6.89	5.93	7.63
Chicago							
NFP / M /	8.16	8.48	8.13	8.38	8.09	8.26	8.63
NFP / W /	8.20	8.44	7.96	8.46	8.19	8.07	8.36
FB / M /	8.49	7.81	7.65	8.31	7.01	7.06	8.04
FB / W /	8.53	7.61	6.72	7.85	7.19	6.88	7.10
Cleveland							
NFP / M /	8.14	8.46	8.11	8.45	8.37	8.44	8.47
NFP / W /	7.90	8.17	7.77	8.50	7.86	8.53	8.07
FB / M /	8.47	8.15	7.84	8.44	7.33	6.75	8.39
FB / W /	8.40	7.22	5.92	7.48	6.88	7.08	6.76
Detroit							
NFP / M /	7.97	8.49	8.06	8.46	8.33	8.01	8.01
NFP / W /	7.72	8.21	7.80	8.09	7.98	8.98	7.96
FB / M /	8.28	8.31	7.97	8.68	7.39	7.56	8.31
FB / W /	8.15	7.49	6.37	7.67	6.41	6.73	7.48
Milwaukee							
NFP / M /	8.12	8.22	7.73	8.03	8.32	9.81	8.40
NFP / W /	7.89	7.82	7.37	7.63	7.81	8.73	8.26
FB / M /	8.22	7.96	7.38	8.06	7.02	9.25	8.49
FB / W /	8.08	7.07	5.77	7.30	6.82	—	—
Philadelphia							
NFP / M /	8.11	8.60	8.23	8.54	8.15	7.65	8.62
NFP / W /	7.93	8.31	7.97	8.34	7.82	8.41	7.74
FB / M /	8.67	8.29	8.18	8.68	7.21	7.00	8.25
FB / W /	8.46	7.49	7.21	7.64	7.15	5.67	8.66
Pittsburgh							
NFP / M /	8.16	8.00	7.59	8.04	7.85	8.14	8.12
NFP / W /	8.01	7.51	7.12	7.64	7.54	8.27	7.30
FB / M /	8.29	8.01	8.00	8.73	6.99	7.16	8.19
FB / W /	8.27	6.77	6.15	7.14	6.45	5.17	6.63

NFP— native of foreign or mixed parentage
FB— foreign born
/ M /— men
/ W /— women

Neighbourhood

Urban Location: a Necessary or Sufficient Basis for Polonian Ethnic Persistence

Eugene Obidinski

As inner city areas of American cities lose portions of their white ethnic populations to less urbanized areas, what will become of the ethnic communities created by Polish immigrants and their descendants? Some of the early immigrants went to rural areas such as Karnes County, Texas, or the Connecticut River valley of New England, but most settled in cities in the Northeastern, Middle Atlantic, and Midwestern states. Urban locations were typical and perhaps, crucial in the development of particular immigrant communities.[1] Golab, among others, examined the functional relationships of such settings to Polonian immigrant adjustment.[2] The relevance of such relationships to community development will be considered in another portion of this paper. A more basic objective of the paper, however, is to investigate the alleged disappearance of Polish American communities in changing urban areas. The investigation will be limited to Polonian communities in the Buffalo, New York metropolitan area. However, this specific and limited examination may help answer a more general question involving necessary and sufficient functions of urban locations in supporting ethnic community life.

Historical development of the Buffalo communities as well as related demographic change and variations in urban-suburban ethnic patterns should be considered in the context of related research findings.

Ethnic Communities as People, Places and Processes

Influenced by classic analyses of Chicago School social ecologists, students of urban life identify communities as subareas of the city which are autonomous ecological units, homogeneous status (or "natural") areas, and forms of human interaction supported by shared symbolic commitment.[3] Communities exist in specific physical locations among persons whose behaviour is influenced—though, not determined—by physical surroundings. For Park, communities were not merely population aggregates but also forms of social order.

> A community is not only a collection of people, but it is also a collection of institutions. Not people, but institutions, are final and decisive in distinguishing the community from other social constellations.[4]

And, to the extent that they consist of persons who are more like each other than different, ethnic groups are a source of "status communities" as defined by Weber.[5] Shared status, common interests, and residential propinquity generate an elemental form of community in "face-block" neighbourhoods described by Suttles.[6] More intensive and autonomous ethnic communities developed in ghetto-like "defended neighbourhoods" in which immigrants and their descendants remained apart from other urban residents, according to Schwiran.

> . . . the ghetto form of organization is not unique to the urban Jew. The Italians, the Greeks, the Poles . . . established defended neighborhoods at one time or another in our large cities. These areas containing the social institutions . . . have been major factors leading to the assimilation of the newcomers.[7]

Perhaps the segregated residential enclaves also impeded elements of social contact and communication essential to assimilation. In any case the ghetto areas—as physical locations—function even after original inhabitants leave and are replaced by successive waves of minority group members. Hispanic residents, for example, occupy neighbourhoods in a formerly Polonian area of Chicago studied by Lopata.[8]

Thus, particular ethnic communities are not permanently grounded in the residential enclaves created by the earliest immigrants. As adaptative forms of social interaction, communities survive—and transcend their original locations. Hunter describes the resiliency of inner city communities.

> I would suggest that the community is not simply a "residue" but, rather, that it is an emergent, socially constructed reality. I think it would be better for us to . . . [study] . . . communal forms and the processes of community formation than to debate the definition of community and then bemoan its predefined demise.[9]

Gannon, in an analysis of supportive elements of urban communities, criticizes announcements of ethnic resurgence or ethnic revival in communities which never really declined or disappeared.[10] A "sense of community" and a "sense of territory" are separate aspects of urban life, according to Warren. Social networks which facilitate communication between friends and relatives in widely separated residential areas provide an integrative sense of community independent of shared territorial location.[11] However, internal forms of social control developed within autonomous ethnic neighbourhoods may disappear—and the "sense of community" may decline—as newcomers replace original residents. In his study of Fairmount, a working-class "European ethnic neighborhood in an inner city area of Philadelphia," Cybriwsky found that as the "revitalized" neighbourhood attracted young professional workers, the quality of life declined.

> The dwindling of ethnic populations, accompanied by newcomer immigration (as well as the area's racial crisis) . . . resulted in a decline in Fairmount's distinctive life styles and close social contacts. While the neighborhood was an isolated enclave, with strongly developed local social relations, order was maintained by internal mechanisms. The effectiveness of these mechanisms decreased with population transformation . . . Fairmount lost its autonomy and . . . has figuratively been annexed to the city.[12]

Ethnic neighbourhoods which survive may do so because they attract relatively homogeneous populations. Among Polish Americans in Milwaukee neighbourhoods described by Pienkos, assimilation was relatively extensive; however, non-assimilated residents—those who shared strong Polonian ethnic orientations—were concentrated in specific South Side neighbourhoods.[13] Similar Polish American enclaves developed in Buffalo, New York, during the past century and remain relatively autonomous residential areas despite general urban to suburban migration trends.[14] After a brief historical description of Polonian neighbourhood development in the city, community-related consequences of such migration will be considered.

Origins of Principal Polonian Residential Areas

Poles did not arrive in substantial numbers on any permanent basis until the 1870s.[15] The Reverend John Pitass, a patriarch of the Buffalo settlement, found thirty Polish families upon his arrival in 1873. A year later, the first Polish parish, St. Stanislaus, was built at Townsend and Peckham Streets in an East Side area later known as the Broadway-Fillmore district. In the 1890s two other Polonian settlements—Black Rock, in the northwestern part of the city, and Kaisertown, southeast of the Broadway-Fillmore district—developed.[16] An area of railroad tracks and stockyards separated Kaisertown from the other East Side neighbourhoods. In terms of Lopata's community typology, the local ethnic community consisted of three settlements of local neighbourhoods clustered around specific churches (such as the St. Stan's neighbourhood).[17] These distinctive segments of the Buffalo Polonian community developed separately and remain somewhat distinct.

Broadway-Fillmore

When Father Pitass arrived in the city as a seminarian in 1873, Buffalo was in the midst of a rapid economic expansion as a railroad centre, a site for large stockyards and grain processing, a convenient location for metal goods production, and a foods processing centre. Such industry demanded a large supply of unskilled workers and from 1875 to 1892, about 13,000 Polish immigrants arrived in Buffalo to help satisfy this demand.[18] The German settlements in the city, however, were established for three generations and contained over 31,000 persons in 1870 and over 52,000 in 1890.[19] Early German immigrants settled in the Fruit Belt area and other East Side neighbourhoods eventually invaded by the Polish immigrants.[20]

> The Polish newcomers had a difficult time when they first started to move to Buffalo's East Side. Their neighbors were members of a large well organized German community. At the beginning . . . the Germans were most helpful . . . later, however, when the Poles overflowed the East Side of the city, the Germans considered them intruders. Many Poles, remembering conditions in their fatherland, were less than cordial to the Germans.[21]

Whatever its source, Polonian antagonism toward the Germans encouraged community cohesiveness. Although Father Pitass generally did not encourage members of his flock to join American organizations, he encouraged affiliation with the Democratic Party during a period when German settlers were predominantly Republican.[22] Father Pitass' influence extended beyond the pulpit of St. Stanislaus and the East Side neighbourhoods. However, these neighbourhoods were the heart of the city's Polonian community because they provided a crucial support system. Broadway-Fillmore was the crossroads of an extensive business centre containing the busy, European-style Broadway Market, bakeries and butcher shops, furniture stores, pharmacies, banks and taverns. The *Dom Polski* building (renovated and known as the Polish Community Center since 1977) and headquarters of fraternal organizations, such as the Polish Union of America, provided meeting rooms for a number of organizations ranging from singing societies (which began to develop in the 1890s) to literary-drama groups and folk dance ensembles. Polish American doctors, lawyers, funeral directors, barbers and other professionals served clients from Sobieski Street or Paderewski Street. The Broadway-Fillmore commercial area was surrounded by an extensive residential area which eventually expanded in an easterly-northeasterly direction past the city's eastern boundary and into Sloan and Cheektowaga. Residential and commercial migration from Broadway-Fillmore since the 1960s is both a symptom and consequence of apparent neighbourhood decline.

Polish American Neighbourhoods of Buffalo, N.Y.

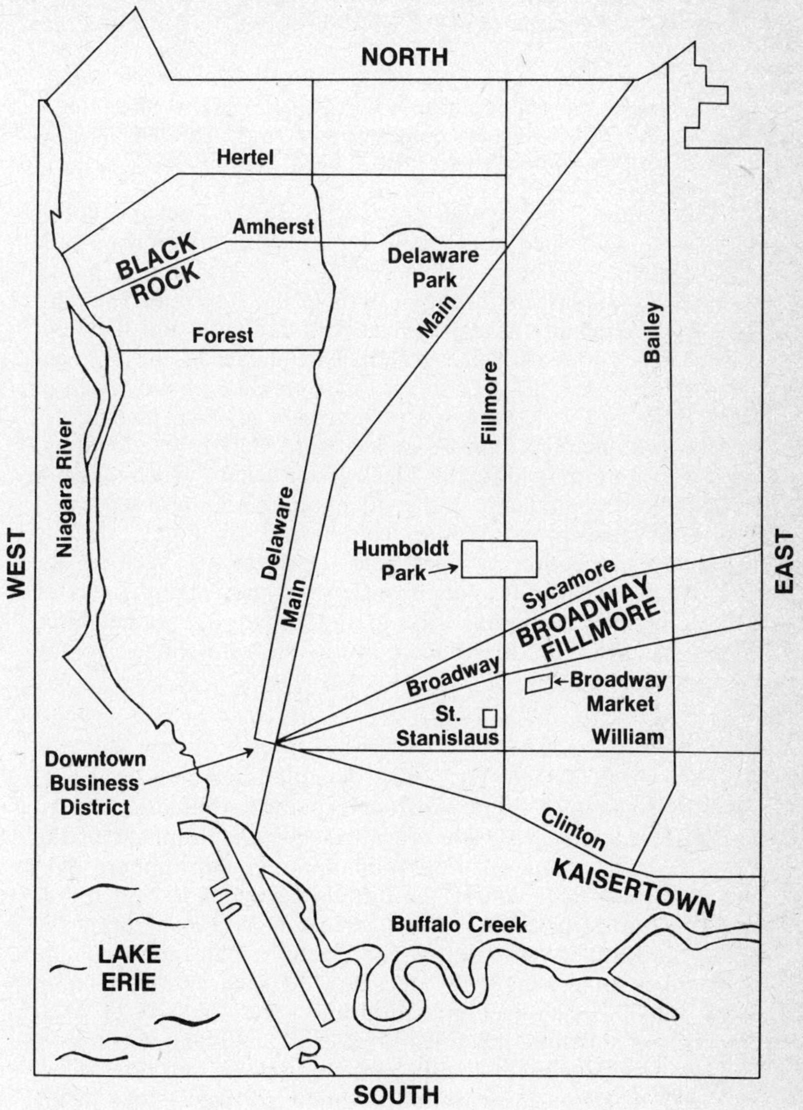

SOURCE: Adapted from map in Stephen Gredel, *People of Our City and County* (Buffalo, N.Y.: Erie County Historical Society, 1965), inside cover.

Black Rock

The Black Rock settlement of Polish Americans may have originated earlier than the larger neighbourhoods on the East Side of Buffalo. Although the "first true Polish-Catholic settler" arrived in the Buffalo area in 1864,[23] a 1923 history refers to an earlier arrival of Poles:

> "Assumption (Roman Catholic Church), at Amherst Street, is largely a Polish parish, and was organized some time later than 1852, when the Poles began to settle at Lower Black Rock.[24]

Another source indicates that "... In the 1890's a second Polish colony was established in Black Rock because of the growing steel industry there."[25] The church and school of Assumption parish were established largely through efforts of the Reverend Theophil Kozlowski, originally an assistant at St. Stanislaus, and the Felician Sisters who staffed the school. Documents of the Felician order indicate that "in 1871, a few Polish families already lived in Black Rock and with increased immigration in 1881, their settlement showed marked increase and growth."[26] Organizational activity was more limited in the Black Rock colony which was not only smaller in population and residential area but also separated from the Broadway-Fillmore commercial shopping district. Through participation in East Side organizations, such as the professional and businessmen's society or the singing societies, and by periodic shopping trips to the Broadway Market area, Polish Americans in Black Rock were—and are—linked to the East Side community.

Kaisertown

Railroad yards, a large post office complex and industrial sites currently separate Kaisertown from Broadway-Fillmore. The intervening railroad lines were crucial in the establishment of the extensive stockyards located off William Street and Fillmore Avenue. According to Jablonski, the Buffalo Livestock Exchange was established at Depot and William Streets in 1893 and during the 1890s, the Buffalo yards were second only to Chicago in volume of livestock processing.[27] By the turn of the century, Clinton Street—the busiest street in Kaisertown—was the site of meat processing companies, metal work factories, and commercial storage facilities. No doubt Polish immigrants from the established East Side neighbourhoods found a variety of factory jobs in the area; however, the settlement of Kaisertown (or Kazimierzowo) may have been stimulated by excursions of St. Stanislaus' parishioners to the rural "Gardenville" area six miles to the southeast.[28] The land adjacent to Clinton Street itself, despite its potential economic value, was not a preferred residential site, according to *Dziennik dla Wszytkich* (Polish Everybody's Daily) in 1912:

> As is always the case, Polish families began to settle not on the main road like Clinton but sought shelter in the most far off corners, near Buffalo Creek. Instead of erecting the church and the school on Clinton Street, they turned toward Buffalo Creek and there they founded a beautiful vicinity beyond Clinton Street. Only later, they realized their mistake.
>
> Why did they fail to settle on the main street—no one knows. Generally, Poles settle far from the center of the city, and secondly, they keep to the side streets. If however, the Poles would reach out for Clinton, many of them would now be wealthy.
>
> Too bad the Poles did not at once inhabit the area on Clinton Street, and that on both sides of it. They would own all the prime lots and the newcomers would be forced to settle by the creek. Today, they regret their actions, but it is like having mustard after dinner and nothing else. . . . That the Poles intended to control all of Kazimierzowo is evident from the names given to the streets there: Gorski, Kazimierz, Fredro, etc. There is also a Pulaski Street.[29]

The Polish American parish beyond Clinton Street is St. Casimir's established in 1890, with forty Polish families and a church on Cable Street. By 1923, the parish school staffed by Felicians enrolled six hundred students.[30] The expansion of the Kaisertown settlement can be traced in terms of the creation of additional churches, with adjacent parochial schools.[31]

Despite the concentration of commercial zones between the Broadway-Fillmore and Clinton Street areas, Kaisertown contains a large residential district where houses tend to have larger yards and are somewhat newer than those in the Broadway-Fillmore or Black Rock neighbourhoods. Many of these houses are comparable to those in middle-income suburban tracts. As in the 1912 description, these houses are located on side streets at some distance from Clinton Street. The newer houses as well as those in more crowded sections of the area are generally well maintained. In a neighbourhood near the site of the former stockyards, there is evidence of residential stability:

> The older Polish American people, particularly those with deep-seated attachment to the homes of the parents, prefer remaining in an older neighborhood like the Dulski Community Center section or the lower Clinton area as it is known today.[32]

Such stability should be compared to signs of change in the old Polish American neighbourhoods. The turn-of-the-century migration to the city neighbourhoods has been replaced by movement beyond Kaisertown, Black Rock and Broadway-Fillmore.

Demographic Trends

No one really knows how many Polish Americans live in the Buffalo area but various estimates usually exceed the partial enumeration provided by the "foreign stock" totals of the U.S. census which include only persons born in Poland or having at least one Polish parent. Polish foreign stock totals are not only an underestimate of Polonian population but also show a constant decline as Polish immigrants and their children die and are not replaced by new immigrants. Apart from such natural decrease, the foreign stock population decline reflects migration from one location to another–from city to suburb. For example, the 1960 Polish foreign stock total for Buffalo (47,589) was much less than the 180,000 Polish American total estimated by a local historian in 1966.[33]

From 1960 to 1970, city population declined by 13 per cent as county population increased by 5 per cent (Table 1). The city population decline continued during the 1970s and a 1980 estimated total is 350,000.[34] Total foreign stock–and Polish foreign stock–also declined; however, the 1970 Polish foreign stock total (31,699) was the largest in the foreign stock categories and considerably higher than the next largest category, Italian, which totalled 29,074.[35]

Table 1: Total Population, Foreign Stock, and Polish Foreign Stock in Buffalo SMSA, 1960 to 1970

	1960			1970		
	Total Population	Foreign Stock	Polish	Total Population	Foreign Stock	Polish
Total SMSA	1,306,957	424,516	93,584	1,349,210	359,948	74,801
Erie County[1]	1,064,688	342,300	82,249	1,113,491	291,635	65,604
Buffalo[2]	532,759	188,482	47,589	462,781	130,822	31,699
Cheektowaga[3]	52,362	16,477	5,519	58,778	17,136	5,648
Lackawanna	29,564	12,484	4,995	28,657	9,877	4,145
Tonawanda	83,771	24,030	2,650	36,012	10,392	2,848

[1] Erie County total for 1978 special census, 1,066,300.
[2] Buffalo City total for 1977 special census, 390,065.
[3] Cheektowaga totals for 1970 are the sum of census tracts (1970) comprising the "Cheektowaga area" as designated in the 1960 Census.

SOURCE: U.S. Census of Population and Housing, *Census Tracts,* Buffalo, N.Y., 1960, Table P-1 and *Census Tracts,* Buffalo, 1970, Table P-2.

Polish foreign stock accounted for 25 per cent of the city total in 1960 and for 24 per cent in 1970. The Erie County proportions of Polish foreign stock were slightly lower–24 per cent in 1960 and 23 per cent in 1970–than city totals. Thus, while the decline in city population was greater than the increase for areas surrounding the city, the change was not reflected in the Polish foreign stock proportions (to total foreign stock) for either area. The relative stability of foreign stock proportions does not mean that

Polish Americans were not leaving city neighbourhoods but only that the first and second generation ("foreign stock") segment declined slightly (by 1 per cent) in both city and county areas from 1960 to 1970. Such change is a function of mortality as well as migration. More recent Polish emigrés and their children may partially replenish the foreign stock population but not necessarily in urban neighbourhoods. Finally, population change involves movement between regions rather than mere transfer between a city and surrounding county suburbs. Explanations of such change based on foreign stock data of the census are limited but do provide some insight regarding demographic trends within the Polonian residential areas.

Census tracts which had relatively high proportions of Polish foreign stock to total foreign stock lost "Polish" residents from 1960 to 1970. The proportions of Polish stock to total populations increased in only three of forty "Polonian" tracts in the city and several adjacent suburbs (see Table 2, tracts 0021, 0103 and 0112). Two of these tracts are in the suburb of Cheektowaga and the third is in Kaisertown. Polish stock proportion of total foreign stock (or PS/TFS) increased in five tracts in Lackawanna, an industrial and residential enclave south of the city limits. Similar increases occurred in two Kaisertown tracts and three Cheektowaga tracts; however, in the Broadway-Fillmore and Black Rock tracts (and several suburban tracts), the PS/TFS proportions declined. Average percentage decline was greater in these city tracts than in Kaisertown, suburban Cheektowaga and Lackawanna.[36] Such variation suggests that change—involving either natural increase or migration—was more diverse than uniform and that a decline in Polish stock residents was typical but not inevitable. Of the three city areas, Kaisertown changed least in its Polish stock proportions.

Both the Kaisertown and Sloan areas had larger proportions of long-time residents than other areas. According to averages derived from 1970 census data which list periods during which residents moved into tracts, only 27 per cent of the Sloan population and 34 per cent of Kaisertown residents moved into the areas from 1965 to 1970 and more than half arrived in the tracts in 1959 or earlier (Table 3). The percentage of long-time residents in other areas varied from 34 per cent in Depew to 47 per cent in Broadway-Fillmore.[37]

The data represent total population movement in the tracts and not merely that of Polish foreign stock residents. However, the data drawn from tracts with substantial Polish stock concentrations suggest variations in residential stability. In this sense, the most stable areas (i.e., those with the least recent in-migration) include a tract within the city (Kaisertown) and an "old" suburban area (Sloan). Both areas are near Cheektowaga tracts where an average of 45 per cent of residents arrived before 1960.[38]

Table 2: Change in Polish Foreign Stock Percentages in Selected Buffalo Area Census Tracts, 1960 to 1970[1]

Tract Number	Name of Area	1960 (1) PS/TP	1960 (2) PS/TFS	1970 (3) PS/TP	1970 (4) PS/TFS	Change from (1)-(3)	Change from (2)-(4)
0004	K-town	.13	.45	.11	.39	−.02	−.06
0005	K-town	.10	.31	.09	.36	−.01	+.05
0012	K-town	.13	.44	.11	.46	−.02	+.02
0016	B-Fill	.46	.85	.37	.79	−.09	−.06
0017	K-town	.34	.72	.26	.64	−.08	−.08
0018	K-town	.19	.59	.19	.49	.00	−.10
0019	K-town	.41	.85	.33	.78	−.08	−.07
0021	K-town	.30	.77	.33	.77	+.03	.00
0022	K-town	.36	.78	.25	.74	−.11	−.04
0024	B-Fill	.24	.55	.19	.50	−.05	−.05
0027	B-Fill	.35	.69	.26	.67	−.09	−.02
0027-01	B-Fill	N.A.	N.A.	.16	.59	N.A.	N.A.
0027-02	B-Fill	N.A.	N.A.	.35	.70	N.A.	N.A.
0028	B-Fill	.40	.85	.34	.78	−.06	−.07
0029	B-Fill	.28	.63	.19	.58	−.09	−.05
0030	B-Fill	.29	.68	.24	.62	−.05	−.06
0055	B-Rock	.39	.69	.30	.61	−.09	−.08
0056	B-Rock	.26	.60	.19	.50	−.07	−.10
0122	Lacka.	.12	.29	.11	.37	−.01	+.08
0123	Lacka.	.32	.67	.27	.70	−.05	+.03
0124	Lacka.	.23	.48	.17	.50	−.06	+.02
0125-01	Lacka.	.12	.31	.13	.33	+.01	+.02
0126	Lacka.	.16	.38	.15	.44	−.01	+.06
0098	Depew	.19	.48	.11	.33	−.08	−.15
0099	Sloan	.29	.73	.23	.69	−.06	−.04
0103	Cheek.	.21	.54	.25	.55	+.04	+.01
0104	Cheek.	.41	.88	.35	.81	−.06	−.07
0105	Cheek.	.22	.50	.21	.49	−.01	−.01
0106	Cheek.	.11	.32	.11	.37	.00	+.05
0107	Cheek.	.20	.55	.19	.54	−.01	−.01
0108	Cheek.	.16	.51	.07	.35	−.09	−.16
0108-01	Cheek.	N.A.	N.A.	.12	.49	N.A.	N.A.
0108-02	Cheek.	N.A.	N.A.	.04	.27	N.A.	N.A.
0109	Cheek.	25	.69	.18	.61	−.07	−.08
0109-01	Cheek.	N.A.	N.A.	.09	.50	N.A.	N.A.
0109-02	Cheek.	N.A.	N.A.	.16	.55	N.A.	N.A.
0110	Cheek.	.30	.78	.20	.60	−.10	−.18
0111	Cheek.	.26	.79	.22	.64	−.04	−.15
0112	Cheek.	.12	.41	.13	.47	+.01	+.06
0113	Cheek.	.12	.39	.12	.42	.00	+.03

[1] Includes tracts in which the 1970 percentage of Polish foreign stock to total foreign stock (4) was 0.33 or greater.

(1) & (3) Polish stock divided by total population.
(2) & (4) Polish stock divided by total foreign stock.

SOURCE: U.S. Census of Population and Housing, *Census Tracts,* Buffalo, N.Y., 1960, Table P-1; *Census Tracts,* Buffalo, N.Y., 1970, Table P-2.

Table 3: Median Value and Length of Residence for Households in "Polonian" Census Tracts in Buffalo Area, 1970

Tract Number	Name of Area	Median Value	(Percentage moved into Units) 1965-70	1964-60	1959 and earlier	Total Population
0004	K-town	$ 6,000	34	8	59	366
0005	K-town	6,300	35	16	49	1265
0012	K-town	9,100	45	20	36	1885
0016	B-Fill	7,300	45.3	13.7	50.1	3251
0017	K-town	7,200	31.1	11.8	57.1	1225
0018	K-town	7,000	39	16	45	633
0019	K-town	15,100	26.4	16.7	56.8	1650
0021	K-town	13,400	28.9	14.9	56.2	370
0022	K-town	12,600	36.2	13.9	49.8	996
0024	B-Fill	11,000	33.9	13.5	52.6	2825
0027-01	B-Fill	7,200	54	15	29	2432
0027-02	B-Fill	8,900	36.8	17.5	45.6	3134
0028	B-Fill	9,300	38.6	11.8	49.7	2845
0029	B-Fill	10,500	41.5	11.3	47.2	2214
0030	B-Fill	12,600	32.7	11.9	55.5	1297
0055	B-Rock	8,800	42.6	8.3	49.2	2084
0056	B-Rock	13,100	47.8	12.8	39.5	1937
0122	Lacka.	10,700	43.8	12.6	43.6	1552
0123	Lacka.	14,800	33.1	13.4	53.5	1583
0124	Lacka.	13,000	44.9	9.6	45.4	1093
0125-01	Lacka.	20,800	36.5	17.2	46.4	2293
0126	Lacka.	18,500	41.8	21.6	36.5	884
0098	Depew	17,800	49.5	17	34	815
0099	Sloan	14,800	26.7	16.5	56.8	1667
0103	Cheek.	18,300	36.7	10.8	52.4	594
0104	Cheek.	16,500	26.5	15.3	58.2	1094
0105	Cheek.	17,900	31.4	12.1	56.6	1083
0106	Cheek.	17,200	32.6	10.1	57.3	1212
0107	Cheek.	18,600	24	17	59.1	1291
0108-01	Cheek.	21,700	50.5	23.8	24.9	1280
0108-02	Cheek.	21,500	89	6	5	3240
0109-01	Cheek.	17,600	37.7	18.1	44.2	1210
0109-02	Cheek.	22,200	60.5	17.2	22.1	1584
0110	Cheek.	15,400	29.7	10.6	59.7	930
0111	Cheek.	16,600	20.8	19.9	59.4	1002
0112	Cheek.	21,900	42.7	14.3	43.1	1455
0113	Cheek.	17,100	35.8	17.4	46.9	1630

SOURCE: U.S. Census of Population and Housing, *Census Tracts,* Buffalo, N.Y., 1970, Table H-1.

In Cheektowaga tracts, the median value of housing units was not only considerably higher than that in established Polonian areas in Sloan, Lackawanna and Depew, but also higher than in the three city areas. The existence of higher median values in the suburbs is less surprising than the variations among separate areas. In Kaisertown, median value of houses in some neighbourhoods was only slightly lower than the least expensive (median value) homes in Cheektowaga; however, median values for houses in Broadway-Fillmore and Black Rock were considerably lower.[39] The census data compiled for housing characteristics, periods of settlement and changes in foreign stock proportions do not indicate a complete dichotomy between Polish American areas in the city and those in adjacent suburbs. Urban and suburban demographic characteristics are more continuous than discrete. Any conclusions from such data—limited to foreign stock categories and lacking ethnic differentiation for housing characteristics—must be tentative and qualified. Interviews with Polish Americans during a 1977 survey in the Buffalo area provides additional and, perhaps, more specific description of urban-suburban differences in the ethnic community.

Polonian Ethnicity in Buffalo's Urban and Suburban Areas

A basic intent of the 1977 field research was replication and elaboration of 1967 dissertation research involving persistence of Polonian communities in city neighbourhoods of Buffalo.[40] Since a complete list of Polish American residents in the area does not exist, a random sample of the population was not feasible in either study. The 1977 purposive sample was drawn from city directory listings for three Buffalo city neighbourhoods, three suburban areas of the city and the adjacent industrial community of Lackawanna. These areas have sizable Polish American populations. For each of the areas, several adjacent streets were designated as "neighbourhood" sampling frames. From street lists, residents with apparent Polish (or Polish American) family names were selected. Apart from these residents, approximately 10 per cent of the sample consisted of other Polish American residents of the neighbourhoods who volunteered for interviews. Interviews involving a pre-coded, structured schedule were obtained from 190 persons. The interview schedule contained 127 items related to demographic characteristics, institutional practices, ethnic self-identity, socio-economic status and attitudes regarding aspects of Polish and Polish American culture. All persons interviewed were contacted in advance and asked to permit interviewers to visit them. Approximately 85 per cent of all interviews were conducted in respondents' homes and the remainder in club rooms of various Polish American organizations. The final sample consisted of 104 males and 86 females. The mean age of persons interviewed was 48. Among those interviewed, 36.3 per cent lived in city neighbourhoods, 49.2 per cent in suburbs and 19.5 per cent in Lackawanna or nearby areas. Comparison of respondents' 1977 place of residence to 1967 residence indicated most movement from all city areas, except Kaisertown, to suburban areas (Table 4). Such migration was not uniform. The largest decrease in city areas (7 per cent) involved respondents who did not live in any of the three Polonian districts (i.e., Broadway-Fillmore, Black Rock, Kaisertown) but in other locations within the city. This movement from locations which were not part of traditional Polish American residential areas deserves more attention in a more detailed analysis than is possible here. The largest in-migration increases (4.7 and 3.1 per cent) were to suburban areas—but not to the more established Polonian areas in Lackawanna and Cheektowaga but to newer (and less urbanized) areas southeast and north of Cheektowaga. Houses and lots in these areas tend to be larger and more expensive than in older suburbs adjacent to the city boundaries.

Table 4: Residential Locations for Polish Americans in Buffalo Area, 1967 and 1977

Location Name	R's 1967 Residence		R's 1977 Residence		Difference	
	#	%	#	%	#	%
B-Fill	38	20.4	34	17.9	−4	−2.5
K-Town	13	6.9	16	8.4	+3	+1.5
B-Rock	16	8.6	14	7.4	−2	−1.2
Buffalo-other	18	9.6	5	2.6	−13	−7.0
Suburb East[1]	41	22.0	44	23.2	+3	+1.2
Suburb Southeast[2]	13	6.9	22	11.6	+9	+4.7
Suburb South/Lacka.[3]	35	18.8	37	19.5	+2	+0.7
Suburb North[4]	12	6.4	18	9.5	+6	+3.1
Totals	186*	99.6**	190	100.1		

[1] Cheektowaga, Depew, Sloan
[2] West Seneca
[3] Lackawanna for the most part
[4] Williamsville, Tonawanda, Amherst

* Excludes: no answer (2)
** Not in Buffalo ten years ago (2)

For residents in suburban areas, there was relatively little discrepancy between current residential location and preferred location (Table 5). For city residents, however, the difference between current and preferred locations was 15.5 per cent. Preference for the Lackawanna/Suburb South location was less (by 3.6 per cent) than current residence, and although none of the 1977 respondents lived in rural areas, 14.8 per cent preferred such locations. More respondents preferred locations in Suburb Southeast (West

Seneca) and Suburb East (Cheektowaga, Depew, Sloan) than actually lived in these areas. The contrast between current and preferred residence, however, was most apparent for city respondents. Of these 69 respondents, 38 preferred current urban locations. Although no comparison was made between current and preferred locations for respondents in each of the three urban Polonian areas, actual migration (Table 4) suggests that preference for other locations may be greater among residents in Black Rock and Broadway-Fillmore than in Kaisertown.

Table 5: Actual and Preferred Residential Locations for Polish Americans in Buffalo Area, 1977

Location Name	Current Residence		Preferred Residence		Differences	
	#	%	#	%	#	%
Buffalo (city)	69	36.3	38	20.8	31	+15.5
Suburb East[1]	44	23.2	46	25.1	−2	− 1.9
Suburb Southeast[2]	22	11.6	26	14.2	−4	− 2.6
Lacka./Suburb South[3]	37	19.5	29	15.9	8	+ 3.6
Suburb North[4]	18	9.5	17	9.3	1	+ 0.2
Other rural area	00	–	27	14.8	−27	−14.8
Totals	190		183*			

* "Don't know" responses (6) and "No answers" (1) excluded

[1] Cheektowaga, Depew, Sloan principally
[2] West Seneca
[3] Lackawanna with a few from areas south
[4] Amherst, Williamsville, Tonawanda principally

Thus, although the survey data indicate a movement from city areas to newer suburban areas, it is not a general exodus of Polish Americans from every established urban neighbourhood. More detailed examination of the urban locations may indicate that some portions—census tracts or blocks—lost Polish American residents while others retained such residents.[41] To what extent are these areas primary repositories of Polonian community life? To what extent does Polish American ethnicity survive in areas outside the city? A comparison of forms of ethnic expression for Polish Americans in the city, suburban and Lackawanna areas provides a partial answer to these questions.

Variations in Polonian Ethnicity

There is a proper time and place for all ethnic subcommunities, including those which developed in Buffalo since the 1870s.[42] Like all communities, the Polish American enclaves are not merely places but also social settings which satisfy economic, biological, associational, cultural and social psychological needs.[43] The study of American Polonia relies upon research and observations in urban settings, for the most part, but the focus of such research has shifted from description of general characteristics, such as sources of "demoralization" or degrees of assimilation, to particular social and institutional processes involving family patterns, political response and forms of "status competition."[44] The 1977 research identified associational, cultural and social psychological elements of Polish American life in city, suburban and Lackawanna residential areas. Specific indices of Polonian ethnicity described below are not only arbitrary, but also a partial basis for comparison of intra-community (i.e., Buffalo area) differences.

Associational indices (Table 6) consist of deliberate, formal response to the activities or products of large-scale ethnic organizations, such as fraternal societies, political clubs and businessmen's associations. Although a large proportion of all survey respondents were not members of such organizations, membership was proportionately higher (57 per cent for city respondents) than for those in the suburbs or Lackawanna (Table 6a). The finding is hardly surprising since organization headquarters and club rooms are more common in the city neighbourhoods.

Most respondents in all areas did not carry life insurance with Polonian organizations. Coverage was more common for Lackawanna respondents than for those in the city or suburbs; however, differences were insignificant (Table 6b). Lackawanna residents were more aware of the Polish American Congress than were city or suburban respondents; however, differences among areas was not significant (Table 6c).

Two-thirds of city respondents received a Polish or Polish American publication as compared to less than half (46 per cent) in the suburbs and Lackawanna (Table 6d). Preference for Polish American congressional candidates was significantly lower among suburban respondents than those in city or Lackawanna areas (Table 6e).

Thus, suburban respondents were less involved in all the associational forms of ethnic expression. However, the differences among the three residential areas were not significant for reactions to Polonian vested interest groups (i.e., the Polish American Congress and fraternal insurance organizations). Such organizations may be less relevant sources of local community interests and attract less personal response than the smaller Polonian clubs, local news stories and neighbourhood political figures.

Cultural elements of ethnicity (Table 7) refer to activities, beliefs and attitudes which reflect a distinctive Polonian orientation or Polish American interests. In general, such responses are more personalized, and less formal, than are associational expressions of ethnicity. Relatively large portions of respondents in all three

Table 6: Associational Forms of Ethnic Expression among Polish Americans in City, Suburban and Lackawanna Areas of Buffalo, 1977 (percentage)

Area of Residence		(a) Member Pol-Am Organizations		(b) Insured Pol-Am Fraternal		(c) Heard of Pol-Am Congress		(d) Receive Pol-Am Publication		(e) Prefer Pol-Am Congressman	
	N:	Y	N	Y	N	Y	N	Y	N	Y	N
City	(69)	57	43	39	61	62	38	66	34	64	36
Suburb	(84)	36	64	33	67	58	42	46	54	48	52
Lacka.	(37)	41	59	49	51	70	30	46	54	76	24

Explanatory Note: N: = number of persons in each area; Y = yes; N = no.

Content of Items (a) to (e):	Levels of Statistical Significance[1] X^2	DF	P
(a) Do you belong to any Polish or Polish American clubs or organizations?	7.410	2	.024
(b) Do you have insurance with any Polish American groups or fraternal groups?	2.569	2	.276
(c) Have you heard of the Polish American Congress?	1.557	2	.459
(d) Do you receive Polish (or Polish American) newspapers or magazines?	6.928	2	.031
(e) Do you prefer your representatives in Congress to be Polish Americans?	9.395	2	.009

[1] Levels of significance is based on X^2 (Chi Square) test of significance which compares actual number of observed responses to those expected by chance. DF refers to degrees of freedom used to interpret raw Chi Square totals. P refers to probability level. Probability levels in this table are rounded to three decimal places. A P of 0.02 means that the observed relationship would be due to chance in only two cases out of 100. A P of 0.000 means the relationship would be due to chance in less than one case of 1000 observed. Generally, probability levels of 0.05 or less are termed statistically significant.

Table 7: Socio-cultural Elements of Polonian Ethnicity in City, Suburban and Lackawanna Areas of Buffalo, N.Y., 1977 (percentage)

Area of Residence	N:	(a) Polish at Home? Y	N	(b) Use of Polish? G	A	L	(c) Polish in Church? Y	N	(d) O.L.C. Legend? Y	N	(e) Pol. Food Weekly? Y	N	(f) Polka Freq.? M	A	L	(g) Polka/ Polonaise? Y	N/d	(h) Trip to Poland? P	O	(i) Visited Poland? Y	N	(j) Write to Poland? Y	N
City	(69)	90	10	44	18	38	78	22	68	32	65	35	35	24	41	32	68	57	43	32	68	41	59
Suburb	(84)	77	23	44	28	28	33	67	65	35	54	46	32	22	46	63	37	56	44	24	76	35	65
Lacka.	(37)	87	13	38	35	27	62	38	57	43	78	22	29	38	33	49	51	77	23	22	78	27	73

Explanatory Note: N: = number of cases in each area; don't know and no answer responses excluded. Y = yes; N = no; in (b), G = good, A = average, L = limited or none; in (f), M = more often, A = as often, L = less often; in (g), N/d = no or no difference; in (h), P = Poland, O = other.

Content of Items (a) to (j):		Levels of Statistical Significance[1] X^2	DF	P
(a)	Is Polish spoken in your home?	4.581	2	.101
(b)	How do you rate your ability to speak Polish?	4.985	4	.288
(c)	Is Polish used in any portion of services in your church?	30.511	2	.000
(d)	Do you know the story of Our Lady of Czestochowa?	1.397	2	.497
(e)	How often do you have Polish food in your home?	6.128	2	.046
(f)	Do you dance Polka more often, less often, as often as other kinds of dances?	2.502	4	.644
(g)	Do you know the difference between a Polka and a Polonaise?	14.472	2	.000
(h)	(Given an all expense paid trip), which country would you most prefer to visit?	5.005	2	.081
(i)	Have you ever visited Poland?	1.795	2	.407
(j)	Do you write to people in Poland?	1.973	2	.372

[1] Levels of significance is based on X^2 (Chi Square) test of significance which compares actual number of observed responses to those expected by chance. DF refers to degrees of freedom used to interpret raw Chi Square totals. P refers to probability level. Probability levels in this table are rounded to three decimal places. A P of 0.02 means that the observed relationship would be due to chance in only two cases out of 100. A P of 0.000 means the relationship would be due to chance in less than one case of 1000 observed. Generally, probability levels of 0.05 or less are termed statistically significant.

areas used Polish in their homes but the percentage was lower among suburban residents than among others. Differences in language usage, however, were not significant (Table 7a). Less than 45 per cent of respondents in all three areas judged their proficiency in Polish as good but differences among areas was not significant (Table 7b).

The use of Polish in church services was more common in the city and Lackawanna than in the suburbs. Only one-third of suburban respondents reported such services as compared to 68 per cent in the city and 62 per cent in Lackawanna (Table 7c). Knowledge of the Our Lady of Czestochowa tradition was greater among city respondents than among those in the other areas; however, differences were insignificant (Table 7d).

Suburban respondents served Polish food in their homes less frequently than respondents in other areas. However, even in the suburbs 54 per cent of respondents served such food at least once a week (Table 7e). For most persons interviewed, Polish food included *kielbasa, pierogi* and *kapusta.*

Contrary to an enduring stereotype, many respondents in all three areas were *not* polka addicts. However, a larger proportion of suburban respondents (46 per cent) did the polka less often than other dances and a higher proportion of city residents (35 per cent) did the polka more often than other dances (Table 7f). Differences in polka preference were slight and not significant. In contrast, a significantly higher proportion of suburban respondents (63 per cent) than Lackawanna (49 per cent) or city respondents (32 per cent) could describe the difference between a polka and a polonaise (Table 7g).

City and suburban residents were less interested in travel to Poland than were Lackawanna respondents (Table 7h). Most respondents in all three areas had not visited Poland, although almost one-third of those in the city areas had previous visits (Table 7i). Area differences in both preference for trips and previous travel were not significant. A larger proportion of city respondents (41 per cent) as compared to other respondents wrote to persons in Poland (Table 7j).

Socio-cultural differences among respondents in the three areas were significant in only three of the ten indices. The more extensive use of Polish in church services in city and Lackawanna areas reflects the survival of parishes in these areas and their relative absence in suburban areas. The less extensive use of Polish food in suburbs may be due to the lack of nearby ethnic food stores, busy schedules of suburban wives, or the unfortunate lack of treasured family recipes among younger homemakers. Finally, the lack of knowledge regarding the polonaise among Lackawanna and city respondents (as compared to those in suburbs) may reflect social class and educational level differences. More interesting than these differences regarding language in church services, food preferences and recognition of the polonaise are the lack of significant differences on the other seven indices. Such similarities, interpreted in a non-statistical sense, may indicate cultural patterns of the three areas are more alike than different.

Social psychological indices of Polish American ethnicity consist of individual, personal response to symbolic elements of persistent Polonian identity. These elements include self-identification, neighbourhood designation, attitudes toward name-changing and intermarriage patterns. Asked to choose from among the categories "Polish," "Polish American," "American of Polish descent," or "American," the largest proportion of respondents in all areas selected the hybrid categories (i.e., Polish American and American of Polish descent). Although the proportion choosing "Polish" were greater in Lackawanna and city areas than suburbs, differences were not significant (Table 8a). Respondents differed significantly in designation of their neighbourhoods. More than half the city respondents (53 per cent) described their neighbourhoods as "mostly Polish" while 56 per cent of those in the suburbs and 47 per cent in Lackawanna said neighbourhoods were "American" (Table 8b).

Respondents in all three areas generally opposed name-changing and differences among areas were not significant; however, the smallest proportion of outright disapproval (49 per cent) came from suburban respondents (Table 8c). Most suburban and city respondents indicated "Polish-sounding names" were not a basis for employment discrimination; however, 51 per cent of the Lackawanna respondents felt such bias existed (Table 8d). Most respondents (84 per cent in both city and Lackawanna areas) said there had been no name-changing within their families. Such changes were reported by 34 per cent of the suburban respondents—more than double the proportions for the city and Lackawanna residents (Table 8e).

Although surprisingly large proportions of married respondents in all three areas had Polish or Polish American spouses, the proportion was greatest (91 per cent) among city respondents. Area differences, however, were not significant (Table 8f). Also, respondents did not differ significantly in preferences regarding children's marriage partners. The proportion of in-group (Polish or Polish American) preferences was greatest in the suburbs and Lackawanna than in the city (Table 8g).

Significant area variations in social psychological indices involve name-changing and designations of neighbourhoods (i.e., as Polish or American, etc.). Name-changing was more common in families of suburban respondents than those in the city or Lackawanna and proportionately fewer suburban residents felt names were a source of bias. This seemingly contradictory data may be explained by the fact that previous instances of name-changing in family occurred in earlier periods of community life when con-

Table 8: Social Psychological Elements of Polonian Ethnicity in City, Suburban and Lackawanna Areas of Buffalo, N.Y., 1977 (percentage)

Area of Residence		(a) Ethnic Self I.D.?				(b) Neighbourhood Designation?			(c) Change Names?			(d) Job Bias Names?		(e) Changed Name?		(f) Pol-Am Spouse?		(g) Children Marry Pol.?	
	N:	P	PA	AP	A	MP	HP	A	Y	N	D	Y	N	Y	N	Y	N	Y	N/d
City	(69)	14	31	45	10	53	28	19	18	54	28	30	70	16	84	91	9	34	66
Suburb	(84)	9	31	48	12	25	19	56	9	49	42	27	73	34	66	84	16	47	53
Lacka.	(37)	19	32	43	5	19	33	47	8	62	30	51	49	16	84	74	26	44	56

Explanatory Note: N: = number of persons in each area. Y = yes; N = no; P = Polish; PA = Polish American; AP = American of Polish descent; A = American; MP = mostly Polish; HP = half Polish; D = depends on circumstances; N/d = no or no difference.

Content of Items (a) to (g):	Levels of Statistical Significance[1] X^2	DF	P
(a) Which phrase (on card) best describes how you usually think of yourself?	3.044	6	.803
(b) Which phrase (on card) best describes your present neighbourhood?	26.094	4	.000
(c) Should persons with long or difficult-to-pronounce family names change their names?	5.886	4	.207
(d) Do you believe persons with Polish sounding last names have a difficult time getting certain jobs in Buffalo?	7.138	2	.028
(e) Have you (or anyone else in your family) ever changed your family name?	8.037	2	.018
(f) What is the nationality of the person you married?	4.195	2	.122
(g) Would (or did) you prefer that your children marry persons of your nationality?	1.692	2	.429

[1] Levels of significance is based on X^2 (Chi Square) test of significance which compares actual number of observed responses to those expected by chance. DF refers to degrees of freedom used to interpret raw Chi Square totals. P refers to probability level. Probability levels in this table are rounded to three decimal places. A P of 0.02 means that the observed relationship would be due to chance in only two cases out of 100. A P of 0.000 means the relationship would be due to chance in less than one case of 1000 observed. Generally, probability levels of 0.05 or less are termed statistically significant.

ventional wisdom explained job discrimination in terms of apparent Polish identity. Perhaps name changes are more likely to occur among younger generations, particularly socially mobile persons in suburban areas, rather than among persons in the older neighbourhoods of the city and Lackawanna.

A more significant variation involves the neighbourhood designation and ethnic self-identity indices. The proportion of city residents who identified their neighbourhoods as "mostly Polish" was more than twice that of suburban and Lackawanna respondents. Despite this apparent awareness of differences in ethnic composition of their neighbourhoods, respondents in all three areas were more alike than different in their designations of self-identity. Smaller proportions of city and Lackawanna respondents than of suburban respondents chose "American" but the overriding preference in all areas was for the hybrid Polish American or American of Polish descent categories. Conceptions of neighbourhood and self-identity appear to be separate dimensions of ethnic response. Obviously, persons in "American" neighbourhoods of the suburbs may think of themselves as "Polish" or "Polish American."

Conclusions: Polonian Neighbourhood Change and Community Adaptation

Although the Polish American enclaves in city, suburban and Lackawanna areas of Buffalo developed separately, responded to ecological processes such as racial invasion-succession differently and retained varying proportions of Polonian residents, a basis for common interests, values and orientations was apparent in survey data as well as demographic patterns derived from comparison of Polish American residential areas. The Polish American community, from its origins a century ago to the present, consisted of separate components rather than a single, well-integrated, geographically bounded ethnic ghetto. Neighbourhoods developed around particular parish churches and differed in terms of occupational opportunities, number of voluntary associations and extent of business-commercial activity. The survival of distinctive area names such as the outer East Side (or Broadway-Fillmore), Black Rock and Kaisertown suggests that all of Buffalo Polonia could be divided into at least three parts. The separate subareas not only developed parallel institutional forms such as parochial schools, district political clubs and neighbourhood shopping districts but also remained interdependent in terms of large-scale service organizations, such as the Felician Sisters and other Roman Catholic groups, fraternal organizations and union associations. Thus, a geographically segmented community developed in an urban setting which provided concentrated areas of similar ethnic population (neighbourhoods), an appropriate employment structure and, most importantly, a reasonably complete institutional structure. In this respect, the urban locations fulfilled necessary functions appropriately.

Demographic change involving migration from the Polonian areas within the city to nearby suburbs suggests that, however necessary urban locations were in the establishment of Polish American subcommunities, they were not sufficient means for unqualified survival. Changes in foreign stock concentrations—an admittedly crude index of Polonian population—indicated general, but not complete, patterns of decline. Movement to "Polonian" suburban areas from particular urban enclaves varied and indicated more stability for one city area than for others.

Survey data suggest that Polish American ethnicity predicated upon associational forms of activity is more persistent in the urban enclaves than in suburbs. Socio-cultural patterns of ethnicity oriented to traditional folk elements are more apparent in the city areas than in suburbs. However, these elements can be transmitted across generations and out to suburbs more easily than the meeting rooms of fraternal organizations or original parish churches. Ethnicity based on more contemporary, intellectual and nationalistic elements of culture, such as recognition of the polonaise, may be more general in the transplanted suburban enclaves than in the city. Finally, if designation of ethnic community survival is based upon social psychological responses such as self-identification, the distinction between city and suburban ethnic areas is blurred. Less individualistic forms of designation, such as ethnic neighbourhood classifications, are more common in the city. The sense of community in urban settings is linked more concretely to location than is the case for newer suburbs.

The Polish American community in Buffalo is no longer confined to its original city enclaves. The community in a physical sense has adapted to demographic and assimilative change. It survives not so much in well-defined physical locations such as Kaisertown or Sloan but as a symbolic community—a form of collective identity—similar to those described by Hunter:

> Residents' perceptions and definitions of their local areas . . . are an independent reality that should not be ignored or discounted. . . . To invoke W.I. Thomas, we are asking people to define the situation, to give the reality they perceive and from which they act. If they believe these communities exist, then they exist.[45]

As Polonia becomes an increasingly symbolic rather than spatial community, urban locations are neither necessary nor sufficient for its survival.

Notes

Census data and related tables in this paper were prepared with the assistance of Allan Roff.

1. William L. Yancey, Eugene P. Ericksen, and Richard Juliani, "Emergent Ethnicity: A Review and Reformulation," *American Sociological Review* 41, no. 3, pp. 391-403.
2. Caroline Golab, *Immigrant Destinations* (Philadelphia: Univ. of Pennsylvania Press, 1978).
3. Mark Abrahamson, *Urban Sociology* (2nd edition) (Englewood Cliffs, N.J., 1980), p. 148.
4. Robert E. Park, *Human Communities* (Glencoe, Ill.: Free Press, 1952), p. 66.
5. Max Weber, "Class, Status, and Party" in *From Max Weber: Essays in Sociology,* translated by Hans Gerth and C.W. Mills (New York: Oxford Press, 1958), pp. 186-87.
6. Gerald D. Suttles, *The Social Construction of Communities* (Chicago: Univ. of Chicago Press, 1972), quoted in Kent P. Schwirian, *Contemporary Topics in Urban Sociology* (Morristown, N.J.: General Learning Press, 1977), p. 201.
7. Schwirian, *Contemporary Topics,* p. 205.
8. Albert Hunter, *Symbolic Communities* (Chicago: University of Chicago Press, 1974), p. 46.
9. Albert Hunter, Reply to Comment, "Is Inner City Alive and Well," in *American Sociological Review* 42, no. 5 (Oct. 1977), pp. 828-29.
10. Thomas Gannon, "Religious Tradition and Urban Community," *Sociological Analysis* 39, no. 4 (Winter 1968), p. 284.
11. Donald L. Warren, "The Multiplexity of Urban Social Ties: An Integrative Analysis," paper presented at 1978 meeting of International Sociological Association.
12. Roman A. Cybriwsky, "Social Aspects of Neighbourhood Change," *Annals of Association of American Geographers* 68 (March 1978), p. 33.
13. Donald J. Pienkos, "Ethnic Orientations Among Polish Americans," *International Migration Review* II, no. 3 (Fall 1977), pp. 350-62.
14. For past studies see Fred Francis Jablonski, "The Dynamics of an East Buffalo Ethnic Neighbourhood-Old (1846) and New (1976)" (M.S. thesis, Social Sciences SUNY at Buffalo, 1976); also Eugene Obidinski, "Ethnic to Status Group: A Study of Polish Americans in Buffalo" (Ph.D. dissertation, SUNY at Buffalo, 1968) (publication forthcoming, New York: Arno Press).
15. Robert W. Bingham, *The Cradle of the Queen City* (Buffalo, N.Y.: Buffalo Historical Society), pp. 166-95.
16. Stephen Gredel, *Pioneers of Buffalo* (Buffalo, N.Y.: Commission on Human Rights, 1966), p. 25.

17. Helena Z. Lopata, *Polish Americans: Status Competition in an Ethnic Community* (Englewood Cliffs, N.J.: Prentice Hall, 1976), p. 44.
18. Gredel, *Pioneers of Buffalo,* p. 26.
19. Walter S. Dunn, Jr. (ed.), *History of Erie County, 1870-1970* (Buffalo: Buffalo and Erie County Historical Society, 1972), p. 296.
20. Ibid., p. 296.
21. Ibid., p. 299.
22. Ibid.
23. Stephen Gredel, *People of Our City* (Buffalo: Erie County Historical Society, 1965), p. 9.
24. Henry W. Hill, *Municipality of Buffalo, New York: A History, 1720-1923* (New York: Lewis Publishing Co., 1923), p. 652.
25. Gredel, *People of Our City,* p. 10. The New York State Census for 1875 listed 17 Poles in Black Rock.
26. Personal communication, Sister Ellen Marie Kuznicki, C.S.S.F., Ph.D., Villa Marie College of Buffalo, July 1980.
27. Jablonski, "The Dynamics of an East Buffalo Ethnic Neighbourhood," pp. 22-25.
28. Sr. Ellen Marie Kuznicki, personal communication, July 1980.
29. Ibid.
30. Hill, *Municipality of Buffalo,* p. 653.
31. Ibid., references to St. Bernard's Church, p. 652 and Precious Blood Church, p. 663.
32. Jablonski, "The Dynamics of an East Buffalo Ethnic Neighbourhood," p. 99.
33. Obidinski, "Ethnic to Status Group," p. 3.
34. Based on estimate by representative of Polish Community Center, Buffalo, N.Y., July 1980.
35. U.S. Bureau of Census, *Census Tracts, Buffalo, 1970,* Table P-2, p. 20.
36. Average percentage declines were Black Rock, 9 per cent; Depew, 15 per cent; Broadway-Fillmore, 5 per cent; Sloan, 4 per cent; Kaisertown, 3.5 per cent; Cheektowaga, 4.6 per cent and Lackawanna, 4 per cent.
37. For other areas, Black Rock, 44 per cent; Lackawanna, 45 per cent; Cheektowaga, 45 per cent.
38. For recent analysis of Sloan, see Francis T. Siemankowski, "The Making of a Polish American Community: Sloan, N.Y. as a Case Study," *Polish American Studies* 34, no. 2 (Autumn 1977), pp. 56-68. For a description of Lackawanna community life, see Richard Sorrell, "Life, Work, and Acculturation Patterns of Eastern European Immigrants in Lackawanna, N.Y.: 1900-1922," *The Polish Review* 14, no. 4, pp. 65-91.
39. See Table 3.
40. Obidinski, "Ethnic to Status Group."

41. Personal observations indicate a series of well-maintained Polonian neighbourhoods east of the Broadway-Fillmore commercial area.

42. For a complete listing of such recent studies, see catalogues prepared by Polish Room staff, Lockwood Memorial Library, SUNY at Buffalo. These studies include: Niles Carpenter and Daniel Katz, "A Study in the Acculturalization of the Polish Group in Buffalo," (Buffalo: Univ. of Buffalo Studies, 1927); Anna Tremaine, "The Effect of Polish Immigration on Buffalo Politics" (M.A. thesis, Columbia University, 1928); Ann T. Skulicz, "Rise of Buffalo Polonia, 1887-1900" (senior thesis, University of Buffalo, 1951); Dorothy Niedzwicka, "The Poles of the Early East Side," *Niagara Frontier* (publication of Buffalo and Erie County Historical Society) 5, no. 2 (Summer 1958), p. 47; Rosemary Switala, "The Political Growth and Development of the Polish Community in Buffalo" (M.A. thesis, SUNY at Buffalo, 1963); Walter H. Borowiec, "The Prototypical Ethnic Politician –A Study of the Political Leadership of an Ethnic Group" (Ph.D. dissertation, SUNY at Buffalo, 1972); Carl Bucki, "A Stacked Deck: Frustration Politics in Buffalo's Polish Community" (honours thesis, Ithaca, N.Y.: Cornell, 1974); Mark Goldman, "Buffalo's Black Rock: Neighbourhood Identity and the Metropolitan Relationship" (Ph.D. dissertation, SUNY at Buffalo, 1974); Fred F. Jablonski, "The Dynamics of an East Buffalo Ethnic Neighbourhood."

43. Irwin T. Sanders, *The Community* (New York: Ronald Press, 1966), pp. 11-21.

44. For a review of such studies, see Lopata, *Polish Americans,* chapters 3 and 4.

45. Albert Hunter, *Symbolic Communities* (Chicago: Univ. of Chicago Press, 1974), p. 70.

Family

Intergenerational Relations in Polonia

Helena Znaniecka Lopata

Two major difficulties face the researcher attempting to study intergenerational relations in American Polonia: a lack of sufficient objective data and the heterogeneity of the population. The sources of available information are mainly the United States censuses—restricted in usefulness by the American hesitation over asking for ethnic and religious identity—and studies of individual communities—which usually have limited information on intergenerational relations (see Sanders and Morawska, 1975). The heterogeneity arises out of the socio-economic and linguistic differences among the emigrants from the various areas of Poland, in "old" and "new" emigration waves, the manner of settlement and the lifestyle developed here, and in generational, age and sex variations (Babinski, 1978; Galush, 1975; Morawska, 1978). For example, relations among the generations of Polish Americans in Los Angeles are quite different from those of Polonians in Buffalo (Obidinski, 1968, 1976; Sandberg, 1964).

The concept of intergenerational relations can refer to either of two sets of relations: those among different generations of immigrants and their descendants in an ethnic community or the society at large; and those among different generations within a family. This discussion refers to both. In the case of Polish Americans the first generation is the one which migrated to the United States directly from Poland as a cultural entity in spite of having been occupied by three foreign political states or after temporary residence elsewhere (Znaniecki, 1952). Apart from the post-1945 emigration, caused by the anti-Polish policies of the Soviets and Nazis, and the displacement caused by the war, the great influx of Polish immigrants to America took place between 1880 and the 1920s. Most immigrants came in the early years of their lives, between ages 20 and 40 in both emigration waves (Lopata, 1976a,

1976b; Pinkowski, 1978; Polzin, 1973). In order to best visualize intergenerational relations in Polonia we can plot the approximate ages of each generation by the decade in which the immigrants entered at age 20+, adding 25 years per generation. By this hypothetical system, immigrants entering America in the 1920s would have been at that time between 20 and 29 years, by 1980 they would be between 80 and 89 years old. Their children would be in their late 50s or early 60s and grandchildren in their 30s. The table below contains the age distributions for decades of the major migrations.

	Age by year of immigration and generation			
If entered America in:	Age and generation (25 years between)			
	Immigrant	2nd	3rd	4th
1880	120	95	70	45
1890	110	85	60	35
1900	100	75	50	25
1910	90	65	40	15
1920	80	55	30	5
1930	70	45	20	—
1950	50	25	—	—

Obviously few people entering America in their 20s in 1920 would still be alive. However, some of those entering before or immediately after World War One as small children would probably have survived till 1980. The gap in the immigration flow between the late 1920s until after World War Two will have produced a relative absence of that age cohort. On the other hand, the 1920s brought to America some older siblings and parents of people already settled here. The new emigration after 1945 contained few older people; most of them were younger people who had served in the armed services or been in labour camps during the war. The cold war prevented these people from bringing their parents from Poland to America.

Census figures of the population of the United States are usually limited to place of birth of the respondent, and his or her mother and father. However, a special "supplement to the November 1969 Current Population Survey" asked for country of origin and a special report contains data of importance to our analysis of intergenerational relations (U.S. Bureau of the Census, 1969). The population of Polish origin was listed as just over four million persons, forming 2.0 per cent of the American population. The median age was one of the oldest, 39.8 years, with the highest median of 45.8 attained by the Russians. The Polish men were younger than the women (38.7 to 40.9 respectively), a fact reflecting the death rate differences between the sexes (Table 1 of the report). Seventeen per cent of the people claiming Polish origin were under age 14 and 31 per cent under age 25. On the other hand, 43 per cent were age 45 and over 12 per cent were over age 65. Only 40 per cent of the Polish Americans reported English as their mother tongue, although 93 per cent claim it as their current language (Table 3 of the report).

Of course, these figures combine all foreign-born with people born in Poland. When these generations are separated for an analysis of people reporting Polish as their mother tongue, the foreign-born had a median age of 65+ years while the native-born had a median age of 47. These figures are based on only 339,000 foreign-born and 1,982,000 native-born people who spoke Polish in their home during childhood (Table 6 of the report). One reason why more people of Polish origin do not currently speak Polish is that only 41 per cent of the men married Polish origin wives (Table 4 of the report).

Another set of figures regarding the generational composition of the Polish Americans in 1969 shows that families of 73 per cent of the fathers who had been born in Poland and emigrated to America had sons born in the United States, and only 23 per cent also had sons who were born in Poland. The figures are similar for the place of birth of the mother and the child. All the statistics indicate a high probability that the Polish-American communities and families have contained members who were socialized in their youth into different social worlds and who have lived their lives in a variety of subcultures, made both more complex and somewhat less heterogeneous by the degree of institutional completeness and the tightness of ethnic community boundaries in America (Barth, 1969; Breton, 1964).

Intergenerational Relations: Sources of Strain

Sociologists since Kingsley Davis have theorized about, and researched, the strains contributed to intergenerational relations by the fact that each generation is born and socialized into different social worlds. The more rapidly the culture and society are changing, the greater the gap between the social worlds of grandparents, parents and the youngest generation (see also LeMasters, 1970). American society is noted for the rapidity of its cultural and social change, especially since the turn of the century. Persons born in, or migrating into, the United States before World War Two, or even before the Great Depression, lived in a completely different milieu than their children born after 1945 or grandchildren currently in school. Furthermore, people of prior generations never "catch up" with the culture of new generations, in spite of television and other aspects of life they allegedly share across time because of the deceleration of the rate of socialization with age. People now going through the early socialization and education process are learning the 1980s culture at a rate unmatched by the learning of older generations. The content of the social world of older generations, the objects and symbols with which they make life meaningful, the definitions of the situations with which they come in contact or about which they hear from others is a different world than that of their children or grandchildren. It is very difficult if not impossible for them to replace meanings and sentiments acquired in their youth just because they became outmoded through cultural change.

These sources of intergeneration strain and conflict apply to families born into the same society and culture which, regardless of the rate of change, at least provide some sense of continuity. But if each generation is born and socialized into different worlds, the differences between them become compounded. In the case of Poles coming to America, the contrast was enormous, not only because the societies and national cultures were so different, but also because of the differences in lifestyle of the immigrants prior to emigration and of their children born here. Many immigrants came mainly from villages, familiar only with their own limited *okolica* (village district) and agriculture as a way of life (Thomas and Znaniecki, 1918-1920). This is particularly true of the vast majority of immigrants in the years before World War Two. Those more educated Poles who came from cities or more urbanized and industrialized areas of Poland, as did many of the "new emigration" Poles, found the contrast between their lives and those of their American-born children less dramatic (Lopata, 1976b; Mostwin, 1969, 1971). The peasant immigrants simply could not learn the new culture or understand the way of life of the American society as rapidly as did their children and future generations. Such learning is not just a matter of rational effort but is complicated by feelings and sentiments, values and deeply held beliefs about the world. Such situational definitions and world views are not shed easily because they form the core of the self-identification. Immigrants thus come with ideas and feelings about family relations, appropriate gender behaviour, the roles of husband and wife, father and mother, son and daughter, family rituals, religious beliefs, health, leisure, beauty, work, and so forth, into which they were socialized in youth and which they do not want to give up or even have questioned. The same world is not available or esteemed in American society into which the children go, no matter how much the parents want to protect them from acculturation. Immigrants are unable to recreate their old country communities and to surround themselves with all the supports which would prevent cultural change in their own families, let alone for future generations.

In addition, the society within which the immigrants settled encourages social change and upward mobility, providing education, job training and mass communication as means of learning the steps needed to move out of a lower social strata, in spite of discrimination barriers. The ideology of such an open and flexible mobility is known and usually believed by members of this society, placing parents in a double bind. The upward mobility of offspring is generally possible only if each generation discards the culture of its forebears and becomes socialized and educated in the dominant culture. This means that parents must allow, even encourage, their children to become unlike them, to believe and behave in different ways, often uncongenial to the older generation. Such permissiveness was very difficult for traditionally socialized Poles in America. It appears from most studies of the Polish Americans that only the most recent generation of young people have been encouraged to become upwardly mobile in American society. Of course, such behaviour did not occur to the early immigrants of peasant origin, since many considered themselves only temporary residents of America, here to collect as many material goods as possible in order to better their situation back home when Poland finally regained its independence.

Another source of potential conflict between generations in Polonia has been the different attitudes toward social change between people brought up in more stable societies such as Poland and those reared in the future-oriented society of America. The older generation had been socialized to see themselves as increasingly important in the society as they grew older. But their American-bred children were seen as providers of a better future for the society and consequently more socially important. Such an orientation encourages change in lifestyles, antagonizing the older generation wishing for stability. The immigrants and the second generation worked very hard to accumulate basic status symbols of property and a respectable, unassuming lifestyle and they often define as cavalier the attitudes of younger generations which take affluence for granted, and even criticize the emphasis on material possessions (Wrobel, 1979). Other aspects of American culture, absorbed easily by the younger generations but a source of irritation to their elders, include the informality and egalitarianism in manner and rights. Mostwin reports that this is one of the main sources of conflict between the new emigration following World War Two, relatively well educated, settled outside of Polonian neighbourhoods and adjusted relatively well to their displacement and their more Americanized children. Bloch, Lopata, Radziatowski and Wojniusz point out that the descriptions of the traditional patriarchal structure of the Polish family neglected the influence of women and that the situation of families in America enhanced their power in the family. Lieberman, on the other hand, found Polish men who scored highest on authoritarianism as the most apt to report life satisfaction. Thus the evidence on the patriarchal nature of the Polish American family and intergenerational conflict is mixed.

Finally, intergenerational conflict can occur as the old Polonian neighbourhoods break up, with the in-migration of groups with different backgrounds and lifestyles and the out-migration of the more economically successful younger generations of Polish Americans. The people who remain are the old and the poor, sometimes joined by the also transitory Poles or the few very recent immigrants. Many a widow and older couple in the old Polish neighbourhoods in America are angry because they feel deserted by the younger generations. They want to remain independent, feeling that they have worked too hard in their lives to now move into the homes of their children and be asked to help with the work and child-rearing, yet they feel left out. Those who move to the suburbs, following their children, are often uncomfortable in an unfamiliar lifestyle and with their offspring's and grandchildren's friends. Conflict erupts in such intergenerational households over the distribution of objects, work patterns and lifestyles and the gap between the elderly and their grandchildren can create enormous family problems. Widows also report difficulties with their own children and in-laws over socialization of the grandchildren. This is especially true if the in-laws are of a different ethnic or religious background.[1]

Intergenerational Relations: Sources of Cohesion

The various waves and social classes of immigrants were aware of the need to prevent their children from rejecting Polish or Polonian culture and becoming too completely acculturated into the American way of life. In an attempt to prevent this, and also in consequence of their own need to create a life which was at least bearable in a foreign country, the Polish Americans within the local communities created a relatively complete institutional system which was eventually integrated into a nationwide and international Polonia (Barth, 1969; Breton, 1964). Finding the Catholic church culturally influenced and politically controlled by a hierarchy foreign to them, they insisted on building their own churches and parish buildings including schools. They imported and then trained their own priests, brothers and sisters so as to ensure that they experience, and the children learn, the Polish form of Catholicism, rejecting its Irish and German versions (Greeley, 1977; Greeley and Rossi, 1968; Kuznicki, 1978; Kuzniewski, 1978; Miaso, 1971; Polzin, 1973; Thomas and Znaniecki, 1918-1920; Wrobel, 1979). Unable to satisfy themselves on this point within the Roman Catholic Church, many Polish Americans joined the Polish National Catholic Church, which even took root in Poland itself.

The building of parish schools to which most Polish Americans sent their children did not result, however, in a generation of Polonians familiar with either Polish culture or much of the Catholic religion. Kusielewicz blames the religious orders for the native-born Polish Americans' lack of knowledge about Poland and Polish culture, but the fact that earlier immigrant generations were restricted in their familiarity to the village or *okolica* must also be taken into account. The building of these schools is not so much a reflection of the interest of the majority of parents in the intellectual content of the curriculum as in the social control of children in an environment familiar to the parents.

A number of researchers have commented on the hostility of Polish peasants and their Polish American descendants to education beyond the mere minimum, even for boys, who might be expected to be the main breadwinners of the next generation. Abel reported that education was considered dangerous because it gave young people strange ideas and decreased their interest in hard work. A further reason families discouraged advanced education, in addition to the fear that it would Americanize children or at least create social distance between generations, was the desire to have each member contribute to the family status through earnings as soon as possible. Internal status competition has been a very important feature of Polonia. Although individuals could maintain and modify their status vis-à-vis others in the community through their own efforts, it has been mainly the family which served as the unit of cooperation in its own *okolica* or area within which its reputation is contained. Only internally important sources of status were acknowledged and this did not include non-parochial and higher education outside the community. Therefore income, converted to homes and other material objects within the community, was an important source of status. The status competition provided the glue keeping families and the community together, although it also produced much externally visible conflict. It contributed to keeping new generations within the community of primary or secondary settlement and active in its voluntary associations rather than outwardly oriented.

The voluntary associations were of themselves important to the life of the Polish American community, creating ties among people and neighbourhoods and providing a superstructure and culture which helped the immigrants and some members of the second and third generation to build a life of relative self-sufficiency apart from the dominant society (Breton, 1964; Gordon, 1964; Lieberson, 1963; Zachariasiewicz, 1978). The complexity of Polonia's structure was developed with the help not only of the immigrants who settled here but also of those Poles who stayed here temporarily, later returning to Poland.

Over a million Poles are listed in the United States immigration and naturalization records as having left America and many returned to Poland during the years prior and just after World War One. Many of these people were political emigrés or members of several different social classes in Poland or in temporary residence elsewhere. These people started innumerable publications and used every means available in Polonia to convert the regionally or village-bound immigrant into a person identifying with the Polish national culture society and the effort to have it reunited into one political state (Lopata, 1976b; Pacyniak, 1978; Sywak, 1978; Znaniecki, 1952). Identifying American Polonia as the "fourth province of Poland" such nationalists obtained enormous sums of money from the Polish Americans for governments in exile, the wars, help to Poles under occupation and assistance in the rebuilding of the country after the wars. Such dramatic and heroic activity helped to unify generations within Polonia; many a second-generation man joined the Polish forces under General Haller and identified with the Polish cause (Haiman, 1948; Lopata, 1976b; Polzin, 1973; Wachtl, 1944).

Even in the interwar years, Polish American organizations have survived the gradual Americanization of each succeeding generation and the transmission of office and activity intergenerationally (Lopata, 1976b; Sanders and Morawska, 1975; Zachariasiewicz, 1978). The economic growth of the community has provided many opportunities for cultural transmission and contact among people of all ages and generations in America. Although the new emigration and the descendants of the old emigration tended to avoid each other in the early years of the "displaced persons" movement to America, social class similarities brought them together in many efforts (Gordon, 1964). For example, the Polish Institute of Arts and Sciences in America, originally almost wholly composed of first-generation immigrants and refugees, has increasingly included second- and even third-generation Polish Americans, to such an extent that the language at meetings is now officially English.

The initial tendency of sons to go into the same occupation as their fathers is beginning to decrease due to the use of higher education by the youngest generation; but the custom while it lasted helped to preserve intergenerational relations. So did the conservative outlook of these generations so that, whatever conflict existed, it tended not to push the children to extremes of liberal thought. There has thus been a transmission of many attitudes toward family roles from generation to generation, even if now the language of socialization tends to be mainly English and Polish observers of the American scene find people identified as Polish Americans to be very little Polish in culture (McCready, 1974; Nowakowski, 1964). Wrobel found the Polish Americans in a working-class neighbourhood of Detroit very similar to the people described in less objective terms by Wood in 1955 in Hamtramck, and McCready found distinct differences between Polish Americans and descendants of other ethnic origins in the combined sample he and Greeley used in *Ethnicity in the United States* (Greeley, 1974).

Conclusion

Most of the immigrants who came from Poland to the United States prior to World War Two are no longer living, and often their fourth-generation descendants are invisible to social scientists. First and second generations were studied by sociologists reflecting the American concern with the size of the immigration and the cultural differences between the entrants and the already established descendants of colonists from other nations. Other researchers have commented particularly upon the amount of open intergenerational and organizational conflict in Polonia. Thomas and Znaniecki documented the type of conflict which reached American courts to which parents brought their children in order to force obedience, economic help or the cessation of some form of perceived anti-social behaviour. Wood portrayed Hamtramck as full of conflict and competition among all generations and levels of relations. The preponderance of Polish gangs in Chicago was studied by Thrasher and the emphasis on delinquent behaviour in this ethnic group was answered by Taft in generation and age-sex terms; the Polish population simply contained the highest number of men in a high-risk age of any other group in the 1930s.

Whatever the conflict level, encouraged by the intensity of the status competition which demanded cooperation of all family members, the second generation about whom so many social scientists worried grew up to be quite law-abiding adults (Finestone, 1964, 1967). Of course, name changes and geographical mobility lost many second- and third-generation Polish Americans from observation. In fact, some of the widows studied in Chicago's old Polonia did not even know where a child was, having lost contact years ago (Lopata, 1977). Wrobel (1979) points out that intergenerational contact at the present time among working-class Detroit Polish Americans is highly dependent upon the stage of the family life course. The peak of interaction occurs when there are small grandchildren in the family, lines of support and pleasurable intercourse strengthening at that time.

Although intergenerational conflict was muted somewhat by the creation of complex, institutionally discrete ethnic communities and decreased with the reduction of cultural differences between the second generation and its own children and grandchildren all of whom shared minimal Polish cultural influences, the dispersal of the community is obvious to all observers. Geographical movement out of the old neighbourhoods of the city has been taking place all along, first into smaller areas of secondary settlement, then on an individual family basis. Even families living in the still heavily Polish American neighbourhood into which Wrobel moved to do his ethnographic study have members scattered in other areas. Interaction decreases as it becomes more difficult to arrange and as people living in different locations and socioeconomic levels develop varied interests. Sandberg's study of the dispersed Polish Americans in the Los Angeles area indicates some of the difficulties in having two or three generations share a modified Polish culture. As the bonds created by Polishness decrease in each generation, other ties must remain to continue interaction. Social security and increased affluence remove economic dependency as a major tie, and some studies indicate that the strictness of manner in family relations is being replaced by more informal affection (Cohler and Lieberman, 1979; Lieberman, 1979; McCready, 1974). At the same time, some of the studies of the ethnic elderly in American cities indicate frequent social isolation or asymmetrical dependence upon one rather than the total set of offspring (Bild and Havinghurst, 1976; Lopata, 1971, 1972, 1973, 1977, 1979). Since fertility has been declining among the Polish Americans, the current older generations have fewer children to use as resources than did past generations so that social isolation and the asymmetry of relations may be even more visible in the future. This trend toward the dispersal of families leaves older members in old neighbourhoods, and for the elderly social isolation will probably continue. It will be offset in the future as higher education and increased knowledge of societal resources equips the newer generations with more personal resources than had been available to the first and second generations of Poles in America, who were heavily dependent upon family and community.

Note

1. In Poland of recent years, on the other hand, a high proportion of rural and even urban older people live with their married children (Piotrowski, 1970). Lobodzinska (1970, 1974) found many of the older generation mothers voluntarily baby-sitting and doing household chores for their children and grandchildren who tend to live nearby, in order to free the middle generation of both sexes to take on full-time employment. The housing shortage in Poland and the tendency to own apartments leads to doubling up in the early years of a couple's marriage with one or the other set of parents and to a subsequent lack of mobility. This is a very different pattern to that followed by Polish American families, though Obidinski (1968) found some third-generation couples of young families willing to live with the grandparents because of the size of their homes and inexpensiveness of neighbourhoods.

Bibliography

Abel, T. Sundeland. 1929. "A study of change in the group life of Poles in New England farming community," in Edmund de. s. Brunner (ed.), *Immigrant farmers and their children.* Garden City, New York: Doubleday, Doran and Company, Inc., pp. 213-43.

Babinski, Grzegorz. 1978. "Zachowanie tradycji kulturowej i narodowej w rodzinach Polonijnych." ["The Maintenance of Cultural and National Traditions in Polonian Families."] *Przeglad Polonijny* [Polonian Review] 4 (1), pp. 71-81.

Barth, Fredrik. 1969. *Ethnic groups and boundaries.* Norway: Johansen and Nielsen Boktraykkeri.

Bild, B. R. and Havinghurst, R. 1976. "Senior citizens in great cities: the case of Chicago." Special issue, *The Gerontologist,* 16: 1, part II (February).

Bloch, H. 1976. "Changing domestic roles among Polish immigrant women." *The Anthropological Quarterly* 49: 1 (January), pp. 3-10.

Breton, R. 1964. "Institutional completeness of ethnic communities and the personal relations of immigrants." *American Journal of Sociology* 70: 2 (September), pp. 193-205.

Cohler, B. and Lieberman, M. A. 1978. "Ethnicity and personal adaptation." *International Journal of Group Tensions.*

Davis, Kinsley. 1940. "The sociology of parent-youth conflict." *American Sociological Review.*

Duncan, B. and Duncan, O. D. 1968. "Minorities and the process of stratification." *American Sociological Review* 33: 8 (June), pp. 356-64.

Emmons, C. F. 1971. "Economic and political leadership in Chicago's Polonia: some sources of ethnic persistence and mobility." Dissertation, Chicago: University of Illinois.

Finestone, H. 1964. "A comparative study of reformation and recidivism among Italian and Polish adult male criminal offenders." Dissertation, Chicago: University of Chicago.

——. 1967. "Reformation and recidivism among Italian and Polish criminal offenders." *American Journal of Sociology* 72: 6 (May), pp. 575-88.

Galush, W. J. 1975. "Forming Polonia: a study of four Polish-American communities, 1890-1940." Dissertation, Minneapolis, Minnesota: University of Minnesota.

Gordon, M. 1964. *Assimilation in American life.* New York: Oxford University Press.

Greeley, A. 1977. *The American Catholic.* New York: Basic Books.

——. 1974. *Ethnicity in the United States.* New York: John Wiley.

Greeley, A. M. and Rossi, P. H. 1968. *The education of Catholic Americans.* Garden City, New York: Anchor Books, Doubleday and Company.

Hutchinson, E. P. 1956. *Immigrants and their children, 1850-1950.* New York: John Wiley.

Kuznicki, E. M. 1978. "The Polish American parochial schools," in Frank Mocha (ed.), *Poles in America.* Stevens Point, Wisconsin: Worzalla Publishing Company, pp. 435-60.

Kuzniewski, Anthony J. 1978. "The Catholic Church in the life of Polish-Americans," in Frank Mocha (ed.), *Poles in America: Bicentennial essays.* Stevens Point, Wisconsin: Worzalla Publishing Company, pp. 399-422.

Lieberman, M. A. 1979. "Social and psychological determinants of adaptation." *International Journal of Aging and Human Development.*

Lobodzinska, B. 1974. *Rodzina w Polsce.* [The Family in Poland.] Warsaw: Wydawnictwo Interpress.

——. 1970. *Małzenstwo w mieście.* [Marriage in the City.] Warsaw: Wydawnictwo Panstwowe.

Lopata, H. Z. 1971. "Living arrangements of urban widows and their married children." *Sociological Focus* 5: 1, pp. 41-61.

——. 1972. "Social relations of widows in urbanizing societies." *The Sociological Quarterly* 13 (Spring), pp. 259-71.

——. 1973. *Widowhood in an American City.* Cambridge, Massachusetts: Schenkman.

——. 1976a. "Polish immigration to the United States of America: problems of estimation and parameters." *The Polish Review* 21: 4, pp. 85-108.

——. 1976b. *Polish Americans: status competition in an ethnic community.* Englewood Cliffs, New Jersey: Prentice-Hall.

——. 1976c. "The Polish American family," in Charles H. Mindel and Robert W. Habenstein (eds.), *Ethnic families in America.* New York: Elsevier, pp. 15-40. Second edition 1981.

——. 1977. "Widowhood in Polonia," *Polish American Studies* 34: 2 (Autumn), pp. 5-25.

——. 1979. *Women as widows: support systems.* New York: Elsevier.

McCready, W. 1974. "The persistence of ethnic variation in American families," in Andrew Greeley (ed.), *Ethnicity in the United States.* New York: John Wiley, pp. 156-76.

Miaso, Józef. 1971. "Z dziejów oświaty Polskiej w Stanach Zjednoczonych" ["The History of Polish Education in the United States."] *Problemy Polonii Zagraniczne* [Problems of Poles Abroad] 4, pp. 19-24.

Morawska, Eva. 1973. "Rola spolecznosci lokalnej w podtrzymywaniu etnicznych postaw i zachowan–proba interpretacji, *Przeglad Polonijny* 4: 3, pp. 34-49.

Mostwin, D. 1969. "Post World War II Polish immigrants in the United States." *Polish American Studies* 26: 2 (Autumn), pp. 5-14.

——. 1971. "The transplanted family, a study of social adjustment of the Polish immigrant family to the United States after the Second World War." Ann Arbor, Michigan: University Microfilms.

Obidinski, E. 1968. "Ethnic to status group: a study of Polish Americans in Buffalo." Dissertation, New York: State University of New York.

——. 1976. "Polish American social standing: status and stereotypes." *The Polish Review* 21: 3, pp. 79-101.

——. 1977. "The Polish American press: survival through adaptation." *Polish American Studies* 34: 2 (Autumn), pp. 38-55.

Pacyniak, Gernard. 1978. "An historical outline of the Polish press in America," in Frank Mocha (ed.), *Poles in America: bicentennial essays.* Stevens Point, Wisconsin: Worzalla Publishing Company, pp. 509-30.

Pinkowski, E. 1978. "The great influx of Polish immigrants and the industries they entered," in Frank Mocha (ed.), *Poles in America: bicentennial essays.* Stevens Point, Wisconsin: Worzalla Publishing Company, pp. 303-70.

Polzin, T. 1976. "The Polish American family." *The Polish Review* 21: 3, pp. 103-22.

——. 1973. *The Polish Americans.* Pulaski: Franciscan Publishers.

Radzialowski, T. 1974. "The view from a Polish ghetto." *Ethnicity* 1: 2 (July), pp. 125-50.

——. 1975. "Reflections on the history of the Felicians." *Polish American Studies* 32 (Spring), pp. 19-28.

——. 1977. "Immigrant nationalism and feminism: Glos Polek and the Polish women's alliance in America, 1898-1917." *Review Journal of Philosophy and Social Science* 2: 2, pp. 183-203.

Sandberg, N. A. 1974. *Ethnic identity and assimilation: the Polish American community.* New York: Praeger Publishers.

Sanders, I. and Morawska, E. T. 1975. *Polish American community life: a survey of research.* Boston University: Community Sociology Training Program.

S-K Chi, Peter and Jerzy Zubrzycki. 1978. "Ethnic origin and social status of the United States population 1978." *Ethnicity* 5 (December), pp. 312-26.

Sywak, Zofia. 1978. "Paderewski in America," in Frank Mocha (ed.), *Poles in America: bicentennial essays.* Stevens Point, Wisconsin: Worzalla Publishing Company, pp. 371-86.

Szczepanski, J. 1970. *Polish Society.* New York: Random House.

Taft, D. 1936. "Nationality and crime." *American Journal of Sociology* 1-4 (August), pp. 724-36.

Thomas, J. L. 1950. "Marriage prediction in the Polish peasant." *American Journal of Sociology* 55 (May), pp. 573- .

Thomas, W. I. and Znaniecki, F. 1958. *The Polish peasant in Europe and America.* Boston: Richard G. Badger, 1918-1920; New York: Dover Publications.

Thrasher, F. M. 1927. *The gang: the study of 1,313 gangs in Chicago.* Chicago: University of Chicago Press.

Wojniusz, H. K. 1977. "Ethnicity and other variables in the analysis of Polish American women." *Polish American Studies* 39 (Autumn), pp. 26-37.

Wood, A. E. 1955. *Hamtramck: then and now.* New York: Bookman Associates.

Wrobel, P. 1979. *Our way: family, parish and neighbourhood in a Polish-American community.* Notre Dame: University of Notre Dame Press.

U.S. Bureau of the Census. 1971. Current Population Reports, Series P-20. *Characteristics of the population by ethnic origin, November 1969.* Washington, D.C.: Government Printing Office.

Zawistowski, Theodore L. 1978. "The Polish National Catholic Church: an acceptable alternative," in Frank Mocha (ed.), *Poles in America: bicentennial essays.* Stevens Point, Wisconsin: Worzalla Publishing Company, pp. 423-34.

Znaniecki, F. W. 1952. *Modern nationalities.* Urbana, Illinois: University of Illinois Press.

Associational Life

The Secular Organizations of Polish Americans: the Fraternals' Role in Polonia

Donald Pienkos

> There are millions of Polish Americans but only one in ten supports our national Polish American organizations. These absent ones represent an enormous store of talent and potential growth for all of our organizations. But the task calls for a realistic appraisal of the Polish American experience in the United States. This meeting may generate some enthusiasm . . . and dispel passivity. It may help to establish priorities and identify the leaders of the future.
>
> Publicity for the 1980 Chicago Conference on American Polonia sponsored by the American Council of Polish Cultural Clubs.

So read a statement whose authors called for a series of conferences, which took place recently in several American cities having large Polish populations. The conference organizers sought to mobilize greater involvement in Polish American ethnic matters among the nine-tenths of the population not belonging to any Polonia organization. The meetings were designed mainly to attract "new blood" to revitalize Polish American activities. Yet, at the same time, the careful manner in which these points were worded showed how much the conference organizers wanted to avoid criticizing the one-tenth of Polonia that belongs to its organizations. Indeed, the organizations of Polish America are so significant in contemporary American society that nothing can be accomplished without them. Rather, any action undertaken in opposition to the organizations would be doomed to fail.

It is my argument that Polish Americans have inherited a great deal from their forefathers in the way of organizational and institutional structures, both secular and religious. This inheritance is in many ways richer than that made available to members of many other ethnic groups. Yet, to some extent it has been underestimated within the Polish American community. As a result, not enough attention has been paid by Polish Americans to the task of better integrating and adapting the existing institutions in Polonia (the term commonly used to describe the organized life of Polish Americans) to contemporary needs, so that more people might be made aware of their existence and their goals. Increased recognition of these organizations might be expected to attract more direct involvement in Polonia life, thereby providing the Polish American population with new cadres of "leaders of the future." Historically, members of Polonia organizations subscribed to the maxim, "the Community–an individual written large" ("Gromada–To Wielki Czlowiek").[1] This concept, borne out of the experience of poor immigrants to America in the decades after the Civil War, was based on the belief that through "hard work, saving, buying from one's own, collective self-help," masses of new immigrants might build the foundations of economic, political and social success in this country.[2] Today, perhaps more than has been the case for a generation, Polish Americans might well reconsider the truth of this maxim. In collective action, more than through individual efforts, people can achieve certain political, social and cultural goals in American society. This principle has traditionally guided Polonia and thus remains valid today.

A number of reasons might be given for the relatively low level of recognition that Polonia's organizations, particularly its secular organizations, enjoy nowadays. For one thing, the great majority of the religious and secular structures, such as the fraternals and the parishes, were created by immigrants of humble economic and social stature to meet their particular needs and those of their children. In a changing American social system, questions are frequently raised as to whether these organizations continue to serve the needs of a Polish American population which is socioeconomically and culturally more heterogeneous in character and no longer a working-class community that is geographically concentrated in particular American urban neighbourhoods. Some better educated, more affluent and professionally trained American-born persons of Polish heritage, as well as foreign-born Poles who have come to this country since World War Two, have complained that organizations such as the fraternals are too parochial in their outlook and non-intellectual in their activities. Fraternal leaders for their part frequently point out that such persons do not participate in their activities in large numbers.

The rather humdrum, routine character of many fraternal activities having to do with recruiting new members into their insurance programs and handling premium payments has also caused criticism. Some of this has its justification because of the very nature of the fraternals' own goals, which are diverse. Selling insurance and holding lodge meetings have always been activities that have co-existed with the grander work connected with political and cultural causes facing Poland and Polonia. The existence of such diverse aims within the fraternal institution has been a source of tension.

The existence of so many Polish American fraternals (nineteen operate at present) with programs that are in many ways very similar, if not identical, may have also led to criticism and an underestimation of their contribution to Polonia. Poles and Polish Americans have lamented the lack of unity of action within their communities, a failing that is often described as a peculiarly national trait. To them, division within the Polish American fraternal movement is in some ways but another reflection of the Polish character. (Such observations however tend to ignore the causes of division within the Polish fraternal movement, which were often rooted in serious perceived differences about its purposes. Even more important, however, is the tendency to minimize the significance of consensus within Polonia at critical times during the past century. For example, in both world wars Polonia's fraternals were nearly completely united in their efforts to work for Polish independence and the well-being of Polish victims of the conflicts.)

For some reason, Poles and Polish Americans have believed that unity within their ranks can be achieved and that disunity and competition within their group is a cultural flaw specific to them alone. One well-respected sociologist has gone so far as to enshrine the concept of "status competition" as the fundamental characteristic of Polonia.[3] Another noted scholar has emphasized in his research on contemporary Poland the persistence in Polish political culture of "basic distrust and disobedience of political or governmental authority; fervent, if not rampant, nationalism; and attachment to certain traditional institutions and social arrangements and structures."[4] Such observations may be accurate enough in themselves, of course. What I question, however, is whether such characteristics distinguish Polish Americans or Poles in Europe from other peoples. In my view, these analyses ought to be made from a comparative perspective and with an understanding that any nationality or ethnic group is best described when it is recognized as being heterogeneous rather than monolithically homogeneous as far as matters of culture, values and socio-economic status are concerned.

If one recognizes this simple point as holding true for discussions of American Polonia, one might better appreciate the fact that the Polish American population has always been somewhat diverse in its members' interests, occupations, religious sympathies and attitude toward the non-Polish culture with which they came into contact. Polish American fraternals became mass organizations during the first two decades of the twentieth century because they best represented the dominant values of the Polish immigrants and their offspring, who were for the most part little-educated people whose roots were in the village. Through collective efforts at mutual self-help, the fraternals were seen as aiding such people in achieving their own personal ambitions by improving themselves socially and economically in a foreign land. At the same time, fraternals helped raise the immigrants' political consciousness by providing them with the opportunities to make some contribution to the independence of their homeland, where so many of their relatives and friends remained.

The fraternals' aspirations to unite Polonia were not achieved in the era of World War One, even though the largely working-class Polish population in America was more homogeneous than it is today.[5] Yet the ideal of a unified Polonia has remained a popular one at the same time when it is increasingly difficult for fraternals to aspire to represent so many different kinds of Polish Americans. For this reason, more than the others, therefore, the fraternals have become objects of criticism, their limitations increasingly emphasized whenever Polonia's future is discussed.

But disinterest in the institutional affairs of American Polonia has not been the province solely of ordinary Polish Americans. Until recently, scholars, even those writing about the Polish ethnic community, paid little if any attention to its organizations. This was particularly true for the Polish American fraternals. Although the fraternals were the largest purely secular institutions in Polonia, and despite the fact that they were its most important single source of human, financial and communications resources, the only research done on the fraternal movement appeared in the form of officially commissioned histories of such organizations as the Polish National Alliance, the Polish Roman Catholic Union of America, the Polish Falcons, the Polish Women's Alliance and others. These histories, nearly all of which were written in the Polish language (thus making them practically inaccessible today) were of varying quality. Some were limited to recording, in a rather strictly chronological fashion, the fraternals' conventions and the official actions taken by their central administrations over the years. Others have a more theoretical focus. The most useful studies of this latter type were those written by Stanislaw Osada[6] and Mieczyslaw Haiman.[7] Osada's work, written on the occasion of the twenty-fifth anniversary of the PNA's founding by a professional journalist who was deeply involved in its politics, remains a spirited defence of the ideological and political foundations of the Alliance. This book also contains an interesting discussion of the rivalry for the leadership of Polonia which dominated the relationships between the Roman Catholic Resurrectionist order, the Polish Roman Catholic Union and the Polish National Alliance in that era. Haiman's book, one of the last of the official commemorative histories and published on the occasion of the PRCUA's seventy-fifth anniversary, is a scholarly study which places the development of the Union within the larger context of the many efforts by Polonia leaders to create a single national representative organization. The theoretical significance of Haiman's effort can be best appreciated when one notes that several recently published works on American Polonia interpret its experience from Haiman's perspective.[8] Of considerable interest are several other somewhat less scientific Polonia histories, such as those by Arthur Waldo and Adam Olszewski.[9] Both of these multi-volume studies have their limitations but they remain useful—Waldo's as a kind of encyclopedic study not only of the Polish Falcons Alliance but of practically every other aspect of nineteenth and twentieth century Polish and Polonia history as well; Olszewski's as a careful official history of the PNA central administration written during the long presidency of Charles Rozmarek (1939-67).

The limitations of a number of the official histories are not solely ones of language or style, however. Perhaps more significant is their tendency to concentrate almost entirely upon fraternal doings in Chicago, historically the largest centre and "capital" of Polonia life, to the virtual exclusion of information about activities in the smaller Polish "colonies" located in Michigan, Ohio, Wisconsin, New York and Pennsylvania. This orientation leaves readers with little understanding of the role of the fraternals in these areas and provides no explanation for the various splits which have occurred within the Polish fraternal movement since the 1880s and which have nearly always had a regional base. (Thus, the Polish Union of America which seceded from the Polish National Alliance in 1890 originally was headquartered in Minnesota; the Alliance of Poles which broke from the PNA in 1895 was centred in Cleveland; and the Polish National Union which was formed in 1908 was based in Scranton. The Polish Association of America, organized in opposition to Chicago control of the Polish Roman Catholic Union in 1895, was centred in Milwaukee.) Of course, given the official histories' commitment to maintaining unity within their ranks, one can hardly fault their authors for not discussing in great detail the regional bases of organizational divisiveness within the fraternal movement.

Recently, a few American and Polish scholars have begun to pay some attention to the fraternals. Overviews of their activities, goals and significance have been written by Joseph Wytrwal, Andrzej Brozek and Frank Renkiewicz, who have each done much to bring serious attention to the fraternal movement. Wytrwal's extensive work represents the first effort by a writer in the English language to give some attention to the fraternals.[10] Its strength lies in its somewhat detailed descriptions of the formation of the various fraternals, their membership size and activities over time. The major limitations of Wytrwal's research are due to his often uncritical presentation of significant information mixed together with relatively less important data about Polonia personalities and activities, as well as his failure to distinguish between the functions of fraternals and those of other organized elements in Polonia. Nowhere in Wytrwal's work does one find either a clear analysis of the role of the fraternal movement in Polonia, or a systematic history of the major fraternals, from their formation to the time in which he published his work. As a result, we get both partial narrative history and partial analysis of fraternal functions but neither in completely satisfactory fashion.

In his work, Renkiewicz has concentrated upon the ideological premises of the Polish American fraternal movement and its origins in post-1863 Polish political and social thought. His work has also placed more acute emphasis upon the diverse purposes which in combination form the bases of the fraternals: altruistic concern for the independence of Poland and the welfare of the Polish immigration in America, and an enlightened self-interest in organizing to provide their members with burial insurance and sick benefits.[11] By means of insurance programs the fraternals established both an important motivation for immigrants to enrol in their organizations as well as an opportunity for fraternal activists to gain useful experience in managing and investing increasingly large amounts of money in "their own" business enterprises. Given their commitment to working for Poland's independence and for an unending succession of worthy charitable and educational needs in Polonia, the fraternals also were involved in directing their members' attention to larger issues of public and patriotic concern. Through the institution of the fraternal lodge, whose meetings were held on a regular monthly basis, members were not only kept informed about their organization's financial status, but were also apprised about local and national political issues of the day confronting them. With the lodge located in the parish-centred neighbourhood, meetings were equally important as social and recreational gatherings. Here, Renkiewicz makes a valid point when he notes that organizations not based on the parish or fraternal principle but solely upon altruistic aims like the *Liga Polska,* the Polish Catholic Federation and the Polish National Council, sooner or later disappeared. Finally, Renkiewicz is the first scholar to attempt to discuss the structural character of the fraternals in some systematic fashion. He notes that while the fraternal lodges were the natural initial entry institution for persons seeking membership at the local level, the structure of the fraternals gave activists a real opportunity to climb the leadership ladder to participate in Polonia at the regional and even national levels. As the number of lodges grew, it became easier for the central office of each fraternal to deal with groups of lodges (combined into communes, circles or councils) and groups of councils (grouped by regions into districts which generally were along state lines). In this fashion, the fraternals developed a sophisticated system of representative self-government, with delegates elected from lodges or councils responsible for choosing national officers and approving fraternal policy periodically at national conventions. Thus, the Polish American fraternals, in addition to their other purposes, enabled members who were so inclined to become involved in the actual government of their organization by holding elective office.

Andrzej Brozek, a Polish scholar interested in the formation of American Polonia has directed his attention to the development of the fraternals up to 1939.[12] Somewhat more systematically than either Wytrwal or Renkiewicz (who do discuss the impact of Polish "positivist" thought which emerged after the failure of the 1863 revolution in shaping the outlook of the Polish American fraternal movement), Brozek examines the connection between Polish nationalist theory (including the ideas of Roman Dmowski) and the ideology which guided the major fraternals, the PNA and the PRCUA, in their formative years. He also traces the ideological heritage of those fraternals which grew out of the two largest and earliest groups, the Falcons and the Polish Women's Alliance. Following Haiman's lead, Brozek notes the distinction between the ideologies of the PNA and the PRCUA, the one emphasizing the importance of working on behalf of the independence of Poland, the latter with its emphasis upon improvement of immigrant conditions in America.

Brozek also argues that the traditional distinction between the original ideological antagonism of the PNA and the PRCUA has been somewhat exaggerated since both fraternals did emphasize the importance of improving the material and cultural conditions of the immigrants. Although the PNA more explicitly called for efforts in support of Poland's independence than did the PRCUA, the latter group eventually adopted views about Poland that were comparable in tone if not emphasis. What seems to have distinguished the two organizations was their leaderships. The PRCUA was Catholic in spirit and its leadership was made up of clergymen and laymen who were willing to defer to them. The PNA, while not hostile to Catholicism, was composed of individuals who would not follow clerical leadership without question. From the beginning, a major issue dividing the two groups was over the willingness of the PNA to admit non-Catholics into their ranks, individuals who could not be expected to be subservient to priestly leadership.

The two organizations did differ originally in their perspectives on the Polish question. Founded on the inspiration of Agaton Giller, a Polish patriot exiled in Switzerland, the PNA was organized by middle-class Poles in America who were committed to preserving the idea of Poland's right to independence. Consequently, it placed a higher importance upon the need for creation of stronger national consciousness in the immigration than its early rival. The Alliance stressed the need to communicate information and ideas about the Polish situation and already possessed its own newspaper, *Zgoda,* by 1881, which was supplemented in 1908 by the *Dziennik Zwiazkowy,* a daily Chicago paper. An aim of both papers was to stimulate greater awareness of PNA programs in Polonia and in American society at large.

In contrast, the PRCUA was more parish-oriented, not surprising in the light of its clerical leadership. Since they believed that Poland's independence was unlikely to occur as a result of any future insurrection, many clergymen viewed the purpose of the fraternal movement as that of assisting the immigrant in his neighbourhood community. As the two fraternals developed, the PNA leadership grew more closely identified with the Republican party (which controlled the American government most of the time from 1861 through 1933 and was seen as most able to do something for Poland and the immigrants). The PRCUA's leadership for a number of reasons, not the least of which was the clergy's preferences, was more closely connected with the Democratic party.

From these studies, we can make a few conclusions. One, the Polish fraternals were mass-oriented groups from the start, created for several interrelated purposes including those of providing their members with insurance while at the same time emphasizing the ethnic cultural basis linking their members together. Formed in the aftermath of the unsuccessful Polish insurrection of 1863 by individuals who recognized the hopelessness of another violent attempt to bring about Poland's independence, the fraternals focused on values such as solidarity, hard work, cooperation and education as the ideals upon which Polish immigrants in America should build their lives. Such principles made the fraternals admirably suited for success in an American society in which they were freely able to engage in social and business activities, to organize for political reasons in a peaceful manner and to communicate their purposes throughout Polonia.

In point of fact, it is extremely difficult to differentiate between the activities of various types of Polonia institutions because they have long been intertwined in terms of their goals, memberships, even leaderships. For analytical purposes, however, fraternals make up one of the four significant institutions of a mass character that have operated in the Polish American community for over a century, the others being the parishes, the veterans' organizations and the newspapers. All four groups share with one another mass membership or participation, and all four have been recognized as leading forces in Polonia life during most of the past century. All have performed important secular functions for Polonia (although the role of the parish has been primarily one of organizing the community for spiritual purposes connected with public worship). These functions include (a) socializing the members of the Polish American community (initiating their members to community values and activities and educating them so that they might participate in Polonia life); (b) recruitment of persons to take leadership roles in ethnic activities; (c) communicating information and opinions about matters of importance to the community; and (d) articulating and aggregating the concerns of community members about a variety of political, religious, social and economic matters and presenting them to non-Polish authorities.[13] To put it another way, one can characterize Polish ethnic organizations and institutions as "mediating structures" which have stood "between the individual and his private life and the large institutions of public life—government, the large corporations, big labor, the church, and modern bureaucracy."[14] Historically, the vast majority of Polish immigrants and their descendants have participated in some way in various Polonia organizations and activities at some stage in their lives. This involvement cushioned their gradual and successful adaptation to an America that was both extraordinarily alien and uninviting to the Poles, even while its political freedoms and material abundance exerted a profound attraction upon them.

The Polish American fraternals have attempted to play all these roles throughout the history of large immigration and settlement of Poles in this country, as have the other organizations that I have identified. (Indeed, it is important to note that prior to World War One at least, it was from the ranks of the Polish clergy and the Polish press rather than from fraternals that much of the top leadership of Polonia came. Under energetic priests such as Vincent Barzynski, Casimir Sztuczko, Wenceslaus Kruszka, John Pitass, Lucjan Bojnowski, Roman Catholic Bishop Paul Rhode and Polish National Catholic Bishop Francis Hodur, Polonia's concerns were stated. In that era, the Polish press under individuals such as Wladyslaw Dyniewicz, Michael Kruszka and Anthony Paryski was similarly influential.) As mass organizations, fraternals, even when their memberships are combined, have included fewer individuals than the Polish ethnic parishes, which have been estimated to number approximately 850, with perhaps one million members or more of Polish birth or descent. Polish fraternal organization memberships presently include about 700,000 individuals in their ranks.[15] In contrast, the combined membership of the various veterans' groups was far less—about 30,000 in the middle 1970s. Monthly readership of the Polish press not connected with the fraternals probably is less than 200,000. In contrast, the major fraternal papers now reach a larger audience. They include *Zgoda* (Harmony) of the Polish National Alliance with about 100,000 circulation every other week, *Narod Polski* (Polish Nation), a monthly of the Polish Roman Catholic Union with about 38,000 circulation and *Glos Polek* (Voice of the Polish Woman), the monthly of the Polish Women's Alliance with another 30,000. The *Polish American*

Journal, published monthly in Scranton, Pennsylvania, has nearly 50,000 subscribers and is the organ for several smaller Eastern fraternals.

Structurally, the fraternals have traditionally possessed both a local or neighbourhood base in their lodges to which insured members have directly belonged, as well as a system of regional and national leadership elected periodically at conventions by delegates representing the mass membership. This national leadership administers fraternal work between conventions and sets policy for the entire organization. Fraternals therefore differ significantly from the other large mass membership institution of Polonia, the parish, which operates at the neighbourhood level only.[16] The fraternal is also distinctive from most business operations as well. Though organized with the purpose of expanding its business operations so that it might provide ever more attractive and low-cost insurance programs yielding high dividends for its members (a growth characteristic shared with private firms), the fraternals in fact are organized as non-profit firms, having no stockholders or corporate owners *per se.* Rather, their administration is closer to that of a government, with conventions, legislatures, judicial bodies and executive officers who have been elected directly or indirectly by the members. These organizational features reinforce the ethnic character of the Polish fraternals by enabling their leaders to present themselves not only as business persons but also as trustees of the Polish American community and its concerns.

Fraternals have also possessed both the financial and the human resources to play a crucial role in Polonia. It is by means of fund-raising activities sponsored by fraternals that major Polonia projects through the years have been realized. Fraternals have underwritten charitable and political action efforts of the Polish American community through the years, including the various national funds *(skarb narodowy)* established on behalf of Poland before World War One, the activities of the Polish National Council during the war, leading the campaigns to collect enormous sums of money in the United States war bond campaigns, support for Polish bond drives after the establishment of the new independent state in 1918, involvement in the interwar World Congress of Poles Abroad, support for the work of World War Two Polish relief agencies such as the *Rada Polonii,* and financial backing of the Polish American Congress since 1944.

Although the assets of the fraternals have never been completely at the disposal of the organizations to be used for whatever purpose they chose, the groups have always had the freedom to utilize a small portion of their funds for social action. Periodically, fraternal members have voted to increase their annual dues for particular worthy causes. Such funds can be considerable when one realizes that the net worth of all the Polish American fraternals in the late 1970s was more than $300 million. The assets of the PNA in 1980 alone amounted to more than $165 million and that of the PRCUA more than $58 million. (Even such relatively small fraternals as Federation Life Insurance of America, headquartered in Milwaukee, possessed assets of approximately $4 million and more than 5,500 insured members in 1980.)

Even more significant to Polonia, however, is the social experience provided by fraternals out of which most of its important political leaders have emerged. The fraternals traditionally provided an early training ground for many politicians who have represented Polish constituencies and an opportunity for politically oriented Polish Americans to make valuable personal contacts with later supporters. One of the earliest major political figures of Polonia, Peter Kiolbassa (who won the office of Chicago city treasurer in 1892) was a president in the PRCUA. John Smulski, a leading Polonia politician, businessman and World War One era activist on behalf of Poland's independence, held high office in the PNA. In the mid-1930s, the PNA published a pamphlet titled *Our Political Heritage.* The publication discussed nearly every Polonia politician in Chicago and it noted they were all PNA members. In other communities as well, local political hopefuls gained valuable experience through connections they made in various fraternal lodges.

Not only has the fraternal movement been an important early training ground for politicians, involvement in these groups has provided crucial opportunities to win recognition for individuals seeking to become active within Polonia itself. Charles Rozmarek, who later became Polonia's main spokesman as president of the Polish American Congress between 1944 and 1968, was president of the PNA from 1939 onward. John Romaszkiewicz, a PNA president between 1928 and 1939, was largely responsible for the creation of the Polish scouts (or *Harcerstwo*), a mass movement which included over 50,000 members at the time of the outbreak of World War Two. Fraternal-based scouting organizations (which were formed by many of the organizations in the interwar era) included as many as 80,000 youths in all and were a constructive and enthusiastic response to the need to instill a sense of Polish ethnic consciousness in the American-born children of their still largely immigrant memberships. This was particularly important because Poland's achievement of national independence had meant that an important early purpose of many fraternals was achieved, and some restructuring of their aims was necessary. In 1894, fraternals were instrumental in organizing the *Liga Polska* under the leadership of the industrialist, Erasmus Jerzmanowski, which was committed to raising funds for Polonia needs. In 1910, the PNA organized a Polish National Congress in Washington, D.C. for the purpose of discussing partitioned Poland's problems and prospects. A large number of representatives from Europe and delegates from other fraternals and Polonia groups also took part in these proceedings.

In World War One, the Polish Falcons movement was largely responsible for the creation of a Polish legion which included approximately 27,000 young men who had not yet been naturalized, under the command of General Joseph Haller, to fight for Polish independence prior to America's entrance into the conflict. After the war, veterans of these units formed the Polish Army Veterans Association.

Fraternals also provided leadership for Polonia itself as an organized element in American society. Major efforts to establish sports and systematic activities, educational institutions, the Polish singers alliance, the construction of monuments to Kosciuszko and Pulaski were inspired by fraternal leaders. Polish banks and savings associations were frequently initiated by the fraternals, which also offered their insured members (and still do) relatively low priced residential mortgage loans at favourable terms. Other institutions initiated by fraternals have included the scores of "Polish homes," or meeting halls throughout the country and immigration hospices in New York, the city of disembarkation for thousands of Poles for decades. During the nineteenth and early years of the twentieth centuries both the PRCUA and the PNA gave much attention to purchasing farm land in the states of Nebraska, Minnesota, Wisconsin and South Dakota for Polish immigrants to establish rural communities in this country. Fraternals and their members have been strong backers of the cultural organizations of Polonia, such as the Kosciuszko Foundation, the Polish cultural clubs, the Polish American Historical Association and the Polish Institute of Arts and Sciences.

Clearly, Polish American fraternalism has represented a highly significant factor in the historic development of the Polish American community. During the past twenty years, however, changes in the social, economic, cultural and residential character of American Polonia have had a negative impact upon the growth and vitality of a number of fraternals. Between 1955 and 1975, for example, the total number of insurance certificates for the ten largest fraternals declined from 751,000 to 656,000 policies, a drop of more than 10 per cent. Since 1975 even the two largest fraternals, the PNA and the PRCUA, have declined, the PNA from 311,000 to 301,000 in 1980 and the PRCUA from 126,000 to 118,000. Furthermore, several of the smaller fraternals have not only suffered far larger membership losses but they have also experienced a net decline in their assets and the total amount of insurance they provide. The future of such organizations is bleak unless such trends are reversed.

The reasons for the decline in membership are numerous and some have to do with factors that are beyond the control of the organizations themselves. Perhaps the most obvious problems follow from the traditional commitment of the fraternals to increasing their membership through recruitment efforts of part-time financial secretaries in the neighbourhood lodges. For most of these individuals, commissions they receive from their insurance sales may represent only a relatively small fraction of their earnings. In the past, reliance on such personnel was a satisfactory and inexpensive way in which to sell insurance since the communities in which the lodge was located were heavily Polish and the lodge hall itself was a centre for socializing and recreation as well as fraternal activity. The resettlement of large numbers of Polish Americans outside of the old Polonia districts has not only eroded the vitality of many lodges; it has also made it more difficult for part-time financial secretaries and lodge organizers to recruit large numbers of new members into their groups by traditional methods. For example, of nearly 3,400 PNA lodges that have been created since 1880, only 1,205 were in existence in 1979, the rest having disappeared or merged with other lodges in their vicinity. Of those presently in existence, approximately 60 per cent are considered to be active—that is, they hold meetings at least four times each year, and are involved in various sports, scholarships, youth or other Polonia-wide functions. The condition of other fraternals may be even poorer since practically none had as large and concentrated a membership from which to start as did the PNA.

Table 1: Growth in the Ten Largest Polish American Fraternals, 1915-75

	1915	1935	1955	1975
Combined membership, ten largest Polish fraternals	318,100	677,700	751,000	656,000
Polish National Alliance	110,300	284,300	337,800	310,600
Polish Roman Catholic Union	85,200	154,600	175,500	126,300
Polish Women's Alliance	14,500	60,700	85,400	82,600

SOURCES: Brozek, Wytrwal.

Such declines are likely to continue as long as fraternals rely primarily upon the lodges in recruiting new members. To deal with this matter, several organizations have already begun to commit themselves to developing cadres of full-time, professional insurance salesmen along with more attractive advertising campaigns to help sell their product, which in fact is very competitive in costs and benefits with the programs of the major commercial insurance companies. Organizations such as the Polish National

Table 2: Major Polonia Organizations, Date of their Formation, Headquarters and Members (c. 1975)

Organization by type	Year Formed	Headquarters	Membership	Affiliated with Polish American Congress*
Fraternals				
Polish Roman Catholic Union	1873	Chicago	126,000	Yes
Polish National Alliance	1880	Chicago	311,000	Yes
Polish Union of USA	1890	Wilkes Barre	14,500	No
Alliance of Poles of America	1895	Cleveland	16,000	Yes
Polish Association of America (Northern Fraternal Life)	1895	Milwaukee	4,500	No
Union of Poles in America	1898	Cleveland	10,000	Yes
Polish Women's Alliance	1898	Chicago	82,000	Yes
Polish Beneficial Association	1900	Philadelphia	24,000	No
Association of the Sons of Poland	1903	Jersey City	12,000	No
Polish National Alliance of Brooklyn	1905	Brooklyn	12,000	No
Polish White Eagle Association	1906	Minneapolis	1,100	No
Polish National Union	1908	Scranton	31,000	Yes
Polish Alma Mater of America	1910	Chicago	5,000	Yes
United Polish Women of America	1912	Chicago	4,000	Yes
Federation Life Insurance	1913	Milwaukee	5,500	No
Assoc. of Polish Women of US	1913	Cleveland	2,000	Yes
Polish Union of America	1917	Buffalo	12,000	Yes
Union of Polish Women in Am.	1920	Philadelphia	9,000	Yes
Polish Falcons of America	1928	Pittsburgh	27,000	Yes
Veterans groups				
Polish Army Veterans Association	1921	New York	8,000	Yes
Polish Legion of American Veterans	1921	Chicago	15,000	No

Polish Veterans of WWII Association	1952	New York	5,000	Yes
Polish Association of Former Political Prisoners	1952	New York	900	No
Polish Home Army Veterans Association	1953	New York	Unknown	No
Cultural-social groups				
Polish Singers Alliance	1889	New York	2,000	Yes
National Medical and Dental Association	1900	Dearborn	1,000	No
Kosciuszko Foundation	1925	New York	3,500	No
Polish Institute of Arts and Sciences in America	1942	New York	700	No
Jozef Pilsudski Institute in America	1943	New York	380	No
Polish American Historical Association	1943	Chicago	500	No
American Council of Polish Cultural Clubs	1948	Detroit	1,400	Yes
Polish Medical Alliance	1948	Chicago	180	No
Gen. Pulaski Heritage Foundation	1959	New York	2,500	No
American Institute of Polish Culture	1972	Miami	150	No
Copernicus Foundation	1973	Chicago	Unknown	Yes
National Advocates Society	No info.	Chicago	1,000	Yes
Polish Highlanders Society	No information found			Yes
Other organizations				
Polish American Immigration and Relief Committee	1947	New York	No information	
Polish American Guardian Society	1962	Chicago	750	No
Orchard Lake Center for Polish Studies and Culture	No information other than headquarters at Orchard Lake Schools, Michigan			

* This refers to the organization's affilition with the Polish American Congress on a national basis. Many if not most of the organizations listed as not affiliated nationally with the PAC in fact participate in one or more of its thirty-one state divisions.

SOURCES: Wynar; Donald Pienkos, "The Polish American Congress—An Appraisal," *Polish American Studies* 36, no. 2 (Autumn 1979), pp. 34-35; and Angela T. Pienkos, *A Brief History of Federation Life Insurance of America, 1913-1976* (Milwaukee: Haertlein Publishers, 1976), p. 26.

Alliance which have been heading in this direction (without, however, giving up on the lodge system for recruitment) have actually experienced a significant increase in their net worth and the amount of insurance in force at the same time they have been suffering a net loss in membership. Still, it may be preferable to enroll one new member into a $10,000 life insurance program that will provide its owner with $50,000 worth of insurance at the age of thirty-five than to sign up five or six persons to $1,000 policies that will be paid up within twenty years. The holder of the larger policy is far more likely to value the policy he or she buys, to continue to keep the program rather than to cash in the policy at the first opportunity, and to become more involved in fraternal activities sponsored by the organization and publicized by its newspapers. While fraternals highly prize all their members, holders of insubstantial amounts of insurance are more likely to regard their policies as insignificant, and to remain ignorant of the fraternal benefits to which they are entitled.

Equally challenging is the need fraternals have to attract greater numbers of the post-World War Two immigration into their ranks. There are many financial benefits fraternals offer that should attract such individuals, particularly their mortgage loan programs and the college scholarships and loans they offer to their children. More emphasis on such practical matters might encourage greater receptivity to fraternalism among the newer arrivals. For Polonia's fraternals, built by earlier generations of immigrant people and their offspring, greater participation by the post-World War Two Polish Americans would also be rewarding, serving to revitalize their own ethnic character and to give new meaning to their role in Polonia as the powerful engines of ethnic activism that they have been in the past.

It would be a mistake to conclude these remarks without re-emphasizing the potential value of fraternal organizations as mediating structures operating on behalf of Polish Americans at both the community and the national levels. Historically, the fraternal lodge was a natural neighbourhood meeting place where people could talk over matters of community-wide concern as well as lodge business. Frequently, persons active in local lodges inspired patriotic manifestations, charitable drives and political campaigns for Polonia's friends. In doing such things, the fraternal "mediated" between the individual members (who otherwise might have remained helpless onlookers observing the great events of the day) and the wider world beyond the neighbourhood. If the existing fraternals could regain this spirit of community service and purpose their activities might have highly satisfying benefits for both their members as well as the larger community.

Similarly, fraternals with their mass memberships and extensive financial resources can be more effective representatives of Polish American concerns and aspirations at the national level, especially if they can develop clearly articulated programs with social and cultural appeal which supplement what they have traditionally offered their members. The task is difficult both locally and nationally because at the present stage of American history, many Polish Americans must be convinced that ethnically based loyalties can make a difference in their lives and in the shaping of public policy. Still, their past record of service and their still enormous human and material resources ought to make fraternal leaders confident that their organizations do possess much to offer Polish Americans in their search for their proper place in American society.[17]

Notes

1. Mieczysław Haiman, *Zjednoczenie Polskie Rzymsko-Katolickie w Ameryce* (Chicago: PRCUA, 1948), p. 29.
2. Frank Renkiewicz, "An Economy of Self-Help: Fraternal Capitalism and the Evolution of Polish America," in Donald Pienkos, Philip Shashko and Charles Ward, eds., *The Eastern European Experience in America* (New York: Columbia University Press, 1980).
3. Helena Lopata, *The Polish Americans: Status Competition in an Ethnic Community* (Englewood Cliffs, New Jersey: Prentice-Hall, 1976), pp. 42-67.
4. Andrzej Korbonski, "Poland," in Teresa Rakowska-Harmstone and Andrew Gyorgy, eds., *Communism in Eastern Europe* (Bloomington, Ind.: Indiana University Press, 1979), p. 45.
5. Edward Kantowicz, *Polish-American Politics in Chicago: 1888-1940* (Chicago and London: University of Chicago Press, 1975), conclusion.
6. Stanisław Osada, *Historya Związku Narodowego Polskiego* (Chicago: Polish National Alliance, 1905).
7. Haiman. For a good bibliography of publications on the fraternals, see Renkiewicz's bibliographical note to his "Economy of Self-Help."
8. Kantowicz, pp. 10-13; Andrzej Brożek, "Próby Zjednoczenia polonii amerykańskiej i ich ideologie," paper presented at the Conference on American Polonia, Kraków, July 21, 1979.
9. Arthur Waldo, *Sokolstwo przednia straż narodu* (Pittsburgh: Polish Falcons of America, 1953-1974), 4 vols.; Adam Olszewski, *Historya Związku Narodowego Polskiego* (Chicago: Polish National Alliance, 1957), 5 vols. The PNA, under President Aloysius Mazewski, commissioned a new history of the Alliance written by this author which was nearing completion in 1982.
10. Joseph Wytrwal, *America's Polish Heritage* (Detroit: Endurance Press, 1961); *Poles in American History and Tradition* (Detroit: En-

durance Press, 1969); and *Behold! The Polish Americans* (Detroit: Endurance Press, 1977).

11. Renkiewicz, "An Economy of Self-Help," and "The Profits of Non-Profit Capitalism: Polish Fraternalism and Beneficial Insurance in America," in Scott Cummings, ed., *Self-Help in Urban America: Patterns of Minority Business Enterprise* (Port Washington, N.Y.: Kennikat Press, 1980), pp. 113-29, 221-24.

12. Andrzej Brożek, *Polonia Amerykańska: 1854-1939* (Warsaw: Interpress, 1977).

13. For example, Gabriel Almond and G. Bingham Powell, *Comparative Politics: System, Process and Policy* (Boston: Little, Brown, 1966, 1978), pp. 52-280.

14. Peter Berger and Richard Neuhaus, *To Empower People: The Role of Mediating Structures in Public Policy* (Washington, D.C.: American Enterprise Institute, 1977), pp. 2-4.

15. In point of fact, "membership" figures for the fraternals record the total number of insurance certificates that are in force at a given time, including policies that have been paid up. Thus, it is estimated that while approximately 300,000 certificates issued by the PNA and 118,000 by the PRCUA are presently being maintained, as many as 130,000 PNA policies and 60,000 PRCUA certificates have already been fully paid up. Such policy holders are not listed as policy holders in current fraternal statistics.

    In general, owners of paid-up policies do not receive fraternal newspapers, nor do they usually take part in lodge activities. There is a small number of persons who hold multiple policies with one or more Polish fraternal. All these factors must be considered whenever estimates of fraternal "membership" are attempted.

    The historic significance of the fraternals as mass Polonia movements can also be better appreciated when one realizes just how many people have belonged to these organizations over the years. A recent estimate of PNA membership that appeared in that fraternal's organ asserted that during its century of activity over 1.2 million individuals had at one time been insured by the Alliance. (*Zgoda,* August 15, 1980, p. 2).

16. In the past, several unsuccessful efforts by clergymen were made to organize national associations of Polish priests and parishes. Groups such as the Polish Roman Catholic Priests Association (1875), the Polish Priests' Society (1886), the Polish Roman Catholic Priests' Conference (1891), the Society of Secular Priests (1904) and the Union of Polish Priests in America (1912) tended to reflect rivalries between religious orders, personalities and philosophies and usually endured for only short periods of time. Historically, only one Polish American religious leader, Bishop Paul Rhode, took an active role in systematically attempting to represent the church in the activities of Polonia, although other bishops such as Krol and Wycislo, among others, have obviously enjoyed great prestige in the Polish American community.

17. See also, Donald Pienkos, "The Polish American Congress—An Appraisal," *Polish American Studies* 36, no. 2 (Autumn 1979), pp. 5-43; Pienkos, "The Polish National Alliance: One Hundred and Two Years of Service," *Zgoda,* 15 February, 1 March, 15 March 1982.

The Local Ethnic Lobby. The Polish American Congress in Connecticut, 1944-74

Stanislaus A. Blejwas

The importance of the Polish parish in the organization, formation and continuity of the Polish immigrant community has been thoroughly documented in numerous scholarly studies. From Thomas and Znaniecki to Paul Wrobel's recent study, the parish's role in the socio-cultural bonding and infrastructural development of the immigrant community is abundantly evident.[1] Conversely, Polish American secular institutions and organizations have not been the subject of systematic scholarly analysis. The local and national fraternals, the cultural clubs and sports organizations, the veterans' groups, and the state and local political clubs, perhaps because many of them first appeared as parish satellites, await the presentation of their contributions to the history of Poles in America.

Secular currents have long been present in American Polonia. Pastor-parishioner conflicts provided some of the most exciting moments in the history of the Polish American community, while socialism found adherents among immigrant workers in Chicago, Detroit and Milwaukee. And as Polish Americans organized and moved into politics at the local, state and national levels from the 1920s through the 1940s, it was apparent that laymen expected to participate in community leadership.

The formation of the Polish American Congress (PAC) in May 1944 was a landmark in the Polish American community. For the first time Polonia was unified in a prominent, nationwide organization which could legitimately claim to speak for it, and laymen as well as representatives of the Roman Catholic and the Polish National Catholic churches shared in its creation. The leadership was in secular hands, and until Pienkos' recent, very balanced appraisal of the Congress, one of Polonia's most important organizations received practically no scholarly attention.[2]

As Pienkos observes, the Polish American Congress has served as "the chief organization voicing the political interests of Americans of Polish descent in the United States."[3] Organized during the last year of World War Two when a Soviet takeover threatened Poland, the purposes of the PAC were to cooperate with the American government in bringing the war to a successful end and ensuring a free and independent Polish state within the framework of a just peace based on the principles of the Atlantic Charter. A genuinely American political interest or pressure group and not a political party, it is a political organization that has remained true to its original goals, defending the rights of the Polish nation abroad and working for the betterment of Polish Americans at home. The most vital era for the Congress was between 1944 and 1952, which coincided to some extent with the Cold War, when it was successful in raising funds and still had at its disposal an active Polish-language press. The Congress criticized the Yalta decisions, supported the Oder-Neisse line, refused to recognize the Soviet-controlled regime in Poland and, in general, presented the case for an independent Poland to the American public. Until at least 1948, the Congress tried to be a stimulus upon American foreign policy, but later supported whatever was in vogue in Washington. After 1956, with the emergence of a more liberal regime in Poland and as increasing numbers of Polish Americans travelled to Poland, the PAC was demoralized because of internal fights over the United States policy of recognizing Communist realities in eastern Europe, and in the early sixties membership declined. With the election in 1968 of Aloysius Mazewski as its second president, succeeding Charles Rozmarek, domestic matters (i.e., upgrading the Polish image, anti-defamation, teaching Polish in schools, publication, government appointments, relations with the Roman Catholic Church and with Jews) seemed to emerge as priority issues. In the 1970s, the issue of human rights in the Soviet bloc enlivened Congress' rigid anti-communism, and the election of John Paul II and the 1980 strikes demonstrated the authenticity of the PAC's policy of distinguishing between the Polish Communist regime and the Polish nation.

Within the Congress, tensions existed over what issues should enjoy priority—the liberation of Poland, or home affairs (i.e., the overall advancement of Polish Americans). This tension between foreign and domestic goals was directly connected with the generational tensions between *stara* (pre-World War Two peasant economic immigration) and *nowa* (postwar political emigrés and displaced persons) Polonias. Uncertain finances, the absence of a communications media and declining membership also plagued the Congress.

Structurally, the PAC is composed of both individual, direct members and organizational, indirect members. Its three basic elements consist of the president, an office that the Congress maintains in Washington and its state divisions, which are relatively autonomous bodies. The state divisions, together with the major fraternals and veterans' organizations, are the Congress' primary units. The purpose of this study is to examine the Connecticut District and its role over thirty years (1944-74) at the grassroots level as, to borrow Pienkos' phrase, "Polonia's chief political interest group." Put in another way, how has this District adhered to and implemented the objectives of its parent body, the Polish American Congress?

Polish migration to Connecticut was part of a larger migration to the Connecticut River Valley dating back to the 1870s and 1880s. The peasant immigrants, mainly from Russian and Austrian Poland, came in search of jobs and cheap land, and the height of this influx occurred between 1890 and World War One. Most immigrants settled in such industrial centres as Hartford, New Britain, Bridgeport, Waterbury and New Haven, but there was also significant rural settlement. By 1930 the total foreign-born and native-born of foreign or mixed parentage was 133,813, or 13 per cent of the state's population, while in 1970 the figure was 304,000, or 10.7 per cent, making Connecticut, in percentage terms, one of the nation's largest Polish states. At the outbreak of World War Two, Connecticut's Polonia possessed a socio-cultural and political infrastructure that compared favourably with Illinois, Michigan or Wisconsin Polonia. There were twenty-six Roman Catholic parishes (many with their own schools), nine National Catholic parishes, branches of all the major fraternals as well as active Falcon nests, a well-known Polish-language weekly, *Przewodnik Katolicki* (The Catholic Leader), and a series of Democratic and Republican clubs. In many ways, the election of Boleslaus Monkiewicz as Connecticut's first Polish American congressman-at-large in 1939 symbolized the groups "arrival" and integration into American life.

By 1939 the interest of Poland's politics was for most Connecticut Polish Americans of secondary or tertiary importance. However, the Nazi and Soviet invasions of Poland in September 1939 altered the situation, especially for those with family and friends in Poland. The war rekindled a common concern for their homeland. Initial efforts to assist Poland were limited to relief work, and between January 1940 and October 1943, $103,770.83 in donations and goods was collected by the Second District (Connecticut) of the *Rada Polonii Amerykanskiej*, in which Dr. Bronisław Smykowski of Bridgeport, a leading figure in the Polish Roman Catholic Union, played an important role.[4] Interest in Polish political and diplomatic developments was stimulated by *Przewodnik Katolicki*, the mouthpiece of the powerful Msgr. Lucyan Bójnowski of New Britain, who engaged in bitter polemics with *Nowy Świat* because of its support of the prewar Polish government of Józef Piłsudski and his successors (popularly known as the *sanacja*).[5] At the same time, there were three branches (Hartford, Norwalk and Stamford) of the *Komitet Narodowy Amerykanów Polskiego Pochodzenia* (KNAPP) in Connecticut grouped around former Piłsudskiites. It is not surprising, therefore, when the growing Soviet threat to Poland led to the call for the creation of a national organization to defend Poland's interest, that Connecticut sent a large delegation to the 1944 Buffalo convention at which the Polish American Congress was created, including Bójnowski, who had serious reservations about KNAPP's influence in such an organization.

The 103-person delegation included 23 priests, two nuns, and a former congressman-at-large (L. Maciora). Representatives came from 24 cities and towns throughout the state, 22 delegates coming from New Britain, the de facto capital of Connecticut Polonia. Additionally, the current congressman-at-large (Monkiewicz), while not a member of the delegation, was one of the Polish American congressmen to address the convention.[6] The local leadership's strong interest in the newly created Polish American Congress was reflected in the organization of the Connecticut State District (one of the first) at a meeting at the Hartford Polish National Home on November 26, 1944. Under the slogan "W Jedności Siła" (In Unity Strength) the initiators appealed to all organizations and individuals to join the District and elected Lucian Maciora of New Britain, the former congressman-at-large, as its first president.

Structurally, the Connecticut District was a partial replica of the national body. While there were provisions for individual membership, the District was perceived as a statewide umbrella organization with Polish American groups represented by delegates at "Congress" (the common term for the Connecticut District) meetings, particularly the annual meeting in Hartford, the state capital. The only persons or groups ineligible for membership were those not recognizing the American Constitution or the right of the Polish nation to independence.[7] In the first year, membership developed slowly because groups considered the question at their regularly scheduled meetings, but it did develop on a statewide basis. The 1970 membership list is representative of the District's umbrella character. Apart from 36 individual members, 64 organizations belonged to the District, including 23 Polish National Alliance lodges, 5 Polish Roman Catholic Union branches, 10 veteran groups, 5 Falcon nests, 5 Polish American political clubs, 3 Polish Women's Alliance lodges, 3 united Polish societies (*Centralas* of Waterbury, Meriden, and Hartford), and 7 additional groups, all of which represented 17 cities and towns.[8]

The stated aims of the Connecticut District coincided with those of the national PAC. According to the projected by-laws, the District's objectives were those expressed in article 2 of the PAC's constitution, to which the District bound itself to engage "in work for the good of the United States, the Polish nation, and Polonia."[9] For the organizers, it was not a conflict of interest or loyalties for Americans of Polish descent to lobby against a Communist takeover of Poland. It was their perception that an independent Poland coincided with American objectives: "in defending Poland and her cause we do so fully conscious that at the same time we defend the cause of America's aims in the past war as in the future peace."[10] Furthermore, as Joseph Kozakiewicz, the District's second president (1945-52) wrote to Rozmarek, it is "our duty, as Americans of Polish extraction, to do whatever we possibly can."[11]

While the threatened Soviet takeover of Poland was a factor motivating the District organizers, the "Congress" was also to serve local Polonia needs. According to the by-laws, the District was a party organization "caring only about the good of Polonia and its position in the political world of America." The State division undertook to support the "political aims and ambitions of Americans of Polish origin without regard to faith, political convictions or party membership," excepting of course, "persons [i.e., communists and their sympathizers] working to the detriment of the Polish and American nations."[12]

In the realization of the Connecticut District's dual objectives, Polish affairs enjoyed priority. The District did not pretend to be able to reverse or alter diplomatic events or foreign policy on its own, but it viewed its activities as part of the "National" (the colloquial for the Chicago headquarters, also called "Chicago"). As a conscious spokesman for Connecticut Polonia, the District articulated constant and strong anti-Soviet and anti-Polish Communist positions paralleling those of the National. By resolutions and letters to Presidents Roosevelt and Truman, the Secretaries of State, and members of the State's congressional delegation, both before and after the Yalta agreement, the District protested the ceding of prewar eastern Poland to the USSR and Soviet behaviour in Poland. The United States Congress was urged to reject the Yalta accords with the warning that satisfaction of Soviet demands was comparable to the appeasement of Nazi Germany. The District insisted that the Polish Communist regime "does not represent the wishes of the Polish people" and called for an end to this state of affairs. Questioning the Potsdam decisions, the District expressed its skepticism about the possibility of holding free elections in Soviet-controlled Poland and later protested those elections in January 1947, demanding a complete Soviet military and police evacuation from Poland. While opposing Poland's new eastern boundary, the District supported the Oder-Neisse Line as her western frontier, a position that led it to criticize American foreign policy when it protested the September 6, 1946 speech of Secretary of State Byrnes, which was interpreted to mean that Poland's new western frontier was merely a temporary demarcation line.[13]

In subsequent years, the District's anti-communism expressed itself in protesting Kruschev's 1960 visit to the United Nations and "Soviet colonialism" while underlining Poland's right to independence and the right of the Polish nation to freedom and human rights. A delegate from the District participated in the activities of the Assembly of Captive Nations, and there were various patriotic commemorations, including the twentieth anniversary of Katyn in 1960, and the fiftieth anniversary of Polish independence in 1969. District members were occasionally reminded that the National's policy of no official contacts with the Polish Communist regime was binding on them, and Senator William Fulbright was criticized in 1973 for his efforts to eliminate Radio Free Europe. The tenacity and consistency of the District's anti-communism, its inherent distrust of detente and the USSR, and its consciousness of its role as a voice in Connecticut speaking for a free Poland, are perhaps best underlined in the Manifesto adopted on Pulaski Day, October 9, 1966 to commemorate the millennium of Poland's Christianity. The declaration reiterated earlier condemnations of "the infamous" Yalta Agreement which led to an "imposed communist regime and neocolonial Russian domination." Disappointed with the refusal of the Polish government to issue Cardinal Wyszynski a passport to visit the United States (including Connecticut), and against the backdrop of intense state-church conflict in Poland, the District went on to praise the Catholic Church and the cardinal for preserving "Poland's heritage in these difficult and trying times," and warned the United States to stand firm against Communist aggression. The demands for free and unfettered elections in Poland, American recognition of the Oder-Neisse Line, and a return to the Treaty of Riga boundaries in the east were also reiterated.[14]

The District's skeptical and cautious attitude in the 1960s toward the American policy of "building bridges" with eastern Europe, which it wanted limited to the Polish nation to the exclusion of any benefit for the Communist government was another example of its consistent anti-communism. The District repeatedly expressed support for American foreign policy in Vietnam during the Johnson and early Nixon administrations, both positions faithfully echoing national PAC policies.[15]

To propagate its views within and beyond Polonia, the Districts hosted major public figures sympathetic to its positions (Jan Karski and Representative Alvin O'Konski, 1945; General T. Bór-Komorowski, 1946; Congressman John D. Lodge, 1947; Tomasz Arciszweski, 1950; Arthur Bliss Lane, 1951; Ambassador Józef Lipski, 1952; General Władysław Anders, 1961) and organized large, well-publicized ceremonies, such as the May the Third *akademias,* as forums for their guests. Distinguished visitors were often presented to the governor and other local politicians, and commemorative booklets printed. The presence of several hundred to a couple of thousand listeners from the 1940s to 1960 at May the Third rallies, or at Pulaski Day parades from 1953 on, assured attendance by most invited politicians, especially in election years. If these events did not bring Poland's liberation any closer, they maintained a vague awareness of Poland's political situation among the politicians, who knew what was expected of them in addressing Polish American audiences. It was not unusual for congressmen or senators to seek the District's opinions or support on immigration matters or American relations with Poland, and the District's views did not go unnoticed. When in 1961 Senator Thomas Dodd, whose anti-communist positions in almost every instance enjoyed District approval, attempted to have Congress cut off all aid to Soviet bloc countries, the District contacted Connecticut's other senator, Prescott Bush, to secure passage of a resolution leaving such decisions to the president.[16] This exercise illustrated the local impact of the PAC through a state division and reflected the District's adherence to national PAC policy, which distinguished between the Polish Communist regime, which it never recognized as the legitimate government of Poland, and aid that would benefit the Polish nation as a people.

Polish affairs were not limited to politics. The District supported passage of the Displaced Persons Act of 1948, and acting on requests from the Washington office, contacted Senator Brian McMahon to support amending the DP Bill in 1949 in order to allow the entry of Polish soldiers from Great Britain. During the Kennedy administration, the District urged amendment of existing immigration laws in order to raise Poland's quota.[17] Earlier, the District also supported humanitarian aid to a war-devastated Poland, but this work was organized and carried out under the auspices of the Connecticut division of American Relief for Poland.

The KNAPP presence in the early District leadership is a partial explanation of the District's preoccupation with Polish affairs. Kozakiewicz (New Britain), the District's second president (1945-52), Walter Maznicki (Hartford), a long-time member of the Political Committee, which in fact occupied itself with Polish affairs, and Frank Rogowski (Hartford), District vice-president from 1944 until 1950, were all KNAPP members. While the three KNAPP branches in Connecticut were small and not very active or effective during the war, in the postwar era, KNAPP influenced the District's tenor in its early years with its members in effect bridging the period from the establishment of the District until the appearance of the postwar emigrés in District politics beginning in the early 1950s.[18]

The District, however, was also committed by its by-laws and in subsequent declarations and resolutions to the political advancement of Polish Americans. When the District president, Ryszard

Mrotek, on Pulaski Day, 1970, demanded political appointments commensurate in "importance and numbers with the percentage of Polish Americans in Connecticut,"[19] he reiterated a basic, if neglected District objective of long standing.

Evaluating the District's role in the political advancement of Polish Americans is difficult. The District, in much the fashion of the National, according to its by-laws was apolitical. Party banners were banned from the annual meeting and the Pulaski Day parade, for it was considered important to have friends in both major parties. When at the 1962 Pulaski Day Parade Representative Frank Kowalski, who was denied the Democratic nomination for the Senate, publicly accused his party of "bossism" and assigning Polish Americans "a beggar's corner in the political bazaar," he was interrupted by the District president, who chided the speaker: "Please, this is a patriotic event."[20]

Nevertheless, the District, while not overtly political, had control over some political levers. Its member organizations included the Pulaski Federation of Polish-American Democratic and the Federation of Polish American Republican clubs, and District members from these organizations sat, at various times, on the respective Democratic and Republican state central committees. The District, furthermore, tried to indicate which candidates it supported: the selection of readers of the Pulaski Day proclamations and speakers at the occasion during election years were careful decisions expressing tacit endorsement of a candidate, either Polish or non-Polish. In the year that Kowalski made his remarks, the Democratic candidate to succeed him, Bernard Grabowski, read the Pulaski Day Proclamation. Additionally, if the District president was a Democrat, the chairman of the Political Committee would be a Republican. This rotation not only preserved an apolitical balance within the organization; it also ensured some access for the District to the respective political parties.[21]

The effectiveness of the District's approach to politics within the state was meagre. Beyond the congressman-at-large slot, which both parties, even before the creation of the District, conceded to the Poles, the Polish presence in the executive and judicial branches was almost non-existent. At the municipal level, Polish Americans scored important gains (for example, the first Polish American mayor of New Britain, 1946), but it was because of the work of local political clubs. The District itself did not organize at the ward level, relying instead upon traditional political modes (i.e., the Polish Democratic and Republican clubs, or simply urging voting for Polish candidates), nor did it campaign for Polish Americans in the name of the Polish American Congress.

This changed with Mrotek's election in 1970 as District president. The Polish-born political emigré, educated in America, after considerable discussion and over very vocal opposition, persuaded the District to wage an active political campaign (newspaper and radio ads, endorsements, a public call for cross-over balloting) on behalf of Polish candidates and to exert pressure on both political parties in demanding local, state and federal appointments. The District subsequently claimed some of the responsibility for the election of thirteen Polish Americans to the Connecticut General Assembly, although the Polish candidate on the Democratic state ticket, because of a three-way race, went down to defeat with his party.[22]

It may be argued that this shift of tactics reflected the apparent renewed emphasis in Chicago upon home affairs promised by Mazewski's election in 1968. The shift, however, did not enjoy unanimous support, but over the next three years the District's Government Action Committee maintained steady contact with the Republican Meskill Administration and by 1973 could point to the appointment of three commissioners (Consumer Protection, Public Work, and Human Rights and Opportunities), a trustee for the state university, the advancement of three judgeships and several lesser appointments. The Polish members of the General Assembly caucused with the Government Action Committee (formerly the Political Action Committee, 1970-71) on various matters, and their role in the 1973 session was crucial in the passage of a bill creating a Polish studies program at a local state college, an action vigorously lobbied for by the District to commemorate Copernican Year.[23]

These successes were concrete examples of the District not only supporting, but actively seeking, in its own name, the "political aims and ambitions" of Polish Americans, and they occurred when the political affiliation of the District president and Connecticut's governor coincided. Of added significance was an aggressive attitude with the District leadership, reflecting the impact and the thinking of the White Ethnic Renaissance. The District supported the Ethnic Heritage Bill in Congress and Mrotek called for an end to the discrimination of Polish Americans in all spheres of life, demanding political representation for Polish Americans in proportion to their percentage (10 per cent) of the state's population. Similar reasoning was advanced in requesting a state-funded Polish studies program at the state university (which was cool towards the idea) and a state college (which accepted the program mandated by the General Assembly).[24] The politization of the District was, based on the record, not in vain.

Beyond the political arena, the preservation and propagation of Polish culture was an important area of District activity. If it is accepted that a knowledge of one's roots is necessary for the successful functioning and advancement of the Polish American in American society, then the Connecticut District was diligent.

The District's by-laws included a cultural commission among

its original standing committees. Its purpose was to "deepen and spread knowledge of Poland and its cultural heritage," to support Polish schools and Polonia youth organizations, and to cooperate with parents' committees at Polish schools. These objectives coincided with the national PAC, which included among its original objectives providing "impartial information to American society about the historical role of Poland, and about its aims and needs" as well as supporting Polish schools.[25]

The committee's work, based upon available resources, appears limited in the 1940s and 1950s. This inactivity in cultural matters prompted the creation of both a Polonia Cultural Committee and a Paderewski Cultural Committee (1954-57) in Hartford. The former, which joined the District, included community activists from the postwar immigration and organized *akademias,* while the latter, consisting mainly of educated members of prewar Polonia, presented a Małcużynski concert. Members of both committees also belonged to the District, and by 1960 were part of the District's revived Committee on Polish Language and Culture, which attracted a mixture of native-born Polish Americans interested in sophisticated Polish culture and community activists from the post-World War Two immigration.

Culture preservation, particularly in the 1960s, was expressed by the committee's organization of Saturday Polish Language schools. In 1960 the committee participated in the creation of three such schools, initially providing textbooks. However, in subsequent years, its support was verbal rather than financial, a fact that provoked criticism from the New Britain school, which was the largest. The appearance of Saturday schools, which numbered five in 1960 with over four hundred students, was described as work for the "rebirth of the Polish language," and viewed as a larger effort to maintain Polish culture in "the Polonia masses."[26] Significantly, the creation of Saturday schools followed the removal of Polish from parish schools and the increasing prominence of postwar immigrants in District affairs, basically satisfying their needs and interests.

Other efforts at culture preservation and renewal were essay contests on Polish themes for students in the elementary and Saturday schools (with modest participation); the introduction, over considerable administrative resistance, of the Polish language for credit in 1971 at the state university; the inauguration of free evening language instruction at a local state college; and the aforementioned successful lobby to have the legislature mandate a Polish studies program at a state college, which was in fact inaugurated in January 1974. Culture propagation within and beyond Polonia was also implemented through cultural exhibits (a large exhibit in 1961); co-sponsored concerts of Polish music; May the Third *akademias,* which from 1945 until 1961 were extensive, well-organized programs presented in Hartford's large

Bushnell Auditorium; a year-long series of events commemorating Poland's millennium in 1966 organized in conjunction with the Association of Polish Priests in Connecticut;[27] and a more modest series of lectures and cultural events to commemorate Copernican Year in 1973. These activities, educational and cultural in nature, were often preceded by an energetic effort to obtain passage of municipal and state resolutions for the event. Local and state Polish American legislators assisted as they knew, for example, that District members expected to see the Polish flag flying over the State Capitol on May 3.

Such activities were planned to stimulate ethnic awareness and pride, which since 1953 manifests itself at the yearly, District organized and sponsored Pulaski Day Parade. Additionally, the District participated in the launching ceremonies of the atomic submarine, the USS *Pulaski,* in New London in 1963, an event that was considered an opportunity to educate Americans about the Polish hero. The District was also an early supporter of anti-defamation initiatives by the National and supported Piszek's "Project Pole" despite the urging of the Downstate New York District to condemn it.[28]

This review of the activities of the Connecticut District of the PAC is not complete, but it presents a picture of an active organization representing Connecticut Polonia. Like the National, the Connecticut District faithfully adhered to the PAC's original objectives, and was well regarded by Chicago. Conversely, the District leadership, while critical of the National for not changing its leadership to coincide with the political party of the current administration in Washington, took its obligations as part of a larger organization very seriously. District officers served as national vice-presidents and the District participated in the quadrennial conventions, which one former officer characterized as "a special event in the life of American Polonia."[29] Additionally, there were at least three instances (1949, 1960 and 1966) when the District engaged in regional cooperation or discussions with neighbouring state divisions.

The Connecticut District is autonomous but it maintains a good relationship with the National. It also faces problems similar to those confronting the National, particularly in the areas of finance, communication and personnel. The complete financial records have not been located, but those that are available present a discouraging picture. Like Chicago, the District never created a permanent financial base, although it readily contributed $35,129.09 to the Congress' Million Dollar Drive in 1946 and 1947.[30] Later efforts to create a permanent fund (1969) did not meet expectations and the financing of District activities came to depend upon membership dues (80 per cent of which go to Chicago), individual donations, collections at May the Third and Pulaski Day ceremonies, proceeds from picnics and dances and occasional interest from a savings account. In the period between 1960 and 1963, for which records are available, the average income was $3,140.61, while expenditures totalled $3,472.50. For the years 1960-62 deficits were incurred, a fact which influenced the decision to cancel central May the Third celebrations at the Bushnell Auditorium and request members to organize appropriate celebrations in their respective localities.[31] The uncertainty of financing is evident when comparing the income of 1970 ($9,661.37), 1971 ($4,966.44) and 1972 ($6,449.47). Income fluctuated over three years and although the District finished 1971 technically in the black, there was a substantial lein ($2,450) on membership dues owed to Chicago.[32] The obligation of local districts to turn over 80 per cent of their membership dues was the subject of frequent discussion between the District leadership and Chicago as well as within the District in the 1970s. The considerable administrative support that the PNA de facto provided the PAC was not replicated at the local level, even though twenty-three state lodges belonged to the District: it was understandable why the District leadership wanted a greater percentage of dues to remain in the state.

The absence of an adequate, permanent source of funds limited the District's effectiveness. While the District met at the Polish National Home in Hartford, it was a guest: except for a brief period during 1970-72, it did not have a permanent office. On the other hand, the District was never financially able to rent such an office, maintain a listed telephone number, or issue a regular newsletter or bulletin, despite frequent calls for such a communication link. It is more than ironic that "Polonia's chief political interest group" at the grassroots is in reality an orphan within its own community. Furthermore, the District's problems paralleled some of the administrative concerns of the national PAC. The District membership in 1968 wanted the National to issue a regular information bulletin and to make the PAC's underfinanced Washington office an important, "active political centre of American Polonia."[33]

The District's financial condition must be viewed in a larger context. The PAC original Million Dollar Drive diverted local resources, and also competed with American Relief for Poland. In the early 1970s when the Congress initiated a drive to establish a Polish room at a local college as an appropriate commemoration of Copernican Year, Hartford's Polonia raised $125,000 for a Pulaski statue, rather startling evidence of both the difference in priorities between the District leadership and the broader community as well as of the District's inability to impose its priorities upon its constituent parts. The District, therefore, was remarkably active, considering the competition for funds. Partial credit for this is due to the generosity of individual members: it was not unknown, for example, for delegates to the national conventions to voluntarily cover their own expenses.

The lack of a regular and widely read means of communication hampered the District's activities. In 1964 *Przewodnik Katolicki* closed, limiting Polonia's printed media access to *Nowy Świat,* later *Nowy Dziennik,* an out-of-state journal providing limited coverage of Connecticut's Polonia. Efforts to publish a bulletin (monthly or quarterly) remained largely unrealized, with the exception of the years between 1970 and 1973 when a *Komunikat* (1970) and a *Biuletyn* (1971-73) appeared with some regularity. Lacking adequate funds radio and television could not be used as alternate means of regular communication. The District relied upon the generous goodwill of Polish American Polish language (*Program Polonii,* Mr. E. Liszka, a District member) and English language (Polka) radio programs to communicate news of District events to its members. As with the printed media, these programs had their own, limited and primarily Polish American audiences.

The lack of regular media access prevented the effective communication of the District's goals and activities, and left the unfortunate impression that the District was inactive or ephemeral. Communication and, thereby, the effective execution of the District's goals, depends heavily upon the organizational ability and initiative of its members, both individuals and delegates.

The District's unpaid leadership has been well motivated, comprising patriotic individuals dedicated to the goals of the PAC and the Connecticut District, to Poland and to Polonia. The leadership reflected Polonia's changing character. Until 1970, all District presidents were American-born, an entirely appropriate development in view of the fact that the Congress and the District were second generation, Polonia institutions. Various presidents perceived of the District as an organization advancing the cause and the image of Polish Americans. Two presidents were former congressmen-at-large (L. Maciora and A. Sadlak), while six were lawyers, one a CPA, another a priest and one a mayor. However, the post-World War Two political immigration made its appearance very early in the District's history. Two of the most active members of this immigration (W. Kejna and A. Sztupak) appeared as officers as early as 1951 and 1952, serving in various capacities until the 1970s.

The co-existence of two immigrations from different social, educational and political backgrounds was, on the whole, successful, although unifying these groups around common purposes was not easy. *Nowa Polonia* was drawn to the Congress as a prestige organization in which they could continue the struggle for Polish independence, which they also believed to be the obligation of *Stara Polonia.*[34] The prewar generation, while sympathetic and critical of the persecution of the Catholic Church by the Communist regime, was concerned with its own advancement and image, which the new arrivals erroneously assumed was high. To make the District work, in the view of a former president, these diverse elements had to be unified despite different priorities, abilities to converse in Polish and entirely different views of Polish culture. It was difficult, and a former District officer from the new immigration conceded that his generation did not pay sufficient heed to *Stara Polonia*'s concerns in the 1950s and 1960s,[35] a fact confirmed by the effort to create Saturday schools and by the Political Committee's preoccupation with Polish affairs in the 1950s and 1960s.[36]

In May 1969, Professor Zbigniew Brzezinski from Columbia University spoke in Hartford at ceremonies organized by the Association of Polish Priests in Connecticut and the District to commemorate the fiftieth anniversary of the regaining of Polish independence and to pay tribute to "Mary, Queen of Poland." Criticizing Polish American groups for focusing their energy toward freeing Poland by resolutions and demonstrations, he urged them to "upgrade the educational level of youth," become involved in American social issues like civil rights if they wanted to match the gains of other ethnic groups, and to tell national leaders "what jobs we want, what positions we demand." Predicting a political rebirth in Poland and the emergence of a new international system spanning national and ethnic boundaries, the speech of Brzezinski, himself a child of the postwar political immigrations, posed the question of priorities for Polish Americans.[37]

Ironically, the question of priorities was disputed in the District with renewed intensity in the early 1970s when the first Polish-born, but American-educated, president was elected (Mrotek). Assuming office under the growing impact of the White Ethnic Renaissance, and only two years after Mazewski's election on a platform that promised greater attention to home affairs, the new president was deeply concerned about the political advancement of the Polish American. His election preceded the appearance of second and third generation American-born Polish Americans who were also searching for their roots and cultural heritage, who were concerned about "Pollack jokes," and who were demanding political appointments for qualified Polish Americans.

Organizational changes reflected the Mrotek leadership's emphasis upon home affairs. The Political Committee in 1971 became the Political Action Committee (in 1972 the Government Action Committee), while a year later a separate Polish Affairs Committee was created to satisfy those wishing to focus their energies in this area. The creation of a Veterans' Affairs Committee was another indication of this reorientation. The shifting of priorities coincided with the departure of a handful of individuals who insisted upon absolute priority for Polish affairs and who ultimately established a stenciled monthly, *Listy do Polaków* (Letters to Poles), a constant District critic.[38] Those believing in the priority of Polish affairs and remaining in the District gravitated to the Polish Affairs Committee, which in 1972 vainly tried to exercise a veto in demanding that all District-sponsored activities obtain the committee's endorsement.

The splits and departures meant the loss of a small, but *engagé*, articulate element, an unfortunate development in view of the general agreement about the ultimate ideal of Polish independence. Nevertheless, the disagreements about priorities and tactics were deep and genuine. The cessionists, perhaps viewing the District as a European political party, demanded that the District be the arbitrator of Polonia life, directing all activity, as well as their own fiercely anti-Soviet sentiments toward the overthrow of the Polish Communist regime. The emerging leadership of the 1970s, while not resigning from the dream of Polish independence, was willing to deal with the Polish reality without, however, recognizing the regime. Furthermore, they approached the pluralism of Polonia and American society in a more pragmatic manner, arguing that the District could not become an arbitrator of Polonia life, or even its chief spokesman (to which the leadership aspired) unless the District offered something tangible to Polish Americans in order to attract membership.

Tensions not only followed *stara/nowa* Polonia lines. The existing reports, as well as interviews, reveal sharp divisions within *Nowa Polonia,* some of which were rooted in personal antagonisms while others carried over from previous political affiliations. If a former member of the wartime Polish underground army and a prisoner of war was skeptical of the unusually timed promotions of former officers who served with General Anders in the West (two promotions immediately prior to discharge in 1945, and a third in 1961, when Anders visited Connecticut!), members of the right-wing, chauvinistic National Democratic Party tended to align with the Republicans while those who belonged to centre or left-wing political groups affiliated with the Democrats.

Polonia's diversity is a strong argument for a non-partisan umbrella Polonia organization embracing all organizations and groups. And yet, in the case of the Connecticut District, the most politically dynamic period occurred precisely when the District engaged in politics under its own name, even though that decision sharpened pre-existing internal tensions. Prior to this period, the most successful harnessing of the District's dynamism occurred during the year-long millennium celebrations, which were, in domestic terms, religious and cultural in character, in terms of Polish affairs, overtly political, and which would not have succeeded without the participation of the Catholic clergy.

The clergy are a Polonia interest group whose relations with the District have been, on the whole, supportive, but also ambiguous. After the initial participation in the Buffalo meeting, the clergy, with a few outstanding exceptions, became passive if not inconsistent District supporters. Parish organizational membership in the District was never high (1970, three, 1971, four, and 1972, five out of twenty-six Roman Catholic parishes), but as one former District president indicated, the support has been there when requested. That cooperation, however, tended to be most evident in events or celebrations underscoring the Christian character of Polish culture, such as the millennium ceremonies (1966) and the commemoration of the fiftieth anniversary of the regaining of Polish independence together with a tribute to "Mary, Queen of Poland" (1969). Furthermore, sporadic District exertions did not bring about the elevation of a Polish bishop, or even auxiliary. There is little that the District was able to offer to the clergy, except cooperation and acknowledgement of the Christian character of Polish culture, a view of Polish culture assumed by the clergy and a view which implicitly reinforces its leadership position within the community. The clergy have retained consistent influence and prestige within Connecticut Polonia, but they cannot be considered an integral, active element in the District organization.

Divisions within the membership and leadership of the community and the District are real problems. Determining active membership is also problematical. As indicated earlier, the District is a representative umbrella organization, and in 1972, after twenty-eight years, counted 84 organizational affiliates, 133 individual members, plus 6 supporting, 9 associate and 21 student members. The problem is that it is not possible to determine the total number of Connecticut Polonia, estimated in 1970 at 304,000, represented by these figures. Only five out of twenty-six Roman Catholic parishes officially belonged to the District, while none of the nine National Catholic parishes belonged. Clearly, there are more than 84 Polish American organizations, clubs and societies in Connecticut, but there was never a time when every Polish American organization or institution belonged to the District. Out of the 304,000 figure, it is fair to estimate that in 1972 perhaps 150 to 200 individuals could be described as actively involved in the District, while the post-1956 economic immigration from Poland was totally absent. This is not to say that the District does not represent the views of the majority of Connecticut's Polonia on Polish questions, only to point out that the District leads a tenuous existence, a fact borne out by membership appeals dating as far back as 1958.

In reviewing the problems and weaknesses of the Connecticut District over a thirty-year period, it is evident that the District's slogan, "In Unity Strength," was achieved only sporadically, most prominently during the millennium celebrations when the clergy and the secular community leaders actively cooperated. The internal tensions, financial problems, lack of a regular publication and a limited active membership all hindered the District in fulfilling the mandates contained in its own constitution and that of the national Polish American Congress. Nevertheless, the District, as the only umbrella Polish American organization in the state, could legitimately claim to represent a broad segment of Connecticut's Polonia. And in doing so, it adhered to the primary mandates of the Polish American Congress. The District never recognized the Communist regime in Poland, and it consistently adopted positions that would create conditions for a truly independent Poland (i.e., free elections, withdrawal of Soviet forces). While not expecting its actions to bring about Polish independence, it faithfully adhered to the same ideal which Polish exiles during the Partitions refused to let die.

The perpetuation of this ideal was reinforced by patriotic events and cultural enterprises which "deepened and spread knowledge of Poland and its cultural heritage." It is in this area that the District enjoyed its most concrete achievements, and it was the Cultural Committee that most often was a fruitful platform of cooperation between *Stara* and *Nowa* Polonias.

The District's poorest area of achievement, with the exception of the early 1970s, was its support for the "political aims and ambitions of Americans of Polish origin." The roots of the problem were both divergent priorities as well as the weaknesses inherent in an umbrella organization which is at least one step removed from the grassroots and lacking a regular means of communication. The failures in this area are most significant because they demonstrate that the District has little to offer potential members from the third and fourth generations. In Polish, cultural and political affairs, the Connecticut District was an accurate reflection of the Polish American Congress.

Notes

1. William I. Thomas and Florian Znaniecki, *The Polish Peasant in Europe and America* (Boston: 1918-1920), and Paul Wrobel, *Our Way: Family, Parish, and Neighborhood in a Polish-American Community* (Notre Dame, Indiana: 1979).
2. Donald E. Pienkos, "The Polish American Congress—An Appraisal," *Polish American Studies* 36: 2 (1979), pp. 5-43. An earlier, useful work is Wacław Jędrzejewicz, *Polonia Amerykanska w Polityce Polskiej: Historia Komitetu Narodowego Amerykańów Polskiego Polchodzenia* (New York: 1954). There is also an excellent chapter in Richard C. Lukas, *The Strange Allies: The United States and Poland, 1941-1945* (Knoxville, Tennessee: 1978).
3. Pienkos, p. 5, *et passim.*
4. "Wykaz ofiar zlozonych na rece II Okregu Rady Polonii Amerykanskiej przez osiedla polskie w stanie Connecticut od 7 stycznia 1940 r. do 15 pazdziernika 1943r." Central Falls and Providence, Rhode Island were also included on this list ($1,981.35).
5. See Daniel S. Buczek, *Immigrant Pastor: The Life of the Right Rev. Msgr. Lucyan Bòjnowski of New Britain, Conn.* (Waterbury: 1974), pp. 121-34.

6. Zygmunt Stefanowicz, ed., *Protokół Kongresu Polonii Amerykanskiej odbytego w dniach 28, 29, 30 maja 1944 roku* (Chicago: 1944), pp. 23-27, 112-13.
7. "Projected by-laws, Connecticut District of the Polish American Congress" (n.d.) Article IVa.
8. "Membership List - 1970," Polish American Congress, District of Connecticut. The 1966 Roster for comparison, lists 63 organizational members and 17 individuals. "Oplaty czlonkowskie na rok 1966," Polish American Congress, District of Connecticut.
9. "Projected by-laws," Article IIIa.
10. "Commemorative Exercises: Sixth Anniversary of the Invasion of Poland. Hartford, Ct.: Polish American Congress, District of Connecticut, 9 September, 1945," (n.p.).
11. Joseph Kozakiewicz to Charles Rozmarek, IV/7/1945. The Kozakiewicz Papers, The Connecticut Polish American Archive (CPAA), Central Connecticut State College, New Britain, Ct. Folder No. 2, 1944-1946.
12. "Projected by-laws," Article IIIb.
13. Letters and resolutions contained in the Kozakiewicz File, Folder No. 2, 1944-1946, and Folder No. 3, 1947-1949.
14. "Manifesto by the Polish American Congress, District of Connecticut, to commemorate Poland's Millennium of Christianity and Pulaski Day celebrations held in Hartford, Connecticut, on October 9, 1966." See also the *Sprawozdanie: Wydział Kongresu Polonii Amerykanskiej na Stan Connecticut* for 1960, 1961, 1962, 1963 and 1973.
15. Instructions for the state delegates to the 1968 convention included demands for 1) an even stronger underscoring of the PAC "independence position" towards the imposed regime in Poland; 2) a renewal of the American "liberation" policy towards Poland and the other east European countries; and 3) support of independence movements in Poland—short of open war. See "Wytyczne dla delegatów Kongresu Polonii ze Stanu Connecticut na konwencję w Cleveland w dniu 28. września 1968, zapronowane przesz Komitet Polityczwy a zaaprobowune na zebraniu kwartalnym Wydziału w dniu 19. maja 1968." [jednogłośnie].

    On the District's support of American policy in Vietnam, see the resolutions adopted by the District at its annual meeting, 25 February 1968. Mrotek Papers, CPAA.

    On the national PAC views see, for example, "Statement of Policy adopted by the Seventh National Meeting of the Supreme Council of the Polish American Congress, Washington, D.C., July 29, 1966." Mrotek Papers, CPAA.
16. "Sprawozdanie Komisji Politycznej," *Sprawozdanie: Wydział Kongresu Polonii Amerykanskiej na Stan Connecticut z prac za r. 1961.*
17. *Sprawozdanie: Wydział Kongresu Polonii Amerykanskiej na Stan Connecticut z prac za r. 1963,* and the Kozakiewicz Papers, Folder No. 3, 1947-1949.
18. For KNAPP's activity in Connecticut consult the microfilm archives of KNAPP (Box 83, roll 235A and Box 88, roll 239) at the Pilsudski Institute of America, 381 Park Avenue, New York.

19. "Przemowienie prezesa R. Mrotka," *Komunikat Zarzadu Wydziału Stanowego KPA w Conn.*, nr. 7/8 (Pazdziernik-Listopad 1970 r.), pp. 5-6.

20. The Democratic Governor, John Dempsey, sitting on the same platform, responded indirectly by reference to his own success as an Irish-born immigrant. He reminded the audience: "We [Irish] weren't given white collar jobs when we came to this country." See *Hartford Courant*, 15 October 1962 and *The Hartford Times*, 15 October 1962.

    There may have been some justification for Kowalski's bitterness. He lost the Senate nomination to Abraham Ribicoff, the candidate of party boss John Bailey. Subsequently, Bailey denied Kowalski renomination for congressman-at-large by ramming through the nomination of Bernard Grabowski. Although the District president openly chided Kowalski for talking "politics" at a "patriotic" event, he was concerned privately about the implications of the Democratic Party's treatment of Kowalski. In a letter to the executive director of the Nationalities Division of the Democratic National Committee, he reported that many Connecticut Poles believed that they were being "fitted for the office of Congressman-at-Large, but not fitted to serve as Senators." Thaddeus Maliszewski to Walter Zaharaiasiewicz, 20 March 1973. Maliszewski Papers, CPAA.

21. Interview with Lucian Daum, 16 November 1980. Mr. Daum was a long-time member of the Political Committee. Another former officer reported that there was a tacit policy to elect as District president someone who belonged to the same party as the sitting governor. Interview with Thaddeus Maliszewski, 30 June 1980. Maliszewski was District president three times (1958-59, 1962-65, 1976-77). It is clear that the District realized the importance of access to both political parties.

22. "Zebranie Zarzadu i Dyrekcji W.S.," *Komunikat Zarzadu Wydziału Stanowego KPA w Conn.*, nr. 6 (Wrzesien 1970 r.), 1, and "Akcja polityczna Wydziału Stanowego," *Komunikat Zarzadu Wydziału Stanowego KPA w Conn.*, nr. 7/8 (Pazdziernik-Listopa 1970 r.), p. 3.

23. Walter L. Galuszka, "The Annual Report of the Government Action Committee, February 16, 1973," and Michael A. Peszke, "The Achievement of 1973, The Challenge of the Future" (Hartford: Polish American Congress, 1974), pp. 1-3. Both reports presented at the annual meeting of the District. Mrotek Papers, CPAA.

24. "Pulaski Day Memorial, 1970," *Komunikat Zarzadu Wydziału Stanowego KPA w Conn.*, nr. 7/8 (Pazdziernik-Listopa 1970 r.), p. 4.

25. "Proposed by-laws," Article XIII, par. 3, and "Ustawy i Reguły Kongresu Polonii Amerykanskiej," Article II, par. 4e and 4g.

26. "Komisja Kultury i Oswiaty Wydziału Stan KPA na Stan Connecticut za rok 1960," *Sprawozdanie: Wydziału Kongresu Polonii Amerykanskiej na Stan Connecticut za rok 1960*, p. 4.

27. Details about the planning and the extensive Millennium activities can be found in *Biuletyn Informacyjny*, nr. 1 (Komitet Tysiaclecia Polski Chrzescijanskiej Na Stan Connecticut); Thaddeus Maliszewski, "Report of Millenium Committee of Polish American Congress, District of Connecticut," (manuscript, n.d.), Maliszewski

Papers, CPAA; and in Józef Ptak, ed., *Protokół Siodmej Krajowej Konwencji Kongres Polonii Amerykanskiej odbytej w dniach 27, 28 i 29 września 1968 roku w Cleveland, Ohio* (n.d.), pp. 181-86.

28. The Downstate NY District objected to the promotion and publication of Andrzej Zieleniewicz, *Poland* (Orchard Lake, Michigan: 1971).

29. *Sprawozdanie: Wydział Kongresu Polonii Amerykanskiej na Stan Connecticut za rok 1960,* p. 2.

30. Reports of the Million Dollar Fund Drive of the State of Connecticut, 1946 and 1947, in the Kozakiewicz Papers, Folder no. 2, 1944-1946, and Folder no. 3, 1947-1949.

31. *Sprawozdanie* for the years 1960-63, especially 1962.

32. "Sprawozdanie Komisji Rewizjnej Przy Kongresie Polonii Amerikanskiej na Stan Connecticut: 1 Stycznia, 1970 - 10 Luty, 1971"; "Sprawozdanie Finansowe, Luty, 1971 - Styczien, 1972"; and "Financial Report, 2/1/1972 - 1/31/73."

33. "Wytyczne dla delagatów Kongresu Polonii ze Stanu Connecticut. . . ."

34. One example of this thinking occurred in early 1963. In 1962 the German magazine *Der Spiegel* reported secret plans of the West German General Staff to use nuclear weapons to destroy Poland in the event of a war with the Soviet Union. The article caused serious concern in Polonia, and Congressman Lucian Nedzi obtained an explanation and denial from the U.S. State Department. At the local level, Koło nr. 10 of the Stowarzyzenia Polskich Kombatantów found the explanation inadequate, and passed a resolution vigorously demanding that the District organize protests against such NATO military plans. The District, headed by an American-born attorney, Thaddeus Maliszewski, preferred to make inquiries and to eschew protest. Consequently, the local SPK voted to refrain from participation in District affairs until the end of Maliszewski's tenure. The relevant correspondence: Koło nr. 10, SPK (Jan Dąbrowski, President) to Tadeusz Maliszewski, 16 March 1963; the President of the State Division to Koło nr. 10, SPK, 2 April 1963; and Koło nr. 10 SPK to Tadeusz Maliszewski, 30 April 1963, Maliszewski Papers, CPAA.

    The local SPK charged that the action taken by the District is "a clear departure from the statutes and moral obligations of the Polish American Congress." (IV/30/63).

    For a general discussion of the "old" and the "new" Polonias see: Stanislaus A. Blejwas, "The Old and New Polonias: Tensions within an Ethnic Community," *Polish American Studies* 38, no. 2 (1981), pp. 55-83.

35. Interview with Alojzy Sztupak, 4 August 1980. Mr. Sztupak was a long-time executive vice-president of the District in the 1960s.

36. The first "Komunikat Informacyjno-Polityczny" of the Political Committee, issued in June 1958, commented upon developments in Poland, Hungary and about American foreign policy, but said nothing about Polish Americans and Connecticut politics. It identified the national PAC's activity on behalf of, "The good of the Polish

Nations and its liberations from communist slavery" as "a great service to American society." Janusz Koryatowicz-Sokolski, "Komunikat Informacyjno-Polityczny," nr. 1/58. Subsequent issues are in the Koryatowicz-Sokolski Papers, CPAA.

The Secretary of the Political Committee, in devoting nearly all space in the *Komunikat* to "Polish" and "foreign" affairs, argued that only a well-informed Polonia could influence American foreign policy. See issue 3/58 (February 1959), p. 1. Space in the *Komunikat* devoted to Connecticut affairs was essentially a listing of District endeavours on behalf of Poland, including May the Third, Pulaski Day, and other resolutions.

37. *Hartford Courant,* 5 May 1969.

38. For information on the split, see the open letter of Czesław Maliszewski (no relation to T. Maliszewski), 1 January 1970; R. Mrotek to C. Maliszewski, 13 March 1970; C. Maliszewski to R. Mrotek, 14 March 1970; and R. Mrotek, "Mili Panstwo," *Biuletyn Wydziału Stanowego KPA w Connecticut,* nr. 9 (Grudzien, 1971).

Polish Immigrants in Sudbury, Ontario, 1883-1980

Henry Radecki

Sudbury, a city of over 150,000 people nearly four hundred kilometres north of Toronto, was founded as a Canadian Pacific Railway camp in 1883. An excellent location and the presence of rich mineral deposits have supported its growth for almost a century. The economy of Sudbury has always been closely tied to the mining and smelting of copper and nickel ores, so much so that even in 1971, 25 per cent of the employment in the region was directly involved in those two industries. The "Nickel Capital of the World," as it became known, gradually absorbed autonomous nearby communities as it developed from an incorporated town in 1893 to a city in 1930 and a metropolitan municipality in 1973.

Though Polish immigrants helped to found Sudbury, their history, as well as that of Polish Canadians generally, has been neglected and almost unknown.[1] This paper seeks to remedy that neglect in two ways: by providing an overview of the area's Polish settlement, especially of its institutions, and by placing that local variation within the pattern commonly used to describe Polish life in Canada as a whole.

The Early Years: 1883-1918

Poles first appeared in the Sudbury area in 1883 among the workers who built the Canadian Pacific Railway through northern Ontario. Others soon followed to cut the forests, work in sawmills, build roads and construct buildings. At the turn of the century several Polish families claimed homesteads in the region, apparently the only Poles east of Manitoba to take up farming, apart from the Kaszubs of Wilno, Barry's Bay and Renfrew. According to one oral account, seven Polish farm families made up the first settlers of the community now called Hanmer, while others were among the pioneers of Blezzard Valley.[2]

Despite the demanding and harsh conditions of work there, it was the mines and smelters that eventually drew the vast majority of Poles to the area and near which, in Copper Cliff, they established their first homes. Employed initially by the Canadian Copper and Orford Copper companies and, from 1902, by the International Nickel Company (INCO), they dug or shovelled the "green ore" or toiled in the heat and pollution of the smelters. Normal work weeks were six days, each twelve hours long. Earnings ranged from thirty-five to forty-five cents per hour (compared to an average of twenty-five cents for manual labour) according to qualifications and experience. Aside from a few boarding houses and five or six small businesses, there were no other sources of income.[3]

The origins of the earliest Polish settlers were probably in the German part of partitioned Poland, but oral accounts indicate that by the 1890s, there were substantial numbers from Galicia and at least a few from the Russian sector. In addition, Kaszubs from Wilno and Barry's Bay sought work (and often married) in Sudbury until 1919, when INCO sharply curtailed production and compelled them to look elsewhere for a livelihood. The Canadian census, showing 241 Poles in the Sudbury area in 1911 and 241 in 1921, probably understates the true number. Scattered references reveal the presence of Polish families and individuals in Copper Cliff, Creighton Mine and Sudbury prior to 1900, and in Garson and Coniston before the First World War. On one occasion in 1896, the Polish community in Sudbury was able to turn out seventy-five people for a marriage at St. Anne's church. From 1901 to 1916, at least sixty Polish couples had their children baptized and over one hundred Poles acted as godparents at St. Stanislaus Kostka church in Copper Cliff. A photograph of Coniston taken prior to 1914 shows part of the town labelled "Polack Town."[4]

Though Sudbury was the centre of one of the largest Polish communities in Canada in the early twentieth century, it long did without the voluntary associations which immigrant Poles usually established. We can only speculate as to the reasons for the absence of any institutional focus—perhaps the instability of employment at INCO, the desire for better work elsewhere, too few people, or the general shortage of Polish clergy. Consequently, the early immigrants confined their ethnocultural life to visits among friends and relatives, occasional dances at private homes, and the more elaborate celebrations of birth, baptism, marriage and death.[5]

Though unfulfilled until the 1930s, the impulse toward traditional religious organization appeared early in the history of the

Polish settlers in Sudbury. Priests from Wilno and Barry's Bay began to visit the area regularly in the late 1890s. One of them or a visiting Jesuit missionary may have encouraged the Poles to erect the imposing church of St. Stanislaus Kostka in Copper Cliff in 1898, the second oldest Polish-built church in Canada. Poles, however, never dominated the parish and were served by a resident Polish priest, the Reverend D.P. Biernacki from Barry's Bay, only briefly in 1911. The members included other Catholics —Italian, French Canadian, Irish and Greek Catholic Ukrainian— and the pastors were French Canadian Jesuits and other non-Poles. The Italians broke away soon after 1900 to found their own parish; then the Ukrainians from 1909 to 1916 to build what was known popularly as the "Polish Church." Poles also collaborated in building St. Michael's Greek Catholic church in Coniston. The diversity of immigrant Polish religious life was illustrated further by a Polish Lutheran church in Copper Cliff in 1914-26.[6]

Revival and Decline: 1919-45

The end of the wartime boom forced most Poles at INCO to seek work elsewhere. Only the railroads and farming continued to offer steady employment for a few until 1924-25, when Poles began to drift back. Spurred by the new demand for nickel in the manufacture of automobiles and other mass-produced consumer goods, INCO reopened many of the mines closed in 1919-20. Prospects for jobs in mining improved further with the founding of another company, Falconbridge Nickel, in 1928. Even in the Great Depression, Poles and many other jobless were drawn to Sudbury by the possibility of work at INCO or Falconbridge. If they were married, Polish immigrants had relatively good prospects of getting a job since management considered them "productive" and "good, efficient, and conscientious" workers. Overwhelmingly, they held unskilled, manual but, in the context of the 1930s, highly desirable jobs. About six or seven small businessmen rounded out the class structure of the community. By 1931, the Polish population of Sudbury had climbed to 393 and in such nearby places as Copper Cliff, Garson and Falconbridge to 909. In 1941, the numbers were about the same altogether but their location was different: 815 in Sudbury, and 478 in adjacent towns.[7]

We still know little about the organized communal life of Poles in the 1920s. Amateur theatrical performances were staged in private homes in Creighton Mine, and a semi-formal part-time Polish school functioned for a while at St. Michael's church hall in Coniston. Only in the early 1930s, when Poles began to settle more heavily in the Donovan area of Sudbury, was there a sufficient concentration for the personal contacts out of which permanent associations were formed. The earliest of these was the Polish Club, established on February 18, 1934. Unlike other Polish organizations in Sudbury, which were branches of Polish Canadian federations, the Polish Club was an autonomous, local group.[8]

The aims of the Polish Club were also somewhat unusual and possibly contradictory. The English-language document of incorporation listed these purposes:

> a) to promote friendly and social intercourse among its members; b) to promote among persons of Polish nationality in the Province of Ontario a knowledge of the requisites of good Canadian citizenship; c) to promote a knowledge of the English and Polish languages among persons of Polish nationality; and d) to aid in the relief of persons of Polish nationality who are in distressed circumstances or who require help of any kind by reason of their recent arrival in Canada.

The Polish version of organizational goals was more assertively ethnic:

> 1) to organize and establish brotherly contacts among all Poles in Sudbury and area; 2) cooperation and defence of the good Polish name; 3) to build own organizational home; 4) to establish a library; 5) to organize and give theatre performances, concerts, and lectures; and 6) to maintain the spirit of Polishness in Canada, and close ties with Poland.[9]

When the club was incorporated, the eighty members purchased shares at $10 each for the construction of the "Polish House," which opened officially on October 25, 1936. Almost immediately the Polish House provided a home for a part-time Polish-language school for children and English-language classes for adults. The Polish school itself established an orchestra, choir, dance group and amateur theatre company which were active until 1945. The House served as a general community centre—the site of socio-cultural activities, patriotic celebrations (both Canadian and Polish), recreational activities, weddings, and visits by prominent visitors such as Lester B. Pearson and Stanisław Mikołajczyk. With the additional support of Group 13 of the Polish Alliance of Canada, the club kept alive the Polish heritage for working-class immigrants and their children.

The history of Group 13 of the Alliance of Poles in Canada, founded on March 16, 1936, with about forty members, roughly paralleled that of the Polish Club. Land was purchased for a building but it was never erected. The group contented itself with using the Polish House much as the club did and acquired instead a picnic grounds and some investment property. It too sponsored a part-time Polish-language school for children in a private home and an amateur theatre group from 1937 to 1945. Two women's auxiliaries—one organized in Sudbury on March 19, 1939, the other in Creighton Mine on January 28, 1940—strengthened the group's ability to carry out its programs. Repeated efforts to amalgamate Group 13 and the Polish Club after World War Two foundered, despite the similarities between them, because the club would have been required to turn over legal title to the Polish House to the Alliance Executive in Toronto.[10]

Church life also assumed a formal aspect between the wars. One Polish-speaking priest, Reverend A. Slominski, spent the time between his ordination in 1927 and his death in 1928 in Sudbury.[11] On April 11, 1936 another newly ordained Polish-speaking priest, Reverend J.S. Nietupski, was attached to Christ the King church. Soon afterwards, a Polish parish committee was formed and a chapel was opened on September 28, 1937 in the Donovan district. It marked the beginnings of Holy Trinity parish. Croatians, Slovaks, Slovenians and Poles, who were about half the parishioners, shared in the campaign to raise money for a church in the next few years. The "Polish" character of this parish was never pronounced. Aside from the purchase of a painting of the Madonna of Częstochowa for the main altar, it is uncertain how regularly Polish masses and traditional religious ceremonies were held at Holy Trinity. What little there may have been came to an end in 1943 when Father Nietupski was transferred to Sault Ste. Marie.

World War Two was a period of intensified and cooperative activity among the Polish associations of Sudbury. A variety of projects—concerts, street collections, drives for funds and materials, in which the auxiliaries were the main force—aided the Polish armed forces abroad, Polish refugees and prisoners of war. Polish organizations also cooperated closely with the local branch of the Canadian Red Cross, and the Polish House became a social club for all Canadian military personnel stationed in or passing through Sudbury. The war years were the culmination of a decade of effort at ethnic cultural maintenance when Poles still lived in close proximity to one another, usually married among themselves, and kept old values and traditions.[12] Then the community began to shrink again. During the last years of the war, people were drawn to southern Ontario by safer and cleaner jobs. At one time fewer than twelve of the original members of Group 13 remained in Sudbury. The schools, orchestra and theatre and dance groups ceased to function by 1945. The Creighton Mine ladies' auxiliary became inactive by 1946, and the Sudbury auxiliary by 1948. The number of socio-cultural and national-patriotic events declined as the organizations lost members.

The New Immigration and the Old: 1945-80

Sudbury's Polonia was rescued from oblivion by a significantly different and large new Polish immigration. As early as November, 1946, fourteen Polish armed forces veterans, recruited in

Italy, came to work at nearby farms on two-year contracts. Most of them remained afterwards as miners or smelter workers. Other veterans and refugees from the camps of Europe were soon directed to Sudbury by Canadian immigration officials. An overwhelming majority of the newcomers entered the mines and smelters as manual labourers, but among them were a few engineers hired by INCO and Falconbridge. Most were single males or had left their families behind in Poland. Their arrival was reflected in the Canadian census for 1951 which showed 2,006 people of Polish descent in Sudbury and 1,565 in nearby communities. The immigration continued in the 1950s, and the census of 1961 recorded over 2,300 Poles in Sudbury.[13]

Many of the newcomers were skilled workers or professionals, accustomed to positions of social leadership. Often living in dormitories and single rooms, they also needed companionship, a place to meet other Poles and to communicate in a familiar language. Meanwhile, the old organizations, their numbers depleted, welcomed their participation. Group 13 experienced something of a revival, but the Polish Club benefited most from the postwar immigration. Taking advantage of the Polish House, the club raised money for projects in Canada and Poland, sponsored visiting lecturers and theatre groups, received special guests from Poland, celebrated the Christmas *opłatek* and the Easter *swięcone,* and observed such national Polish holidays as the Third of May and November the Eleventh, the Day of Polish Independence. Once more the Polish House became a centre for social-civic occasions ranging from the showing of Polish films to weddings and the selection of Beauty Queens. Some cultural activities did not take very well in the atmosphere of the 1940s and 1950s. A new amateur theatre group and orchestra seem not to have outlasted 1949-50. A dance group, organized in 1954, also disappeared after a year or two. The club's "Polonez" choir did only somewhat better with an active life from 1965 to 1968.

The successes of the club probably reflected the tastes and values of the newer immigrants. After a false start in 1948, the club firmly re-established the Polish school in 1953. Language maintenance was supported in other ways as well. A library, only a dream before the war, was opened in 1949 in conjunction with a reading room for single men and women. With about three hundred volumes, the library–reading room operated until the mid-1960s. Together with Branch 24 of the Polish Combatants, the club sponsored a weekly radio program, the "Polish Hour," in early 1952. A soccer club, "Polonia," was also organized under its auspices in 1949. Eventually many of the new programs were taken over by organizations founded by the new immigrants. Though still active in 1980, the club had only thirty-one members (two more than Group 13), fewer than the forty of the ladies' auxiliary which had been founded in the first flush of ethnic renewal in 1948.[14]

The relationship between the prewar and postwar Polish immigrants, especially in the early 1950s, was often strained as a result of misunderstandings about priorities and appropriate behaviour for the organizations. The veterans were preoccupied with the power of the Soviet Union and with communist rule in Poland. They saw Canadian Polish institutions as bulwarks of the anti-communist Polish government-in-exile in London. The needs of Polish war invalids and the maintenance of Polish military traditions were also important considerations for them. Though sympathetic, the prewar members of the Polish Club and Group 13 had other goals, largely to do with the local needs of more Canadianized Poles. There were besides questions of leadership, style and decision-making which further divided the new from the old immigrations. As early as 1946 veterans who had been recruited for farm work had begun to organize Combatants Associations to deal with their specific concerns. On January 23, 1952 the Sudbury veterans established Branch 24 of the Polish Combatants Association in Canada.

The Sudbury Branch of the Combatants soon became the most dynamic Polish organization in the region. Its *Information Bulletin,* first published in 1952, still appears. It took responsibility for the Polish radio hour from August 1953 to May 1956, and opened a library in 1953. From 1952 to 1954 it supported the local soccer club, now renamed the "White Eagle," before the team became autonomous. The headquarters building which it purchased in 1955 quickly became the centre for a range of activities parallel to the Polish Club's, except that its patriotic celebrations emphasized such events of recent Polish history as the Battle of Monte Cassino. A successful credit union, established in 1956, significantly extended the services the branch offered its members. A woman's auxiliary took permanent root in 1960, providing additional institutional strength. With about 150 regular members and about thirty in the auxiliary in 1980, Branch 24 remained the largest Polish lay organization in Sudbury since the early 1950s. By then, the rivalry with the Polish Club had largely disappeared. An agreement was reached, for example, for the club to organize the Third of May celebrations in its House, and for the Combatants hall to be the site of the commemoration of Poland's Independence Day. Indeed, it might be argued that the competition of the 1950s and 1960s had a positive effect by heightening the self-awareness and enriching the institutional life of the Polish community.[15]

The needs and influence of the new immigrants also permanently altered the organized religious life of Poles in Sudbury. The petitions for a Polish-speaking priest from Branch 24 were followed on December 23, 1953, by the arrival of Reverend Eugene Jastalski to minister to Poles from Holy Trinity Church. He promptly set about organizing a Polish parish, and a church, St. Casimir's, was ready for use by the end of 1955. Additional construction the next year—a belfry, parish hall and parsonage—and the cost of furnishings raised the parish debt to over $60,000. When that debt was retired in 1970, the parish acquired land for a summer retreat, St. Casimir's Youth Camp, about eighty kilometres south of Sudbury. Reverend E. Jastalski and Reverend Edward Wawrzyk, who succeeded the first pastor in 1966, encouraged the formation of the societies one might find in many Catholic parishes as well as major Polish religious traditions. The parish was also closely integrated with secular organizational life. In 1966-67, three Polish Ursuline nuns assisted the pastor and taught at the Polish School. The Polish Scouts and members of Branch 24 regularly appeared in uniform at special services. The parish hall was used by most community organizations, and members of other organizations were usually also parishioners of St. Casimir's. The 260 families and 60 individuals who were members of the parish in 1980 were also the core of organized Polonia in Sudbury.[16]

The third major institution to grow out of the postwar immigration, the regional office of the Canadian Polish Congress, was founded on May 15, 1956, after about eight months of discussions among the Combatants, the Polish Club and Group 13 (which withdrew in 1957). The other charter members were the auxiliaries and the Polish-Canadian Agrarian Association in Sudbury, a group founded in 1955 with the encouragement of Stanisław Mikołajczyk to support the Polish Peasant Party in London. The Sudbury Congress assumed a wide variety of functions, usually of a non-political nature. It coordinated social services directed to and by the Polish community—the "Aid to Poland" drive in 1956-57, fund-raising for a cobalt bomb for a health centre in Poland in 1962, relief of needy Polish families during the lengthy INCO strike of 1958, assistance to the families of several Polish victims of industrial accidents, and the reunification of Polish families separated by World War Two. The Congress was also a convenient vehicle for major communal cultural activities. In 1957 it took over the Polish radio hour for the duration of its run until 1967. Congress committees sponsored the sequence of cultural events and fund-raising projects in the years leading up to the commemorations of the millennium of Poland's Christianity in 1966 and the five hundredth anniversary of the birth of Copernicus in 1973. Officers of the Congress normally represented Poles at larger civic events, especially those of a multicultural character.

Some of the Congress' most successful efforts at cultural maintenance and community service have been in educating young children. In 1957 it established the Parents-School Committee to build support for a better program at the Polish School. Renamed for the Polish Canadian engineer Sir Casimir Gzowski in 1962, the school emphasized the language, history, geography and music of Poland. At its peak in 1964, it enrolled one hundred children. With three teachers and a director, the school still served forty-five children in grades from kindergarten to six in 1979. The Congress also sponsored the Polish Scouts in Sudbury from 1957 to about 1960 (when the lack of qualified leaders caused a suspension) and from 1970 until 1979 (when lack of interest among boys left only a small troop of seven girls). The rise and decline of the Polish school for children coincided roughly with the life of one of its major support organizations, Link 5 of the Federation of Polish Women in Canada. Founded by Dr. M.C.A. Zurowska in 1959 and lasting only a few years after her death in 1972, Link 5 helped to finance the Polish School and Scouts, donated Polish books to the public library and joined in Sudbury's multicultural celebrations.[17]

As educational programs for young children declined in the 1970s, the number and stability of associations for teenagers and young adults seemed to grow. An independent youth club, "Syrena," in 1959-61 and a youth auxiliary to Branch 24 in 1972-75 had been active briefly at the Combatants hall. St. Casimir's youth camp, dedicated in 1976, represented another effort to provide continuity between generations. Late in 1975 an independent Polish youth club began to hold semi-weekly meetings at St. Casimir's parish hall. With no written rules or organizational aims, the club still managed to pursue a variety of Polish-oriented activities and to participate in the community's major Polish patriotic events. Nearly all of its thirty-five members in 1980 were Canadian-born. Finally, in 1979 the Ottawa-based Friends of the Catholic University of Lublin established a branch in Sudbury to assist the only Catholic university in eastern Europe. A few months later, the presidents of the Catholic University and of Sudbury University agreed formally to the exchange of students and faculty between their institutions.[18]

Demographic change and social mobility based on education probably accounted for the shifting pattern of institutional life among Sudbury's Poles. The census of 1971 indicated a further increase in the number who claimed Polish descent in the area to 2,900. The aging of the population was revealed in the formation in 1978 and rapid growth of a senior citizens' club in the community. Most of the men were active or retired blue-collar employees of INCO and Falconbridge. The years of hard, dirty and often dangerous work, punctuated by lengthy and costly strikes, had resulted in relative material well-being. Most owned their homes, and their children attended colleges and universities. Those children seemed likely to add to the number of Polish-origin businessmen, managers, white-collar workers, skilled tradesmen and professionals who had appeared during the previous generation. But they are likely to leave Sudbury. The network of organizations erected since the 1950s faces the loss of its base and an uncertain future.

Notes

1. On Poles in Canada see: Henry Radecki with Benedykt Heydenkorn, *A Member of a Distinguished Family; Polish Group in Canada* (Toronto, 1976); Henry Radecki, *Ethnic Organizational Dynamics; Polish Group in Canada* (Waterloo, Ont., 1979). The major secondary works on Poles in Sudbury are: John George Janota, "The Polish Community in Sudbury" (B.A. thesis, Laurentian University, Sudbury, 1972); Henry Radecki, *100 Years of the Polish Community & 25 Years of St. Casimir Parish in Sudbury* (Sudbury, 1980). Simultaneously with the author's research, Mrs. Irene Dembek carried out a research project for the Multicultural History Society of Ontario, and her cooperation in sharing information is greatly appreciated. Miss Jadwiga Plewko of the Department of Sociology at the Catholic University of Lublin has also conducted research on the Poles of Sudbury recently.
2. L.W. Luke, "Citizenship and Immigration," paper delivered at 28th Annual Meeting of the Canadian Chamber of Commerce, Victoria, B.C., October 3, 1957, p. 5; interview of Mrs. Adele Swiernik by Mrs. Irene Dembek, 18 February 1980.
3. Józef Samulski, *Pamiętniki Emigranta Polskiego w Kanadzie* [An Autobiography of a Polish Emigrant in Canada] (Wroclaw, 1978); Henry Radecki, *The 1978-79 Strike at INCO; the Effects on Families: A Report* (Sudbury, 1979).
4. *Sudbury Journal*, 29 October 1896; St. Stanislaus Kostka Church, *Registrum Baptismorum*. . . . Also see the church records of St. Anne's parish and Vernor's Directories for Copper Cliff in 1916-26.
5. Interview of Mrs. M. Czajka (born in Copper Cliff in 1900) by H. Radecki, 2 February 1980; Radecki, *The 1978-79 Strike;* Samulski, *Pamiętniki;* Radecki with Heydenkorn, especially chapter 8.
6. Rev. J. Cossette, S.J., to the author, 25 February 1980, citing material in the Archives of the Society of Jesus in St. Jerome, Quebec; interview of Mr. Mike Solski (a union activist since the early 1940s) by H. Radecki, 4 June 1980; Vernor's Directories for Copper Cliff, 1916-26.
7. Interview of Mr. John Warenda by H. Radecki, 12 December 1979; interview of Mr. Frank Ressel by H. Radecki, 22 January 1980. Mr. Ressel's father was a senior foreman with INCO in the 1920s and one of the founders of the Polish Club in 1934.
8. Interview of Mr. John Narozanski by Mrs. Irene Dembek, 3 June 1980; interview of Mr. Mike Solski by H. Radecki, 4 June 1980.
9. *Książka Rocznych Zebrań Akcjonarjuszy Klubu Polskiego, 1955-1976* [Book of the Annual Meeting of the Shareholders of the Polish Club, 1955-1976]; *Canadians All: Poles in Canada* (Winnipeg, 1938). The translations are the author's.
10. *Księga Pamiątkowa Związku Polaków w Kanadzie; 1906-1946* [Memorial Book of the Alliance of Poles in Canada, 1906-1946] (Toronto, 1946); *Złoty Jubileusz Związku Polaków w Kanadzie; 1907-1957* [Golden Jubilee of the Alliance of Poles in Canada, 1907-1957]

(Toronto, 1957). There is some dispute about the foundation date of Group 13, but *Złoty Jubileusz* and the recollection of one of the charter members agree on 1936.

11. Interview of Mr. John Bowers (Bała) by Mrs. Irene Dembek, 7 May 1980.

12. Interview of Rev. Chester Warenda by H. Radecki, 4 December 1979; interview of Mr. Mike Solski by H. Radecki, 4 June 1980.

13. Interview of Mr. Leon Stefańczuk by H. Radecki, 4 August 1980; Janota, "The Polish Community in Sudbury."

14. Henryk Zins, *W świecie anglosaskim; Studia i szkice o Anglii i Kanadzie* [In the Anglo-Saxon World; Studies and Sketches of England and Canada] (Lublin, 1975), for a discussion of one of the Polish activists in Sudbury; *Książki Protokołowe Polskiego Klubu w Sudbury* [Minute Books of the Polish Club in Sudbury], Nr. 1: 1947-1954, Nr. 2: 1956-1968, Nr. 3: 1969-1980; Jan Dubis, "Historia Polskiej Piłki Nóżnej w Sudbury" ["History of Polish Soccer Teams in Sudbury"], unpublished manuscript, 1980.

15. On the Combatants see: *SPK w Kanadzie; 1946-1971* [The Association of Polish Combatants in Canada; 1946-1971] (Toronto, 1971), for a general description of the Association and historical sketches of the branches; SPK Koło 24 [Association of Polish Combatants Circle 24], "Sprawozdania Prezesa" ["Report of the President (for 1953)"] (Sudbury, 1954); Koło Pań Przy SPK Nr. 24 [Women's Circle No. 24 of the Association of Polish Combatants], "Pisma na Rok 1961-62" (Sudbury, n.d.).

16. On St. Casimir's see: *St. Casimir's Parish Weekly Bulletin,* May 1966-; Radecki, *100 Years.*

17. On the Sudbury Regional Office see its "Sprawozdanie" ["Report"], 12 May 1956-17 February 1957; "Protokoły" Rok 1956/57, Rok 1957/58 ["Minutes for 1956-57, 1957-58"]; and "Roczne Sprawozdania z Działalności Zarządu KPK, Okręg Sudbury za Rok . . . " ["Annual Reports of the Activities of the Executive of the Canadian Polish Congress, Sudbury Division for the Year. . . . "], 1964-. On cultural work see: Milenium Protokoły "Koncert Malcużyńskiego i Zebrania Milenium, 1962-1966" [Minutes of the Millennium "The Malcuzynski Concert and the Millennium Meetings, 1962-1966"]; *Księga Kasowa Funduszu Milenium Polski, 1962-1967* [Financial Book of the Polish Millennium Fund, 1962-1967]. On the Polish school see: "Sprawozdania Komitetu Rodzicielskiego od 10.2.1962 do 6.10.1973" ["Reports of the Parents' Committee from 10 February 1962 to 6 October 1973"]; Komitet Rodzicielski Przy Szkole Polskiej im. K. Gzowskiego w Sudbury, Ont. [The Parents' Committee for the C. Gzowski Polish School in Sudbury, Ont.], *Księga Protokołowa, 1973-1978.* On the Scouts see: Towarzystwo Przyjaciół Harcerstwa Polskiego w Sudbury, Ont. [Association of the Friends of Polish Scouts in Sudbury, Ont.], *Książka Protokołowa, 1971-1978* [Minute Books, 1971-1978]; Irene Dembek, "Harcerstwo Polskie w Sudbury, 1970-1980" ["Polish Scouting in Sudbury, 1970-1980"] unpublished manuscript. Also see: Federacja Kobiet Polskich w Kanadzie, Ogniwo Nr. 5 [Federation of Polish Women in Canada, Link 5], "Sprawozdania, 20.2.1966-17.10.1971" ["Reports, 20 February

1966-17 October 1971"]. In 1965, apparently at the time of its dissolution, the Agrarian Association sent its unique flag and a seal to Mr. S. Mikołajczyk, then living in Washington, D.C.

18. A branch of the Montreal-based Friends of the Catholic University at Lublin was active in Sudbury from 1958 to 1960.

Prospects

The Future of Polish Organizational Life in Canada

Jan K. Fedorowicz

In speculating about the future of Polish organizations in Canada, one should begin with salient aspects of the present as some indication of the crisis which they may be facing. This paper will begin with a statistical profile of the Polish Canadian population, after which it will consider the implications of that profile, and conclude by suggesting several strategies for meeting the challenges posed by the Polish community's present condition.

The statistical portion of this paper is based on a study conducted in Canada in the wake of the report on Bilingualism and Biculturalism which initiated the entire multicultural debate in this country. Because multiculturalism had not been expressed as a coherent governmental option before the report, there was a notable lack of statistical information pertaining to Canada's ethnic groups, their languages and their aspirations. The study to which this present paper will refer was conducted by K.G. O'Bryan, J.G. Rietz and O.M. Kuplowska as a partial response to this need and was published in 1976 under the auspices of the federal government under the title *Non-Official Languages: A Study in Canadian Multiculturalism.* There is a wealth of statistical information about Canada's ten largest non-charter ethnic groups contained in this book and most of it still awaits proper study, evaluation and interpretation, but for the purposes of the present discussion, I shall extract a few salient features of the study as they pertain to the Polish community in Canada and present them for the reader's consideration.[1]

To begin with the most basic question of self-perception, fully 50.6 per cent of the Canadians of Polish descent surveyed considered themselves to be simply Canadians, with no further ethnic appellation, while only 40.8 per cent described themselves either as Canadians of Polish origin (18.4 per cent) or as Polish Canadians (22.4 per cent).[2] On the basis of these figures, one may seriously question the size of the real constituency which the Polish organizations in Canada claim to represent, and indeed one may also wonder what, if any, affiliation the vast majority of Polish Canadians may have with Polish institutional life in the future.

The survey in question was primarily directed at the issue of language and in this area we find results which suggest a general advance of assimilationist trends throughout the Polish Canadian population. For example, on the question of language fluency, the following table may be constructed from the study results:

Table 1: Self-Perceptions of Fluency in Polish among Polish Canadians (percentage)

	Fluent	Some knowledge	No knowledge
First generation	64.6	35.1	–
Second generation	9.8	59.1	31.1
Third generation	4.9	24.8	70.3
All generations	35.8	41.5	22.7

SOURCE: *Non-Official Languages,* pp. 45-46, 48.

This table alone is sufficient to suggest the drastic erosion in the use of the Polish language with the passing of generations. Even in the first generation, that is those born in Poland, not all are fluent in the Polish language, since they either came over to Canada at a very young age, or they forgot much of the language through years of not using it. Obviously, with subsequent generations the case is far worse.

One basic reason for this deterioration in language retention is simply that only 36.9 per cent of those surveyed used the language every day, only 6.5 per cent used it often, and a further 15.7 per cent employed it occasionally. At the same time, 7.7 per cent spoke it rarely and 28.8 per cent claimed insufficient knowledge of the language to use it in conversation.[3] When one investigates further, it turns out that the family remains the chief focus for the transmission of Polish, as is borne out by the following table:

Table 2: Percentage of Those Surveyed Reporting At Least Some Use of Polish

Social context	Fluent speakers	Total Polish sample
Family	96.9	63.7
Close friends	76.0	35.4
Clergy	46.3	20.9
Grocer	10.3	6.5
Doctor	16.9	8.8
Classmates/co-workers	18.3	7.2

SOURCE: *Non-Official Languages,* p. 64.

Clearly there are few opportunities available for using Polish on an everyday basis and the family remains the chief focus for this. Perhaps the only surprising feature of Table 2, given the central position of the church in Polish society, is the small percentage of people reporting using Polish in conversation with their clergy.

We know that historically the church was the first and chief bulwark of Polish immigrants to Canada, both spiritually and culturally, but recent statistics suggest that this role is waning. Not only is church attendance falling off, but there are trends towards mixing ethnic populations in the churches which promote assimilation. Only 19.7 per cent of the Polish Canadians surveyed attended a church where the only language used was Polish, while 21.5 per cent attended churches where there were few or no other Poles whatsoever. Furthermore, 32.7 per cent of those studied were associated with no church or had no religious preference at all, suggesting that at least in Canada traditional spiritual values wane hand-in-hand with ethnic identity and language use. Only 11.3 per cent of Polish Canadians surveyed attended church services conducted exclusively in the Polish language, 18.9 per cent attended services in which English or French was also used, and 32.1 per cent attended church where only English or French, and no Polish whatsoever, were used. Again, 32.8 per cent in the survey claimed not to be associated with any church.[4] The conclusion one may draw is that the church alone can no longer be relied upon to act as an effective transmitter of Polish language and culture. On the other hand, since church attendance seems to be declining in proportion to interest in maintaining Polish language and culture, it may be in the interests of both the church and secular Polish organizations to cooperate more closely in the future to combat these trends.

Another transmitter of Polish language and culture is the mass media: newspapers, radio and television. In the statistical discussion which follows, it will be seen that the Polish community has not really employed the media to its fullest advantage in securing the interest and adherence of a large part of the Polish Canadian population.

Table 3: Percentage of Polish Canadians Who Read a Polish-Language Newspaper or Bulletin

Never read	Over 10 years	6-10 years	3-5 years	2 years	1 year	Less than 1 year
61.4	18.4	6.7	5.5	2.5	2.4	1.5

SOURCE: *Non-Official Languages*, p. 68.

Not only do Polish-language papers have little impact on the Polish Canadians, but what little interest there is seems to be waning inasmuch as there are fewer and fewer new readers being recruited as subscribers, as is borne out by the decreasing percentages reading these papers for two years or less. Generally, of those fluent in Polish, 73.9 per cent had read something in the language within a year of the study but of those with only some knowledge of the language a scant 29.7 per cent had done so.[5]

The same can be said of both radio and television.

Table 4: Percentage of Polish Canadians Listening to Radio or Watching Television Programs in the Polish Language

Frequency	Radio	Television
No program available in area	32.0	65.8
Regularly	6.9	1.2
Sometimes	14.1	.9
Rarely	7.8	1.3
Never	14.5	5.8
Insufficient language	23.9	23.9

SOURCE. *Non-Official Languages*, pp. 71, 73.

Table 4 obviously shows that the first and most basic problem is simply that a large proportion of the Polish Canadian population are not served by any programs in their own language, and therefore do not even have the opportunity to make a choice, while another large group of the Polish Canadian population cannot make such a choice because they lack enough knowledge of the language to take advantage of such programs even if offered. On the other hand, if a concerted effort were made to improve the quality of the media available, as well as its quantity, the results would be quite different for radio and for television, as Table 5 shows:

Table 5: Interest of Polish Canadians in Additional Polish-Language Programs (percentage)

If available, they would be	Very int.	Somewhat int.	Unint.	Depends	Programs available or no language knowledge
Radio	6.7	6.4	14.2	4.7	66.3
Television	24.9	17.6	16.0	7.8	32.5

SOURCE: *Non-Official Languages*, pp. 148-49.

Clearly, if the Polish community is to invest its already slender resources in any particular direction, it would do better to put them into television programming rather than into radio. The same conclusion can be drawn when comparing television with the written word as in Table 6.

Table 6: Attitudes of Polish Canadians Towards More and Better Newspaper and Television Services (percentage)

	Very important	Somewhat important	Indifferent	Unimportant	No answer
More newspapers	13.7	19.5	8.1	43.0	10.6
Better newspapers	13.3	25.6	9.9	30.4	11.0
More television	24.4	30.8	4.6	25.9	10.6
Better television	26.4	30.3	5.5	20.2	11.4

SOURCE: *Non-Official Languages*, pp. 145-46, 150-51.

Obviously a considerably larger group of people would be interested in more and better television programming than in any improvement in newspaper facilities, which perhaps suggests that in an age of MacLuhanesque 'hot media,' no matter what the quality of newspapers, television simply has more appeal and impact than does either radio or the printed word. If the Polish community is to invest in the media, it would be better served, therefore, to concentrate its efforts on television, something hitherto only marginally attempted. Whether this takes the form of securing greater access to community television facilities, or ensuring that more Polish materials appear on the regular network broadcasts, is something the community will have to decide.

There is, as we have seen, a general tendency to use Polish in the family to a greater degree than anywhere else, and this is reflected in the fact that most Polish Canadians feel that the family is the single most important agent for preserving the Polish language and culture. Fully 46.7 per cent of those surveyed felt that parents had the primary responsibility to teach their children Polish history and language, while only 22.2 per cent in areas where the Polish Canadian population is concentrated thought the schools should undertake this. Interestingly enough, another 22.6 per cent placed the burden of this responsibility on the Canadian educational establishment across the country.[6] If schooling in the Polish language were available, however, a significant proportion of Polish Canadians would encourage their children to attend such classes, as can be deduced from the following table:

Table 7: Attitudes of Polish Canadians to their Children Taking Courses in Polish (percentage)

	Would Insist	Encourage	Indiff.	Discourage	Inapplicable*
First generation	10.3	42.9	11.5	0	30.7
Second generation	2.8	34.8	20.7	2.7	39.0
Third generation	1.1	25.0	28.4	2.4	36.1

SOURCE: *Non-Official Languages*, pp. 132-33.

* Includes those without children.

Even though there is an evident weakening of commitment to education in Polish over the generations, as many as a quarter of the parents in the third generation would consider sending their children to courses in the Polish language. A more direct expression of interest in Polish-language education is displayed in Table 8:

Table 8: Attitudes of Polish Canadians Towards Schooling in the Polish Language (percentage)

	Very important	Somewhat important	Indiff.	Unimportant	No answer
More schools	15.4	27.9	5.9	34.6	10.6
Better schools	13.2	29.8	6.0	26.4	11.0

SOURCE: *Non-Official Languages*, pp. 136-37.

According to this, something over 40 per cent of the Polish Canadian population would like to see more and better schools in their own language, and this is a significant enough group that the Polish institutions now in existence should seriously consider how best to meet this potential demand. On the other hand, whatever response is made must be realistic enough to acknowledge that a substantial majority of Polish Canadians have already lost interest in education in their ancestral language.

Paradoxically, a considerable number of Polish Canadians continue to see language retention as desirable, even if they are not convinced that the schools are the best place for this to occur. Table 9 shows that language retention is favoured, even in the third generation.

Table 9: Attitudes of Polish Canadians Towards Language Retention (percentage)

	Very desirable	Somewhat desirable	Indifferent	Not desirable
First generation	21.0	62.1	12.3	4.5
Second generation	19.8	42.5	28.8	8.9
Third generation	12.8	45.8	34.5	6.9
Total Polish sample	19.5	52.3	21.6	6.5

SOURCE: *Non-Official Languages*, pp. 75, 95-96.

What emerges from these figures is that well over 70 per cent of Polish Canadians have a general feeling that retention of the Polish language is at least theoretically desirable, though most of them are not clear how this might be achieved outside of the family. The family does manage to transmit attitudes even if it does not always transmit facility in the language itself. Fully 43.5

per cent of the children of parents strongly favouring language retention were also strongly in favour, while 22.6 per cent favoured it and only 30.7 per cent were indifferent. None were opposed. On the other hand, among parents indifferent to language retention, 66.0 per cent of their children were similarly indifferent with only 17.5 per cent strongly in favour, 11.2 per cent somewhat in favour, and 2.5 per cent opposed.[7]

Even though much reliance can be placed in the family, it is clear from the above statistics that the family alone cannot successfully resist the forces of assimilation, and among the programs which Polish organizations develop for the future there must be concrete proposals for saving the Polish language on this continent.

There is clearly a serious crisis in the Polish community, at least as far as language goes, and yet it is a crisis which is not even perceived by many Polish Canadians. The decreasing use of the Polish language was thought to be a serious problem by only 34.1 per cent of those surveyed while 35.8 per cent did not think of it as a problem at all. The same pattern is observable in considering the loss of ethnic traditions and customs. A majority (51.3 per cent) did not view this as a problem and only 20.4 per cent thought of it as either a very serious or somewhat serious issue.[8]

If Polish organizations wish to secure their future, therefore, they must direct their efforts in the first instance towards the struggle against complacency. From the above survey it emerges that there is still a substantial group of Polish Canadians who are interested in preserving the Polish language, in supporting schools, and in expanding the use of Polish in the media, but this group needs leadership. It needs to be informed of possible alternatives, it needs to be mobilized to press for effective programs to halt the erosion of the community's identity, and it needs to be attracted with relevant and effective solutions. And in addition to the 10 per cent or so of Polish Canadians who are seriously committed to the ideal of preserving the community, there is a considerably larger group who are still concerned, who are willing to at least encourage language persistence, and who have a limited knowledge of Polish. Clearly this should be the target group for any future organizational drive; and because this group is as yet not entirely convinced, Polish organizations must concentrate more on the reasons for maintaining their ethnic identity. Rather than simply assuming that those of Polish descent recognize the obvious advantage of preserving their Polish heritage, Polish organizations must realize that these advantages may not in fact be obvious at all, and without a concerted campaign of persuasion and reinforcement, the commitment of many will continue to weaken and disappear.

If Polish organizational life on this continent is to have a future, then the Polish community as a whole must retain some sense of group identity which transcends differences of geography, class, cultural level, and the like. Perhaps the fundamental problem here is that no consensus exists as to what Polish culture really is. Indeed there are a host of Polish cultures, defined by region, by social class, by historical tradition, by the time in which particular groups emigrated from Poland, and even by the foreign models imposed or adopted at different times by different groups in Polish society. Polish culture is not monolithic, nor indeed are its offshoots on this continent, but somehow as a group it has been difficult for Polish North Americans to accept their diversity and accommodate it within the framework of larger cooperative ventures.

This cultural diversity is an important problem for the future, since in their attempts to mobilize the support and energies of the hitherto uncommitted, Polish organizations cannot enforce some rigid cultural stereotype which may at best conform to the real condition of only a small fragment of the whole ethnic Polish community. Rather than imposing one definition of "Polishness," their strategy should be to provide a forum for the interchange of cultural models with all versions accorded equal consideration. Perhaps one way of illuminating this problem is to study successive waves of Polish immigration to this continent which brought with them the language and cultural assumptions of their particular region and class in Poland at the time that they left it. Disagreements between these successive waves of Polish immigration are not entirely due to different socio-economic backgrounds, nor to different levels of education. They are also due to the fact that the Poland of 1870 was very different from that of 1940, or even 1980.

The one common element in the various forms of "Polishness" is, of course, the Polish language itself; yet the language is threatened with complete extinction on this continent as the forces of assimilation continue to advance. If Polish organizations seriously intend to safeguard their future existence, they must place more emphasis on language retention as the one means by which the cultural diversity of the Polish community may be overcome in a larger sense of group identity. There seems to be an absolute need for preserving the Polish language as a living element in the community's existence, as a transmitter of its cultural values and as a token of its group commitment and identity. Both language and culture are living things which develop together and which reinforce each other. Without language there is repetitive tradition but no understanding, ritual but no culture. It is familiarity with the Polish language which allows successive waves of Polish immigrants to return to the roots of their tradition, thereby modifying and enriching their understanding. Instead of a culture frozen in time like an exhibit in a museum, language allows for a developing and growing culture by continually transmitting the latest and best of what the root culture has to offer. Without the Polish language which enables the Polish community to continually return to its roots and compare its own evolution with that of its cousins in Poland, that community will contribute little to North America save a still-life of a world or society long vanished.

If it is true that a knowledge of the Polish language is the single best safeguard against assimilation, then a concerted effort to preserve that language should be the first concern of all Polish organizations on this continent. In general terms, cooperative strategies should be developed by which community resources are efficiently applied to this purpose, and we should not assume that the unaided family milieu will be sufficient to transmit the sophisticated language skills which make the exercise worthwhile in the first place. Ultimately what is needed is a regular system of schooling which would offer courses in Polish subjects in addition to the regular curriculum. How this can be best achieved obviously depends on regional conditions, but some form of private institution operated by the Polish community itself may be the only answer to this problem. If the resources of the Polish community alone seem inadequate to this task, then serious consideration should be given to efforts involving the cooperation of other ethnic groups whose interest in their own language retention parallels that of Polish Canadians. A joint private school offering several alternative linguistic and cultural options in addition to the regular curriculum would avoid duplicating resources, and still achieve the objective of preserving heritage languages.

Before any kind of ambitious educational program of this nature can be undertaken, extensive preparatory work must be undertaken to interest and motivate those who at present manifest only a weak inclination to participate in the life of the Polish community. Perhaps the time has never been quite as favourable as it is today for this kind of work: the community has established itself firmly on this continent and with the struggle for economic survival no longer of such pressing importance, other issues may now be considered; events in Poland in the last decade have attracted global attention so that people of Polish descent around the world can be conscious of belonging to a commonality of some significance; the election of a Polish pope, the awarding of a Nobel prize for literature to a Pole, has done much to revive ethnic pride and perhaps even overcome the pernicious effects of those ethnic slurs which had undermined group solidarity; and the general sense of inadequacy in North American cultural and educational alternatives may promote a move to rediscover roots and renew interest in the community's ethnic identity. These opportunities are real and they should be utilized by Polish organizations in their drive to attract committed members. Such a drive should emphasize the great advantages which can be derived from a closer association with the ethnic tradition, in terms of personal enrichment as well as in terms of the larger questions of the day.

One hopes, of course, that in their efforts to attract a younger generation of members, Polish organizations will eschew traditional, patriotically exaggerated descriptions of Polish culture which are counter-productive. Formulations which in some way stress that Polish culture is in one way or another "the best" must be scrupulously avoided. On the other hand, Polish culture does represent a coherent and worthy set of values which offer a unique view of the world. Poland's history has led to the evolution of a tradition of democracy, liberty, patriotism, family loyalty, piety and courtesy which sets it off as distinctive within the European context. Even if these values existed at times as ideals to be striven for rather than as concrete descriptions of Polish reality, nonetheless, they exerted a powerful effect on the Polish national consciousness which can be seen to operate in Poland today as strongly as at any time in the past.

Like any culture, it offers a personal orientation in what might otherwise seem to be a disorienting world and by becoming familiar with Polish, as with any other culture, one has to confront the very concept of culture itself and thereby enrich one's experiences, create aesthetic criteria of judgment, develop a scale for comparison, and refine one's taste. In this broader sense, Polish culture can be one doorway to a richer intellectual existence for those who find it familiar and accessible. Furthermore, such a confrontation with Polish culture necessitates a process of selection among various cultural elements, in search of those which seem relevant and useful to one's own existence and development, and this in turn forces one to think, reflect and evaluate. Consequently this type of cultural experience may be regarded as one form of safeguard against apathy or mediocrity—not because Polish culture itself does not contain mediocre elements of its own, but because the entire process allows and even demands that one continually choose between mediocrity and the truly excellent.

When making their appeal to the uncommitted on the grounds of more universal issues, Polish organizations might legitimately argue that Polish group identification offers a unique insight into the elemental questions of the struggle for human rights, and the campaign to restrain the arbitrary exercise of government power at the expense of the rights of the citizenry. If North American Poles maintain their links with and interest in Poland, they will have a remarkable opportunity to observe the struggle at close quarters, and also to transmit the lessons of the struggle to their adopted lands. The human rights issue affects all peoples throughout the globe and is of critical importance in all times and all places, but unless one experiences it directly, it takes on a distant and theoretical colouration which might breed a dangerous indifference to the question. Those of Polish descent, like those descended from numerous other nations which currently find themselves faced with violations of human rights, have their own particular and valuable insight into this problem. It is a form of experience which of necessity must sensitize one to the larger issues at stake and enrich one's political understanding. If the price of liberty is eternal vigilance, then an aware and vigilant citizenry is essential to the functioning of our democracy and Poles, like other nations in similar positions, have important lessons to offer, while Polish North Americans can make a valuable contribution by transmitting those lessons. Such arguments have their own inherent validity, but they must never be cheapened by exaggerated notions of national destiny or mission, which have too often in the past served merely to alienate those interested in making the connection with Poland relevant to their own lives. The Polish case represents one of many such opportunities for raising the level of political awareness on this continent, but it is after all only the one with which the Polish North American community happens to be most familiar.

It is to be hoped that arguments such as these can act as a focus for organizations interested in revitalizing their membership and securing a future for themselves. Perhaps the most important thing for all such organizations to remember is that no organization will ever long survive without a concrete set of objectives, and such objectives must be clearly enunciated in a rational form. Of course one cannot then stop at the statement of objectives, but must make concerted efforts to achieve these goals in the most effective manner possible. Here the experiences of other groups, scholarly research, studies of the community's composition and needs, surveys of opinion and similar data all have an important role to play. Unfortunately the modern techniques of fund-raising, media utilization and motivational research have not been adequately exploited by the Polish community on this continent; yet they are a crucial element of public life today, whether one approves of them or not. Armed with such concrete information, Polish community leaders will be in a better position not only to sound out the opinions of their real or potential constituents, but also to influence and lead that opinion in constructive directions. Therefore as one important priority, I would suggest that Polish organizations everywhere on this continent study the possibilities of adapting modern information-gathering techniques to their own needs. By this, I mean more than just the hitherto existing research centres which tend to concentrate their efforts on historical and sociological studies. I also mean data-gathering institutions modelled more on public surveying groups and public opinion pollsters.

As a second recommendation, I would propose that concrete political action groups be formed directed at specific ends. Whether such groups have as their objective the erection of a school, the collection of funds for a cultural centre, or political lobbying on behalf of the workers' struggle in Poland, such activities impart a concrete goal to the community, they transcend existing organizational differences or rivalries, and they can unite the community in a common sense of purpose and thereby also stimulate a sense of identity. Without a strong, purposeful and vigilant public profile, the community will never make its presence felt, will never exercise its own voice within the larger national communities to which it belongs, and will be consistently ignored by national political leaders. Though many admirable objectives have already been achieved in the past, one must resist the tendency to think that the Polish North American community's best days have passed and that it will not be able to exercise an even stronger political influence in the future. In fact it can exercise such an influence if it can mobilize and motivate the community in concrete and productive directions.

As a third recommendation to Polish organizations for the future, I would propose that contacts with Polish language and culture be maintained and if at all possible strengthened. Such a return to roots will strengthen group identity and solidarity, and enrich the contribution which the community as a whole can make to society on this continent. Community organizers should urge wherever possible that Polish-language courses be introduced, that parents support such courses and children attend them, that religious, counselling and informational services be provided in Polish, that appropriate cultural exchanges with Poland be organized, and that media services, especially television, be provided in Polish wherever feasible. Admittedly such a general program of language and cultural promotion will be costly and many may question the possibility of its realization, but without such a program, the community will simply not survive as a distinct entity on this continent for very many more generations. If its organizations wish to safeguard the Polish community's future, then they have no other alternative. Of course in undertaking such an ambitious program, or continuing and developing it wherever a beginning has already been made, only the strictest collaboration among organizations offers the slightest chance of success and therefore such campaigns must be kept emotionally neutral in order to attract the broadest possible base of support.

Similarly ambitious projects need to be directed at the younger generation in the community, but here the objective should be to create programs which the youth can run by themselves as much as possible, and which once started can take on a momentum of their own. A promising alternative could be a cultural and drop-in centre which might be utilized by the young from different socio-economic and cultural sections of the Polish community as a centre for the interchange of ideas and experiences, as a focal point for group projects and activities, and as a means for transmitting values, interests and even the Polish language in everyday usage. Such centres should be organized as collaborative ventures wherever numbers of ethnic Poles warrant, and again only the cooperation of various organizations offers any hope that they might be successful.

As a final recommendation for the future, I would offer the perhaps obvious suggestion that the community as a whole learn to use its resources more sensibly in concrete and directed projects which have some definite purpose to them. This seems obvious, and yet considerable sums continue to be spent on ephemeral items such as conferences whose impact is limited, rather than directing those sums towards cultural centres or educational institutions whose impact would in fact persist and accumulate. Strict priorities need to be worked out according to which financial resources will be assigned to the community's most important immediate objectives, not to the agreeable but largely cosmetic activities which have only a limited impact at the grass roots of the community. Again, as with all of these recommendations, this one will remain at best a pious resolution unless the community's leaders acknowledge the gravity of the crisis they face, and choose to undertake the necessary action to meet it. Perhaps the community as a whole has been too modest in the past, either in its ambitions or in its capacity to carry out those ambitions. It cannot afford to be so in the future. Only a bold, imaginative gamble will offer Polish North Americans a chance of preserving their own unique ethnic identity in the face of the ever stronger forces of assimilation.

Notes

1. K.G. O'Bryan, J.G. Reitz, O.M. Kuplowska, *Non-Official Languages: A Study in Canadian Multiculturalism* (Ottawa, 1976). The Polish sample in the study consisted of 91,066 who identified themselves as Polish in some way in five major cities (Montreal, Toronto, Winnipeg, Edmonton, Vancouver) in 1973. Consequently it over-represented immigrant, especially recent immigrant, population and may exaggerate attitudes in favour of maintenance. In the 1971 Census, 316,425 Canadians claimed ethnic Polish origin. Of the census total, 129,435 or 40.9 per cent lived in the five major cities surveyed later in the languages study. Percentages in some of the tables below may not always total 100 since miscellaneous responses were not always included in the published results.
2. Ibid., p. 192.

3. Ibid., p. 55.
4. Ibid., p. 143.
5. Ibid., p. 69.
6. Ibid., p. 125.
7. Ibid., pp. 120-21.
8. Ibid., p. 82.

The Adaptation of Polish Professionals in Canada: Traditional Roles versus Middle Class Realities

Alexander J. Matejko

Social mobility between societies which are differently structured, represent cultures well apart of each other, expose themselves to different historical challenges, and are governed differently, offer an exciting topic for creative writers as well as for social scientists. The comparison of Poland and Canada is illuminating in many respects. First, both societies have been very much conditioned in their development by the presence of a "big brother" on their borders. Secondly, the historical place and role of the middle class in Poland and Canada has differed considerably even if at the present time there is some evidence of similar trends and problems, such as the mass production of post-secondary education graduates, rapidly changing styles of thinking and living, limited career opportunities, a commitment to egalitarianism.

Members of Polish intelligentsia who settled in Canada have brought with them from their old country their traditional cultural and social aspirations of the "governance of souls" at the national level not applicable to the Canadian scene, except within the Polish ethnic community. Earlier Polish immigrants who arrived before World War Two were mostly of a lower class background and they had been exposed to the Canadian material and social values long enough not to accept the leadership aspirations of the postwar arrivals from the intelligentsia. This has led to some distances and even tensions within the Polish ethnic community, as well as to the adaptational problems of intelligentsia.

The latest Polish immigrants are mostly from the ranks of the middle class, and they differ widely in their values, orientations and commitments from Poles belonging to the previous waves of immigration. Differences in their socio-cultural upbringing and in their major goals are combined with the different approaches among various generations of Polish Canadians to their Polish heritage. Polish Canadians differ in their understanding of Polish patriotism and this is justified when taking into consideration the very substantial social and cultural transformations in Poland since World War One, and especially after 1945.

The Polish arrivals to Canada during the 1940s and 1950s consisted of the demobilized soldiers, previous civil servants, manual workers and farmers taken by Nazis to Germany, as well as of the Polish free professions. There had been until then a great shortage of the white-collar workers among the Polish Canadians. In 1941 the clerical, financial and various professional categories constituted around 2 per cent of the Polish Canadian labour force, but in 1961 they constituted already around 12 per cent (in addition 9 per cent of the managerial staff not considered before). In the 1930s the shortage of well-educated people had been a major obstacle in developing the organizational life of Poles. "We do not have enough lawyers, doctors, and even businessmen and merchants. We must ensure that our youth possesses the enthusiasm and love for study, as well as a measure of initiative" was the plea of Polish ethnic leaders in 1938.[1]

The postwar arrivals greatly invigorated the Polish ethnic life, and also prevented it from being dominated by the official authorities from Poland, which had been the case before the war. The reason for this was not only the strong anti-communist sentiments of the ex-soldier immigrants but also a general feeling of antipathy for the new government amongst Polish Canadians. The Polish immigrants had the organizational experience as well as the ambition to secure the continuity of Polish life on Canadian soil. At the end of the 1970s almost two hundred Polish associations were consolidated within the Canadian Polish Congress. According to H. Radecki, "the Polish group maintains over 300 various institutions, organizations, and associations with a membership of about 20-25 per cent of the total Polish ethnic category (if the church and parish affiliation is taken into consideration)."[2] This well developed organizational structure is to a large extent the product of the postwar immigration of the late 1940s and the 1950s.

The ambition of these immigrants to establish a consolidated Polish framework in Canada did not receive any major resistance from the Poles who arrived in Canada much earlier and became sufficiently Canadianized to lose interest in the exclusively Polish identity. With the availability of mass education and a booming economy lower-class Poles had many opportunities to improve their social and economic status. This upward mobility corresponded with the decline in the use of the Polish language and the growth of mixed marriages, both higher among Poles than among Ukrainians.[3] The fact that the latter have been more effective in the preservation of their native language and ethnic identity is interesting considering the much higher Polish postwar immigration, better access of Poles to the culture of their old motherland, and approximately the same development of the organizational structure in both ethnic groups. According to Kogler, "the process of assimilation was retarded [among Ukrainians] through intensive cultural programs, strong organizational links with increased influence emanating from cultural centres and institutions, as well as close cooperation between church and lay organizations."[4]

During the 1970s Polish ethnic life has become increasingly handicapped by the lack of involvement of the younger generation. There are only a few young people in the Polish organizations and there is not much chance of the successful replacement of the older generations as long as the traditional goals of the Polish associations that outlived their purpose and usefulness are not seriously reconsidered. Originally, "the primary organizational aims reflected the needs and views of people who saw themselves either as Poles in Canada, or Polish Canadians, not able or willing to enter and participate in the organizational structure of their hosts."[5] Now the question is how to redesign the ethnic organizational life in order to secure the continuity of generations as well as an adequate place for Polish Canadians in the main stream of the Canadian cultural, social and political life.

Communist Poland is of no attraction for the majority of ethnic Poles who make a clear distinction between the Polish nation and the Polish communist state. If taking into consideration that only a tiny part of Polish associations remain on friendly terms with the Polish communist state, and on the other hand that the Polish government in exile loses its influence in Canada, the external control is not a problem. However, the major question remains how to reorient the Polish ethnic life from an inward orientation to an outward orientation. Several Polish associations have already succeeded in orienting themselves outwardly by cooperating with the Canadian universities, providing data and insights on Polish issues to the mass media, making presentations to the governmental bodies, etc. According to Radecki, "modifications and changes in organizational aims did not consider the needs and values of the Canadian-born generations, reflecting rather the changing expectations of the foreign-born members," and this was the factor that prevented the Polish associations studied by him in 1974 from attracting and serving the needs of the Canadian-born individuals of Polish descent. There is also not much chance for the development of new ethnic associations because the latest arrivals from Poland are in general not organizationally oriented, and the Canadian-born Poles activate themselves almost exclusively outside the Polish ethnic group.

Ethnic Leadership in the Mass Society

There is an obvious need to provide some new dimensions to the Polish ethnic life but the question remains who will offer the leadership. In Poland traditionally it was the function of the intelligentsia to provide the inspiration and leadership. Even under communism the intelligentsia remains a highly influential stratum, especially in Poland and in Hungary. The official leadership has to take into consideration the demands of the intelligentsia at least to some extent, especially when students, artists and intellectuals, together with the blue-collar workers, provide the main source of an organized and semi-legal opposition, as happens particularly in Poland. Rising to the ranks of intelligentsia remains very attractive among blue-collar workers and farmers, who will do everything possible to place their children in the appropriate schools. Social inequality under state socialism remains not only in terms of income, power and privilege but also in the field of culture, lifestyle and personal perspectives. Membership in the intelligentsia still stands for something valuable and at the same time inspires a feeling of responsibility. The negative reaction to the authoritarianism of the ruling communist establishment is constantly fed by the still vivid attraction of the intelligentsia as a stratum of enlightened and patriotic people willing and able to take responsibility for the whole nation.

A similar attraction has inspired the postwar leaders of the Polish community in Canada to spend time and effort tirelessly for the common good. In addition, many among them had also in mind the political motivation identifying themselves with the Polish nation remaining under the authoritarian rule of Soviet communism. The ex-soldiers brought with them an unequivocal devotion to the idea of Poland free from Soviet rule. Their close ties to the Polish government-in-exile in London led to several politically inspired actions and an insistence upon a united front with other anti-communist emigrants. Any emigrants who for various reasons were unwilling to pay at least lip service to the values and norms of establishment emigré ideology were treated with suspicion or even hatred. Actions by Polish immigrants to Canada outside the accepted channels were ostracized by local ethnic activists. For example, the discussion club established by the local members of the Polish intelligentsia in London, Ontario, has been for several years ostracized by the local Polish community as an "elitist" initiative that does not fit into the local pattern. The club organizes lectures and debates on various social and cultural issues and is not committed to any particular political orientation. But the difference in style and activity is enough to create tension between the club and its traditionalistic ethnic surrounding.

What keeps the Polish Canadian ethnic group community alive is to a large extent status competition. The prestige hierarchy inside an ethnic community has been for many ethnic Poles a convenient and fully acceptable occasion for status crystallization. Having in general great difficulties to establish their status outside of their own community because of language difficulties, differences in the religious background, low educational level and the lack of strong achievement motivation, immigrants have had to rely mainly on their own religious congregations, mutual benefit associations, centres of patriotic activity, families, friends and neighbours. The internal diversity and fragmentation of most ethnic groups in Canada and the long tradition of internal splits and struggles may be explained by the intensive search for status, as well as by the structural transformations. The fund-raising activities have remained in many cases highly decentralized probably because this has enabled a large number of local leaders to enjoy power and prestige. Conflicts between various ethnic leaders and officers frequently have dramatized the status competition.

From time to time some people are denounced and attacked in the Polish ethnic press for their nonconformist views, and even mild criticism of the ethnic life or Canada in general is strongly rebuked. The climate of mutual accusations and denouncements nourishes the tensions. The nature of them may be easily found in the letters to the editor in the Polish weeklies. Two approaches are clearly evident in these letters. One of them is representative of the uncritical loyalty to everything related to the Polish past, as well as presenting the Polish nation as the scapegoat of Russian oppression and exploitation under the disguise of communism. The other approach represents the intellectualized understanding of the past as a source of learning and experience. Both approaches reject communism as the solution for Poland (as well as for Canada) but differ in understanding what actually happens in the old motherland and how the Polish Canadians should define their own attitude.

And probably even more important is the difference among the ethnically active Polish Canadians with regard to the role for them in Canada. Is it a place of temporary residence until Poland is "liberated" from Soviet communism or is it a new motherland? The young generation of Polish Canadians is definitely committed to Canada but also even they have some problems related to self-identification in this multicultural society.

The Characteristics of Present-Day Canada and their Impact on Poles

Canada is an ethnic mosaic although the reduction of the whole society to the two statutory ethnic groups appears to be gaining momentum with the spread of mass education and the socio-economic upgrading of several ethnic groups that traditionally used to be underprivileged. Polish Canadians in practice are exposed to strong pressures to conform to the dominant values among which the Anglo-Saxon heritage plays a major role.[6] It is an interesting question as to how much this image of Canada has been changed and what consequences it has for Poles.

We may consider this question in relation to another question, namely, whether present-day Canada differs in any substantial respect from the image portrayed by John Porter in 1965 in *The Vertical Mosaic,* using data from the 1950s and early 1960s. This image still dominates the Canadian social sciences, inspiring research and stimulating debate on the nature of Canadian society.[7] The image of an ethnically fragmented and stratified society ruled at the top by Canadians of British origin still has validity. According to data for the period 1953 to 1973, in the governing elite the British have remained heavily over-represented, the French slightly under-represented, and all others most heavily under-represented (Panitch 1977:199-218). The traditional establishment is still well entrenched, closely linked to American business circles, and shows an evident tendency for self-perpetuation.[8]

On the other hand, some new trends have entered the Canadian scene and have become of growing importance. One of them is the rising educational level of the whole population, and especially the younger generation. The level of expectations in Canada is rising rapidly thanks to the impact of mass media and universal education. The class and ethnic differences in educational aspirations are diminishing even if the actual attainment remains unequal.

The ethnic factor seems to change its role in comparison with the past. Most of the ethnic groups have shared in the socio-economic achievements of the country and their relative positions have improved—even if their relation versus the establishment has changed little, except in the case of the Quebecois. In anglophone Canada, English dominates universally at the family home, although many ethnic groups still preserve their traditional allegiances without meeting any substantial discrimination. There has been a partial fulfillment of Porter's prediction that cultivation of ethnic differentiation would necessarily lead to the weakening of the Canadian identity and perpetuation of the social inequalities. Porter is right that ethnic differences have been important in building up the bottom layer of the stratification system in both agricultural and industrial settings. However, he had underestimated the processes of educational and economic upgrading experienced by several ethnic groups during the 1960s and the 1970s.

This educational upgrading, as well as the impact of urbanization and the increasing percentage of Canadian-born among the Poles, have contributed to the speed of assimilation and the influence of trends to which all Canadians are exposed. One of them is the decline of religion. Traditionally religion provided a strong social bond and cohesion in society, but in the Canadian case it has never worked this way because of the denominational diversity. More recently, public opinion polls have shown that during the 1960s and 1970s church attendance has slumped in Canada. The churches are experiencing difficulty in maintaining moral authority over their members. The young generation is particularly vulnerable to anti-clericalism and secularization.

All this does not necessarily mean that Canadians are becoming atheists or agnostics. Only one-tenth of Canadians, in comparison with one-fifth in the Benelux countries, Britain and France, think that religious beliefs are not at all important for them. Canadians are now too preoccupied with the practicalities of their daily lives and leisure to consider seriously the philosophical basis of their existence. Religion is part and parcel of a relatively comfortable lifestyle and only some higher measure of social instability may stimulate a more active approach to religious problems.

Poles of previous immigrant generations, who entered Canada with strong reminiscences of a highly stratified society and the much lower standard of living, had to adapt themselves to a different set of values and conduct. Poles who now arrive from communist Poland meet in Canada a society differently stratified than in their motherland, as well as following a different system. Canada is not one of those countries which has wide disparity of income levels, yet there is an evident and persistent inequality. The share of the lowest 20 per cent of Canadian households from the 1950s until now has been 4 per cent of the total income, while the upper 20 per cent have consistently controlled over two-fifths of the total income. Not only in Canada but also in several other developed countries there are pockets of poverty that survive or even grow not because of some evident negligence among their members or among the society in general, but because of much more objective reasons.

Canadians, and among them Polish Canadians, share with the remaining Western world the advantages of a fast historical growth of material well-being, but also face the socio-moral costs of a developed market society burdened with social welfare services as it reaches the limits of growth. The Canadian society enjoys the status of a service-oriented welfare state at a high level of consumption. However, the realities shared by Canada and several other Western countries make necessary a gradual change towards a conserver society and major adjustments in the economy in order to defend the present high standard of living. Canada's heavy dependence on the United States has helped historically to develop the economy but at the same time has also contributed to short-sighted consumerism and welfarism not adequately substantiated by the industrial development.

Canada consists of people who differ in their religious and ethnic background but the impact of a market society reduces them to the role of consumers who all strive for a high standard of living. The increasing decline of religious beliefs and practices in Canada reinforces the one-sided egoistic approach to life and society that leads to excessive demands and anxiety. The centrifugal tendencies in Canada originate to a large extent from the widespread anomie which feeds dissatisfaction and makes people particularly vulnerable to negativism as an easy answer to the current problems of their own society. Primary groups, the basic sources of any genuine socialization, have become weakened by the development of a depersonalized mass society based in large measure on the U.S. pattern. Several major problems in Canada today have their roots in the narrow scope of interests and concerns of individuals and groups who are unwilling or unable to reach beyond their own micro-world and pay serious consideration to the broader public interest. The Canadian body politic, so effective in the struggle for popularity and votes, is helpless when dealing with the crucial disintegrative trends related to inflation, unemployment, poverty, the crisis of education, relationships between French and English, aggravated industrial relations, industrial underdevelopment, etc. These critical issues go beyond traditional bureaucratic policy formulation and require a demonstration of courage, imagination and ability by the whole country in problem solving. There are problems associated with strengthening family ties and developing a network of substitutive "extended family" institutions.

The mass consumer society may be highly beneficial for the aggressive and highly ambitious individuals, as well as for the business concerns, but it is disastrous for the socio-moral fabric of the society, which becomes internally split into various conflicting interest groups and bureaucratized institutions among which each has only its own privatized goals in mind. The traditional socializing agencies, primarily the family, have become highly endangered under such circumstances. The welfare state has been in general unable to fulfill the integrative role due to its impersonality, anonymity and bureaucratization.

The ethnic background of Poles helps them at least to some extent to face effectively challenges of a developed mass society by sticking to the family as a basic socializing institution, the universalistic religion (predominantly Roman-Catholicism) and the tradition of liberty. In the modern mass society the close social ties existing among Poles and widely cultivated by them help to resist the consequences of alienation and anomie so typical for the highly urbanized modern environment.

The problem is who would be able and willing to redesign accordingly the ethnic life of Poles in Canada and how effectively. Professionals and intellectuals have become absorbed into the Canadian middle class and many of them are practically lost for the ethnic cause. The leadership function in the socio-cultural field largely remains in the hands of people who have political and administrative aspirations. The contacts with the cultural and academic Canadian centres remain underdeveloped.

The Ethnic Intelligentsia

What is the potential of Polish intelligentsia as a factor able and willing to inspire the rest of the Polish ethnic group or at least its part still fluent in Polish? In order to find the answer to this question in 1975 the author did a survey among Poles mainly in eastern Canada who were on the rosters of Polish ethnic organizations and played a more or less active ethnic role. A questionnaire in the Polish language was mailed to the members of the predominantly middle-class ethnic parish in Ottawa and to all members of the Association of Polish Engineers in Canada located mostly in Ontario and in Quebec. This questionnaire was also published in the Polish semi-weekly *Alliancer* and a few additional responses were obtained this way. One-third of the questionnaires were returned (350 responses).[9] Of those who replied, nine-tenths of them are married men; two-thirds are aged 45 to 64, and one-fifth over 65; 70 per cent have a post-secondary education; half are engineers and 27 per cent are other professionals; nine-tenths were born in Poland and the same proportion declare themselves Roman Catholics; 85 per cent own houses; most are well off (nine-tenths own a car and 24 per cent own two cars; 44 per cent own a colour TV, 27 per cent own a cottage).

All this means that the population of our survey constitutes the upper level of wealth, income, education and occupational position within the social category of around 70,000 people in Canada who still speak mostly Polish at home. What happens within this population is of crucial importance for the survival of the Polish ethnic group within the Canadian society. The basic question is whether the population surveyed is willing and able to fulfill the leadership function for the rest of the Polish Canadians.

In our analysis we distinguished among the respondents according to their educational level (primary, secondary, post-secondary) and occupational position (engineers, other professionals, clerks and technicians, labourers). We must remember that our population does not include those people of Polish origin who are substantially Canadianized or who for other reasons have lost contact with the Polish community. All our respondents are ethnic activists at least in the sense that they are on the rosters of the Polish ethnic institutions and are regularly being informed about the current ethnic events (balls, banquets, public lectures, festivities, artistic performances, etc.).

This survey shows a remarkably good adaptation of Poles to the Canadian way of life, as well as a harmonious reconciliation of the Polish identity with the Canadian identity. At the same time a gap seems to be growing between the well-adapted members of intelligentsia, particularly their offspring, and the network of the Polish traditional ethnic institutions that follow Etzioni's "survival model" rather than the "efficiency model." Such institutions are expected to survive and to prove, simply by existing, that Poles are present in Canada. The attention of ethnic leaders is focused on requirements which, if fulfilled, allow the ethnic group to continue. How to make the group more effective in fulfilling its goals is secondary. A survival orientation is more evident in the newest generation of immigrants of Polish descent than among older generations of intelligentsia. The social functions of ethnic institutions seem to dominate over their cultural and innovative functions, and this influences negatively the adaptation of the Polish Canadian institutional infrastructure to the socio-cultural transformations of Poles in Canada.

The Polish intelligentsia of our survey showed a relatively high level of ethnic commitment of an informal nature. They spoke Polish, were interested in the Polish issues, read Polish and had many friends among Poles. Their ethnic identity went together with the more or less successful adaptation to the local Canadian environment. At the same time a considerable part of this intelligentsia remained lukewarm to the Polish ethnic institutions, even including the Polish Catholic parishes. Those Poles who belonged to the working class or who were only on the margin of the intelligentsia showed in several cases a much higher level of devotion to the Polish institutionalized life in Canada.

There are probably three basic reasons for the differences existing among the Polish Canadian intelligentsia in their organizational commitment. First is the high level of formalized activity in Canadian society and the shortage of time. For the blue-collar workers, clerks and technicians the ethnic organizational life appears quite often as one of the few opportunities to meet other people after work and the household chores. For the Polish intelligentsia attendance at ethnic meetings is at the expense of attractive cultural and social activities in the Anglo-Saxon environment or even of their professional commitments.

The second reason is that among the more recent arrivals from Poland there is in general a negative attitude to formalized commitments similar to those that used to be imposed on them by the authoritarian communist regime in their home country. These people dislike any long and boring organizational meetings and are mainly interested in pursuing their own private pleasures.

The third reason seems to be the most important one. Polish ethnic institutions had originally developed on the basis of mutual aid and were oriented mainly to the preservation of the tradition. Being treated as inferior by their foreign environment, the earlier immigrants had remained mostly within their own institutions which had offered them security, prestige and entertainment. For the intelligentsia these institutions have only a limited attraction.

Some of the recent immigrants from the traditional Polish intelligentsia for various reasons could not fully establish themselves in the Canadian world and the Polish ethnic institutions became the only field available to them. However, these institutions were mostly dominated by the people from the lower classes in Poland who had come up considerably in the new world and were very hesitant to accept new pretenders to the ethnic leadership. New ethnic institutions have developed and a split of vested interests has become evident between them. The traditionalistic character of the most well-established ethnic institutions was difficult to accept by the liberally oriented part of the intelligentsia, especially by those among them who came lately from Poland. They rejected the concept of a Polish ethnic ghetto and were in general cosmopolitan. They did not want to be led by people from the older generation who had much more limited knowledge of the Polish drab reality under communism, but at the same time pretended to be experts on communism, Poland, and anything else concerning eastern Europe. The ethnic institutional life would have to change substantially in form and content to interest these new immigrants, but in this they ran up against the vested interests of the entrenched leadership who for many years treated the ethnic institutions as their own domain.

Ethnic Commitments

There are several ways in which people are able and willing to express their ethnic commitments. Several of them were explored in our survey, and we tried to estimate their relative importance depending on the time of arrival in Canada of our respondents, their educational level, and their occupation.

First of all we should look into the issue of language. The percentage of Polish couples using only Polish in their daily life did not differ among our respondents between those who came earlier (before 1956) and those who came later. On the other hand, those who did not use Polish at all were more likely to be the pre-1956 group. The use of Polish among the children, as well as the Polish identity of parents, was more common among those who came later. No significant differences were found between these two categories in subscription to the ethnic press and attendance at Polish meetings.

Respondents in general evaluated their own knowledge of present-day Poland in a favourable light. Two-thirds of them had characterized as good their orientation in the political and economic situation of present-day Poland. In orientation about Polish issues, or at least in the self-estimate of it, there were not any basic differences between these people who came to Canada earlier and those who came later. On the other hand, the eventuality of returning to Poland was more often mentioned by the latter, and there appeared a stronger desire of later arrivals to marry only Catholics. There was also less satisfaction among later arrivals with the achievements of the Polish ethnic group in Canada.[10] The later arrivals seemed to be less active in the Polish ethnic community but at the same time they read more Polish and financially helped more of their relatives left in Poland. Only very few of them regretted being outside Poland.

When it came to interest in Polish issues in Canada two subjects dominated: the Polish culture, and the local ethnic organizations. A concern for Polish society and its current problems loomed much larger than any involvement in the politics of present-day Poland (this was much before the establishment of Solidarity!). The political factor was of a relatively low importance for most Poles even if they felt well informed about politics. It was probably the result of an awareness among our respondents that not much could be done against the current political system in Poland even if the great majority of them were not in favour of the regime there. Help to relatives in Poland was quite substantial among our respondents.

In our survey the role of various factors in the successful adaptation to Canada was of particular importance. The respondents gave priority to personal contacts with other Poles, and their own religious convictions. These factors were mentioned as significant much more often than membership in Polish associations, Polish parishes or non-Polish associations. On the other hand, the help gained in their adaptation by Polish people, and particularly by the younger generation, from their own religious convictions went together with church attendance. The same was valid for the help gained from the parish.[11]

Both the level of education and the occupational position of our respondents affected the role of various adaptational factors. At the upper level of education the ethnic factors and the personal religious beliefs played a much lesser role—or at least our respondents felt so. Professionals depended for their success on their connections outside of the ethnic group. However, this did not necessarily mean that they lost interest in maintaining their ethnic contacts. The Association of Polish Engineers is one of the most vital ones in the Polish ethnic community. The traditional warmth and hospitality are widely cultivated among the Polish professionals who find many things in common beyond purely business affairs.

The family life of respondents still exhibited strong Polish ingredients. Four-fifths of them had Polish spouses, and three-quarters spoke only Polish at home; 57 per cent spoke even to their children only in Polish, and an additional 27 per cent spoke Polish to them at least sometimes. Their circle of friends and acquaintances consisted to a large extent of Poles; nine-tenths of them met Polish friends more often than once a month. There was also still a remarkable interest among our respondents in reading Polish. The Polish connection was therefore widely cultivated. It is significant that the length of stay in Canada did not seem to make any difference. However, the Polish ingredient differed among respondents depending on their level of education, occupational location, adaptation to the local environment, and exposure to the external influences. The Polish ingredient was stronger in several respects among the less educated people. Respondents at the post-secondary level of education felt themselves better adapted to the Canadian environment and at the same time they were less active in the Polish community, less often practised Polish in daily life, and in general were less inclined to cultivate "the Polish connection."

Our respondents identified themselves either as "Polish Canadians" or as "Poles." The data available in the questionnaires have allowed us to analyse the "Polish" identity. The respondents were requested to associate this identity with three factors voluntarily selected by them. Their answers show the strongest association of "Polishness" with childhood, followed in descending order by family life, Polish history, World War Two and Polish traditional holidays. It is significant that only few associations were made with the political life of Polish emigrés. The association of the Polish identity with visiting present-day Poland was also relatively weak. In other words, a Polish identity was mostly connected with the past and not the present.

Pride in the achievements of the Poles in Canada was a debatable issue among respondents. Only one-fifth of them were very satisfied with these achievements; another fifth were critical, and the remaining three-fifths declared these achievements as only fair. Younger people were less satisfied than the older people.

Professionals appeared as less satisfied with their ethnic group than others: they were also more sceptical about the possibility of achieving unanimity within this group as well as any possible contribution by the new Polish immigrants to secure ethnic survival. However, professionals were more optimistic than others regarding the future of the Polish ethnic group in Canada.

The future of the Polish ethnic group in Canada depended mainly on preservation of the language and tradition according to one-third of respondents, on new immigration according to one-fifth, and on unanimity according to 16 per cent. The remaining 30 per cent mentioned a whole variety of other factors. Unanimity as a condition of survival was mentioned by more respondents who came to Canada later than by respondents who came earlier. The later arrivals seemed to be a little more optimistic regarding the survival of Poles as an ethnic group in Canada. They were more action-oriented than the earlier immigrants, who were oriented mainly towards the preservation of tradition.

Only few of our respondents regretted that they were not in Poland, and only one-fifth considered the possibility of returning to Poland sometime in the future, mostly for retirement. This shows that the great majority of respondents treat Canada as their permanent home.

Comparison of respondents according to their occupational status shows that people in the higher brackets estimated their achievement in Canada and future perspectives definitely more favourably than people in the lower brackets. However, at the same time blue-collar workers had less regret at not being in Poland, and were less inclined to think about an eventual return. This was probably the result of the better social position of labour in Canada than in Poland.

In order to evaluate the general adaptation of our respondents to Canadian conditions we have decided to apply the following classification:

(a) poor adaptation: no or meagre material achievement; no or poor economic perspectives; high regret of not being in Poland; poor English or none at all
(b) good adaptation: good or very good material achievement; good or very good economic perspectives; no regret at all of not being in Poland; English good or very good
(c) fair adaptation: all remaining cases.

According to this classification, we found 1 per cent of our respondents fell into category (a), 28 per cent into (b), and 71 per cent into (c).[12] It is not surprising when taking into consideration that all these people had to change their cultures and faced in this respect many problems. Probably the most difficult issue was to accept the generation gap much more evident between parents and their children in Canada than in Poland.

Even the relations of our respondents with people from the other ethnic groups seem to be quite satisfactory. English was not a problem: most of the respondents claimed that their English was good or very good. Rapport with the non-Polish speaking people in Canada was evaluated by two-fifths of respondents as good or very good. Among retired people one-sixth complained about the difficulty of establishing friendly relations with non-Polish speaking people, but much less among all remaining respondents. We checked the differences between respondents depending on the length of their stay in Canada. More people who came later treated their adaptation as good, but at the same time less of them gained some help from the Polish associations. In other respects the differences were not significant.

In finding a job or in promotion at work Polish descent could be a handicap, but this was far from common: the negative role of Polish descent in finding a job or in promotion was mentioned only by a few respondents.

The role of Polish ancestry in the family life was evaluated by our respondents much more often as an asset than a liability. The same was more or less valid for social life of respondents, their relations with neighbours and even political activity. This means that discrimination was not a problem for the great majority of our respondents.

The results of our survey suggest that the public proclamation of a Polish Canadian identity among members of the intelligentsia is far from being of a defensive nature, as happens with the previous generations of Polish immigrants to the North American continent. For example, people surveyed by us seem to bother much less about "Polish jokes," and they do not necessarily feel offended by the fact that somebody teases Poles. The well-established professional status of intelligentsia within Canadian institutions and the close contacts with other ethnic groups, mainly Anglo-Saxons, excludes their confinement to an ethnic ghetto preoccupied with its own survival and with its relative status versus other ghettos. This is probably the reason why among intelligentsia there is now much more continuity of the ethnic identity than in other social strata, where Canadianization is often equated with the upgrading of the young generation from the "lower" social milieu of an ethnic character to the "higher" Anglo-Saxon middle-class identity. The relatively high status of the intelligentsia provides its members with the self-assurance that is very often missing in those who still gain their livelihood from manual or clerical work.

Conclusion

Poles in Canada, unlike most Polish Americans, have not yet blended into a melting pot in which nothing is left of their ethnic identity. Nevertheless, they and other Canadian ethnic groups face questions of identification as their commitments shift from the old motherland to their newer home. The problems of mass society—anonymity, the reduction of standards, the revolution of rising expectations—as well as peculiarly Canadian issues further complicate the transition. It is the argument of this paper that the Polish heritage can assist in dealing with those problems, and that, furthermore, a culturally pluralistic Canada is more likely to preserve her national identity than a nation based on standardized mass culture and conformism.

The steady decline of ethnic languages is one of many evidences of how Canadian life has been impoverished by an ambition to become "like others." Even among immigrants, only seven in ten report full fluency in their mother tongues.[13] Among metropolitan Poles fluency in Polish diminishes from 65 per cent in the first generation to 10 per cent in the second generation (compared to 19 per cent of Ukrainians) and 5 per cent in the third generation. The use of Polish is limited mainly to the family and is otherwise rare, even when talking to close friends. Only one-fifth of metropolitan Poles read non-official language newspapers or bulletins regularly; and three-fifths never read them. Only 7 per cent of ethnic Poles listen regularly to non-official radio programs, and a mere 1 per cent regularly view non-official language television programs. At the same time, surprisingly, almost one-fifth of metropolitan Poles treat Polish language retention as desirable and over a half of them treat it as at least somewhat desirable.[14] Among ethnic problems the decreasing use of the ethnic language is treated by ethnic Poles as more important than other problems, among them the ethnic group being too much apart or the loss of ethnic traditions and customs.[15]

The attraction of the ethnic language will remain at a high level only with the growth of ethnic cultures as non-parochial entities that enlarge horizons, help in dealing with the Canadian problems, and open a window to the world. Our survey of the ethnic Polish intelligentsia shows that a considerable socio-cultural potential remains idle. People who feel comfortable in the Polish environment as well as in the Anglo-Saxon world, whose skills and experiences represent a considerable leadership potential, remain nevertheless at the margin of the ethnic organizational life and are dissatisfied with the state of ethnic affairs without however stirring themselves to action. Active participation in ethnic Polish associations remains secondary in the individual adaptation compared to informal connections with personal friends and acquaintances. The ethnic identity of Polish Canadians is now far less a result of background and difficulties in adaptation (in such matters as language, socio-economic status, education, relations with other groups) than it is something chosen voluntarily within a multicultural framework.

Polishness based mainly on birth and inability to adapt, though a powerful basis for community at first, tends to diminish in value for the ethnic institutional life as its traditionalistic adherents age and die. The decline is evident in the loss of younger generations, conflict between "traditionalists" who emphasize the continuity of emigrant life and "adaptors" who give priority to Canadian reality, a preference for gestures over deeds (especially evident in the large number of formal declarations which lack practical conclusions), vulnerability to manipulation by outside interests, mythologization of the past, and failure to recruit or expand leadership. Every ethnic group must renew its leadership and program from time to time in order to survive under changing circumstances. The model of ethnic life satisfactory to those leaders whose roles are defined by ascription is not entirely relevant to others, usually more oriented to the use of English, who would sustain their ethnic identity in a modernized form. An estrangement between generations frequently appears in the failure to respond to calls from the old leadership for sacrifices and in charges by younger people that the leadership is intolerant of dissent and indifferent to contemporary realities.

The ethnic intelligentsia ought to be able to lead the Polish Canadian community toward participation in a multicultural society, expressing itself in an east European tradition of devotion to the public interest, tolerance of differing values and disinterested pursuit of "high" culture. During the 1970s, moreover, the ranks of the Polish Canadian intelligentsia have grown considerably through a selective immigration policy and the advance of young Canadians through the schools into the professions. Their potential influence has remained largely unrealized for a number of reasons. In the consumer mass society, "high" culture must appear alien and the power of its bearers must remain limited. The intelligentsia cannot compete with professional, profit-oriented moulders of mass opinion. Structural changes in the population of Canadian Poles have not yet been matched by a renewal of ethnic culture and reinvigoration of communal leadership. Partly that is the result of the resistance of established leaders to admitting new and unknown people to their ranks. However, the major reasons are the general resistance of "ascribed" ethnics to modernization and the lukewarm attitude of Canadianized Poles to the content of their ancestral culture.

The weakness of the Polish intelligentsia in Canada lies also in the position and composition of the class itself. The wide political gap between Canadian Polonia and contemporary Poland has inhibited contact with the culturally creative intelligentsia of the old country. The influence exercised by the local ethnic intelligentsia is much reduced by being widely scattered geographically and deeply divided by education (in the United Kingdom, the United States and Canada) and generational perspectives. Lacking adequate demand for their services or interest in their elitist culture, they have turned, with modest success, to their own organizations (the Society of Polish Engineers and the Canadian Polish Research Institute, for example). Finally, the ethnic intelligentsia remains heavily influenced by Anglo-Saxon middle-class standards which give priority to the attainment of income sufficient to maintain a comfortable lifestyle and satisfy leisure aspirations. Under Canadian circumstances, an ethnic intelligentsia driven by a social-cultural mission beyond material comfort is a myth actually unattainable.

However, Canada is in the process of constant transformations and the search for a national identity different from American mass culture demands an original ethnic contribution. On the other hand, the traditional ethnic identity is in decline and only a strong cultural infusion will overcome that process. For years the Polish ethnic press has discussed the issue of "what to do in order to preserve ethnic continuity." Still Polish periodicals persist, and new ones are established from time to time. The performances of Polish artists and films attract large audiences. Polish culture remains mostly isolated from the main stream of the Canadian life, but the growing number of intellectuals of Polish descent in

Canada may open channels for its dissemination. As Poles enter the primary group level of cliques, clubs and institutions of Canadian society, assimilating structurally to the host nation, they bring new elements with them. Provided they do not entirely abandon their native cultural patterns and are proud of their heritage, they enrich themselves and other Canadians. The growth of Polish national culture, even under constraints of communism, continues to provide satisfaction in being a Pole and an appropriate inspiration. The traditional elements of Polish social culture have survived under changing circumstances and gain in attraction with the growing disillusion with modernization in developed societies. The future and the influence upon that process of the Polish Canadian ethnic community, on the other hand, depends on its ability to adapt by taking advantage of the atmosphere and official policies of multiculturalism. In that, Canadian Polonia might look to the example of the Ukrainian community in Alberta, but it will have to rely heavily upon the energetic leadership of its native or newly arrived intelligentsia.

Notes

1. See B. Heydenkorn, *The Organizational Structure of the Polish Canadian Community* (Toronto: Canadian Polish Research Institute, 1979), p. 35.
2. H. Radecki, *Ethnic Organizational Dynamics. The Polish Group in Canada* (Waterloo: Wilfrid Laurier University Press, 1979), p. 2.
3. If one considers ethnic origin only, the proportion of endogamous families among Ukrainians in 1961 was 61 per cent, Jews (92 per cent), Native Indian (92 per cent), French (87 per cent) or British (81 per cent) among Scandinavian (32 per cent), German (51 per cent), Dutch (55 per cent) and Polish (51 per cent).

   In the period 1921-71 the proportion of mother-tongue Ukrainians among all ethnic Ukrainians has declined from 92 per cent to 49 per cent, among ethnic Poles from 78 per cent to 38 per cent, among Germans from 53 per cent to 36 per cent, among Scandinavians from 79 per cent to 20 per cent, among Jewish from 91 per cent to 17 per cent, among Chinese from 99 per cent to 76 per cent, among Japanese from 100 per cent to 42 per cent, and among Indian and Eskimo from 94 per cent to 54 per cent.
4. R. Kogler, "The Polish Community in the Light of the 1976 Census Results," in *The Canadian Alternative,* ed. by H. Bouraoui (Downsview: ECW Press, 1980), p. 62.
5. Radecki, *Ethnic Organizational Dynamics,* p. 98.
6. Anti-American feelings are also often interpreted as unifying Canadians. How much negative orientation towards the U.S. really does exist in Canada may be a matter of debate. According to 1974

comparative survey data, only a little over 20 per cent of the Canadian respondents, approximately the same among the elite as among the general public, felt that the proximity of their country to the U.S. was too close; this was similarly felt in France but much less so than in Italy, Brazil, Mexico or Japan. On the other hand, the Canadian general public felt in a little over 20 per cent of the cases that the proximity of their country to the U.S. was not close enough —not much less than in West Germany in general or among the French elite. *Social Indicators 1976* (Washington: U.S. Department of Commerce, 1977), p. XLIX.

7. See James L. Heap, ed., *Everybody's Canada: The Vertical Mosaic Reviewed and Re-examined* (Toronto: Burns & MacEachern Ltd., 1974).

8. See W. Clement, *The Canadian Corporate Elite* (Toronto: McClelland & Stewart, 1975).

9. I would like to thank Dr. Elizabeth Nowicka of Ottawa who coded and prepared the computer program, and the Association of Polish Engineers in Canada, and St. Hyacinth Parish in Ottawa who provided the lists of their members. Father Antoni Rabiega from Ottawa announced our survey in the St. Hyacinth Parish. The same was done by the director of the Polish TV program in Ottawa. This study was done during the one-year visiting professorship of the author at Carleton University in Ottawa during the academic year 1974/75. It was sponsored by the Department of the Secretary of State, Canadian Citizenship Branch (The Multicultural Programme).

10. Very satisfied in this respect were 27 per cent of those who arrived in the period 1940-56 and only 12 per cent of those who arrived after 1956.

11. Seventy-six per cent of the regular churchgoers have found this help very positive, when only 21 per cent found it so among people attending church only sporadically.

12. The adaptation of our respondents seems to be satisfactory if taking into consideration that our population included two and a half times more people on pension than the average in the total Canadian population. Obviously, pensioners would have good reasons to be dissatisfied to a higher degree than the younger generations.

13. K.G. O'Bryan, J.G. Reitz and O.M. Kuplowska, *Non-official Languages: A Study of Canadian Multiculturalism* (Ottawa: Supply and Services Canada, 1976), p. 165.

14. Among the first generation Poles, the language retention is treated as desirable in 83 per cent of the cases. In the second generation this percentage drops to 62 per cent and in the third generation it is at the level of 59 per cent; ibid., pp. 95 and 96.

15. O'Bryan et al., *Non-official Languages*, pp. 46-75.

Polish Youth in the West: a Preliminary Reconnaissance

Danuta Mostwin

Arthur Koestler has observed that, "A concept has as many dimensions in semantic space as there are matrices of which it is a member."[1] The concept "Polish immigrant" has as many dimensions as there are scientists and artists whose fields of observation and discourse include the "Polishness" of an immigrant. The "matrices," or topics, of this symposium are drawn mostly from the sciences of economics, sociology and history. They are concerned with the immigrant's adaptation to a new environment, with his social status and occupational trends, and with the history of groups of immigrants.

A Holistic Approach to the Study of Generational Change in Polonia

The Polish immigrant, or any other immigrant for that matter, however, cannot be perceived only in a group, only as a member of an institution or social class. She or he has to be studied as an individual whose psycho-social needs were not only formed by but helped to form groups, organizations and churches. Furthermore, a holistic view of a person who is the structural and dynamic component of a group or community requires an understanding of the most fragile, yet most important and intriguing matrix of an individual's humanity: his inner, psychic life. Respecting that dimension, we should ask such questions: Why did they emigrate? What was happening within themselves—their inner life—when they did it? What inner restructuring was or is taking place when social change confronts them with the need for a decision? What relations exist between cultural factors and the resolution of crisis in the life of an individual of Polish heritage or in the life of a family of Polish heritage?

The stresses which usually lead to a confrontation of forces—those derived from subconscious psychic strata, the memory traces of early socialization, and later social interaction—may reach a point of crisis. Guided by a holistic view of a person, psycho-social and historical research might, for example, consider hypotheses such as these: that cultural factors promote the crystallization of ethnic identity in response to a crisis experienced by an individual of Polish heritage; that cultural factors help to alleviate a crisis experienced by a family of Polish heritage; that cultural factors exacerbate a crisis experienced by an individual of a family of Polish heritage. It is the argument of this paper that the outcome of a crisis, whether life or situational, depends on the degree of a person's vulnerability. The degree of vulnerability is a function of several factors such as the individual's personality, previous experiences, the state of the ego and the stage of maturity.[2] Loyalty to parental cultural values acquired in the processes of socialization becomes an integral part of the individual's personality, influencing his or her lifestyle and perception of the world. These cultural factors, whether buried in the person's subconscious or experienced in day-to-day life, affect the degree of vulnerability to stress. They may support a person or a family in a stressful situation, or they may be a force leading toward a crisis. The crisis may either generate creative energy or disturb the mental health of a person or a family system. However, the unexpressed cultural component is seldom recognized or included in the diagnosis and treatment of persons of Polish heritage. Even if recognized, the cultural factor is rarely approached on a deep level of understanding.

"Wholes, in the technical sense of the word, are never entirely undifferentiated, but are always structured and articulated into parts. This characteristic distinguishes them from homogeneous masses and from chaotic aggregations."[3] We may argue whether ethnic Polish generations in the world constitute a whole or are only a homogeneous mass or a chaotic aggregation. However, I believe that there is a need to study Polish ethnic generations as *unitas multiplex* and that such a study can be conducted in three different yet interrelated directions.

The first research direction, building on the experiences of people everywhere, should develop models that relate social change to all aspects of the lives of individuals and families of Polish heritage abroad. The study will inquire into how, under what conditions, and in what ways generations changed over individual life spans and historical time. Its goal will be to provide new insights into the structure and function of that holon in *statu nascendi* that we refer to as Polonia of the world. The second purpose of the research project should be to develop a model of Polonia—a holon composed of parts structured by generation and class differences. The independent variables would include reasons for immigration, and mental and physical health. The dependent variable will be the degree and kind of Polishness experienced by the respondents and expressed by them verbally or in action.

The third line of inquiry will analyse the Polish ethnic community as one of the systems within the suprasystem of the country of settlement. The focus will be on interaction with other ethnic groups, and with the country's socio-cultural environment. Existing studies of Polish communities, though numerous, are primarily historical or social works rather than interdisciplinary investigations which deal with psychological aspects of the population. They focus primarily on the sociology of adjustment, with less emphasis on the contribution of Poles to the countries of settlement. Except for a few publications, Polish communities have been shy in telling, or possibly are not even aware of the nature and degree of their cultural investment in the countries which have become their homes. We are not yet sufficiently knowledgeable about the symbiosis between Polish culture and the cultures of the new environments. Polish folk dances, for example, enthusiastically acclaimed by the onlookers for their spontaneity, openness and *joie de vivre,* stand in contrast to the budding Polish American poetry. Unheard until now, or maybe not admitting their heritage until now, the second and third generation descendants of Polish peasants are creating a sad, even painful, yet moving poetry in which Polish themes return like an echo of a distant cry.[4] The flamboyance of the folk dances and the mystique of the timid young poetry are both components of a culture transmitted across generations and merged symbolically with the culture of a new environment. René Dubos, the microbiologist and experimental pathologist, has described the mode and consequences of cultural symbiosis:

> The interplay between cultures commonly takes the form of associations analogous to biological symbiosis—that is, characteristics transcending those of the component parts. If this analogy is at all justified, one can postulate that symbiosis between different human cultures will enhance their differentiation and thus increase the diversity of social systems. . . . There is evidence that, as in purely biological systems, diversity encourages the emergence of organs of communication which generate a new and higher level of unity. Each nation, region, or city acquires uniqueness—its peculiar genius—through the interplay between the traditional culture of its population, the resources and other characteristics of its natural environment, and the foreign cultures to which it is exposed.[5]

A holistic approach to the study of Polish generations, cutting across discipline as well as embracing diverse cultures, will show patterns and lines of development not yet revealed by specialized studies.

Polish Youth in the West: The Study

The binding threads of ethnic generations consist of many human needs. One of them is a need for loyalty. By repaying one's own obligation and by investing oneself in an unending chain of give-and-take, a person fulfills that need. While loyalty can be defined variously, I follow the conceptual approach of Boszormenyi-Nagy who defines it as an "unconscious commitment to a group," and as "surpassing the simple behavioral notion of law-abiding behaviour."[6] Failure to obey unconscious obligations leads to guilt feelings and disturbance of a person's mental health.

Over thirty years ago Kurt Lewin discussed the meaning of forces drawing a Jew toward or away from his group. He concluded that "... an early build-up of a clear and positive feeling of belongingness to the Jewish group is one of the few effective things that Jewish parents can do for the later happiness of their children."[7] In this sense, loyalty to parental cultural values is a force acting on a person and guiding him in the search for ethnic identity. The pilot study, "Polish Youth in the West," provides us, in addition to factual information, with insights into loyalty to parental cultural values. The study was initiated by Jerzy Gierdroyć, the editor of *Kultura* in Paris, who constructed a questionnaire which he printed in No. 11/262 of *Kultura.*[8] His purpose was to learn about the population of young Poles and persons of Polish heritage residing outside of Poland. The survey was not limited to the readers of *Kultura.*

The status of the editor, and a long and distinguished tradition of the publication, paved the way for the questionnaire. It was reprinted in the Polish papers in various countries of Polish settlement. Social leaders, teachers and interested individuals were instrumental in distributing the questionnaire to the non-readers of *Kultura.* In spite of this effort, only 367 self-selected responses were returned to the editor. The responses were entrusted to me for analysis. Because of the absence of a scientific process in the preparation and distribution of the questionnaires, the survey cannot be considered a valid research study. However, to the best of my knowledge it is the only survey of young Poles in the world and suggests enough of interest to be counted as a preparation for further scientific research.

Each response was approached as an individual document, and a content analysis was performed which resulted in preparation of a more complete questionnaire into which all the answers were reintroduced. The 367 persons who responded were from 13 countries (the United States, Argentina, Australia, Canada, Germany, Great Britain, Belgium, Holland, France, New Zealand, Sweden, Denmark and Switzerland). Of the 367, 336 met the criteria for age (between 15 and 40). The majority of the respondents were in the 15-19 year age bracket (39.5 per cent), and only 4.5 per cent were between 36-40 years of age. Two-thirds of the respondents were born outside of Poland, one-third were university students, and over 27 per cent were college graduates. The majority knew the Polish language well (72.5 per cent), or had a fair knowledge of it (27.5 per cent). More than half of them learned the language at home, the rest in other situations (school or vacation in Poland). The majority (88 per cent) are satisfied with their countries of settlement. This satisfaction varies with the country of birth; those born in Poland are less satisfied than those born, for example, in the United States or Canada. Unfortunately the questionnaire did not inquire about such variables as sex, family composition or social status, which would have enriched the findings. The content analysis of the questionnaires revealed 75 variables. The statistical computations resulted in over 200 tables. For purposes of this essay, the findings may be grouped around four topics dealing with attitudes toward parental cultural values: (1) attitudes toward Polish ethnic organizations; (2) attitudes toward prominent individuals in Polish history and culture; (3) attitudes toward the Polish language and culture; and (4) attitudes toward Poland and its current situation.

Findings

1. Over half of the respondents maintained some contact with Polish organizations However, there was more interest in ethnic (cultural) organizations (65.4 per cent) than in Polish political organizations (16.5 per cent). The activities of the organizations were evaluated by the majority as fair, or even efficient (43.1 and 38.7 per cent); only 18.2 per cent considered the function of the organizations as poor. There were 303 responses to a question concerning attitudes toward the Polish government-in-exile, which continued to function in London long after the Great Powers withdrew recognition in 1945. The attitudes were mostly neutral (53.1 per cent), with 21.1 per cent positive and 25.7 per cent negative.

The value of Polish organizations outside Poland is evident in the attitudes of the respondents. Even the value of the Polish government-in-exile, an institution less familiar than traditional Polonian organizations, was rated favourably by the majority of the respondents. One may hypothesize that attitudes toward Polish organizations were influenced positively by parental participation in those organizations and by feelings of loyalty to parents.

2. The two most popular figures in Polish history and culture among the respondents were Józef Piłsudski, the national military

hero (named 84 times as the most fascinating individual in Polish history), and Henryk Sienkiewicz, famous for his historical novels of Poland in the fifteenth and seventeenth centuries (named 131 times as a preferred Polish writer). Other fascinating individuals appearing in the responses were military leaders in World War Two (Sikorski, Anders), leading national statesmen (Dmowski, Witos), scientists (Maria Sklodowska-Curie) and Catholic church leader Cardinal Wyszynski. Only about 55 per cent of the sample responded to the questions regarding prominent individuals; the rest were either not knowledgeable or not interested. However, the available findings suggest that the values of struggle for independence, honour and bravery tend to be internalized by some young Polish persons in the West, and are expressed in their attitudes toward prominent personalities in Polish history and culture.

3. The degree of interest in Polish language and culture, and the reading of the emigré press, served as measures of attitudes toward "Polishness." The interest in the language and culture was great for the majority of the respondents (66.6 per cent) with about 1 per cent uninterested. The degree of interest increased for those who read at least one emigré publication (173 persons) and became even greater for the persons who read *Kultura* (86 persons). The reading of Polish publications associated with the place of birth and the country of residence provided some interesting findings. (See Table 1.) For example, although Canadian and New Zealand-born respondents made up 12.3 and 6.3 per cent of the total sample respectively, they only made up 6.3 per cent and 0.0 per cent of the group that read at least one Polish emigré publication. In addition, only 4.6 per cent of the respondents born in the English-speaking countries of the new world read *Kultura.* This is in spite of the fact that they make up nearly 40 per cent of the entire sample. The residents of Canada and New Zealand tend to be less likely to read Polish publications than their counterparts in other countries. While part of the explanation for this probably lies in the age and educational differences of the particular groups, we may also speculate that assimilation in these two countries is taking place at a faster rate than in other countries of the world.

It is also possible that the Polish generations in the four English-speaking countries are evolving a new form of ethnic identity, different from the identity of Polish generations elsewhere. We may assume that while "Polishness" is a component of their identity, it is integrated not as "Polishness" is understood in Europe or non-English speaking countries but in some newer emerging form. The holistic study, which I propose, may inquire into this area of ethnic identity.

As expected, Polish-born respondents overwhelmingly indicated a great interest in Polish language and culture. However, the American-born as well as the New Zealand-born respondents also expressed a strong interest in this area. Those nations with a high percentage of Polish-born respondents showed a larger interest, the other countries less so. One exception to this was New Zealand, where only one Polish-born respondent resided, and yet 75 per cent of the New Zealand residents exhibited great interest in the Polish language and culture. The older age groups were more likely to indicate great interest than the younger age brackets. Education proved marginally significant; yet the more education, the more interest.

The place of birth and the place of residence were found to be strongly associated with the source of language learning. Polish-born respondents overwhelmingly depended exclusively on family as their source of learning, while British-born were least likely to depend on the family as the source of learning Polish. It is interesting to observe that Canadian and New Zealand respondents, although similar in many other characteristics and attitudes, differed substantially on this question. Canadian residents largely depended on their family for knowledge of Polish, while New Zealand residents took advantage of a combination of sources: Polish language classes, visiting Poland and family.

Since the Polish language is both a cultural value and a psychological value in the mental health of the first and second generations of immigrants, its importance should be recognized by the researcher and the mental health practitioner. Only fairly recently has the language of the country of origin become a subject of psychiatric research. Louis R. Marcos, writing about language as an emotional barrier, states: "Patients whose mother tongue is not English comprise a significant proportion of the psychiatric population.... True communication is hampered by this language barrier."[9]

The inability to learn English, especially among immigrants of limited education, undoubtedly led to many life crises. Some may have rejected the Polish language as a stumbling block to acceptance in the new environment, to a better life and to higher social status. It is also possible that the drawback created by language limited the role of Polish to casual, superficial communications and barred it from ever developing into a medium for more sophisticated exchange among the generations of Polish immigrants.

One second-generation Polish American poet admits that "her mother knew no English before she started school, and this experience so traumatized her," she refused to allow her daughter to learn Polish.[10] However, language does not need to be spoken for its symbolism to be understood and to remain in the subconscious. John Gogol, another Polish American poet, writes of the meaning of language:

God spoke to us in Polish
spoke purple silk banner
only partially comprehended,

divine words intuitively understood,
drawn into nostrils
from burning candles and incense,
through flowers, and grandmothers.

English, language of schoolbooks
What god would speak such a boring language?[11]

4. Polish youth in the West tend to take a pragmatic, conservative view of contemporary Poland but reveal some socialistic sympathies. For example, over half of the sample (53.8 per cent) believed that the socialistic system of economy was more just, but the majority (84.8 per cent) considered capitalism to be more effective. The entire sample, as well as those who read emigré publications, tended to associate with conservative political labels, while more than half of the *Kultura* readers associated themselves with socialist or left-leaning labels. However, in spite of the fact that *Kultura* readers had a socialist/labour orientation, they, more than the other respondents, believed that capitalism is a better economic system.

The majority of the sample (63.5 per cent) evaluated the current (1977) situation in Poland as in need of radical change through evolution (148 respondents) or revolution (122 respondents). The younger the respondent, the more he was likely to choose evolution as a way of change in Poland. The exceptions were the Australian respondents who tended to choose revolution.

The survey included two challenging questions which, in spite of their hypothetical nature, permitted an insight into attitudes toward Poland and solidarity with the nation: 1) If revolt against the regime breaks out in Poland, would you join in the fight? 2) In case of World War Three, would you join a Polish army organized in the West? Out of 281 respondents to (1), only 89 would join the revolt. This sample tends to be rather older, dissatisfied with their place of residence, and to reside in Germany, Scandinavia, and the United States. More respondents were interested in joining a Polish army in exile in case of World War Three than in joining any revolutionary movement in Poland. Out of 293 respondents to (2), 129 would volunteer, and 163 answered in the negative. Only 52 persons out of those who would volunteer to join the army were born in Poland. The rest were born in Great Britain, the United States, Australia, Canada, Germany, Argentina and New Zealand. The respondents who "would join the army" tended to be younger than those who "would join revolution." They were interested in the socio-political situation in Poland, spoke Polish, were deeply religious, in touch with Polish emigré organizations, rather conservative and admirers of Piłsudski, Mickiewicz and Zeromski.

The characteristics of the sample and the findings suggest that the respondents were the first or second generation of Polish post-World War Two immigration, rather than the grandchildren of the "bread immigration" earlier in this century. The findings, therefore, cannot be generalized to all Polish background youth in the West; they pertain only to the self-selected sample of the respondents. However, the sample generated enough information to provide a beginning of insight into the Polishness of young persons of Polish heritage. It also inspired some new research questions which may be included in a more rigorous, scientific study. What, for example, are the differences between Polish Americans and Polish Canadians in the degree and kinds of satisfaction derived from their countries of settlement? How do the attitudes of New Zealanders differ from those of Australians in relation to the generations of Polish immigrants who settled in their respective countries? What are the emotional problems of young persons of Polish heritage in various countries, and what preventive measures exist in these countries to safeguard the mental health of Polish generations? In what ways, and to what extent, do the Polish generations participate in the creative cultural exchange with the countries of their settlement?

Conclusion

To conclude, let me draw a profile of Polish youth in the West. It is a hypothetical venture, a result of research, clinical observation, writing on the subject of Polish American identity, and reflection on the subject.

Young persons of Polish heritage, first, second and subsequent generations residing in the various countries of the world, tend to be satisfied with their place of residence, their socio-cultural environment and their economic situation. Their interest in Polish culture and solidarity with the Polish nation is an outcome of their psychological needs to be loyal to their parental cultural values. Not to be loyal means not to fulfill one's own obligations and to experience the uncomfortable pangs of guilt. These parental cultural values, adjusted, refined, and sometimes even distorted, are compressed into a nucleus of "Polishness" and become a much-needed structural component in the formation of the young person's ethnic identity.

The feeling of guilt caused by unrepaid obligations towards one's own parents, and the feelings of emptiness and confusion which flow from not being a part of a cultural heritage, may lead to a depression and even a crisis.

Interest in Polish culture and solidarity with the Polish nation, limited for the majority to an overt expression of joy in folk dances, customs and traditions, and to the inner, often unrealized need to belong to a historical tradition of a nation, is primarily a family affair. Only a selected group of creative individuals among the Polish youth in the West will develop a meaningful, conscious relation with their "Polishness," which will be but tinted, but not overwhelmingly coloured, by the need for loyalty to parental cultural values.

Table 1: Interest in Polish Language and Culture and Place of Residence

	Interest in Polish Language and Culture							
	Fair		Great		None			
Place of Residence	#	M%	#	M%	#	M%	Miss	Total
U.S.A.	14	17.9	64	82.1	0	0.0	2	80
Canada	25	43.9	32	56.1	0	0.0	2	59
Great Britain	35	55.6	27	42.9	1	1.6	1	64
Germany	1	7.7	12	92.3	0	0.0	0	13
Switzerland	1	25.0	3	75.2	0	0.0	0	4
France	7	43.8	9	56.3	0	0.0	0	16
Belgium-Holland	0	0.0	7	100.0	0	0.0	0	7
Australia	20	42.6	27	57.4	0	0.0	2	49
Argentina	0	0.0	1	100.0	0	0.0	0	1
Sweden-Denmark	0	0.0	18	100.0	0	0.0	0	18
Others	0	0.0	2	100.0	0	0.0	0	2
New Zealand	2	10.0	15	75.0	3	15.0	2	22
Total	105	32.2	217	66.6	4	1.2	9	335

Tests of Independence	Statistic	Significance
Maximum Likelihood	76.189	< .0001
Chi-Square	84.908	< .0001

In the *Anthology of Polish American Poetry* several passages seem to support my thinking. One can hear in these verses a sad, even funeral, note which connects "Polishness" with the memories of parents and grandparents. John Calvin Rezmerski ends a "letter" to his grandfather, written on the anniversary of his death:

> Your children are prospering
> and you have dozens of great grandchildren.
> Since you died we have acquired new one-way streets
> and another stoplight.
> And they're finally going to pave your street.
> And according to the papers
> Poland is still there.[12]

And in a touching lullaby, John Pijewski sings a last goodbye to his father:

> Before they lowered him into the grave
> I climbed inside his coffin
> In darkness I held his cold hand,
> Sang Polish nursery rhymes,
> Told fables, recited alphabet.
> When my voice gave way
> I dug myself out.[13]

Joseph Lisowski best expresses the meaning and the strength of family ties:

I looked in the mirror long enough
To see my childhood still sucking the dug
Of my mother and noticed how her blue eyes
Lulled me to sleep with a song of grandfather
And father and grandmother and all the children after.

I was stunned at first then curious.
But when I decided to turn away I saw
Myself suck harder and felt the cord draw tighter
Until it seemed that I was gathering again in her belly
And heard nothing but the echoes of family funeral cries.[14]

Notes

1. Arthur Koestler, *The Act of Creation* (New York, 1967), p. 642.
2. Donna C. Aguilera and Janice M. Messick, *Crisis Intervention, Theory and Methodology* (3rd ed.; St. Louis, 1978).
3. Andras Angyal, *Foundations for a Science of Personality* (New York, 1941), p. 13.
4. Victor Contoski, ed., *Blood of Their Blood, An Anthology of Polish American Poetry* (St. Paul, Minnesota, 1980).
5. René Dubos, *Beast or Angel? Choices that Make Us Human* (New York, 1974), p. 187.
6. Ivan Boszormenyi-Nagy and Geraldine M. Spark, *Invisible Loyalties: Reciprocity in Intergenerational Family Therapy* (Hagerstown, Md., 1973), p. 37.
7. Kurt Lewin, *Resolving Social Conflicts* (New York, 1948), p. 183.
8. Danuta Mostwin, "Młodzież Polska Na Zachodzie" ["Polish Youth in the West"] *Kultura,* June-August 1979, nr. 7/382-8/383, pp. 128-57. The statistical computations were performed by Marian Jan Krzyżowski from the University of Michigan in Ann Arbor. Also see the author's "Post-World War II Polish Immigrants in the United States," *Polish-American Studies* 26, no. 2 (1969), pp. 5-14; "The Transplanted Family: A Study of Social Adjustment of the Polish Immigrant Family to the United States after the Second World War," in *American Ethnic Groups: The European Heritage,* ed. Francesco Cordasco (New York, 1980); "Emotional Needs of Elderly Americans of Central and Eastern European Background," in *Ethnicity and Aging,* eds. Donald E. Gelfand and Alfred J. Kutzik (New York, 1979).
9. Louis R. Marcos, "Bilinguals in Psychotherapy: Language as an Emotional Barrier," *American Journal of Psychotherapy* 30 (1976), p. 552.
10. *Blood of Their Blood,* p. 116.

11. Ibid., p. 94.
12. Ibid.
13. Ibid., p. 89.
14. Ibid., p. 69.

The Pastoral Care of Poles in America

Andrew Woznicki

Close to two hundred years have elapsed since the arrival of the Polish clergy in America.[1] Since then, in the United States alone, they have established about eight hundred parishes and missions. Many Polish missionary societies and congregations of both men and women, some founded in the United States, took as their primary concern the spiritual growth of Polish migrants.

They did not limit themselves to pastoral care alone, however, but contributed greatly to the conversion of these immigrants into American citizens. Polish priests did not base their efforts on changeable political tendencies, which often encourage national disunity and the establishment of ghettos. Loyal to the principles of the Catholic church, Polish priests, by implanting in the hearts and minds of immigrants values shared by all men, attempted and still strive to incorporate the Polish ethnic group into the mainstream of the American society. Still, they preserved the Polish language among the migrant population while propagating and continuating their highest national cultural values. Finally, Polish priests in the United States also directed their energies towards the good of the Polish nation through such organizations as the Catholic League and American Relief for Poland.

We are witnessing today great changes in the Catholic church.[2] It could be said that a new vision of Christ's church is evolving in front of our eyes. Vatican II encouraged the faithful to realize God's Kingdom on earth, according to the demands of our times. The migrant clergy faces therefore new tasks and new perspectives of development. Polish priests ought to reassess their position in regard to the church, American society and the Polish nation, since many misunderstandings concerning the pastoral care of immigrants have arisen with the changing times. And although the Polish clergy usually remains incorporated into the diocesan ministry, yet, due to the specific character of their work, priests in following their particular calling often find themselves isolated and dependent on their own resources and ingenuity.[3]

In order to properly understand the socio-religious activity of the church in regard to particular ethnic groups, it is necessary to reflect on the need for a specific kind of pastoral care among immigrants. This action is of necessity different from the one carried out in the old country. Immigrants face entirely new sets of problems, and the issues concerning their native lands are, of necessity, of different significance. In the following paper we will analyse the Polish ethnic group in the United States as an example of such a divergence of problems.

The pastoral care of an immigrant population has tended towards two fundamentally different approaches: a reduction of the entire problem to the area of strictly religious life; or a concentration on a cultivation of ethnic distinctness of particular national groups.

How should this divergence of attitudes be viewed and interpreted? In evaluating the pastoral care of the Polish immigrant community in the United States, the socio-cultural situation of the entire American population has to be considered. If American society has a pluralistic character and if the cultural life of individual ethnic groups is still vital, then the apostolic activity of the church ought to be aimed not only at the preservation but also the development of the religious life of individual social groups of faithful within the framework of their own system of cultural values. No one has the right to arbitrarily decide which values of cultural life are to be considered as most appropriate for any given society. The decree of Vatican II, "Christus Dominus," guarantees the right of immigrant groups to self-determination in their cultural life: "Special concern should be shown for those among the faithful who, on account of their way or condition of life, cannot sufficiently make use of the common and ordinary pastoral services of parish priests or are quite cut off from them. Among this group are many migrants, exiles and refugees, seamen, airplane personnel, gypsies, and others of this kind."[4]

The problems of the pastoral care of immigrants in the United States cannot be reduced to the issue of national parishes alone. In apostolic action all characteristics of individual social groups have to be considered. The resolution of problems stemming from the inter-relation existing between the religious and national life depends on the appropriate attitude and understanding of the particular spiritual needs of immigrants by the church authorities.

One of the most vital topics in the Post-Vatican church is without any doubt the problem of the community of the faithful. It is the new vision of the church herself, which in her very essence represents and personifies a community of the faithful striving for eternal salvation, that should be considered as one of the most important achievements of Vatican II, and which opened the door for further discussions in this field. Two of the Constitutions of Vatican II, namely, "On the Church" and "The Church in the Contemporary World," as well as some of the numerous Declarations and Decrees, relate directly to the ecclesiological issues in the life of the believers.

In searching for new structural forms for religious communities within the Post-Vatican church, two tendencies come to the forefront. One of them, referring to the unchangeable structure of the church, both as a depository of faith and in her hierarchical forms, stresses the permanent and stable character of the communities of the faithful. In everyday life such communities, however, based strictly on stability and unchangeability, tend towards an excessive institutionalization of life of the believers, and towards over-legalization of individual behaviour of the particular members as well as entire groups. This consequently leads to a formalization of religious beliefs and to subordination of eternal salvation to a strict observance of all rules as applied to one's vocation or occupation. Such a rigorous adherence to norms either established by the hierarchy or simply inherited by tradition, can result in an ossification of religious life and create an immobilization of the patterns of everyday moral behaviour, as expressed by the attitude of mere formalistic application of the principles of ethics, excessively regulating the life of individuals or entire groups.

Every community, be it a social or a religious one, is formed on and expressed by a unity of convictions, aims or specific activity. Depending on the unifying element, different types of communal forms can be observed in any social life. Applied to the contemporary church, although there are still elements tending towards the stable character of religious communities, we also find communities based on instability and mobility. Inasmuch as the adherents of the unchangeable elements of faith founded their life on the precise formulas handed to them by the instructions of the hierarchy, the followers of the mobile elements base the forms and types of their communities on the charismatic character of the church, and stress the *praxis* of Christian life of an individual.

Vatican II, by defining the church as a universal sacrament of salvation of all men, underscored the invisible character of the church. This understanding of the church stresses the significance of grace and thus appeals more to the particular conscience of an individual as the invisible character of God's reality in the life of the faithful. A religious community based on this vision will consequently be more sensitive to the needs of a propagation and actualization of the premise of faith in the everyday life of the believers; the question of doctrinal correctness or the hierarchy's role in the communal life becomes a secondary one. The life of such a community takes on a character of spontaneity, bordering often on pure emotionalism, and in consequence it tends towards the formation of an alleged underground church.

Both these tendencies, by stressing either the stable or the mobile elements of unity exclusively, result in a distortion of the proper understanding of the role and meaning of Christian life. From a social point of view, the adherents to the idea of stability, calling for solidarity, tradition and the necessity for subjugation, experience a process of ghettoization. Any deviation from the established rule or norm is often met with intolerance, resulting from a fanatical conviction of extreme conservatism. On the other hand, those proclaiming the mobile character of the religious community lean towards a spiritual nomadism. The Christian idea of freedom as a prerogative of the children of God grows into a cult of individuality, which taking on aspects of sentimentalism and quietism, changes faith itself into a kind of religious excitement. Both the unhealthy activism of the "mobilists" and the extreme conservatism of the "stabilists" cause of necessity a growing tension in the entire community of the faithful, or at least bring about a disorientation as to the authentic understanding of God's signs in a given situation, place or time. The well-known controversy existing within the church in the Netherlands, or the intensification of the sense of uncertainty among Catholics in the United States, are obvious examples.

In searching for new and relevant structures for religious communities in today's church, a proper balance has to be reached between the elements of stability and mobility; between deliberation and spontaneity; between doctrine and *praxis.* In applying this rule to immigrant communities of the faithful, the additional problem of differentiation between various needs in respect to the structure and form of apostolic action should also be taken into consideration. Pastoral care in these circumstances should make allowances for all the unifying or diversifying elements of the ethnic group, since the necessity for complying either with stable or with mobile requirements stems from the ethnic origin as such. Ethnicity can be understood in a twofold manner: either as a given group, or nation (*ethos*), or as an expression of a character, custom and culture (*ethnos*). Comprehension of an immigrant society in terms of a group, tribe or nation points to and comprises the existing pluralism within the group, since every social grouping is formed by a given number of members, differing from each other in their individual and personal characteristics. Yet these members, although different in their individual characteristics, are nevertheless united by supra-personal, national, cultural and religious bonds. Thus we have an immigrant society divided by *ethos* and at the same time united by a given nation.

The specificity of a particular ethnic society relates to the diverse elements which characterize a given group or nation, such as language, tradition and common cultural values. A unity thus understood forms the basis for a further development of culturocreative values which promote and safeguard the vitality of a particular group, regardless of time or place.

Religiosity and common beliefs are without any doubt one of the fundamental unifying elements of any group, since religion in its very essence as a mystery of salvation of man, places it in the framework of Christian community. Thus it is faith which, as an invisible element, remains at the basis of Christian unity. Principles of ethics and moral behaviour of the members of a given group, however, although formed according to common norms, differ in their application to everyday life and in actual realization of the commands proclaimed in the Gospel. The codices of moral behaviour of an individual can be considered therefore as the visible characteristics of an individual member of any community of the faithful.

In planning religious communities for particular ethnic groups the principle of pluralism should be taken into consideration since, as a congregation of individuals united by the principle of faith, such a community will also reveal its different values and patterns of behaviour. Principles of behaviour, as depending on particular characteristics of a person or group, are of necessity manifold and diversified. Acting upon the principle of unity in the church, ethnic groups should therefore be granted the right to create various and independent communities, according to their authentic and actual needs, and conforming with the specificity of national or cultural structure.

The principle of pluralism permits a crystallization of various communities of faithful. Thus applying this rule to ethnic groups does not mean the establishment of religious communities in the framework of national or territorial parishes alone. Past experience proves that confining pastoral planning to personal or territorial parishes leads in reality to conflicts among different groups.

Properly understood, the principle of pluralism should then be directed towards creating authentic communities, satisfying religious needs of a given group. The role of the bishop or of any corresponding church authority should be passive in character and anticipate rather the activity on the part of particular groups. Too forceful an interference or desire to solve all the religious and moral problems of an ethnic group without taking account of all its desiderata and actual needs will be an expression of arbitrariness and authoritarianism, resulting in tension and mutual dissatisfaction.

Past experience shows that an effective spreading of Christ's Gospel can be best realized in the framework of communities having both the stable and mobile character. The interrelation between the conservative element inherited by tradition and the element of innovation, stemming from ever new and actual needs of the believers, leads to a development and deepening of communal awareness of a given group of faithful.

According to Vatican II, "the good of the souls" ought to be the main and basic goal of every apostolic action. In the light of this principle in planning of the pastoral care among immigrant groups the church should aim at developing a new awareness of religious consciousness through installing in their minds a conviction that the migratory situation is but a temporary step leading towards the ultimate destiny of every man, namely, God. Apostolic action among an immigrant population so understood will aim at the benefit of each person, both as an individual and as a member of a given society.

The religious experience of the immigrant situation rests on two factors: a free acceptance of migration as a form of a Christian life and growth towards the fullness of Christ's grace; and a striving towards a sense of co-responsibility for the fate of a given national group as well as a cultivation of the sense of solidarity embracing the whole of humanity in the spirit of Christian universalism.

In the process of religiously experiencing these two factors an equilibrium between them should be maintained, and a striving towards a full growth of Christian personality both as individuals and as social migrant groups should be developed.

The formation of Christian personality in a migrant should lead, according to Pius XII, towards the "education of a whole man."[5] This education consists of the integration of all the potentialities of an individual into one harmonious entity and the development of all the best possibilities of a particular human being. Thus understood, the religious education of an immigrant will lead to the flourishing of all his values, both personal and social. In the process of the religio-moral integration of immigrants one can distinguish the following steps:

(1) the formation of a supernatural life, with preservation of the personal intangibility of an individual;
(2) the cultivation of the personal integrity of each individual by promoting his personal freedom;
(3) the conservation of the spirit of equality and justice for all men through the awareness of the truth proclaiming the spiritual unity of the entirety of mankind, its common origin and destiny; and
(4) the sustaining of a cultural life of all faithful through the cultivation of the traditions of particular social groups.[6]

The religious education of a whole man includes, therefore, all areas of an immigrant's life and strives for the cultivation of his best possibilities common to all men. Man, as an individual and a person, is the only true deserving and proper object of the spiritual care of the church. The church, in her concern for the immigrant, leaves him the right to his own way of thinking and working, his sense of personal responsibility and even encourages his attempts at achieving self-dependency. But such a process of religious education of a whole man is possible only within a properly formed religious community.

The religious communities can be established in different ways, depending on the needs of the faithful. The imposition of a particular mode of action and the reduction of the entire sphere of social life to one form only is, in the view of Pius XII, contrary to the teaching of the Catholic church, and certainly contrary to the precepts of individual freedom. In the Apostolic Constitution, *Bis saecularis,* Pius XII writes as follows: "The Church in no way supports limitation of the spontaneity of life, which would reduce the entire sphere of apostolic action solely to one organization or parish."[7]

In the process of the establishment of a particular religious community, it is imperative to fully appreciate the character of a given social group of faithful and to pay respect to their specific moral-religious life. With this aim in mind, Vatican II puts the bishops under the obligation of planning appropriate apostolic action, with regard to the need of the particular social group of faithful. The religious communities should be the expression of the true demand for a moral-religious life of man.[8]

Generally speaking, in planning apostolic action one could take as the criterion either the common territorial habitation of a given society, or the specific system of values of a particular group of faithful. In the former case we will have local communities, in the latter, particular congregations.[9] The local communities, having as their goal the common fulfillment of the moral-religious needs of the faithful, organize their life around a particular church administration or a particular place of worship: for example, the parish church. The particular communities, because of a specific selection of faithful, are of necessity oriented towards satisfying the specific needs of the moral-religious life of the members of a certain congregation of the faithful.

The need to distinguish these two types of religious communities stems from the differentiation of human societies in respect to the various degrees and manners of the moral-religious integration. In this process of socio-religious integration, one can distinguish two states: the state of anonymity, and the state of crystallization. Anonymity in the church denotes all that which is not yet disclosed in the striving of the faithful for a full participation in the life of the church. The state of crystallization, on the other hand, includes all that which is already being actualized and realized, or consciously and personally cultivated by a particular individual. The local community, which includes all the inhabitants of a given territory without being differentiated, has an anonymous character, since the only condition of belonging to such a community is a passive participation in the sacramental life of the church, requires from the faithful a special involvement in the life of the church and a conscious cultivation of certain social values in its framework and thus acquires the character of crystallization. Thus understood, the process of socio-religious integration of the faithful in the church will demand the creation of a particular community which will support the local ones. In such a way, the life of the religious community of the faithful will evolve from the state of anonymity to the state of a full crystallization of the life of grace.

Now, the different national origin and the diverse system of socio-cultural values of the immigrant requires, and at the same time favours, the creation of special national communities in the church. These national communities in the church would be the proper manner of integrating their moral-religious life. The goal of the process of integration of immigrants into the church should consist in the cultivation of the physical and spiritual abilities of an individual based on the Christian virtue of patriotism, properly understood. Of course, membership in such a religious community would demand from the immigrant both goodwill and a certain maturity in regards to the socio-cultural as well as moral-religious life. For this reason establishing specific religious communities possessing a particular character should be considered as a postulate for the greater development of the religious life of immigrants, and cannot be either forced upon them or limited in any way.

In times past, in planning religious communities, the social unity of the faithful was reduced either to a territorial or personal element. The territorial elements of a stable and unchanging character built the religious life of the faithful on the framework of territorial parishes. The differences between parishes in the framework of territorial administration applied only to the social characteristics of the faithful in specific areas and consequently the distribution of parishes followed the particulars of social religious groups. The specificity of territorial parishes consisted of a uniformity of religious life, regardless of individual spiritual needs resulting from the education or social background of the faithful.

In contrast to the territorial parish, the one-time planning of pastoral care also provided a possibility of establishing religious communities in the framework of personal parishes. The personal communities could have been of varied character and responsive to the specific needs of various groups, and could be organized as academic chapels, discussion groups, military chapels, and so on.

Taking into consideration the multiplicity of races, nationalities and minority groups constituting the population of the faithful in the territorial ecclesiastical units in a given society, planning pastoral care and spiritual assistance for these diverse groups poses a serious problem for the ecclesiastical authorities. Generally speaking, the weakness in former planning of pastoral care for immigrant groups was demonstrated by the tendency to subordinate the spiritual needs of particular religious communities of minority groups to the legal demands and general structure of ecclesiastical administration. In other words, following the legal administrative requirements, the needs of religious communities were to be locked into the framework of regional or particular administration as such.

In papal documents prior to Vatican II, the organization of national parishes, both territorial and personal, depended on the decisions of the Apostolic See; these also were the directives of Pius XII expressed in the Apostolic Constitution, *Exsul Familia*. The documents of Vatican II, on the other hand, foresaw the planning of immigrant pastorates on the level of a particular church. Such were the instructions with respect to the solution of pastoral care proposed in "Pastoralis Migratorum Cura" in 1969.

As far as the general community is concerned, a decentralization of church authority is of course of great benefit to them, since smaller administrative units can improve and satisfy the religious needs of the faithful more efficiently. With respect to immigrant groups, however, the situation is diametrically opposed. Generally speaking, a correlation exists between the geographic structure of a given area and the demographic movement. The smaller the geographic unit, the greater the possibility of reaching a point of demographic saturation. Population expansion will have to take place in adjoining localities. On the other hand, the smaller an area, the greater the density and adherence of population. Now, in applying this rule to an immigrant population, it is evident that the decentralization of church authority brings about a rather unfortunate situation. Dispersed into different territorial ecclesiastical units, such as parishes, or deaneries, the immigrant population does not represent in any of them a group which would warrant establishing a specific pastorate for them. A national minority living in an artificially divided area is subjected to a further breaking up of its ranks, and consequently is deprived of any possibility of satisfying its real needs.

A geographic structure, determined by nature, is a stable one. Demographic movement, on the other hand, constitutes a constantly changing element. Demographic changeability results from the following interdependency: the greater the territorial density, the greater the social adhesiveness. The stability of a geographic structure is then a favourable element for the decentralization of authority; the specificity, however, of the density and adhesiveness of the ethnic population does not advocate the decentralization of authority based on the geographical structure of an area.

The question then arises: How can one solve this dilemma in planning pastoral care for immigrants, and in organizing religious communities for national minorities in the framework of the multi-ethnic structure of a given society?

With respect to the decentralization of church authority, neither the centralistic idea of *Exsul Familia*, nor the concept of a particular church, due to judicial reasons, encountered any basic difficulties. In view of the fragmentation of the minority groups living in different ecclesiastical units, as well as of the insufficient reasons for establishing either territorial or personal parishes, the church jurisdiction did not foresee the necessity of a pastorate for particular national groups. On February 22, 1975, however, the Apostolic See, in the document *Ecumenical Collaboration at the Regional, National, and Local Levels,* stated that "the ecumenical spirit must find a concrete application at the level of the local Church."[10] The term "local church" is applied in this document in a broader sense than the term "particular church," which was identified as a concept of diocese. The local church, according to this document, not only substituted the previous understanding of a particular church, but broadened it in respect to parishes (be they territorial or personal) and dioceses, and even to the entire territory within the competence of the National Conference of Catholic Bishops, that is to the whole church of the country. The document clearly states that the expression "local" is used in a wider and more readily understandable meaning than the "particular church."

The change in terminology, from a "particular" to a "local" church implies a serious shift in the administration of church authority. Generally speaking, the previous centralization on the level of the universal church reflected the centralization of religious life on the level of the particular churches, whereas in the Post-Vatican period of universalism of church authority, the care of the spiritual life of the faithful is planned on a local level. In other words, the term "local church" stresses its meaning as "universal" church, endowed with considerable autonomy, specific goals and particular responsibilities, and as such, its authority is not delegated.

> Ecumenism at the local level—we read—is a basic element in the ecumenical situation as a whole. It is not purely secondary or derivative. Ecumenism at the local level answers to specific needs and situations and has resources all its own. It has a range of undertaking proper to it and its function is not reducible to the simple application within a limited sphere of ecumenical directives meant for the world as a whole. . . . Therefore, the local Church, or a grouping of local Churches in the territory of an episcopal conference or a synod, may be in a better position to enter into contact and establish a brotherly relationship, at their own level, with other Churches and Christian communities.[11]

This concept of the local church is in complete agreement with the "Decree on the Bishops' Pastoral Office in the Church," which states that:

> Since pastoral needs increasingly require that some pastoral undertaking be directed and carried forward as joint projects, it is fitting that certain offices be created for the service of all or many dioceses of a determined region or nation. These offices can even be filled by bishops.[12]

The concept of a local church seems to be particularly appropriate when applied to ethnic populations, since a local church:

(1) is not defined either by the size of the community nor territorial boundaries, and can therefore avoid many of the administrative and legal restrictions which often arise from a strictly formalized constituency of faithful;
(2) opens the way for establishing a variety of ecclesiastical units, based on the origin, nationality, tradition, heritage, and cultural values of different socio-religious groupings. Thus, pastors can emphasize and support pre-existing preferences and cultural responses while giving proper guidance and instructions to their communities;
(3) leads to mutual cooperation between different ecclesiastical administrative units such as parishes, deaneries, or neighbouring dioceses;
(4) promotes the new spirit of collegiality with respect to the spiritual needs of ethnic population of faithful because it includes both the authorities of the place of their factual origin (*a quo*) and the hierarchy of their actual residence (*ad quem*); and finally
(5) encourages and prepares the ethnic population for organical integration into a given society at large, enabling a free exchange of views and inherited values with the way of living in the country of their residence.

In order to extend proper pastoral care to a greater number of ethnic groups who are deprived of systematic pastoral support in their language and tradition, it is vital that the concept of a local church be applied to them as it is in the case of ecumenical groups. That means that whenever in a diocese there are small scattered ethnic groups but no territorial or personal parish to provide proper systematic pastoral care in their language and tradition, additional diocesan or inter-diocesan faculties should be granted to already existing ethnic pastoral centres or parishes. If the situation requires it, facilities would extend to such matters as baptisms, marriages, funerals, religious instructions, pastoral care of the sick, the elderly, the destitute, fallen away Catholics, converts and new immigrants.[13]

Notes

1. On the first Polish priest in America in 1805, see Miecislaus Haiman, *Polish Past in America, 1608-1865* (Chicago, 1939), p. 65; Joseph Swastek, "Pierwsi polscy księza w Stanach Zjednoczonych," *Sodalis* 30 (1949), pp. 12-14; Józef Krzyszkowski, S.J., "Kto pierwszym polskim kapłanem w Ameryce?," *Sodalis* 38 (1957), pp. 179-84. For a review of the role of the Poles in the American church, see: *The*

Contributions of the Poles to the Growth of Catholicism in the United States, published as a sixth volume in: *Sacrum Poloniae Millennium* (Rome, 1959).

2. Cf. *The Crucial Questions on Problems Facing the Church Today* (New York, 1969).
3. For analysis of the attitude of the Church of Post-Vatican II towards migratory population see: *Migration in Light of Vatican II* (Center for Migration Studies, New York, 1967); Andrew N. Woznicki, "Faithful and religious life in Post-Vatican Church," *Migrant Echo* 1, no. 4 (1972), pp. 150-55.
4. *Acta Apostolicae Sedis* (AAS) 58 (1966), p. 682.
5. Ibid., 38 (1946), pp. 145-46. Cf. also "Populorum progression," ibid., 59 (1967), p. 278.
6. Cf. Andrew N. Woznicki, *Socio-religious Principles of Migration Movement* (Toronto, 1968), p. 35.
7. *AAS* 40 (1948), p. 398. Cf. also Nils A. Dahl, "The Essential Nature of the Congregation," *Catholic Mind* 68, no. 1242 (1970), pp. 23-24: "As far as we can see, a uniform order of congregational life never existed within the primitive Church. Structure and forms of organization were, it would seem, not the same in Jerusalem, Antioch, Ephesus, Corinth and Rome. Charismatic and institutional ministries, presbyterial and episcopal order may exist simultaneously, or they may be combined in one way or another" (p. 25).
8. Theodor I. Jimenez-Urresti, "Gemeinschaft und Kollegialität in der Kirche," *Concilium* 8 (1965), pp. 627-32.
9. Joseph P. Fitzpatrick, "The Importance of 'Community' in the Process of Immigrant Assimilation," *International Migration Review* 1 (1966), pp. 5-16: "Community. The meaning of community can be presented in descriptive terms, the way in which it would come to one's attention when empirically observed. It signifies a group of people who follow a way of life or pattern of behavior which mark them out as different from people of another society, or from other people in the larger society in which they live or to which they have come. They are people who have generally come from the same place, or who are identified with the particular locality where they now live or to which they have come. They speak the same language, probably have the same religious beliefs. They tend to 'stick together' to help and support each other. They have expectations of loyalty one to other and methods of social control" (p. 6).
10. *L'Osservatore Romano,* July 7, 1975.
11. Ibid.
12. *The Documents of Vatican II* (New York, 1966), p. 427.
13. This is the substance of a proposal made by the author and unanimously accepted by the Bi-Centennial Congress of the National Catholic Conference of Bishops in Detroit in 1976. See: *Origin* 20 (1976), p. 334. For a similar view, see Józef Bakalarz, *Parafie personalne dla emigrantów w prawodawstwie powszechnym Kosciola zachodniego* (Lublin, 1978).

Polish Emigrants' Search for Equality of Opportunity

Jerzy Zubrzycki

Emigration from Poland to North America has been the subject of a large number of historical, sociological and demographic studies which had their beginning in Father Kruszka's personalized account of Polish settlements in the United States and Canada (1905-08), reached a zenith in Thomas' and Znaniecki's monumental study of Polish peasants transplanted to the new world (1927) and continues to this day on an unprecedented scale as witnessed in the massive preliminary bibliography published by the Polonia Research Institute in Krakow. The bulk of this massive outpouring of scholarly studies is, however, concerned with descriptive accounts of the processes of migration and settlement and rarely does it raise theoretical issues appropriate to this branch of study.

In this paper I propose to argue that the crucial theoretical problem which has to be tackled before embarking on discrete monographic accounts of Poles in particular communities, industries and other institutional structures is to what extent assimilation of culture and education of the receiving North American society by the consecutive ethnic generations has in fact meant equality of opportunity, especially occupational opportunity for Polish immigrants. Further, to what extent the utilization of actually existing opportunities—i.e., social mobility of the second and consecutive immigrant generations in comparison with social mobility of non-immigrant groups—has meant free acceptance into close social relationships by the dominant white Anglo-Saxon Protestant group.

The case for development of a viable theoretical approach to the study of the process of migration and settlement cannot be restricted to the Poles in North America. Indeed, it applies to the study of international migration as a fact of history.

During the past one hundred years international migration has assumed considerable importance as a factor in population redistribution among a growing number of countries and regions of the world. Social, economic, political and demographic disparities, as well as political pressures, have exercised considerable force in affecting the international distribution of population, skills, knowledge and welfare. Yet the causes and the consequences of international migration, as well as the volume, function, direction, type and selective character of movement have not remained fixed. Indeed, even policies designed to control international movement have been altered to reflect the changing views and needs of both the sending and receiving countries. The significant changes which international migration has undergone, coupled with the recognition of the growing importance of international movement as a variable affecting the demographic and economic development of a number of less developed countries as senders and/or receivers of migrants, argues strongly for more conceptual work and intensive empirical research in this field. In particular, there is an urgent need for assessment of the interrelations between international migration and development that will have direct relevance to policy formation and evaluation for both the sending and receiving countries, and for guidance to international agencies concerned with these problems.

I would argue that an understanding of the circumstances and consequences of Polish transatlantic migrations would be greatly enhanced if attention was focused on the theoretical perspectives of opportunity structure, the determinants of social mobility and the relationship between these variables and that of assimilation/integration. A theoretical discourse so focused might indicate whether or not cultural assimilation and acquisition of education by the successive generations of Poles in North America has in fact, meant equality of opportunity. By the same token recent evidence presented might also reveal that social mobility has often meant competition with members of other ethnic groups, dominant or otherwise, with a consequent increase rather than decrease of social distance between groups.

In what follows I shall review several possible approaches to the study of equality of opportunity centred on the notion of ethnic stratification in a plural society. By stating my objective in this fashion I am deliberately reversing the order of discussion of ethnicity in American sociology which has been dominated by an argument between the assimilationist and pluralist perspectives with its emphasis on the cultural origins of ethnic groups.

Digression on Ethnicity and the Ethnic Group

Most sociologists agree that ethnic stratification is a system of status distribution by which status is determined according to membership in an ethnic group, the group being somehow based on cultural or physical criteria such as race, language, religion, ethnic origin, common history.[1] Various factors come into play, however, in determining the membership of an ethnic group. When defined objectively, an ethnic group is composed of individuals having a common ancestry, religion, race, heritage. Others choose to define ethnic groups subjectively; the members must conceive of themselves as being alike. They must have a shared sense of peoplehood, identify with the group and be united by emotional bonds.[2] Particularly for Shibutani and Kwan this is the essence of an ethnic group. The members must think they have a common ancestry—it matters little whether or not this is the case. Ethnic groups are, therefore, cultural constructs and not necessarily biological groups.[3] For some sociologists, being a member of an ethnic group further entails participating in the activities of the group, thereby becoming involved in a unique culture. Another factor sometimes considered is outside pressure which may impose a common identity on individuals. The pressure may be in the form of prejudice or discrimination, which causes the individuals to identify with one another in the context of a group in order to adjust to, or oppose, majority prejudice. This consciousness of kind develops from consistent reactions of people which tend to reinforce the ethnic group's cohesiveness.[4]

Furthermore, an ethnic group can be viewed functionally, as an institution providing a source of group self-identification, and a network within which the individual can remain to conduct his primary relationships.[5]

Out of this myriad of conditions which determine the nature of group membership and degree of group identification and which give rise to a corresponding myriad of definitions, one major conclusion is important: scholars studying ethnic phenomena must make the vital distinction between ethnic groups and ethnic categories and "how salient ethnic identities are to the 'members' of these collectivities."[6] For example, when Sandberg claims his scale measures "ethnic group cohesion" among a sample of Polish Americans, it can readily be seen that he is actually dealing with ethnic awareness among members of several ethnic categories.[7] Consequently, in conceptualizing about experience of social mobility of the Poles in North America we must bear in mind that we are dealing with not one group of people who all share a consciousness of kind and exhibit the same sense of belonging, but with a spectrum of ethnic categories that differ in terms of the degree of ethnic awareness as well as in terms of such objective characteristics as length of residence, educational and occupational achievement and other criteria. Thus the monolithic treatment of ethnicity used in much contemporary empirical research is clearly not applicable to Poles in North America.

Opportunity Structures and Social Mobility

Systematic evidence collected in North America in the fifties and the sixties (Hutchinson, 1956; Lieberson, 1963; Porter, 1965) indicates that persons born in Poland or of Polish ethnic origin were initially located at the lowest levels in the occupational structure of the United States and Canada.[8] To understand the occupational concentrations of Polish immigrants and their children it is necessary to consider both the diverse educational and occupational skills which immigrants brought, as well as the specific working opportunities which were available at the time of their arrival.

I do not wish to dwell at any length on the well-known facts concerning the character of mass movement of peasant Poles to the anthracite coalfields of Pennsylvania, the stockyards of Chicago and the prairie provinces of Canada during the last decade of the nineteenth century and up to World War One. This has been documented. In short, we know that they "were not the erudite, sophisticated, cosmopolitan city dwellers, nor were they men of wealth or influence."[9]

The American economy at the turn of the century was becoming more diversified and industrial, with substantial concentration initially in the older port cities on the eastern seaboard and, later, in midwestern cities. These expanding centres of manufacturing industry attracted the newer immigrants from Russia, Poland and Italy who lacked the skills of such well-established groups as Germans, Scandanavians and the Irish. Given similarity of occupational status, immigrants from Poland tended to develop significant territorial enclaves which in turn encouraged a high degree of institutional completeness and group consciousness. Much the same pattern was to be found initially in the rural settlements of Manitoba and Saskatchewan where agriculture offered the only outlet for settlers.

There is little evidence of significant change in the sources and composition of Polish migration to North America in the interwar period when the quota legislation in the United States and worsening economic conditions in Canada seriously curtailed employment opportunities. A break in this pattern came after World War Two when both countries opened their doors to large numbers of Polish ex-servicemen and political exiles with relatively superior education and occupational skills. This had occurred at the time when the United States and Canada were about to enter the stage of development characterized as post-industrial.

While economic opportunities became diversified as a result of a shift from secondary to tertiary and, more recently, quaternary industry, the sons and daughters of the first generation of peasant settlers experienced some mobility the full extent of which, regrettably, has not been fully documented. Consequently, the main purpose of this paper is to stimulate scholars to develop such a research. In what follows I shall attempt to outline an analytical framework that might be suitable for this purpose. Unfortunately the limits of space imposed on the paper will preclude any discussion of suitable methodological approaches.

The key concept which must be applied in a study of differential mobility experience of the individual cohorts of Polish immigrants in North America is that of ethnic stratification. Economic forces of supply and demand for labour have created the inequalities of ethnic stratification. Over time the marked differentiation at the point of entry can either harden into a permanent class system or change in the direction of absorption or integration as a result of which the relationship between ethnicity and class disappears.

There are two important aspects of this process which should be distinguished analytically: the pattern of individual and group mobility, and its relationship to assimilation.

There is plenty of empirical evidence to suggest that an upwardly mobile immigrant can make one of two choices: he can choose the relatively "safe" course of pursuing whatever opportunities exist within his ethnic group, or he can take a more adventurous course by competing in the opportunity structure of the wider society. The essence of this choice lies in the metaphor of the ethnic mobility trap.[10] If the first choice is made it may have social and psychological effects which may make it irreversible for a person who follows an occupation in an ethnic-specific institution or occupation. He will become deeply embedded in a close network of ethnic ties—family, church, occupation and club membership—from which he can extricate himself only with considerable effort. In short, he may be trapped.

The duality of intra- versus extra-group mobility is further complicated if the group is moving upward as a bloc in the ethnic system or in the larger society. In the former case, however, opportunities for mobility may be severely restricted, thus reinforcing the ethnic entanglement of the individuals concerned. Here the concept of institutional completeness may be relevant denoting an ethnic-specific institutional structure which, in its extreme form, will be a microcosm of the opportunity structure of the larger society and, consequently, will offer a complete range of mobility perspectives. Such a high degree of structural pluralism would normally be associated with endogamy, pronounced ecological segregation, institutional clustering and rigidity of group definition.

What about the relationship between social mobility and assimilation? An adequate theoretical framework for the purpose of study of the historical experience of groups such as the Poles in North America can never be complete without some discussion of the manner in which certain groups and institutions in the receiving society, at different times, have exhibited varying degrees of inclusion and exclusion to the newcomers. The analytical propositions to be developed here must relate to the actual circumstances of inter-group relations in another way, also, for there is an historical relationship between beliefs about status and assimilability of minority groups on the one hand and forms of social closure and exclusion on the other. Hence an analysis of this particular relationship must be concerned with an historical trend in the development of chief ideological stances and corresponding policies beginning with Anglo-conformity through the melting pot to cultural pluralism.

The questions then that have to be asked include some or all of the following. What is the nature of monopolistic practices that by giving one group an advantage over other groups contribute to the creation of boundaries that, in turn, create ethnic categories and stereotypes (e.g., that of an uneducated "Polack" in an ethnic joke)? How do these monopolistic practices limit access to scarce resources and affect life chances of individual members of minority groups? What is the relationship between inclusion/exclusion in areas like employment, education and community relations to the prevailing social difficulties that create ethnic categories and stereotypes? When does a group with a low entrance status lay claim to have joined the charter group?

Participation in the Larger Society

So far I have stressed the importance of social mobility in the evolution of ethnic stratification into a system in which ethnicity ceases to function as a stratifying variable and boundary maintenance is decreased to promote inclusion rather than exclusion of groups and individuals. Inclusion applies to a wide variety of segments of the receiving society and its principal charter groups ranging from micro-structures of the primary group and the neighbourhood through education, employment to the sharing of power. Participation in these structures opens up new channels of communication; those who were strangers are now able to share their experiences and in time become more alike culturally. When minority groups share common cultures they are no longer visible —a condition which, in turn, enhances social, occupational and geographical mobility. This process has been described by Richmond as an exchange relationship, a series of inputs and outputs in which the ethnic system and the society of which this is a part both change.[11] Briefly stated, the conceptual framework of this process is as follows. Social change is a continuous process and while, for analytical purposes, one can break into this process at any point, changes in ideas always evolve in a structural context and changes in structures always evolve in a pre-existing context of meaning (the "always" modified only in extreme cases of cultural annihilation, and usually the annihilation of individuals— and the imposition of change by external force). Change in the demographic composition is not necessarily followed by change in social structure, but one source of change in social structure is response to demographic change. Response is a multi-stranded process (although the strands are sometimes chronologically quite distinct) of denial and awareness, the concealment, non-production and production of "knowledge," the development of interpretations and explanations and the initiation of structural change in the form of eliminating, creating and modifying roles, groups, functions, resources and sanctions. Finally, response is always meaningful response, even though what is given meaning may be only a part of the phenomenon in question.

Once a response of the larger, receiving society to newcomers has become crystallized and particularly if groups with power adopt and legitimize it, there is a tendency for it to become self-generating, which means that perception and the accumulation of knowledge are selectively geared to confirming its truth, morality and expediency. However, in politically plural, anti-centralist and anti-authoritarian societies like Canada and the United States, consensus of response across institutions does not happen easily. What looks like consensus is often composed of a lot of discrete indifferences. Moreover, the mechanisms that an institution will adopt with the object of encouraging agreement with its chosen response will often uncover or even generate a diversity of meanings and of approaches to structural change.

My contention in presenting an outline of theoretical perspectives on the central issue of the Polish immigrants' search for equality of opportunity in North American Society is toward a reorientation of research away from its present preoccupation with largely descriptive monographic studies of particular communities and institutions. Let me repeat again, in conclusion, that future macro-sociological research in this area must begin with the development of a framework that would facilitate an understanding of the dynamic processes that resulted in the placement of Polish settlers in a particular social status category at a given point of time. In summary, a conceptual framework designed for this purpose must include at least the following propositions each concerned with one particular independent variable and each close enough to the operational level to be directly or indirectly testable:

(1) the nature of opportunity structure of the receiving societies;
(2) the response of established institutions in recognition of the relevance of immigrant interests, needs, characteristics, situations and problems;
(3) the occupational and educational levels of immigrants entering Canada and the United States at different points of time; and

(4) culturally determined differences in achievement motivation of groups listed in (3).

A common element to all of the above propositions and, in particular, to (1) and (2) is an assumption about a particular belief and ideological stance concerning the status and assimilability of minority groups on the one hand and institutional forms of social inclusion or exclusion on the other. Thus any worthwhile analysis of the search for equality of opportunity on the part of Polish immigrants in North America must consider their experience within a framework of the dominant ideologies of the time, ranging from Anglo-conformity and assimilation to cultural pluralism.

The transition from an assimilationist to a pluralist policy is dictated by the philosophy of liberal democracy. There can be no question that the pursuit of equal opportunity demands innovative programs to benefit members of minority groups. The problem, however, is twofold. First, can ethnic groups resist processes of absorption, integration and assimilation and at the same time avoid ethnic stratification? In other words, can collective mobility replace individual mobility? This applies in particular to North America where, as John Porter argued, "collective mobility programmes are relatively new and their consequences unknown the question may concern the choice between mobility and ethnic group survival."

The second problem concerns pluralism and its relationship to equality. The merit of pluralism is that it opens up additional options through which people can gain access to whatever rewards (material or non-material) a society has to offer and through which they can pursue self-fulfilment. While in many industrial countries at the present time some individuals and some minority groups are urging the case for pluralism on these grounds, large numbers of people of ethnic origin do not see this as the route they wish to take to rewards. What they want for themselves is open access to what they see as the way to success and satisfying acceptance in the established society. Equality of opportunity, not pluralism, is their concern; often they cannot see pluralism as anything but a perpetuation of the distinction between first- and second-class citizens.

These are some analytical theories that, in my judgment, must feature prominently in a sociological assessment of Polish emigration to North America and the impact it made on the receiving societies.

Notes

1. Stanley Lieberson, "Stratification and Ethnic Groups," *Sociological Inquiry* 40, pp. 172-81; Donald Noel, "A Theory of the Origins of Ethnic Stratification," *Social Problems* 16, pp. 157-72.
2. Milton Gordon, *Assimilation in American Life* (New York: Oxford University Press, 1964), pp. 24-30; Tamotsu Shibutani and Kian M. Kwan, *Ethnic Stratification: A Comparative Approach* (London: The Macmillan Company, 1972), pp. 40-41; and W. Lloyd Warner and Leo Srole, *The Social System of American Ethnic Groups* (New Haven: Yale University Press, 1965), p. 28.
3. Shibutani and Kwan, *Ethnic Stratification,* p. 589.
4. Gordon, *Assimilation in American Life,* p. 29.
5. Ibid., p. 38.
6. James McKay and Frank Lewins, "Ethnicity and the Ethnic Groups," *Ethnic and Racial Studies* I (1978), pp. 411-27.
7. N. Sandberg, *Ethnic Identity and Assimilation: The Polish-American Community* (New York: Praeger, 1974).
8. Edward P. Hutchinson, *Immigrants and their Children, 1850-1950* (New York: John Wiley, 1956); Lieberson, *op. cit.;* and John Porter, *The Vertical Mosaic* (Toronto: University of Toronto Press, 1965).
9. Joseph A. Wytrwal, *Behold! the Polish Americans* (Detroit: Endurance Press, 1977), p. 90.
10. Norbert Wiley, "The Ethnic Mobility Trap and Stratification Theory," *Social Problems* 16, pp. 147-59.
11. Anthony H. Richmond, "Sociology of Migration in Industrial and Post-industrial Societies" in J.A. Jackson, ed., *Migration* (Cambridge: Cambridge University Press, 1969).

Contributors

Grzegorz Babiński is Associate Professor of Sociology and a member of the Polonia Research Institute at Jagiellonian University. He co-edits the institute's *Przegląd Polonijny* and has himself written frequently on the assimilation and evolution of ethnic groups in the United States. He is the author of *Lokalna społeczność polonijna w Stanach Zjednoczonych w procesie przemiań,* published by Ossolineum in 1977.

Stanislaus Blejwas coordinates the Polish Studies Program and is Associate Professor of History at Central Connecticut State College in New Britain. His published works deal with the history of modern Poland as well as with Polish Americans. He has edited the *Newsletter* and been Assistant Director of the Institute on East Central Europe at Columbia University.

John Bodnar, Associate Professor of History at Indiana University in Bloomington, is the author of many articles and several books which integrate migration, kinship and work during the American industrial revolution. His most recent work, *Migration and Urbanization: Blacks, Poles and Italians in Pittsburgh, 1900-1950,* was published by the University of Illinois Press in 1981.

Daniel Buczek, Professor of History at Fairfield University in Connecticut, is a student of medieval and modern Catholic religious institutions. *Immigrant Pastor,* his biographical study of Rev. Lucyan Bojnowski, the patriarchal leader of New Britain's Polonia, appeared in 1974.

Leonard F. Chrobot is President and Professor of Sociology at St. Mary's College in Orchard Lake, Michigan. He has lectured and written widely on the sociology of religion and ethnic groups.

Jan K. Fedorowicz teaches history at the University of Western Ontario in London. His research interests have focused on the history of early modern Poland, and he is the author of *England's Baltic Trade in the Early Seventeenth Century: A Study in Anglo-Polish Commercial Diplomacy,* published by Cambridge University Press in 1979.

Krzysztof Groniowski is Associate Professor at the Institute of History at the Polish Academy of Sciences in Warsaw and the author of many basic works on the agrarian and economic history of modern Poland. His latest book, *Robotnicy rolni w Królestwie Polski 1817-1914,* was published in 1977.

Benedykt Heydenkorn is the former editor of *Zwiazkowiec* and co-author (with Henry Radecki) of *A Member of a Distinguished Family: the Poles in Canada* in the Multiculturalism Directorate Generation Series. He is the author and editor of many monographs of the Polish Research Institute, including the two-volume *Memoirs of Polish Immigrants in Canada* and *Topics on Poles in Canada.*

Rudolph K. Kogler serves as Chief Demographer, Central Statistical Services, in the Ministry of Treasury of the Province of Ontario. He has specialized in population estimates and projections and in the ethnic composition of the Canadian population. As President of the Canadian Polish Research Institute in Toronto, he is active in encouraging the study of the Polish ethnic group in Canada.

Marcin Kula is Associate Professor of History at the Institute of History of the Polish Academy of Sciences, where he has dealt with the social history of Latin America, particularly with black and ethnic settlement in the region. Most recently he has edited the collective work, *Dzieje Polonii w Ameryce Łacińskiej.*

Anthony J. Kuzniewski, Assistant Professor of History at the College of the Holy Cross in Worcester, Massachusetts, is the author of *Faith and Fatherland: The Polish Church War in Wisconsin, 1896-1918,* published by the University of Notre Dame Press in 1980. In addition to his interest in the history of religion, he is active in the ministry as a member of the Society of Jesus.

Helena Znaniecka Lopata, Professor of Sociology at Loyola University of Chicago, has frequently oriented her major interest in women and the family toward the analysis of Polish American life. Her major synthesis, *Polish Americans: Status Competition in an Ethnic Community,* appeared in 1976.

Alexander Matejko, who is Professor of Sociology at the University of Alberta in Edmonton, has written extensively and lectured throughout Europe and North America on the sociology of work and of organizations. He is the author of *Social Change and Stratification in Eastern Europe,* published by Praeger in 1974.

Joanna Matejko received her Ph.D. in History from the University of Warsaw and has carried out extensive research on Polish settlement in western Canada. Among her published works on that subject, the most recent is *Polish Settlers in Alberta,* published in 1979 and for which she acted as editor.

Ewa Morawska is now affiliated with the Department of Sociology of the University of Pittsburgh. Her research has focused on social change with particular reference to Polish immigrants in America. She is, with Irwin Sanders, the author of an important bibliographical study, *Polish-American Community Life,* published in 1975 by Boston University and the Polish Institute of Arts and Sciences in America.

Danuta Mostwin is Professor of Social Work at the National Catholic School of Social Service in the Catholic University of America. Her teaching, research and writing have emphasized the ethnic factor and mental health issues in family services.

Eugene Obidinski, Associate Professor of Sociology at the State University of New York at Oneonta, has written extensively on various aspects of Polish American studies. He is the author of *Ethnic to Status Group: Polish Americans in Buffalo,* published by Arno Press in 1980.

Laurence J. Orzell is currently a research analyst with the United States Army at Fort Bragg, North Carolina. His published writings have dealt with Poland's role in international affairs as well as with ethnic dimensions of religious history, including *Rome and the Validity of Orders in the Polish National Catholic Church,* published in 1977 by Savonarola Seminary.

Dominic A. Pacyga has collaborated with Glen Holt on *Chicago: A Historical Guide to the Neighborhoods.* He earned his doctorate at the University of Illinois-Chicago Circle with a study of Polish workers' responses to industrial role definitions on Chicago's South Side.

Joseph J. Parot is the author of *Polish Catholics in Chicago: A Religious History,* published by Northern Illinois University Press in 1981. He is Professor and Head of Historical Studies at Northern Illinois University in DeKalb.

Donald Pienkos, the co-editor of *Aspects of the East European Experience in America,* contributes frequently to scholarly journals on such topics as the social and political development of rural Eastern Europe and the political behaviour and ethnic identity of Polish Americans. He is Associate Professor of Political Science at the University of Wisconsin in Milwaukee.

Henry Radecki is Assistant Professor of Sociology at Laurentian University in Sudbury. His interest in the structure and evolution of ethnic institutions is reflected in his major published works: *A Member of a Distinguished Family: The Polish Group in Canada* (with Benedykt Heydenkorn) in 1976, and *Ethnic Organizational Dynamics: the Polish Group in Canada.*

Thaddeus Radzialowski is on leave from the Department of History of Southwest State University in Marshall, Minnesota to assist the Director of the National Endowment for the Humanities. His writings on immigration have dealt with all aspects of Polish American social history; those on eastern Europe, his other major interest, on Russian and Soviet foreign policy and historiography.

Frank Renkiewicz edited *Polish American Studies,* the journal of the Polish American Historical Association, from 1971 to 1981. He is Professor of History at St. John Fisher College in Rochester, New York, has written broadly on Poles in the United States, and is active in local, state and national ethnic associations.

Irena Spustek is Associate Professor of History at the Polish Academy of Science in Warsaw. In her research and writings she specializes in the problems of emigration for Poles. She published a monograph in 1966 on Poles in St. Petersburgh, 1914-17.

Andrew Woznicki, Professor of Philosophy at the University of San Francisco, has written extensively on the relationship between religion and ethnicity. He is most recently the author of *A Christian Humanism: Karol Wojtyla's Existential Personalism.*

Jerzy Zubrzycki is Professor and Head of the Department of Sociology at the Australian National University in Canberra. He has written some forty articles or chapters in books, largely on international migration. His *Polish Immigrants in Britain: A Study of Adjustment* pioneered the study of Polish ethnicity in the aftermath of World War Two when it appeared in 1956. His most recent work (in collaboration with L. Broom and F.L. Jones) is *Opportunity and Attainment in Australia,* published by the ANU and Stanford University Presses.